RESISTANCES TO
FEARLESSNESS

RESISTANCES TO FEARLESSNESS

A Philosophy of Fearism Approach

R. Michael Fisher & B. Maria Kumar

Copyright © 2021 by R. Michael Fisher & B. Maria Kumar.

ISBN:	Softcover	978-1-6641-0508-9
	eBook	978-1-6641-0507-2

All rights reserved. No part of this book may be reproduced or transmitted in any form or by any means, electronic or mechanical, including photocopying, recording, or by any information storage and retrieval system, without permission in writing from the copyright owner.

Any people depicted in stock imagery provided by Getty Images are models, and such images are being used for illustrative purposes only.
Certain stock imagery © Getty Images.

Cover art by R. M. Fisher

Print information available on the last page.

Rev. date: 05/06/2021

To order additional copies of this book, contact:
Xlibris
AU TFN: 1 800 844 927 (Toll Free inside Australia)
AU Local: 0283 108 187 (+61 2 8310 8187 from outside Australia)
www.Xlibris.com.au
Orders@Xlibris.com.au
791530

Dedicated to...

Those who know the path, like Iyania Vanzant, who wrote, "We die to fear of Spirit to be reborn into the Spirit of fearlessness."
-R. Michael Fisher

I am extremely grateful to my wife Vijayalakshmi for her unfailing inspiration to all of my endeavours.
-B. Maria Kumar

CONTENTS

Figures and Appendices x
Acknowledgements xi
Preface xiii
Introduction 1 xxv
    Highlights of What is to Come 1
Introduction 2 liii
    The Gift of Fear lxi
    Highlights of What is to Come cv
Introduction 3 cix
    (Defense) Intelligence cxi
    Terrorism, Fearism, Futures: Fearlessness Exercising Its
        Muscles cxvii
    Fearism's View of Fearlessness cxx
    Highlights of What is to Come cxxvii

PART I   FEARLESSNESS AS/IS LEADERSHIP

Chapter 1   Fearlessness as/is Leadership 1
    Escape: The Elephant in the Room 4
    Fearless Leadership In and Out of the 'Fear' Matrix 17
    What's Not Right About This Picture 31
Chapter 2   Does The World Need Us To Be Fearless? 35

PART II FEARLESSNESS AS/IS BEAUTY

Chapter 3   Fearlessness as/is Beauty 69

Chapter 4   Fear (The Ugly) Idealized 105
            The Problem of Appearance(s) 131

PART III FEARLESSNESS IS/AS MOVEMENT

Chapter 5   Fearlessness is/as Movement 141
            Wake Up! 144
            Fearism, Fearlessness & Politics 157
            Fearlessness: Conservative? Liberal? or Radical? 170

Chapter 6   Affective Potency: The Force of Esteem(s) 179
            History of an Omission 'Crime' 179
            Highlighting Esteem(s) 183
            Fear of the Sacred Warrior: Emancipatory Leader(ship) 200

PART IV FEARLESSNESS IS/AS PHILOSOPHY

Chapter 7   Fearlessness is/as Philosophy 213
            Fearlessness: A 'Fear' Vaccination Process Philosophy 214
            In Search of Fearlessness Community: Living Philosophy 222
            Philosophy of Fearlessness *cum* Fearlessness Philosophy 227

Chapter 8   Double Talking Fearlessness 238
            King Fear vs. King Fearlessness: A Telling of the Truth 263
            Dialogue, Morphing, Mutation and Unplugging 283

PART V FEARLESSNESS IS/AS "UNCANNY"

Chapter 9   Fearlessness is/as "Uncanny" 287
            Fourth Conceptual Revolution: Fearlessness 310
            Deciphering History, Deciphering 'The Crime' 312

    "Our 20th Century is the Century of Fear" 313
    Camus' Path to a Century of Terror 328

Chapter 10 Recommendations 335
    Questions/Exercises to Practice True Fearlessness 339

References 345

Endnotes 363

Index 409

FIGURES AND APPENDICES

Figure 1 Tripartite Esteem Model: Fear — Fearlessness — Love........xliii

Figure 2 *"Elephant in The Room"* 4

Figure 3 Stages of the Soul's Journey: Defense Intelligence Systems (DI) 53

Figure 4 A-D/ness Images..79

Appendix 1 Soliciting Questions for the A/D-ness Survey............102

Figure 5 Four-Layered Meta-Motivation Map 207

ACKNOWLEDGEMENTS

There are many diverse voices we have drawn from in this book. Their experiences with fear and fearlessness have been especially valuable throughout our writing. We thank Desh Subba and the Fearism community of thinkers, writers and educators he has built around his philosophy of Fearism over the last few decades. The specific research and experience on Fearlessness as a way to live and run organizations has come from many sources, too many to name them all. In the West, these have circulated around the social experiments like the founding of the The League *for* Fearlessness with The Baileys et al. in 1931. Then, came the In Search of Fearlessness (ISOF) Project, co-founded by R. Michael Fisher and Catherine Sannuto, and then continued soon after with the partnership of Barbara Bickel and her committed leadership to make this Project a real possibility with longevity. To all the ISOF community members and others who studied Fear and Fearlessness, we acknowledge their work to enhance this new era of adult education for the purpose of liberation. Fisher wishes specifically to thank the late Dr. Carl Leggo, his co-supervisor of his dissertation as well as a gracious colleague, who took Fisher's work seriously and eventually in 2011 wrote a first significant educational publication on the role of Fisher's book in Leggo's life and work.

PREFACE

We have a (capital) Fear[1] Problem on our hands. How would a Fearlessness Paradigm within a Fearism approach help? How would the *resistances* or barriers to such a paradigm and approach equally contribute to their disablement? To understand that, we ought to resist falling into Fear's Empire[2] as it tries to shape the discussion in this book.

There's a battle going on. From a fearlessness spirit, we have to resist the resistances to a Fearlessness Paradigm within a Fearism approach. As co-authors, our choice to engage the topic of resistances can sound like a rather *negative* thing to focus on. Yet for us, resistances are not merely negative and not merely against something. They express and contain enormous creative energy and great wisdom too. More obvious, they can be positive, like in liberating revolutions and/or the resistance of Greta Thunberg, the teen-star from Sweden, who resisted her society and school, and who led the most powerful activism campaign against the Global Warming threat to planet earth than anyone before her in history. She's been nominated for a Nobel Peace Prize.

In regard to analysis of resistances to Fearlessness, so far there has not been this kind of critical analysis offered in depth anywhere. As co-authors who shy away from grand proselytizing and overt street activism, we take a philosophical and creative way to intervene. We think the time is right. We make Recommendations in Part VI for individuals and groups to explore ways to put the ideas in our book to practical use, as well as to improve one's critical literacy of fear/ fearlessness as a dialectical and dynamic phenomenon in constant evolution. Our book is *not* a self-help guide but it is also *not* an abstraction so far removed from real experience that it is only for the powerful leaders and elitists and/or the educated academics in ivory towers. We try to strike a balance. Fearlessness is for everyone—it's our birthright. Unfortunately, history books have not been written on this Fearlessness Movement that lies and operates, rather invisibly most of the time, beneath the visible history of Fear.[3]

We wish to dramatically influence, if not correct, the dominant discourses on fear/fearlessness in this world. Promoting Fearlessness and Fearism, like those who promote courageousness in order to face our troubled times as individuals and as a species, is *not* enough on its own. Our orientation makes a strong 'shift' from the promoting/positivizing discourses, although no doubt, we will at times swerve into writing about our passion for Fearlessness today and its offering a 'gift' for the future of a troubled world. The discourses are largely out-of-date relative to the challenges we face in the 21st century, an argument Fisher made in his first major book.[4] It's hard to ignore how ridden life is today with its excesses derived from a toxic "culture of fear"[5] spreading everywhere like a virus. Our negative emphasis however is not one sourced from our despair, angst, worry and pessimism. We argue from and for Defense Intelligence (Fearlessness IQ) having both a negative and positive role in human affairs. Our aim is to utter the *best* of Fearlessness as exemplar of great fear management/education—that is, of great Defense Intelligence that Mother Nature provides our species, and all species, with.

We understand the rationale and pragmatism that one has to be *positive* about the thing being promoted in order to 'sell' an idea, service and/or a commodity. All business people know this, as well as the positive psychologists and educationists. For example, health and wellness promoters know they have to, often dramatically, emphasize (or exaggerate) what good health practices and positive attitudes will benefit you as a result of making some change. They know breaking unhealthy habits and thinking is hard to motivate. Typically their lists of benefits is longer than harms of not changing; because, today we are in a *culture of positivism* where that's what people want to hear about if they are going to motivate themselves to change. This positivism, according to Fisher, harms advances in Fear Studies.[6] This positivism is also called the 'carrot' approach to learning and change; or in more technical terms it's called cognitive positive imagining, which needs to be accompanied by behavioral positive reinforcement. Overall, we call this the Positive Paradigm (PP) and it could be called the Love Paradigm. Marianne Williamson a spiritual leader and politician in the 2020 U.S. Election, promoted a "Politics of Love" to end all divisiveness and inequality in her country.[7] It's seemingly good old common sense, it's compelling to explain how change happens, and it is all extremely popular, like 'motherhood and apple-pie.'

To express doubts about this paradigm and to question and critique the PP and/or even to offer a 'better' alternative, is in some ideological positivism circles perceived as a threat to 'the Good' itself. These people have made the PP their new mantra and 'God.' So, you'll hear "Be Positive!" swung around the room or the culture as if it is the answer to everything—which is just another version of "Love is the answer" to everything. And, if you are operating on and promoting the PP you can bet there are a tonne of resistances against the alternatives and/or the critiques coming their way.

Fisher and Subba began to challenge the broadcasting PP *via* discourses on Love as better than studying Fear(ism).[8] Fearlessness and Fearism are both going to have to deal with this domination of the PP. Fisher's specific articulation in the late-20th century of the Fearlessness Paradigm, as originally opposed to the domination of the Fear Paradigm was a start. We talk a good deal about this in our book. Relative to the Fear Paradigm, Fearlessness is positive. However, Fisher has recently realized that to promote a Fearlessness Paradigm is not always perceived as a positive alternative—or, more the case, it is not perceived by the majority as positive enough.

Fisher has been critiqued many times that his philosophy is "too negative," because it is about "lessness" and that is a negative movement and attribute of the lower-vibrations.[9] Also Fear equally is lower-emotional vibrations not of a higher spiritual resonance. These critics would sometimes say, "If you focus on fear, you'll merely attract fear." All of this was an assumed truth they spoke. They were acolytes of the New Age and a variety of Positivists of the Human Potential Movements and Positive Psychology/Attitude followers. All of them have real trouble with Fearlessness. They typically tell Fisher he ought to have named his "In Search of Fearlessness Project" by a more positive name with good energy like "In Search of Love Project." It is not that they disagree with Fisher's calling out of the horrible consequences of the "Fear Project" but that they just think his approach is going the wrong direction and thus it can't be very 'Good.' The moralism and defenses of those operating in the PP is immensely problematic when one wants to offer another positive alternative, like Fearlessness.

We offer in this book a largely *negative philosophy* approach,[10] yet a comprehensive integrative one, because we see the Fearism approach of Desh Subba and the Fearlessness Paradigm as taking a road-less-traveled, more 'negative' as critics may argue because Love is not fore-fronted, in order to achieve the 'better' way for humans to go. We invite readers into this controversial territory to make up your own minds about the PP and Fearlessness Paradigm in contrast—and yet, clearly they *both* are necessarily parts of the 'big picture' reality of how human beings are trying to cope with their circumstances. The bigger picture of the big picture, however, seems to us to involve some deeper investigation than merely arguing back n' forth about the positive vs negative.

Even constructing "fear" along that reductionist and boring spectrum is dubious, as we'll show in this book such an attempt of moralistic locating of Fear is an impossible thing to do in the first place because of the complexities of layers of meanings and definitions possible for Fear and for Fearlessness. We offer an open-minded creative investigation and understanding. Yet, we do suggest strongly the impulse to *locate* our subject matter here is probably a good direction to go (see Chapter Nine) but just not to fall into the trap of dualism/moralism and their ideological consequences which tend to close down intelligent dialogue because they pursue addictively only the 'right' understanding. We as co-authors want 'deep' understanding before we search for the 'right' understanding. The PP typically is already too biased towards the positive/the right to see the deep. Fisher has long argued, there's little room for such protective righteousness *in the search for true fearlessness.*

The world's cascading crises from the ecological, economic to political and combinations thereof, now place human kind in a vast predicament. We are not only in struggle to make it through the day but we have this creeping sense, especially with the mutating waves of the COVID pandemic since 2020, that our struggle is personal *and* communal. It's a struggle of evolution of consciousness itself. Will we regress or truly progress in our battle with this foe? Often this immensity is recognized by people's awareness we are all on the 'same sinking ship.' We can either work together and stay afloat and minimize the losses or we can compete and retract into our fear-based defenses behind our walls and compete for limited resources and/or for the privileged, easier it is to deny there is anything or anyone of concern over on the other side of the wall. At the same time, the double meaning of 'wall' means—"Enemies are everywhere." Depending on which side of the wall, each side defines the enemy!

Indeed, a certain "Immobility and Fear" has taken over most of the large cities around the world with COVID 19 and "lock down" emergency planning. As co-authors it behooves us to write a book on Fearlessness that takes into account this mega-context of unreal proportions. Few of us living today have experienced such a global lethal pandemic. The international expert on trauma, Dr. Peter Levine, spoke to our issues in a recent lecture on this immobility and fear dilemma we all face. It's worth citing at length:

> Our nervous systems, our brains, our bodies, have evolved over millennia to deal with threat. So, if there's something novel in our environment we'll orient towards it. We locate it, we localise it, and we express whether its friend or foe, whether it threatens us.[11]

Indeed, to "locate" and "localise" is a powerful tendency, when it comes to threat/risk/fear phenomenon. In Chapter Nine, intrigued by the "uncanny" as an actual location for Fearlessness, we suggested three questions could be very useful for advancing knowledge: (a) Where is Fearism located?, (b) Where is Fear located? and, (c) Where is Fearlessness located? Levine along with our questions overlap in a potential unlearning and re-learning some fundamentals of a critical literacy of fear/fearlessness dynamics. Levine indirectly is noting that "fears" are easiest to talk about and locate. With identifying a "fear of x, y, z..." then there is a 'place for fear.' It seems to comfort us. But then, comes the paradigm and philosophy which challenges all that and says we need to look at *fear itself* not merely where we end up boxing fear into a type or specific attachment to an object or situation *via* the hundreds of fears or phobias. Some theorists argue anxiety is the more nebulous aspect we experience as well, before that anxiety finds an object—but it always does—because it can always default to a fear of death, so say the existential philosophers. Yet, that's only the surface of the problem of locating fear and Fear. Fisher answers the three questions from Chapter Nine in a simple but complicated scenario by suggesting all of them (Fearism, Fear, Fearlessness) are located in paradigms, worldviews, consciousness itself. He's not being only playful here but is pointing to the underlying need to grasp the very structures of our thought and languages in order to determine good ways of understanding. It is a little like saying: 'to really understand fear, then know thy self.' More accurately, 'know the predominating ways of constructing knowledge' and that will guide you to 'knowing the ways you construct fear.' This is a definite postmodern form of constructivism and requires a new self-awareness of our role in 'making reality' as much as being in reality. Humans have that kind of power of cognitive and symbolic operations. We are a unique animal that way. To return to Levine's lecture, he never gets outside of a simple dualism philosophical frame as he sets up the 'observer' (experiencer) over here as 'A' and the 'emotion' (experienced) over there as 'B.' This is an old and worn strategy and in regards to fear studies it has to be challenged today, from a new approach. Let's continue with Levine's words in stating the problem today with the pandemic as global threat:

> We locate it, we localise it...If it threatens us then we will respond biologically, respond either by fleeing or fighting? That's the fight-flight response; that's very

well known. But what if you can't localise the source of the threat? And you keep searching...but it's not there but at the same time it is everywhere. Every person could be the carrier of this...potentially lethal enemy. So it's sort of like, everybody is our enemy, which is [very] dangerous because we need to pull together with this kind of thing. So we have to find a way that we can come out of this, what it is really, it's actually a state of shutdown. You know so many people are reporting [during this pandemic] symptoms like exhaustion, that they can't think clearly...and that they're on edge...and [it's] easy to get angry. All of these things are...what we're left with. But we don't really have any way to respond to it.[12]

So it looks like a major teaching of the pandemic, if we really get it, is that our enemy is everywhere and it is right inside of us too. Look not always out there for the worst enemy. It is like right in there, in you, in us, in our worldview itself. The way we live, reflecting our worldview, is the big problem—a point we make in this new book. The good news behind that lesson is that we have to look at how we have made ourselves alien and an enemy to our living and ecological companions on this planet. Who is really responsible for this mess? Yet, Levine is pointing to only the understanding so commonly assumed that fear can be understood by the "fear response"—like "fight-flight." This behavioral location of Fear is highly reductionistic, and we'll argue in this book that it distorts mostly in that it individualizes fear and Fear unnecessarily and it swerves around the undercurrent of what is even more important (perhaps) than fear and its responses. It is the forgotten and unseen response—better put—that is lurking and awaiting to be seen. Fisher's dictum guides much of our thinking throughout this book: *When fear appears, so then does fearlessness. Fearlessness is latent, and we trace that for readers into the Freudian world of the Id and the Indigenous worldview of the "primal" and many other tracks of argumentation. But let's not become distracted in the Preface into such details. It is merely a symptom of ignore-ance that even someone of the stature of Levine missed to inform humans that "fearlessness" is the way—in contrast to his conclusion "we don't really have any way to respond" to pandemic collective fear/threat. In that light, we dedicate this book to the COVID-19 pandemic, and more.*

We dedicate this book to the good will of humans as well when in crisis. We have seen neighborhood signs, during the pandemic "shut down" isolation, put up on windows and street corners by adults, and often adorned with rainbows and hearts painted by children, that say things like "Don't give up," "Love," and "We can make it through this together." One apartment senior's high rise in one city passed out hundreds of large bright red hearts to all the residents to place in their windows, of which many cooperated to create a group display of hope for everyone on the streets. On the negative-side, there is a plethora of unspoken, unsymbolized messages not put up on display but kept inside the psyche of the majority, who are trying to come to terms with their sense of frustration, anger, if not betrayal, at what this collapse of 'normal' life is doing to them and their loved ones and their livelihoods. The sense of threat and fear, dread and despair is becoming extreme. By nature, *We* are a social species and thus resist being "shut off" and "shut down." Freedom is no. 1, but so is health, and the two values are in a dangerous competition right now. Yet, Levine is suggesting many humans at this time are "shut down" emotionally, with potential real harm because of the immobility in these times.

On the positive-side of what a deep crisis pulls out of humans is the interest *to care, to help* and at our best *to serve* and at the highest ideal to enact *compassion-in-action* with no expected rewards to come back for the 'good' we have done for the Other. This latter evolution of caring has a natural philosophy of 'the gift' at its core. As co-authors we are well aware that the current predatory capitalist economic structures and ideologies have *not* been ecologically aligned with the laws of Nature and Her 'gift' to all of us—the gift of Life. Air is one of Her gifts. Milk is another gift from the mother. And, we argue in this book in various ways, that *Fearlessness* is a gift as well. These gifts can be made sacred or when that fails due to inaccurate ways of perceiving, thinking, propaganda and self-need obsession and greed, the gifts are turned into commodities to 'buy and sell' and even 'steal and horde.' We've seen far too much of the latter in a desacralization of the inherent caring that all these gifts in Creation offer. Faux "fearless" prescriptions and commandments are everywhere, along with the red hearts. Yet, there is a great shallowness in those interventions when they are not accompanied by a good fear management/education and discernments of what a true Fearlessness Paradigm can be.

"Right now," exclaimed the international health guru Dr. Deepak Chopra, "the entire world is facing the same existential anxiety directly." It appears we have a medical emergency not just on the outside but on the inside. The dis-ease and 'virus of fear' is taking over everything. It is real threat at our door, for sure. However, it is also an inflated threat that swerves from the rational to the irrational and panic. As a species were are facing an existential crises of proportions never seen before. The very awareness of our extinction potential, along with a whole lot of other species, is very near in the shrinking future. Young people feel this contracting sphere of joy, abundance and hope and reel with the losses of their future options—of which the climate change and global warming crises are more than evident of disasters to come. The global political scene however is slow to act and change. People are slow to change. There seems a chronic apathy, if not growing pessimism, that will not be helpful—recall Levine's "shut down" inside people's psyche and soul.

That said, some rebel spirit, like the *spirit of fearlessness* itself, is not willing to play victim to the forces of oppression and stupidity. "Right now," says international child-star environmental activist Greta Thunberg, "is where we draw the line." Many, including the likes of Chopra and Thunberg must also be wondering, as we are as co-authors, "How scared should we be?" Should we be made to feel more fearful in order to motivate us to stand up and speak out ethically against injustices, and resist, and do something useful to face these problems? How can we make people care more, if at the same time we are to make people fear more? There's no easy answers and yet in this book there are important directions offered to probe and explore the truth beneath the surfaces of what is happening in this world.

dimension of reality. We offer as very different authors a unique journey into this quest, which Fisher labeled in late-1989, while having an uncanny experience of the mystical sort, "in search of fearlessness."

To conclude, we are pleased to offer to our other fearism colleagues, and those who are unfamiliar to the philosophy of fearism approach, an application of many of its methodologies and ideas to the issue of *resistances* to Fearlessness. We ought to know our 'enemies' intimately not to eliminate them by moral judgements but to help them transform to their higher potentialities in the 'big picture' of evolution itself. We are indeed, even our 'enemies,' all on the same ship.

At times we are somewhat critical of our colleagues' work in specific areas, but we also appreciate their offerings. All of us are on this ship learning together. We trust this book will bring about more productive dialogues for all in the near future. We end this Preface with a pertinent quote, and an example of the use of negative philosophy and description, from the developmental, integral, artist/philosopher Jean Gebser:

> We have only one option: in examining the manifestations of our age, we must penetrate them with sufficient breadth and depth that we do not come under their demonic and destructive spell. We must not focus our view merely on these phenomenon, but rather on the humus of the decaying world beneath, where the seedlings of the future are growing....[14]

****

INTRODUCTION 1

State of the Youth in Democracy: Fear and Fearlessness

> Cassandra of [the] Trojan episode [story] is an unheeded prophetess for she knows everything including the future but is always disinclined to speak or even if she reveals her [youthful] forecast, no one believes. When she predicts that Troy is set to be doomed, none of her family members cared about her words.
>
> -Kumar & Sushmita[15]

n 2017, we (Fisher in Canada; Kumar in India) met each other online for our first of what was to become a set of ongoing book projects with Desh Subba, who is the founder of the *philosophy of fearism*. This initial contact was arranged through our mutual acquaintance of Subba, a Nepalese philosopher, novelist and poet, who was born in Dharan and now lives in Hong Kong.

Fisher and Subba met online a few years earlier in late 2014. The attraction was due to their mutual interest in fear(ism), as a central motivational and organizing principle for a new philosophy and psychology for humanity. Independently writing intensely about fear (Fisher since 1989; Subba since 1999), these two diverse thinkers joined forces, thus creating a first East-West dialogue on fear(ism). Their work has kick-started an intellectual global (r)evolutionary movement that would reset the inadequate and dangerous direction humanity was heading. Their humanistic and ecological vision and critical analysis would support an enlightened better developmental trajectory; because it foregrounds a profound understanding of the critical *nature and role of fear*. Subba wrote a subtitle for his classic philosophical tome on the subject, that "Life is conducted, directed and controlled by the fear." And Fisher would write that humanity has developed enough that it is time to grow-up and face head-on its collective "Fear Problem."

The three of us have grown to respect each other and nurture our overlapping interest in this enlightenment project—which is basically an Educational project. All of us have been concerned with the inadequate philosophies and psychologies available to people, and especially young people. The educational systems have not well served youth in terms of guiding them to recognize the reality of human behavior *via* the two-sided coin of motivation: fear/fearlessness. This dialectical relationship we believe is a key to freeing the human mind and building strong healthy communities and democracies.

Here we would also like to clarify what a *true democracy* is rather than going onward unmindfully by traditional and habitual ways of thinking about democracy. Traditions usually conform to the past modes of practices, perhaps suitable to the then prevailing customs and contexts. As the new wave of technologies emerged, so did the human mind evolve as *per* the existing and ongoing scenario. For example, the Constitutions of various democratic nations formed centuries or decades ago hardly incorporated explicitly 'fearlessness' among the ideals and virtues like liberty, equality, fraternity, dignity, justice, pursuit of happiness etc. The notion that autocratic systems of government alone are the centres of oppression and fear is no longer restricted to them as we currently observe certain democracies where the weaponization of fear has become a norm in the game of politics. Hence the time has also come to redefine the idea of a democracy—and, do so in referential new terms *via* the unique fear/fearlessness yardstick.

Education as a whole needs to critically re-evaluate its entire curriculum, while societies need to re-design their socialization processes from basic parenthood to work life to elder years and the dying process (e.g., where *fear of death* becomes a disproportionate reductionistic molding of human behavior as *survival*). Human beings are much more complex and capable than merely surviving under this old habit of indoctrination that fear of death (as our dreaded enemy) discourses have wrought upon human kind. Rather, a more complete holistic-integral view of human nature and motivation has been our radical aim, whereby human beings can powerfully *re-imagine* themselves anew within a more liberated (fearlessness) potential; rather than one that is largely oppressed and driven by fear-based designs and motivations. Individually and collectively, *all fear* can be transformed into a better ally for civilization to thrive, rather than constructing humans into slaves or merely agents of the State of Fear. Clearly, we are not suggesting "fear" is all bad (see Introduction 2).

Education, as we envision it, has now the immanent ethical task to catch-up, as well as Psychology and Politics etc., to enact a positive *leadership* role that Fisher calls "Fearless Leadership" for the 21st century. He has called for a "culture of fearlessness" to replace the dominating "culture of fear"[16] found near everywhere in the modern era. He has designed a new *Fearlessness Paradigm* (discussed in this new book) in order to think about *fear management/education* (FME) as part of everything that humans do daily. Of course this will be resisted by many. Fearlessness will be coded by the mainstream as even pathological. This latter point, of mis-representation of fearlessness, will be discussed throughout this new book.

Unfortunately, Fisher's research shows, nearly all people typically do not think of their lives in terms of fear management practices, nor do they realize their habits of thought and behaviors which are typically an unaware replaying of the patterns of *fear education*[17] that were taught to them by their elders (their culture) when they were young. Bringing this unconsciousness to consciousness is a major educational and therapeutic intervention built-in to the emancipatory agenda of a philosophy of fear(ism), fearlessness paradigm[18] and FME.

We imagine (dream of) a progressive dramatic event in human history, like never before, when the leaders of nations, and leaders of education, one-by-one gather to assess what has happened in their societies, especially in terms of youth development. And, in doing so they important now in a world that is turning more and more to fear as the way to socialize, educate and carry on politics. Kumar and Subba well know the negative barriers and signs that youth creativity is decreasing in domains of communication competency, while they become exclusively tech-savvy "netizens."

They are "like Cassandra" with "infinite loads of information on their fingertips," wrote Kumar. Yet, the world mostly is not ready to believe them. Unfortunately, too often amongst themselves as youth, they are suspicious of one another. There is so little trust because of the mass of dis-information and 'post-truth' skepticism. As well, they commonly don't communicate or integrate information overload very well, and it "often goes unattended."[23] Yet, they also know there are alternatives to the dominant fear-based ways—and, Kumar's book on youth fears and the future cited Subba's poem regarding a 'bridge' way, like a path to fearlessness, which can be founded upon new images of guidance from a trusted source—that is, from Nature, especially when Culture fails.[24]

All three of us agree that no part of society and all its institutions go untouched or untainted by the insidious seduction to (mis-)use fear as a form of power to dominate others (i.e., fearmongering). In this opening chapter we (Fisher and Kumar) wish to dialogue specifically on some of the issues that play out in the realm of Education and Politics. We believe that the grave problems in India where Kumar lives are very similar to Canada (and USA) where Fisher lives. With our initial diagnosis here we'll offer some initial guideposts and roads to travel in bringing about this new enlightenment for societies everywhere.

> **RMF:** First, as fearists who view the world through the critical lens of a fearism perspective, I declare, and I am suspecting you agree Maria, that the impact of *fear* and the potential of its twin *fearlessness*, ought to be staged and mapped in a radically new way compared to what history has provided us. It is like with the philosophy of fearism through Subba and my own fearlessness philosophy, a 'new story' of the very purpose of existence is unfolding. That may sound hyperbolic

but I am actually not trying to be dramatic but rather merely asserting what the data from Fear Studies shows us. At least, the new types of studies of fear(ism). I mean, that it is time to present these actors, fear and fearlessness, in a new dialectical story—that is, in their more accurate and holistic-integral relationship, within an emancipatory new theory, paradigm and worldview. Specifically I wish to focus on a *Fearlessness Paradigm*.

BMK: I agree Michael. Your twin metaphor is an interesting one theoretically but also in the realm of myths and psychodynamic complexes, for there is a universal application to make sense of what you are describing in more rational terms. This duality has been evident in Nature. Darkness doesn't exist without light. Space doesn't exist without time. They are two but exist as one. Likewise, we cannot understand the world only from a fear perspective and so we need to look at it also from the angle of fearlessness. Ancient Indian Puranas are replete with stories of '*bhaya*', meaning fear and '*abhaya*' means fearlessness, as occurring simultaneously and getting resolved in reciprocal relationships.

RMF: Thanks for that information, as I have not directly studied the Puranas, but some eastern philosophers I've read draw on them somewhat. You basically mean the Twin Myth as an archetypal mytheme phenomenon?

BMK: Yes. In Greek myths too. If there is Ares, god of violence, war, then... Aphrodite, goddess of love, is also there.

RMF: That dialectical 'balancing' imperative fits my dictum: *When fear arises, so then does fearlessness*. Regarding the mythic pattern, I've recently been exploring that somewhat superficially as a phenomenon with deep collective roots in the historical memory of groups and cultures; and, I've written about how this collective Twin phenomenon is a useful analytical concept in understanding opposites generally. In particular, applying it recently to my understanding of the problem of the healthy Republic as a governance structure and how various political leaders can, and often do, serve battling roles as iconic Twin oppositions. In my new book on Marianne Williamson, I proceed to investigate her leadership for the Democratic Party in the USA in 2020 *contra* the enemy—but in disguise, really a Twin—phenomenon—of Donald Trump Jr., former President of the USA and provocative leader of the Republican Party since 2016.[25] It makes me wonder if the ideal of the Republic, anywhere in the world where democracy is trying to take hold and succeed, may someday be fully realized. I wonder what that might look like?

BMK: On first glance, we can see Opposites or Enemies easily. But it takes a much more nuanced deeper investigation to see they are Twins, or at least potentially so. Yes, it is a challenge to not get hooked on only the surface of the battles of oppositions and polarities. That's the big danger of politics generally today. Oppositions and polarities need to be based on impersonal attitudes because self-oriented Ego will not go well for the collective good. The Republic is not a personal issue *per se*. It is a commons matter, much on the lines of the commons and goods, such as air, water or land. Whatever the deliberations or arguments are between the ruling party and opposition party, they ought to be able to reach a more impersonal level with an aim, with an overall perspective, for something of a larger cause—for the good of the nation or society or world for that matter. For generations. As Max Weber propounded, bureaucracy is to best be founded on an impersonal approach to manage affairs. If nobody weaponizes fear, we can call it a fearless Republic. Thomas More's 'Utopia' is a particularly interesting and an outstanding example of good futurist vision.

RMF: I agree. I've often looked for new thinking that includes but transcends binary oppositions—and the dualism philosophy that accompanies it. That old paradigm of thinking I believe has really run its course—with rather disastrous effects overall.

BMK: True Michael! The Constitution of each country, for example, lays down procedures for national businesses. The interpretations of legal provisions should be in favour of the collective good, and at the same time without causing any smallest inconvenience to the innocent. On the same lines are the international laws, covenants etc. for peace and friendship among the nations. But the issue gets worrisome when nations *weaponize fear* not only against their dissenting voices within their countries—like opposition party leaders or civil society members, etc.—but also against other nations. All of which leads to intractable oppositions in destructive unhealthy conflict—and wars. Such wars can be found not just in nations against nations, businesses against businesses or tribes and religions against tribes and religions, but they can exist in families and in many relationships. Because opposites do seem real. But such opposites should integrate in the same way as Hegelian synthesis emerges from dialectic treatment of thesis and antithesis.

RMF: I agree the Hegelian dialectic is one of others; yet, it still has some basic value today in how to approach problems. I think of them as opposite qualities and values, for example, say with an intimate couple or an employer and worker.

BMK: When opposite qualities are in moderation, it is like a balanced personality, having no extremity at either side of scale. Some may interpret it as equanimity when a person is neither too submissive nor too aggressive. Buddha was famous for his middle path theory of life. This type of moderate conduct is the general trait of the 'normal' healthy human being. Extremely good and extremely bad people come to be viewed as abnormal when the former are respected as saints and the latter frowned as criminals. Here too, we see the duality working in opposite direction much the same way as Id is too selfish and superego is too socially-oriented and conformist. And it is Ego that acts as the moderator. If people in a given group are polarised on the scale with goodness at one extreme and badness on the extreme, it is up to the government or society in general to moderate so as to reform the bad. Practically speaking, both the extremes will be in negligible numbers and the maximum will be in the category of moderation. An American proverb reads, 'you have to take the good with the bad.'

Or a child and their school teacher and so on. If we focus our attention on the surface conflict between X and Y, for example, we'll not see the deeper dynamics as you have pointed to in our discussion here. Fear and Fearlessness look like opposites. They could be seen as enemies. But as I understand your work Michael, and the use of a dialectical rather than a dualism methodology or framing, you end up with a different picture of what is going on in their dynamic relationship. I hear you have done the same manoeuvre with Williamson and Trump as leaders fighting it out for how the Republic ought to be. Political conflict is everywhere, even in our personal intimate relationships.

RMF: Oh yeah, even if we don't call it political. It's there operating as a power struggle. Politics is fundamentally about how to share power—either well or not so well. So, that's part of my interest in conflict management/education (CME)[26] from my early graduate studies. In those literatures I studied on conflict resolution dualism was prevalent in use for setting up the architecture of conflict analysis—and resolutions. It is the obvious way we can understand conflict as X versus Y. However, I was never satisfied with that. It was too reductionistic and functionalist—lacking in any real psychological depth. I had studied Carl Jung's depth psychology and the concept of the Shadow prior, and I was looking to see if it could provide a mytho-psychological and philosophical theory applicable to real conflicts between obvious oppositional peoples and forces. I mean even Good vs. Evil is archetypal just like say God and Satan as personifications, as Shadow Twins—and of stories of battles in the cosmos. It seems these labels are more primal and universal than merely personalities like say Williamson and Trump. Maybe there's a lesson or two there for our understanding of Fear and a fearism perspective.

I wonder...what would we make of the conflict situations of these dramatic oppositions that we see so often operating—and, thus turn the interpretation—and try to imagine them as if X and Y are at some level of reality, Twins? As overt enemies they may be, from another perspective, really *disguised* Twins? In other words, I suspect they have the same intimate 'source' or 'parent.'[27] Dialectically, they are co-evolving and shaping each other, perhaps. Can studies of mythology of Twins help us here? And, then, can you apply that learning from the mythic aspect of reality, and our psyche, to the dynamic of fear and fearlessness, which I have also called two-sides of the same coin?

BMK: Yes, it can be applied. For example, Janus represents the resolution of conflicts between the mutually opposing qualities in the same person. He is the god of beginning/doorways in Roman mythology. He is double faced, one face looking backward and the other forward. He has two mutually contrasting traits, one of which is past-based and the other is future-oriented. Moderation of the two optimally keeps the present in a balanced, stable and feasible manner.

RMF: Past-Present-Future are held in this Janusian thinking[28] as a co-creative embrace and dynamic feedback loop. Each of the three parts a One—as you say, they keep in 'balance'—in a holistic-integral way. The Fearlessness Paradigm truly seeks this way as well.

BMK: Fear and fearlessness are like past and future. Past means 'the life lived thus far' and future means 'the life ahead.' It's the combination of the two in present life—which is an integration of both past and future; as one passing by and the other taking off. And it is always dynamic, on the move.

RMF: Typically our *fear education* in school systems, analogous to say sex education, does not typically take this complex dynamic into account; thus, learners suffer with a rather dead and static notion of what fear is, and what fearlessness is, if they even get taught about these things period. We need a holistic, relational-based, evolving systems paradigm. The 21st century knowledge fields are already telling us, especially in the new sciences of chaos theory, complexity theory, cybernetics and adaptive systems, that we have to shift from the old Newtonian understanding of reality.[29]

BMK: I agree. In application to resolution of conflict occurring at the point of one passing by, the past—and the other taking off, the future—lies a zone of creative integration and a moderation or balanced state, or simply persistent 'reality' which is in front of our eyes...happening now. The point of dialectical thinking in Janusian fashion as a dynamic system, at least theoretically, keeps us from becoming fixated on *only one* perspective like say the past, or the future, or the present. They all are equally valid in this holistic paradigm. This undermines pathological ideologism. I guess that is what you are attempting to pull out as well in your Fearlessness Paradigm and in the fearism perspective. Keep things moving; keep elements of the whole 'communicating' with each other—rather than splitting off, dividing, and each part trying to control the whole—that is, trying to dominate and/or convert other parts to the *one and only* perspective on reality. Thus, a complexity perspective is sought as best in thinking about fear and fearlessness or any set of binaries. You and Subba definitely bring this dynamic creative space to fear studies, like I have never seen before.

If we take a model/theory of three-identities in one; an archaic form of a *trinity* mytheme that is common in myths around the world, I see the same adaptive logic is comparable to the Freudian tripartite theory: Id concept—which represents the mostly unconscious primitive, evolutionary, and past memories, like instincts; there's the Superego, which represents the evolving-edge in the form of society and the future course of life. Regarding the psychic conflict that Freud made us realize is so important, we can see the 'conflict resolution manager' in any present moment, is the Ego. It is there that the skills and abilities are enacted, negotiating Id and Superego demands and knowledges, including the Ego's needs, upon this triangulating motivational template, which one's entire life takes its twists and turns. In Id itself, the duality of life as *libido* and death as *destrudo,* interrelate, resulting in conflict between the two, like opposites; and it is the Ego which does its best to resolve those forces, whether positively or negatively, healthily or unhealthily, or most probably if all goes well, in a moderate way which brings about the integrated and functional outcome desired.

RMF: How interesting. I have a similar notion of the triad of human nature, human condition, and human potential. Anyways, over the years I have naturally been attracted to that creative and Janusian growth process in developmental terms and have read other theologies, philosophies and psychologies that utilize some form of trinity notion as well. It's archetypal. Yet, readers in particular here, may note in my work that I have made a big deal about my critique of Love,[30] and those that think love is the elixir, the answer, the 'beginning and end' to all current human and ecological problems.

What I have found so lacking in their thought and theories is that they are rarely able to get beyond the rigid ontological idea that: Fear is merely the absence of Love.[31] They therefore disregard trying to learn anything more about fear as a positive force, and a complex co-evolving and morphing reality that is part-n-parcel of what love is and can be. There is no artificial separation or dualism, is my point. It's romantical to think otherwise. That's the problem when anyone asserts a philosophical idea about only the virtues, as if they are ontologically pure—abstract, as Plato did as well. And worse, these love-mongers typically ignore fearlessness pretty much or simply call it a pathology. The Western philosophers and psychologists generally are most prone to that mis-interpretation.

To apply your take Maria, I situate Fear and Love at opposite poles, perhaps the Janus metaphor is appropriate as well. The arche-motivational opposites are found represented in a good deal of wisdom literature throughout history and across cultures.[32] But I then combine a new space for Fearlessness as in between. Fear <---> Fearlessness <---> Love. Readers can check out my publishing on this trinity dynamic[33] and also see Figure 1 below. But that's getting ahead of ourselves.

BMK: A *philosophy of fearism* perspective helps. For starters, you cannot find anything in that new philosophy that locates fear as opposite to any one thing. There is virtually no dualism in fearism thought. It is quite intriguing that Subba and yourself, do not have only one definition or meaning for *fear*.[34] I feel that both of your perspectives (re: fear and fearlessness) are complementary to each other. They elucidate both aims for a progressive moderate and/or holistic-integral approach.

RMF: Equally, I've not provided only one definition for *fearlessness*. My preference is to search out an architecture for a Fearlessness Paradigm which sets a new emancipatory reference point for understanding fearlessness, fear, love, or anything else in the realm of human activity. I guess I am always walking a razor's edge to tip into binary world reality—because I have, in some ways, constructed the Fearlessness Paradigm in contradiction to the oppositional Fear Paradigm, which the latter is near totally dominating the planet. Anyways, the rest of this book you and I are writing will go into that more carefully for readers to make sense of it. A lot of the problems I stir up with the 'norm' ways are because of my complexifying the very definition of fear—making it also a notion of 'fear'[35]—that is, culturally-modified fear. Subba and other fearists don't really attend to 'fear' in a postmodern critical culturalist lens the way I do. Yet, I see room in the fearism perspective to address it.

BMK: Right. This fearism perspective for our new book here is important for a much bigger project of dealing with opposites generally. And, as you say, it could help with CME practices too. And, for the Republic and democracies—no doubt, there is a good deal of learning to integrate there. I recently published a newspaper article[36] arguing that, "In a way, the most vital feature which is embedded in all the sacred tenets of the Republic is nothing else than 'fearlessness.'" I encouraged in India, where the oldest Republic existed in the Licchavi state in 6th century BC, to return to the concepts of fearless and fearlessness in every day, and to recalibrate ethical political and economic discourses. I believe it is Dr. B. R. Ambedkar, the architect of the Constitution of India, who had offered such a beginning framework for true liberation within a Republic. Unfortunately, it appears that fear-based concepts and thinking have dominated since, and continue to grow worse in this nation. That is why I initiated the topic for the recent book, *India, a Nation of Fear and Prejudice*, with you and Subba.[37]

RMF: I don't know Ambedkar's philosophy and activism but it sounds somewhat like the foundational principles of what I have called "fearless leadership"[38]—with some great examples in history like Mahatma Gandhi. But Maria, I'd like to steer you back to my earlier question: Can you apply that learning from the mythic aspect re: Twins to the dynamic of fear and fearlessness,

BMK: Sure. Apart from the Janus example, we see that everything is explainable in terms of the synthesis of opposites. Often in cosmogenesis mythemes we see this. For example, the Bible says that it was Dark in the beginning and God said, "let there be light." And Light was there. If we look at it, we understand that darkness is nothing but absence of light.

RMF: Analogously, Death is the absence of Life.

BMK: Similarly, Fearlessness is nothing but the absence of Fear.

RMF: The danger, in my mind, is to take these rather objectivist, logical, rational representations, as words and concepts and to overly conflate their literal meaning with the phenomenological reality of what is going on holistically. The latter is a whole other problem needing attention and methodological sophistication. I am all for such representations as words, but they are like 'theories' and that's about all. They have to be continually deconstructed, reality-tested in empirical and experiential ways. They also can become just another dualism, looking like a monism or nondualism, but merely articulated in a different form than the standard X vs. Y form of dualism. Okay, I want to move on...

I'm thinking of the youth of today, everywhere in the world. I'm thinking of caring activists and others fighting for a strong democracy, liberty, justice. My question to all of you, and to the school teachers, mentors, leaders you will encounter who greatly influence you: Do you have a good curriculum of FME? of CME? Will you know what such a curriculum would look like and feel like? Are you currently capable of discerning a Fear Paradigm in your educational model and practices compared to a Fearlessness Paradigm? Are you being exposed to a fearism perspective OR are you merely being taught about fear and its management just like the ancestors before, who may have been doing their best, but they had not had access to the best information on fear management and on the nature and role of fearlessness?

Simply to start, a Fearlessness Paradigm sees the entire world/cosmos through a fearlessness perspective. That becomes more complicated as we go throughout this book and attempt to define fearlessness—but for now, that gives readers a first meaning of what we are going to talk about. This approach is by no means the only way to understand fear/fearlessness, and we embrace other's investigations; but we believe we have one of the most potent images—as Figure 1, in the form of a processual and in-progress mapping and model that shows explicitly the visuality of their relationship. It has greatly influenced my own designing, teaching and therapeutic work on this subject. Let's glance over the diagram, and you can ask questions and comment Maria, while I describe the basic meaning of these parts of the diagram and their implications.

SYSTEMS INTEGRAL META-DYNAMICS of LOVE and FEAR

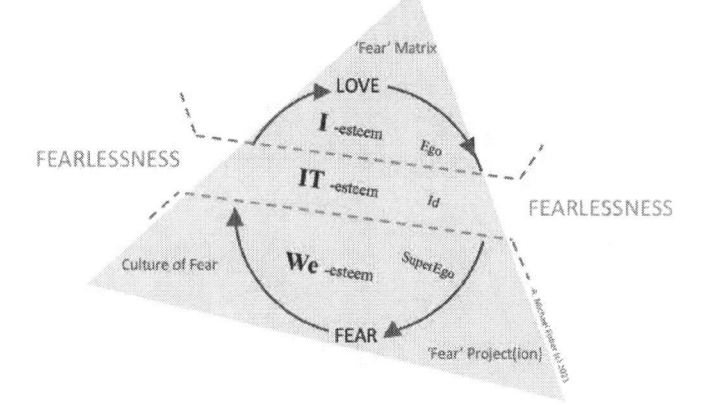

Figure 1 Tripartite Esteem Model: Fear — Fearlessness — Love

Several layers of complex dynamics are going on in this Figure 1. In the core of the model is the circular-cyclic relationship of ever evolving forces and meta-motivations we might call Love to Fear and back again. They are not absolute opposites but function as binary poles. They are part of a circular flow, in connection; that is, continually and dialectically moving and growing, self-correcting in excesses, *via* intimate interrelationship.

I have uniquely amongst the other theories, added Fearlessness as a 'middle' zone between the dropping down from Love and increasing Fear. This zone is a place to temporarily halt, and turn the trend of loss of Love and gain in Fear with other possibilities of resolution, correction, self/system regulation. Fearlessness is best suited to this task of Descent but not just this path. For on the other side of the circle path, when Fear is dropping down and there is an Ascent to Love again, Fearlessness is best suited—as a middle Fearlessness Zone offers a location to turn in and not rush too quickly to Love but only to do so after being informed by Fearlessness (e.g., the Fearlessness Paradigm).

Why the Fearlessness Zone? It was constructed as an idea, but is thought to also be a real phenomenon, in order to counter the larger meta-contextual forces that are in light blue color that interpenetrate all the psycho-cultural dynamics of the situation. The Fear Paradigm I have mentioned earlier in our dialogue, operating as dominating Culture of Fear, 'Fear' Project(ion) and 'Fear' Matrix, are constructs I have created over the decades to account for the chronic, often low-grade, often invisible, tug-forces of these larger dynamics on everything. In other words, the flow between Love and Fear in the center is not "pure" but tainted—that is part of what I have also called the global Fear Problem—and, yes, it is also a global Love Problem. It seemed to me that a mid-zone turn out would be a more 'free space' theoretically, and not hooked so totally on the direct Descending-Ascending path which operates within the Fear Paradigm. In another sense, the Fearlessness zone/paradigm offers the restoration, and re-learning space—the de-hypnosis zone to get out of illusions brought about by the incessant social propaganda and conditioning from the 'norm' ways of knowing and being—that is, from the Fear Paradigm.

I've then added Freud's three conceptions as I imagine where they operate on this model and named three resonant types of Esteem(s) that go with the zones.

There's a much larger conversation, for later in the book in Chapter 6, where I make a case that the Fearlessness zone is most potent to counter the Fear Paradigm (the Fear Problem) when it is founded in the Id and It-esteem. This is the instinctual and Natural layer of our motivational template. I realize this may sound all rather abstract at this point, and it is, but over the pages to come, hopefully this will become more clear and meaningful, with even associated practices for these layers in Figure 1. I'll make a philosophical distinction, as does the integral philosopher Ken Wilber, that a good holistic-integral model of reality, is both dialectical, but it is also vertical and developmental. The Fearlessness Paradigm is both of these. Wilber asked us to recognize the *foundational* levels of the spectrum of consciousness[39]—as the most basic, simpler, and ancient. They offer great wisdom. The Id included. Of course, we don't want to take everything they offer as great because some of it is not.

Then along the spectrum of evolution of consciousness arise other structures and motivational forces that become more and more *significant* or higher in advancement and complexity. Yet, as we have been saying in this dialogue, Maria, one ought not make any one of these levels of reality, lower or higher, absolutely 'better' than another. Each has their role of specialization and wisdom. They're holarchical in development, argued Wilber—but neither is better; for we need both ends of the spectrum for the whole to function well—as you've said, in 'balance.'

I would be so delighted if schools everywhere were teaching children and youth from the start, how to begin to think well in such a way. It would solve so many later problems in life. The holistic curriculum is intended to do this but over its 50+ years of offering a new philosophy of holism and systems thinking etc., it has yet given fear and fearlessness the due attention it requires. That neglect of content is disastrous, as far as I am concerned.

BMK: I've no reason to doubt your educational expertise in regard to designing a progressive 21st century curriculum that encourages a type of thinking that most of us never learned. A rare few of us maybe have picked-it-up but we did it on our own account because we were looking for better perspectives to use to critically analyze our worlds. They are alternatives and often are not supported by the 'norm' systems of education. In fact, sadly in India, evidence shows that youth are continuing to be overwhelmed and unnecessarily distracted, and not very alternative in their outlooks.

They have become susceptible to social influences, like new media, and cell-phones, TV, etc., to such a large extent that they are losing the sensitivity to adapt and change to reality. Their virtual reality bubbles may be interesting and useful at times, but on the whole they narrow down youth's overall perceptions and skew accuracy as to what is really happening in the world. It is not all their fault.

RMF: I get really concerned how easily they can fall prey to what Marianne Williamson has called "ideological capture"[40]—and, that is even more prevalent when children are severely poor and highly traumatized. Terrorist groups amongst others of nefarious intent will prey on these youth and bring them into their 'flocks' and organizations.

BMK: It's a massive problem. Those kinds of youth are searching for some sense of security, even if it is within an authoritarianism that oppresses them. They need to allay their fears however they can. They find adults or even peer gang leaders to identify and find purpose with and such leaders may seem 'fearless' to them. Although, as you have pointed out often in your work Michael, that kind of 'fearless' is more bravado than true mature fearlessness. Anyways, the issue of today's Indian youth attention and attitudes is startling. The Centre for the Study of Developing Societies, by Konrad, Adenauer, Stiftung and Lokniti, surveyed in 2016 Indian youth's attitudes, aspirations and anxieties. They point out in their research that the youth are inclined more towards traditional ideas than progressive and futuristic ones.

Of course, the traditional social system of 'norms' and authorities and institutions are still perpetuating an age old caste consciousness of prejudices and fears, exacerbating inter-caste conflicts, all of which regularly make headline news. Another study was conducted in 2017 by an NGO entitled *Pratham*. It was reported that a large proportion of the teenage population are not aware of basic facts like the name of the national capital and its location, etc. It hard to have a strong citizenship or Republic under this failure of basic knowledge of issues of governance in the country. So, the state of the youth is such that most of the political parties are eager to exploit the conditions of young people by indoctrinating their own beliefs and ideological traditions. Since there are many religions and thousands of castes and tribes, certain mischievous ideologues will assault the gullible youth with propaganda along divisive lines. With such growing fear is inevitable hate speech, be it online or offline. So, democratic processes often involve demonic practices and strategies of 'divide people to rule them'—of which election campaigns are ubiquitously known for. The resultant mutual enmity is triggered and reciprocal fears, creating a climate of fear, takes over many respective groups and communities. The youth find themselves at their wits end as the things roll out naturally in an unexpected manner. Recently in politics the lack of good political education shows through. Their youthful votes made them partners in victory in elections but it did not make them wise. Their party leaders emerged as winners in forming the government but not as the unifiers of the country. Their ideologies promoted them as policy makers but not as the benefactors of the society. This is the unfortunate state of affairs in those democracies where the electorate is not enlightened, not practicing fearlessness, and tend to be largely misguided on socioeconomic and political realities.

RMF: Youth are suffering in the real and at the same time how they feel and behave is symbolic. The culture is always trying to make sense of youth because of their symbolic power to represent something well all long for. Youth represent innocence, energy and creativity. How they handle the future and envision and enact an innovative life is really important. If adults end up fearing youth's despair, then they will be fearing the future in despair; and as youth allow themselves to be caught up in a climate of fear and culture of fear, then the future to them is always going to be threatening. If they feel threatened and withdraw, adults become more terrified as to where the world is going—and thus, these masses of youth are often projected upon by adults, often mis-informed adults, as threatening. It's a vicious fear-cycle, hard to break that both generations play into, if they are not critically aware of this dynamic. The archetypal pattern, a kind of universal conflict in this regard, is probably demonstrated well through the mythic conflictual forms of the *Senex*, as *old* tradition, and the *Puer*, as *new* ways of doing things. Such archetypal forms also play out, said Carl Jung, in our individual psyches. We'll return to this issue later in this book.

I want to point to another problem with adults and what I have observed about their learning styles that is troubling. In the last three years I have published nearly a hundred teaching videos, and 11 FearTalks, mostly on my thoughts and critiques about how humans relate to fear and fearlessness. I typically invite viewers to enter conversations and ask questions, and I await for their curiosity to go with that. For five years I have facilitated the Fearlessness Movement ning, and have also promoted fearlessness education in hundreds of published papers. Unfortunately, amongst the thousands of viewers and readers of my work, there is nearly no such interaction, no such curiosity. These contemporary adults are sadly becoming very distracted by the plethora of things to watch on the Internet and it is turning out a mass of passive learners. Indeed, there is a good deal of *resistance to fearlessness* and a lot of it is resistance to change! I think underneath resistance one will find both a good form and a bad form—that is, a positive righteousness and indignation to oppression driven by a quest for freedom; while on the other-side of the coin of resistance there's a weakening of will, cynicism, apathy, helplessness and hopelessness and neurotic pathologies—all driven by fear. Our new book will address many of these issues and offer recommendations for dealing with resistance in a holistic way—a fearlessness way. I think that will be innovative and enlightening for many people to find out more about.

When it comes to planning how to better educate a population, the factors you point to above and my own teaching experience add up to a most challenging problem. I'm glad we are talking about it. And, I invite readers of our new book to engage with us and form coalitions of a Fearlessness Movement globally that can really make a difference. We have a lot of work to do yet to find learners who have an ignited a *spirit of fearlessness* for that collaborative mission.

Highlights of What is to Come

Because we've chosen to write three distinct but overlapping Introductions to this book, there is nothing conventional in our style. We wanted the trio of Introductions to reflect the very idea of triangulation and holistic-integral sensibility to everything in this book and as part of representing what fearlessness is to us. The trio gives a different angle in on how best to introduce this book's content. We felt they all had a valuable role to play.

So, let us first briefly summarize what is the main angle we intended with this Introduction 1. We both felt that it was important to start with a concrete situation that was universally recognizable to all readers. That is, the state of youth today in the world. And, we then thought it important to draw out how *youth itself* is symbolic of our future, and that we can paralyze ourselves as a nation, a Republic, a democracy, if we don't give good attention to the needs and desires of youth. In many ways Introduction 1 ends up being a 'guide' for parents and teachers to a large extent, although it is for all adults and mature youth who want to read it. This good attention will require an educational transformation overall. New priorities. We point to the inadequacies of so much of our Education systems, but equally we could have talked about Psychology and Health systems, Political and Economic systems, and so on. No one system is worse than another, that is, IF all of the systems are still dominated by Fear's Rule—that is, what we called the ruling Fear Paradigm.

Although, we did not try to define the Fear Paradigm and the Fearlessness Paradigm we propose as a counter project, we hope that readers will start to get a feel for what these concepts and phenomenon might mean. With reading further in the book, no doubt the pieces of the complex puzzle will come together. Because we chose from the start to emphasize that reductionistic and overly simplistic notions of fear and fearlessness are not part of the fearism perspective of this book, it behooves all of us to upgrade our education and critical literacy on these topics, and one of the first strategies is to make one's perspectives and knowledges more complex. The Fear Problem is complex and will not be understood in its full depth and breadth without a complexity mindset and thinking that is dialectical.

Our bringing in mythic aspects into this discussion ought to excite pre-rationalistic and creative modalities of feelings, images and thoughts to everything in this book. Clearly, both of us as co-authors can be rational, but we are convinced that the human psyche, and our societies do not function on rationality[41] alone. Implicitly, we trust that we conveyed to you all that in such troubled times of cascading global crises, including the youth crisis we touch upon here, that now is not a time to be too conservative and shy about trying new ideas, theories, philosophies and perspectives. The broad and deep fearism perspective we introduced is a start to a re-translation of how to even approach fear knowledge—never mind that it also gives us a set of new opportunities ideally to manage fear better than we ever have as individuals, and as collectives, before.

We are at the cusp, says the great fearist, Desh Subba, of passing from an "Extreme Fear Age" to a "Fearless Age."[42] As co-authors, we'll do our best to continue building 'bridges' in our writing in this book so more of you may find a way to also pass, even if there are *resistances* that may seem like an 'abyss' or 'wall' impossible to overcome. With new conceptual tools, like new vocabularies, and ideas, maps and theories that catalyze new imaginaries—with a focus on fear and fearlessness—we are confident humanity won't miss this grand event of a transition, a passing, a transformation, towards a new future that is both positive and negative—but, we'll be smart enough now armed with the new tools and perspectives to not get hooked on only one way of seeing reality—and thus, of seeing ALL of ourselves and ALL of our possibilities be they negative and/or positive. From that vast array of holistic open-mindfulness, of sincere and disciplined embrace—then, and only then ought we make our decisions and act. That's the beginning of true wisdom.

In terms of a practical recommendation: *Try out what it is like to carry around the term **fear**, every time you see it, hear it, feel it, talk about it, but do so with a new handle—add the '**ism**' to it. Never let fear run around without the handle (leash).* Report your results of this shift. Study fearism. Create with fearism. Critique fearism. Share your findings with others. We offer two philosophers' quotes of inspiration regarding Education, one from the West and one from the East.

> One generation...could transform the world by bringing into it a generation of fearless children....Education is the key to the new world.   – Bertrand Russell[43]

> [O]ur whole education should be based on fearlessness, and so should the whole social and political structure.... The goal of education must be freedom from fear.... Until education is really based on fearlessness there is no hope of any change in society.
>   –Vinobā Bhave[44]

INTRODUCTION 2

Gift of Fear—Gift of Fearlessness

My research for 32 years on this topic shows that until we can shift our thinking to *fear itself* and then to *fear is social*—we will continue as a species to create and reproduce knowledge about fear (i.e., fear management/education) that falls far short of that which is critically required to undermine the insidious and deadly growth of the global Fear Problem.

– R. M. Fisher[45]

Fear and anxiety have a magical ability to open new doors of perception, giving us information about our situation and prompting us to look carefully at our circumstances [including who we think we are].

- Four Arrows[46]

Look carefully. Listen deeply. Resist not what Fear has to teach. We begin with Four Arrows (*Wahinkpe Topa*), our Indigenous elder brother, author of 22 books, speaking as a Western Indigenous-based educator, hypnotherapist and Lakota Sioux pipe-carrier. Fisher has collaborated with Four Arrows since 2017, respecting him as a mentor, warrior, a 'medicine' man, and a great practitioner of fear/fearlessness; both who have committed to the path of learning, within a truly *transformational dimension*.[47] They well-know the deep architecture of the global Fear

Problem, and of the mass hypnotic trance most humans are currently caught in, and rarely are such people aware of it. According to Fisher's recent intellectual biography of Four Arrows,

> Not by any means a household name or recognized by most mainstream educators, professionals or academics, Four Arrows offers a unique holistic perspective on human potential, curriculum, and pedagogy as an alternative to the destructive path modern economic and technological-based societies are on. The path of Fearlessness he offers radically intervenes into the enslaving Fear-based hypnotic processes of everyday unconscious individual and cultural trance that plagues most societies today. He [Four Arrows] recently concluded:
>
> In my mind, this mass hypnosis syndrome, I now call Trance-based Learning [TBL] gone awry, is the only explanation that makes sense of how modern educated societies, especially, have rationalized their technologies of domination, their polluting of their own nest, and their addictions to ways of life that paradoxically destroy Life. My own vision of rehabilitation from this destructive path is that Fear and courage concepts are essential to understand as they drive learning and development in a "good way" or "bad way"....This is the ethical core to all my environmental and social reform work. I offer an intentional transformation learning theory and critical praxis as an initiative to build a society and world that is able to resist and reconstruct current hegemonic fear-conditioning—the latter, which has unfortunately become "normalization" socialization—a "culture of fear."[48]

As co-authors, we do not wish to side-step the immense challenges humanity faces in the 21st century, and Four Arrows captures much of that challenge in this quote. From our view, the diagnosis points to a rehabilitation which could be called the making of a *social vaccine*—a *fear vaccine process*—whereby, everyone, including our institutions, ethically re-calibrates what it means to live a life that is Good, True and Beautiful. Of course the solutions are to be found in the details, So, let us proceed to open some doors on our ideas and include some stories that revolve around the Gift of Fear notion that several writers have already pursued. But first we wish to contextualize those ideas and prescriptions, by re-emphasizing methodology and approach, and ultimately how we make sense of a fearism perspective on everything in these pages.

Readers will notice that the first five of the six PARTS of this book are titled to repeat the phrase "Fearlessness is/as...". One reason for this emphasis on *is* or *as* is because there is an implicit attempt to define *fearlessness*. Yet, typical of our holistic-integral approach[49] and fearism perspective we (Fisher and Kumar) are not going to search for or settle for just the *one and only* approach to a 'proper' or 'certified' normal definition of fear or fearlessness. We've adopted strategically, and with a good deal of philosophical back-up, fear/fearlessness as a *dialectical reality* (as argued in Introduction 1), and thus to really separate a definition for only one-side of the dialectic and not the other is already undermining of a holistic-integral approach. Equally, throughout this book you will notice that as co-authors we bring each a different voice and set of experiences and perspectives to this topic.

Although we overlap in agreement at times, we also will slightly verge from each other's preferences and thoughts. However, that tension we believe is what will make this a more creative work than not. It is clear to us that a fearism perspective is a relative wide-open inquiry. And even the heavy emphasis on rational philosophical argument and theory or even science at times, ought not be read as that is the only set of modalities to bring to imagination and thinking about fear/fearlessness. Our attitude is one of deep listening to not just ourselves inquiring into "what is fear?" for example, but it is critical we ask what is the subject "fear" for example, equally offering up as insights, if not hidden secrets, and perhaps gifts, to help us as inquiring fearists along the way of our study. Simply, we are reinforcing here that fear/fearlessness is a dialectical form much like a 'mirror'—the slash (/) is really the threshold of both distinction of phenomenon and it is a mirror device that asks us to be conscious as much as possible that each side is informing the other.

So, regarding the difference in the inquiry that this attitude brings one can say it is a transformative learning approach. For example, *what is fear/what is human* or *fear/self* (?) is a transformative fearist way of inquiring. Fear management/education (FME) on this planet, according to Fisher has not yet fully understood how transformative the study of fear/self can be. Or as his Indigenous-based colleague, Four Arrows, has argued with his invoking our ancient "primal mind," we have as humans the imperative as earth-beings to re-locate ourselves in relationship with all Mother Earth's 'teachers' (and beyond)—including *Fear* as a great teacher—and, the best place to look, listen, learn about fear is from the greater-than-human beings we share this earth with. Thus, we encourage readers to alter their paradigm of knowing from the conventional, anthropocentric[50] (i.e., overly human species-centered), ways of dominating knowledge and inquiry and open with us along this journey with a fearism perspective that embraces a diversity of ways of knowing.

In other words, *fearlessness* and *fear* are up for grabs, somewhat at least, as we write this Introduction 2. Fisher has used the 'fearlessness' and 'fear' code at times as a methodological means of identifying a subject with (') marks, which tells us to be cautious of falling into the habitual norm and dictionary meanings alone for such terms.[51] Although, useful, we've chosen here not to overly and tediously use those signifying marks; but rather to have merely set forth the cautionary awareness for you as readers in the Introduction, and that will suffice.

Our conscious tendency, especially as English-speakers but also with our own *resistance* to its dominating ways, is thus to avoid making the subject of our study a noun-based conceptualization alone. For example, like the common dictionary, 'fear *is* a state of experience...'.

Note the *fear is* component, which composes a standard format for many definitions of concepts and representations of phenomenon.

We know at times that our fearist colleagues use "Fear *is* one of them [i.e., "consciousnesses"]"[52] or "Fear *is* a beast."[53] Beyond those colleagues, one can find other writers defining our subject as "Fear *is* a dragon....is the father of ignorance, superstition, and prejudice."[54] Many of these authors like to label "positive fear" and "negative fear" for example,[55] of which such a labeling promotes the nouning tendency.

English language and its habitual dualistic binary thinking moves quickly to create a noun form out of a real flowing, dynamic, and organic processual phenomenon in Nature. Indigenous-based primal languages, according to Four Arrows, tend not to do this but keep everything named as verbs, as living words/spirits.[56] Of course, using metaphors, like in the above examples as well, we see another tendency to nouning that we ought to watch for. What impact does it have in biasing our imaginaries, imaginations and discourses on, and our teaching about, fear/fearlessness?

'Fear is a gift' and 'Fearlessness is a gift'—are two specific phenomenon (processes) we are going to center our dialogue on for Introduction 2 (see below). As readers you can discern how well we do with our use of words in promoting, not distorting, the spirit of livingness of fear/fearlessness as dialectical reality.

By now you ought to have been prepared for a little more of a roller coaster ride with our presentation of the subject at hand. Ernest Hemingway was onto this ride: "Life isn't about finding yourself. Life is about creating yourself." Part of the roller coaster approach to defining and making meaning has to do with our eschewing the over-emphasis on the noun-forming static-forming tendency, be the subject fear or fearlessness or even one's identity—and, one's identity when they are becoming a fearful or fearless subject. No living subject is ever a mere total embodiment of fear or fearlessness. One's subjectivity is much grander than that. Our humanistic-existential philosophical understanding in a 21st century new paradigm of growth and development calls on us to envision humans as *beings becoming*. This radical image of ourselves (our species) is central in the Fearlessness Paradigm that threads itself throughout this book.

Becoming is a *creative action process*. Thus, we (as co-authors) believe in a systems way of thinking about *subjectivity* formation, going so far to say that even the 'human being' is a verb-in-transit, is a co-creative adaptive process of relationality, of complexity blended with the environment by means of porous boundaries, and is a flowing identity with many layers, an ever-shifting open-ended process; rather than a mere bounded noun (object-self). The noun tends to fixate and become static—making all parts seem as if they are *separated* dualistically from the whole. Joseph Campbell in conversation with Bill Moyers, once spoke of the ancient understanding from his life-career study of the world's myths:

> **Campbell:** The [Infinite before time and space] divine power [of Oneness] is antecedent to sexual separation [division of Twoness]....Everything in the field of time and space is *dual*...metaphysical duality.... This is represented in the mystery religions, where an individual goes through a series of initiations opening him [sic] out, inside into the deeper and deeper depth[s] of himself, and there comes a moment when he realizes that he is both mortal and immortal, both male and female [Twins].
>
> **Moyers:** Do you think there was such a place as the Garden of Eden? [as noun]
>
> **Campbell:** Of course not. The Garden of Eden is a metaphor for that innocence that is innocent of time, innocent of opposites, and that is the prime center out of which consciousness then becomes aware of the changes [and itself eventually].

Moyers: But if there is in the idea of Eden this innocence, what happens to it? Isn't it shaken, dominated, and corrupted by fear? [the Ego]

Campbell: That's it. There is a wonderful story of the deity, of the Self that said, "I am." As soon as it said "I am," it was afraid.

Moyers: Why?

Campbell: It was an entity now, in time [separated]. Then it thought, "What should I be afraid of, I'm the only thing that is."[?] And as soon as it said that, if felt lonesome, and wished that there were another, and so it felt [insecure and] desire. It swelled, split into two, became male and female, and begot the world. *Fear* is the first experience of the fetus in the womb....shortly before birth the rhythm of the uterus begins, and there's terror! Fear is the first thing, the thing that says "I."…. That is the breaking into the world of light and the pair of opposites.[57]

Campbell's grasp here of some basic truth about the relationship of fear/fearlessness is a theme we shall come back to as we explore which does come first(?)—fearlessness, then fear(?)—as seems to be the mythic story that Campbell presented. And what is of this initiation path, as a gifting of adventure for the hero explorer, to find the truth beneath the waves of fear and courage—if not fearlessness(?). Lots of questions to ponder as we proceed.

What is worth mentioning as well and that is crucial to our interest as co-authors, is that Campbell and Moyers proceed in their dialogue from origins of fear to origins of *rebellion*—that is, "Life really began with that act of disobedience,"[58] which can be found in the Eden myth (e.g., Eve's desire) and it is also found as a universal (archetypal) rebelliousness in youth and in many of the myths throughout the world.

lix

This concept is a useful attempt to explain human nature—and our will power, and many other things re: why humans don't always get along. Again, this is something key in our thinking and writing because the focus of this book is on *resistances*. Rebellion-resistances-revolutions; one way or another, change and dramatically change things—becoming, at their best, evolving transformations. It is this latter transformative dimension of learning and growth that really interests us, on many levels of existence and in societies. Fear/fearlessness dialectic has got to be part of that rebellious story. OK, moving on...

Our holistic, rather than reductionistic (separationist) emphasis from the start of this book is a contradiction to nouning and objectifying everything, which dominant Science (and its paradigm) has tended to do for centuries. Such 'scientific' objectification is particularly one of the main linguistic and worldview characteristics of the English language, which we are privileging in this book.

Finding a truly living and subjectifying organic language to reinvent the human being and fear/fearlessness dynamics is a challenge. We are just beginners here. However, in a brief review of another book entitled *Exotic Fearology* by one of our fearist colleagues,[59] Dr. Aurelian L. Stiopu generously captured the processual spirit of interrelationship with fear, which we desire as co-authors here. Stiopu perceptively wrote in process terms,

> Fear reinvents itself under the investigation of the followers of this new branch of philosophy, philosophy of fear, maybe more exactly [the] philosophy of fearism.[60]

Indeed, "fear reinvents itself" and equally so does fearlessness. The creative-relational paradigm underpinning these words is crucial. It demands we as investigators and fear managers etc. be creatively reinventing our theories, philosophies, *and ourselves* as well. Add the component of identity to the mix and there is a *Self-Fear-Other* trialectical unit to attend to, which in some ways (in part) co-creates nearly all motivational aspects of the consciousness (psychic) system of individuals and groups. Interesting to think that way but that is a side-tracking theory we best turn from in order to continue on task for this Introduction 2.

In regard to the earlier discussion, the convenience of such a dualistic language disposition, as English, does not mean we (as co-authors) are not critical of it for its grave limitations of capturing the nuanced grain of actual phenomenon/reality. We thus want to make it known that we utilize a *process philosophy*[61] underneath everything in these pages. Equally, we utilize a mind-based *consciousness philosophy*,[62] that keeps all things discussed in a more spontaneous, fluid, alive, and organic evolutionary flow. Subba's fearist perspective demands that we ultimately see fear/fearlessness *as consciousness* in one of its manifest and multiple forms (if not disguises).[63] You may recall in Figure 1 (Introduction 1) the intentional use of arrows circling/cycling was to remind us of the flow of motivational forces that are typically not always visible to our everyday perceptions, thoughts and actions.

The Gift of Fear

> Fear is a multifaceted instinct. It is one of the most primitive emotions....It depends on the individual being whether to use if for good or to be harmed by it. It is just like a kitchen knife or any other technical gadget. It is a double-edged weapon....a necessary force.
> – B. M. Kumar

> I think everyone will to a certain extent...we probably all could agree on a common definition of fear....
> - James (host of Hermitix)[64]

Commonly, most humans have a relationship with fear that is both good and not so good. For many in history "*Fear* became the multi-edged weapon,"[65] as everyone can more or less learn from the relationship with fear and target fear's powers in various ways with diverse ends. That said, arguably, however, each group of humans does not wield the same powers and thus the same set-of-choices re: the *fear factor*, in order to enact those powers and be successful and influential in the society. Kumar explained this in terms of the historical relationship to *benevolent fear*, which in this section of our book we'll call the *gift of fear*. He wrote of the history of security *via* the elites of India:

> Benevolent or *positive fear* motivated the members of the royal clan [elites] to learn a variety of effective skills like sports, military exercises, and activities of physical robustness. They believed that such skills would ensure their strength and supremacy to continue [to rule and to dominate]. Military skills involved raising the army's capacity and its preparation for facing dissent or any invasions. Their planning abilities sharpened their expertise in strategizing and tactical approaches. Fear of failure in war made them alert and cautious while making decisions. Positive fear helped the members of the royal, priestly and business castes seek more knowledge and information *via* systematic education. Such motivational factors [with the help of the *fear factor*] turned them not only worldly-wise but also skilled manipulative tacticians.[66]

RMF: I'm curious Maria where you learned such things? Did you always, for example, going back to your youth, think about the *fear factor* and how it played out in your everyday life and the local world around you?

BMK: That's a good point on the fear factor Michael to ponder because such subtle components of emotional nature in behaviour will have perceptible impact on actions. First, I'll share my subjective and autobiographical awakening to these issues in the everyday life; and second, I'll share some more on Indian society historically.

Fear factor had always been there. I felt it especially during my childhood. I was born in a Catholic family where somewhat traditional rigid practices were followed; for example, it is a sin if you don't attend mass on Sundays; or unless you make confessions, you will remain a sinner waiting for the wrath of God etc. Church was constructed in my village in 1850, that's more than 150 years ago. There are other religious groups there as well.

The Indian society, whether it is my village or a distant metro city, continues to run more or less based on a prejudicial ancient caste system, which means you find people in groups or communities divided by birth status to a caste somewhat like being born into a tribe in more primeval eras. With castes especially, they don't marry into each other's groups. On that ground, reinforced by customs and traditions, each developed in each caste distinctively despite the fact that people belonging to various castes come under different religions. In the same caste, you find some families practising Christianity and some Hinduism. But caste affinity is more foundational in impact than religion generally because of marital and kinship exclusivity reasons.

From this long casteism we can see, and I felt it too early in life, that India is divided both horizontally and vertically much more rigidly than the societies elsewhere in the world. Hence fear factor in various forms: suspicions, biases and prejudices are the consequences. Associated with all these ambiguities and uncertainties, there are intractable superstitions in all religious groups cutting across castes and subcastes, which in turn have their own sets of superstitions. Given this social scenario, which is very volatile as far as interpersonal relations are concerned, there is another worsening factor that makes everyone wary, and that is economic uncertainty. The landowners are not secure if there are no rains. As such the rivers and other water bodies are drying or disappearing in the whole of India. The farm labourers are far more insecure because they are dependent on the landlords for employment and they comprise most of the illiterates, meaning thereby they don't have other skills other than agricultural labour work. Businesses in rural areas depend upon the state of agriculture whether it is good harvest or not. The better social security system, which generally exists in the West, is not promoted by the government in India. Every family is left to fend for itself. Therefore existence is uncertain and insecure.

To handle such a state of affairs, people take solace in the supernatural, like religion and superstitions. If something good happens, they owe it to God's hand or to superstitious ritual. If bad happens, they feel it is due to *karma* which means an unfounded belief that the so-called misdeeds of the past life are taking their price in the current life in the form of punishment. Such are the overall hopes, beliefs, practices, which were prevalent during my childhood in my village. I lived there until my 15th year. I was brought up by my grandmother, as my grandfather had died, in that village. When I was five years old and had just joined the Roman Catholic Elementary School, my father, a civil contractor, secured a good work in a metro city about more than a thousand kilometres away from my village. My parents left me with my paternal grandmother, as I had already joined the school and they migrated to that metro city. My father started earning handsomely there and so he never again thought of returning to my village.

Having been in the school already for some three years, my parents didn't disturb my studies. Every month my parents would send money for my studies and all comforts, and I would visit them on every periodical vacation. By 15 years of age, I could understand the differential and prejudicial status people's lives and the reasons of how these differences between people influenced living in my village, and in my father's metro city. There was no sense in me at the time, that fear was a gift. I didn't reflect on the nature and role of fear then.

I became independent quickly because as a child, I used to travel alone for more than one thousand kilometres to my parents' place. That way, till I turned 15, I was almost independent without direct parental control over me except for a little bit supervision by my aging grandmother. After school, I went for collegiate education to a bigger town about a hundred kilometres away, where I joined a hostel. Eventually, my grandmother left the village to unite with my parents. By that time, I had already become a self-made youth, mostly on my own. I was privileged however by getting security through a handsome monthly money from my parents. So I could enjoy life, albeit studying attentively. From early childhood I was very inquisitive to learn and to know the world. I was also a movie maniac right from my village days. The plot of each movie would thrill me. While in college, I was regular at the release of every Hollywood film in the theatre. After reading many Greek and Roman myths and after having watched some classical western movies, I had an ambition to visit Athens and Rome some day in future. This college age dream was fulfilled in 2012, when I attended a course at London Business School and made my return journey to India *en route* Athens and Rome with a one day stay at each place. I was impressed.

RMF: Ah, now that makes sense to me why you often bring in references in our past dialogues and co-writing to Greco-Roman stories, myths and history. I'm curious why that may have been more intriguing to you as a young person from India, than Eastern myths and history? Maybe, you weren't impressed by India and its casteism connected to religion and myth. As a Westerner myself, I'm always ambivalent when I hear stories of people in the East, much like Desh Subba, who get a large fascination for the West. Interesting both of you were brought up in small villages. I was brought up in the big city. I can't help thinking a bit like Mahatma Gandhi and others in the East, who have been very critical of Western imperialist and colonialist education agendas in India, and other developing nations, especially in the East.

There's always been this underlying and unspoken tension since 2014, when I met Desh, between how I see the West and how you and Desh see the West. I am much more negative and skeptical; while you both are much more positive. It's all relative I suppose to where we live and grew up and were conditioned and socialized. Then, I hear also that you had a W. Catholic missionary educational upbringing from the start. You were rather Westernized then, at least in part, it seems.

A macro-level question lurking in my mind has been for years now: Is the West or the East more fear-based? Is the religious world or secular world more fear-based? And so on. And, the answer to those questions may be part of the inquiry we are doing here as co-authors—by which I mean, specifically: Where would the most *resistances* to Fearlessness be? East? West? North? South? Secular? Religious? Okay, that's enough. I didn't mean to distract from your story.

BMK: I understand somewhat your context re: the West, and British colonial rule in India. From my view, it was only during the two century old British Raj that the people of more than six hundred separate dynastic kingdoms and principalities of the subcontinent developed a certain sense of oneness under the umbrella term of Indianness. It was a W. idea, although not exclusively because also B. R. Ambedkar within India's shaping a Constitution also tried this, and ironically the oppressive aspects of the British invasion actually helped in many cases to bring India out of the Middle Ages—yet, it was never fully a workable solution. Even after the British have gone, more than seven decades ago, the caste-based divisiveness is as fresh as it was earlier. The curse of immutable divisive caste hierarchy creates ongoing exploitative socioeconomic inequalities, reinforcing caste-based fears particularly among those who are in the lower rungs of that system.

Since childhood, I was especially fond of reading. My village high school, St. Joseph's, a missionary institute, has a small library. I could read William Shakespeare's dramas, which were translated into my mother tongue Telugu as condensed editions. Reading characters like Orpheus, Eurydice, Atlas, Theseus etc. at the age twelve or so made me curious to know more about Greek mythology. On the other hand, my village, being a traditional society has all the Hindu festivals celebrated pompously with cultural events, which would have Mahabharata and Ramayana episodes as background themes. My church attendance and the regular catechism classes by nuns and priests enabled me to grasp Biblical knowledge to some extent. So I developed equal interest in Greek myths, Bible and Indian legends and myths. Occasionally I would write poetry and dramas basing on the characters from the three varied disciplines.

RMF: In contrast to my working poor upbringing and impoverish W. education, you are quite middleclass, eclectic, keen and astute—a real East-West thinker.

BMK: I joined the arts, quiz and literary club while in college and later on at university also. My frequent participation in cultural and intellectual programmes enthused me to read more and more to fare well in the competitions.

RMF: Again, in high contrast to me in my youth, you were sociable and involved in the 'normal' community of learners and a competitor-learner at that. I was none of those things, and chose a much more reclusive and highly rebellious life since I was 14 years old.

BMK: Michael, what you've shared about your parents, especially your mom coming out of the grips of Nazism raging in WW-II Belgium, amongst other factors in your life, no doubt these were catalysts to awaken your unconscious fearlessness instinct to rebel against the system. The reason I may infer for your rebellion was your audacity that enabled you to stand against the invasive efforts of fear perpetrated by the forces of inequality. Hitler and his followers were delusional in feeling that all humans are not born equal. Nazi ideology was based on racial prejudices. And, in India too, social inequalities have been perpetuating. Fears abound.

RMF: Good points. Unlike yourself, I had no religious upbringing but the lightest spattering of Christianity that was in my mom and dad's backgrounds, yet they were not really practicing religion at all. I was free to just be 'me.' I guess that made me a free-thinker without traditional influences from early on. The sub-cultural radical revolution of the 1960s-70s in the West, especially in W. coast USA, highly influenced my attitudes and shaped my desires. I still carry that influence. It was a generation, now called 'Baby Boomers' who wanted to turn the world into a paradigm of Love not Fear. I was a rock-star wannabe musician and artist in those years of the 1960s but by early 1970 I was heavily influenced by the first Earth Day official celebration and the kick-off of what was to be known as the Environmental Movement. Anyways, that's a bit of my background in contrast to yours, which I think readers may find helpful somewhat as they are reading our dialogues.

BMK: Though I was a student of chemistry at the graduate level and of international trade at an MBA[67] level, I took a lot of interest in arts and humanities. I used to be a daily visitor to the government library, where I invariably would lay my hands on different encyclopaedias. My friends used to ask me as to how those "irrelevant" books would help me. I would reply, that they are the *real* books of *real* life though they might not fetch me a job or livelihood.

One day a friend in the hostel looked worried. He lost his wrist watch. I consoled him saying that he would find it. Then, being a devout church going youth of about

19 years, I had immense faith in Saint Anthony, who is the patron saint of lost things. That night, I prayed and prayed for my friend's wrist watch. I had big faith that my prayer would be answered. Next day, nothing happened. My friend could not find his watch even after a week. It was then that I started doubting the efficacy of faith in religion. That faith weakened further when I joined the MBA in the university though I occasionally would go to church as a matter for socialising purposes, like meeting with friends and acquaintances.

I was growing intellectually and self-actualizing somewhat, as Maslow might call it because of my growing independence streak from early youth. Due to my regular reading habit at the library, I also touched on Marx. His ideas influenced me a great deal and his views on religion reinforced my view that blind faith is of no use, and rather, it is actually detrimental to the awakening and development of our innate potential and abilities. This Marxist 'new enlightenment' improved my thinking in a clear manner rather than in a foggy way. Earlier, I was afraid of the unknown, especially if I missed church on Sunday. That fear has now gone. Superstitions like a cat crossing the road, crow cawing on the house, sneezing before starting a journey or work etc. were quite fearsome earlier too, but later on those fears diminished.

As the fears of socioeconomic and political nature got reduced due to analytical rational thinking, my self-confidence and optimism levels also increased. After my university study was over, I competed in an all India level examination to join the government service and I succeeded, as I realised that my confidence in my own honest efforts would be the game changer. This led to developments, like a career as a police officer. I became well-acquainted with people of all walks of life so closely. And I put in efforts to alleviate their problems. The outcomes enriched my practical knowledge. Fear factor became very much more conscious for me. Most of my work was with those who are fear stricken due to crimes, difficulties, exploitations, atrocities, animosities, insecurities, victimisations and so on. Such situations are usually dealt with by standard operating procedures as per law. But I felt that something extra needed to be done to mitigate the miseries of the people. Whenever possible, I tried to apply philosophical and psychological principles to a considerable extent, when the people encountered dilemmas or anxieties/fears. Such experiences were so fulfilling during the course of a 33 year span of police profession from 1985 to 2018, mostly in Bhopal.

RMF: Wonderful. It's a gift to offer that solace. I too am a life-long career care-giver, therapist, and a kind of 'missionary without a church.' Hey, I'm spiritual but not religious. I have lots of doubts about organized institutional religion and its role in the historical and cultural evolution of the culture of fear phenomenon that has taken over much of the contemporary world. Anyways, it has always intrigued me that you are a police officer with all that experience you've had, and how we have been able to find some solid common ground in our philosophies and teachings about fear management. So, I grew up fearing, not trusting police. I had not one good experience with them. So, you are a first, of which I am grateful.

BMK: Now for a few more things about the fear factor in India's history, still influential to where this nation is today. Besides religion and caste, there is division on the grounds of political party, regions and languages. Economic status forms another reason for division. Sometimes, different caste men find identity in the same economic class or same region or in the same political party. Marriage divides them again. So do rituals and customs. As a result, the whole society is further divided diagonally or by whatever arithmetical angularities that are applied. Such diverse and divisive separateness tends to cause not only confusion but also hesitation about how to deal with people in society. Social trust is undermined by the fear factor continually.

The upper echelons of ancient Indian society benefited hugely from such fear-based strategies. The same was true of Western society also in regards to the nobles or upper classes or estates. Both the groups i.e., the highly privileged and lowly placed in the social ladder will grow fears and mistrust towards each other. The entire political sphere of social life is surrounded, if not engulfed by this dynamic, unfortunately. The former are afraid of revolt against them by the lowly placed; and the latter, will feel threatened by the oppressive power of the former. As a reflex of defence mechanisms, both sides will be cautious and alert to counter in the eventuality of any clash. Had the clashes occurred, it is more likely that the former, though numerically small but armed would easily crush the latter, who happen to be in large number but not equipped enough with arms. The reason being that sophisticated psychological tactics will have the better edge over brute physical strength in most of the cases. Such is the history of warfare. The key is in fact the high social status that invigorates the mental energy of the upper elites, whereas the lack of standing in the society dampens the spirits of the lower classes and they are less innovative and strategic in competing.

Dr. Peter Belmi and his research colleagues from the University of Virginia found in their studies that the people who are posh and are in higher social strata do have higher confidence levels to do better, despite the fact that their real worth might not be actually so. The lower class people on the other hand tend to show low levels of confidence, which in turn affects their performance adversely. The crucial difference lies in the element of morale. Napoleon once said, "morale is to physique as three is to one." That's why the upper elite of the ancient Indian society and of course even the royal or corporate dynasties of the medieval West had additional psychological advantage besides economic and social privileges. Dr. Belmi concluded that "advantages beget advantages." The ancient Indian example and Dr. Belmi's experiment suggest that fears could be channeled in favour of personal benefits more effectively by those in the top than those at the lower rungs of the hierarchy. In this context, for the elites, they made fear into a gift more effectively than their lower compatriots.

RMF: Your historical summation of India as a nation is probably not that different than most nations of the world, as you suggested above. Basically I hear you are saying, that at first humans, like elites, were and still are, differentially predisposed to be more skilled at building more skills—and, you are saying that *fear of survival* really helped. *Fear of insecurity* really helped. *Fear of failure* in re: to both survival and security really helped. The first relatively benevolent humans/elites gained advantages over the crowd because they better managed fear. They seemed to befriend it.

OK. This is enough of a logic of relationship of humans with fear that it is worth dubbing "benevolent" or "positive fear." Surely, this is common sense thought. The stories below from several authors, including Gavin de Becker, will give more details on this common and dominant way of looking at *fear*—as an emotion that is a gift to Life. Of course, there are also times in history when fear is only seen as mostly negative. This gifting benevolent view also is not just a gift to one's own life or one's own family's; but also the life of the tribe's, the culture's, and/or the nation's, life. And, ultimately, this basic positive position argues that fear is a gift to Life itself, because it existed and still exists, from the beginning of Life. In a sense, Fear is Life—both are well-honed complementary partners—a duo of Intelligence. Fisher often refers to Fear in this largest sense as contributing to and/or virtually equivalent to, the natural Defence Intelligence System.[68]

Your articulation of this story seems to posit that fear is an essential multi-faceted and good, if not brilliant, *instinct*, with all kinds of uses that help humans, as with other creatures, to survive and reproduce successfully. Your quote above raises issues about the 'story' of how we understand human nature itself, that is, our evolutionary animal nature—and further, our cultural nature or what might be called the human condition—and clearly, these thoughts and stories will significantly impact our vision for what's our human potential. So, big issues are at stake.

BMK: You are right to point out that all hi*story* is a '*story*' too. We are always interpreting 'facts,' and even facts are constituted within the context of stories. Because nothing we learn or know of as historical data is without a degree of subjective and cultural mediation. But yes, I think there are enough facts available throughout history and our own experiences as humans, to be confident and find some agreement, for example that the fear factor is both positive and negative, depending on how we manage that fear as it arises.

RMF: And what if fear is *not* merely a *factor* of history but a *paradigm* of history? Where a paradigm is the hidden organizational regime for how to make sense of the world[69]—very similar to worldview. In other words, what if fear itself, unbeknownst to us, is right now shaping the very way we are understanding the history of fear itself? Okay, I'll not pursue that dilemma here but we have to at least think about that question. And, yet, I suppose if fear is only benevolent, as some might think, then there's no problem if fear is shaping the way we understand the history of fear itself? I'm not one of those believers.

But you and I know there is more going on than benevolent fear. The great E-W. Christian mystic Thomas Merton, also paraphrasing Pope John XXIII, said we have to examine the "Law of Fear" and whether that is what we want to follow or follow the "reign" of Love(?). As much as I like that quote by Merton,[70] it raises questions about what kind of "fear" or what quantity of "fear" is he talking about when it crosses a threshold and becomes *the ruler* of our lives? Maybe it is a good thing for fear to rule our lives, as the philosopher Thomas Hobbes had extensively argued in the 17th century, because of its basic instinctual functional properties.

Yet Maria, you indicate the elite of India may have started with good intentions to let fear instinct push them forward to progress; yet, at some point they merely became, at least more and more of them proportionately, to become "manipulative tacticians"—diminishing their role as benevolent. They turned a good thing into a bad and oppressive thing and used fear against others in the process; especially the less powerful and less elite got hit hardest by fearmongering in the culture as a whole. No doubt, everyone in a society will fearmonger, to some degree. For some it is highly consequential and for some less so. But then that begs the philosophical question of how to define what fearmongering is?

BMK: It is logical to say that the makers of certain traditions in ancient India were not only manipulative tacticians but also doomsdayers-cum-doomsdoers of the times because they created such fears as never existed in other parts of the world. For example, the reading of scriptures or touching or standing close to an elite person would invite more wrathful repercussions than one could ever imagine. Hence reduced level of education and lack of interpersonal interactions led to the downfall of medieval Indian society intellectually, socially, economically and politically. Those who suffered the wrath of such systematic diminution stood as living examples of the victims of fear regimes. These fears were transmitted genetically like that of primitive environmental fears or fears of predatory wild animals—and, also physically from generation to generation by word of mouth, as well as by written word as means of conveyance for the spread. That was the convenient form of fearmongering in those times.

RMF: Anyways, this turn of the elite, let's say, builds up great divisiveness in a nation of which India has still not solved, and you have written a good deal about this, for example, with casteism. I'll come back to this meaning-making problem later below in my studies of why the "gift of fearlessness" cultures in S. Asia, evolved there in the East and not apparently in the West, but that's getting too far ahead of ourselves.

Your point Maria: *we are always learning from fear* and learning how to manage our instincts and gifts, whether we are conscious of that or not and, whether we manage them well or not. Freud was very intrigued by that 'learning' problem re: the Id or instinctual layer of motivation in human beings and their civilizations.

Anyways, my problem is that I don't know always how people are defining *fear* when they write or talk about it. They talk like fear, be it good or bad fear, is 'out-there' or 'in-here'—and, it is fixed like a solid object—which can, apparently, be so easily placed, then looked at under a microscope or through a telescope to measure, to study and comment on. This is so disembodied knowledge as far as I am concerned. And I don't really trust it is connected to something living, whole, human, invisible and even mysterious. It pretends to be a knowledge forgetting its source, that is, an intimately involving knowledge dialectically related to the very self-structure-system—that is, the Ego at every turn—that is, the structure that is talking about where fear is or isn't and where fear *should* be! The Ego can be a bossy sort of micro-management, if not authoritarian-type of entity. But not always accurate or wise.

Clearly, the self will admit its *fears* now and then—typically, in common discourse. So, that's not my concern. Rather, my concern is how will we know *fear itself,* or *fear is social*—as I have eluded to prior in Introduction 1—when we keep cleaning, domesticating, and paring fear down *via* reductionism and slicing off fear as an object to measure, assess and manage instrumentally. This is a like a cold 'scientific' approach to fear alone, which tends to dominate in modern societies. It has to be challenged by this philosophical, if not therapeutic approach to fear and its management, *via* fearism; as we have both agreed as co-authors, the latter is the better way to go.

It is like most people, less systematic in their thinking and less philosophically-oriented, have agreed "fear" is that much of a thing, a noun, a measurable entity. The neurobiology of fear discourse certainly hasn't help improve this nouning and materialistic functionalistic tendency. It seems we often as societies just accept certain common sense configurations of meaning, or scientific ones, and then they are accepted as the 'norm' or the 'correct' way to define or make meaning of fear or anything we want to name by a word. A *fearlessness paradigm*, with a process philosophy, as I work with it, is built on a troubling critical-edge of both accepting and questioning or resisting such 'stories' and 'science' that are told about fear and its positive role.

Positive fear, means the positive role fear plays. It is the chosen focus of our conversation here because of the foregrounding of the idea of a, positive, "gift of fear." Okay, but there still has to be questioning of all positives, all facts, all takes on the *history of fear* claims and so on. You may hear in between the lines right now, that fear and security are too closely linked—and that may really skew *the why* and motivation of certain stories about fear and its positive role. I bring that up at the moment, only because it will potentially be a concern as you Maria and I attempt to understand better the architecture and mechanisms of defenses people have that will create *resistances* to fearlessness.

At the same time that I have my complex preferences of how to speak and write about fear and fearlessness, I also have to figure out how to converse with non-scholars, and thinking people, like yourself, who seem comfortable talking about fear, like in the quote above, as if it is already figured out and agreed upon, assumed to be a 'good enough' or 'convenient script' as a way to speak/write about fear.

BMK: For sure, I have found a certain comfort with talking about fear and writing about fear the way I do. You on the other hand, have made me aware of my ease, and some of my assumptions, and that I now also have to think more philosophically, not just psychologically about the nature and role of fear. Desh Subba and the philosophy of fearism perspective also make me think more carefully but that doesn't mean when I am writing I always am conscious and careful enough to take that into account. I tend to write to keep things simple.

RMF: There's a useful place for that too. You are sure not alone on that. Both you and I are still trying to figure our way through this maze of complexity and how to best communicate and teach about it. I'm raising deep epistemological problems and discourse problems that arise once one uses the philosophy of fearism perspective on the topic of fear itself. I came across this overtly, in a conversation recently when talking to the host of a popular philosophical podcast entitled Hermitix. I'll share an excerpt of my views around this issue of language re: fear:

James: To jump into fearism, I'm not just going to...flat out ask you to define it. So I think everyone will to a certain extent, we probably all could agree on a common definition of fear...fear is something you're scared of, and you attempt to avoid or as you say something that you are going to develop ways to cope with it. But is there a different definition of fear in relation to fearism?

Michael: Yeah....I appreciate the question of definition because as a philosopher-type...I'm going to use the analogy, I was thinking of, it's been going around for years, the story...if you talk to...an Eskimo or Inuit or Dené...Indigenous person who lives in the north... way north, where there's snow most of the year, and a Westerner comes from the south and asks them: "What's your definition of snow?" An Indigenous person...the story goes, they will look at you and say, "Well, we have 23 different definitions of snow, which one do you want to know?"

I kind of use that same analogy...and this is related to fearism. Why did fearism appear as a way of understanding fear. And of course, a way of understanding the world, reality? Is that, I think we've gone down a very narrow...convenient track, not all bad, not all wrong, but very partial in our understanding of fear. Just as we have, and it would be easy to go down the track of trying to understand snow and having a definition for snow, and we might have 2-3 different nuances of different kinds of snow. Well, with fear, it's very interesting, once you start to listen to the W. world, it's got 450+ phobias named, because we're putting fear into all these different containers. So fearism, and the philosophy of my own thinking, even before I came to the notion of fearism of Desh Subba, I was interested in fear itself before it gets casted down into all the phobias, all the fears, of spiders, fear of this and that, fear of 13. And I thought those would not be all that useful to actually understand the processes for the mechanisms and the philosophy that fear itself is bring into the world. So, I was interested in an expanded notion of fear right from the start.

I had a couple strategies I want to share, in how I started that—in respect [and contradiction] that it's basically fear [typically] is just an abstract term and then we can define it and that may be very convenient and then we think we have located fear right where it is supposed to be. It's the mechanism in the amygdala in the brain, and the fear is my fear of heights, or we have these natural fears...loud sounds. Now, all of a sudden I'm like this hermeneutics of suspicion guy, you know in Ricoeur's sense, the philosopher—I'm always doubting. I start with the doubt that I don't want to be following any convenient conventional easy way down, to be able to locate fear, so then we can say "We have a common understanding of fear now, it's in the dictionary, it's in our medical encyclopedias." As soon as I see all that, I go "OK, partially true." Partial truth there no doubt, but can we deconstruct that, can we start to take that apart? And I even go as far to put the question, which fearism does as a philosophy: "How do we know that our understanding of fear, our convenient definition, is not itself fear-based?" So that's the epistemological question. We could ask that about anything....How do you know you know the truth, your confidence in the truth? How do you know that that [truth] is not fear motivated?....in other words, it's a truth you've used for convenience [common sense] that makes you feel less anxious, that makes you feel a bit more protected [in control] and safe because you've got that definition fixed. And then you can be very confident about it. Right? You can even be ideological about it. You can want to try to change the world and try to convert the world to your definition.

So, that's where I sort of start the epistemological inquiry...so...in a lot of my writing I actually put the word [fear] and you can do this in writing, it's harder to do when we're talking, I put apostrophes, a single one... on the world 'fear'. Scare marks. And that immediately is to raise the awareness to the reader. I define this for people. I do that because I want to raise the awareness: Let's not let ourselves get into a convenient discussion about fear that falls down a very comfortable definition and meaning. I want to always be in questioning....So, why I am saying all this as you and I are going to be going into talking about fear—is, we have to both, and this is my challenge as a fearologist...as someone who practices this philosophy of fearism, I have to continually talk at multiple levels. I talk at the level of, OK, this person I'm talking with right now wants to talk about fear as if we know exactly what it is, as if it's already defined... [that is,] in the traditions of Psychology or Philosophy or whatever, and the conversation and (have to use that language because the word is there. [But] I want to leave space for the 'fear' with the marks because I put everything that we're saying about fear in a different conversation based on an inquiry—a critical inquiry—a critical philosophical analysis—a fearanalysis of fear itself. A fearanalysis of our language of fear that we use, the way we construct sentences that have the word fear in it or a story or a film or an image. All of these can be analyzed. As in, how are we representing?

This is the problem of representation, the basics to all philosophy and perception. How do we represent reality—this reality of fear? So, all of a sudden fearism discussion, and I enter this 'ism' and Desh Subba and I came to this uniquely on our own....We basically said by adding the 'ism' onto the word fear, it actually does the same effect as putting the (') marks on...it all of a sudden puts fear in a different context. Well, that's what artists love to do; you take an apple and it looks like an apple then you put it in a certain kind of landscape... painting...and you've changed the meaning of the apple....Fear is not exactly what you may think it is. Well, you known what I've learned? That scares the shit out of people. It's so much of an interesting irony and paradox, we're actually trying to develop a philosophy of fearism to enlighten our understanding of fear in a more expansive way than generally we have been taught and falling into these conventional ways of knowing fear—but at the same time, it's incredibly scary. And I know it myself. I've gone through this myself, and I've gone through it having many conversations— people don't want to talk about something so complex that it might disrupt the very very comfortable definition of fear itself....

James: It's interesting what you say about fearism, because I think it's key, that it would be awkward to do the click sounds every time [re: 'fear'], so fearism does work as that. OK, we're now having this more of an epistemological genuine investigation into fear....[71]

BMK: Yes Michael! Fear is a universal topic. Its definitions vary like that of types of snow or phobias. Disciplines such as psychology, philosophy, psychiatry etc. have only superficially touched it so far. They have not prioritized it nor attended to it in the deeper ways it should have been. That's why Subba and yourself are pioneers, taking initiative to create an apt place for the discipline of fear and fearlessness in the world of knowledge. If there's any inquiry pertaining to the human condition, without involving the fear factor, it means that there is no depth of meaning to their approaches, or even the so-called holistic approaches. Now that fearism/fearology/ fearlessness are established as a new orientation and movement of thought, a lot more is to be done to refine our understanding of fear, to reorganise it, to reinvent it, to experiment with it, to develop literature for it, to explore and research it, and to model theories of it—as you said, to formulate an effective *cura* and *therapia* for its management or treatment.

I agree with Subba, that *fear is as vast as universe* itself. It is like darkness, all pervading. I view it as the invisible manifestation of time. Then light becomes space. Coming to the minutest unit of universe called the individual species or animal species, then fear takes hidden manifestation as death, whereas light symbolises life and is represented by fearlessness. Then the critical nature of fear could be known to the extent that the riddle of consciousness is solved and explained. And I think that fearologists, as the future goes, will have been shown to have had a big role to play in unravelling the nitty-gritty surrounding consciousness.

RMF: STORY A (from de Becker, 1997)

Meg is a woman who works with violently inclined mental patients every day. She rarely feels fear at her job, but away from work, she tells me, she feels panic every night as she walks from her car to her apartment. When I offer the unusual suggestion that she'd actually be safer if she relaxed during that walk, she says, "That's ridiculous. If I relaxed, I'd probably get killed." She argues that she must be acutely alert [i.e., fearful] to every possible risk.

Possibilities, I explain [rationally], are in the mind [calculations], while safety is enhanced by perception of what is outside the mind [moment-to-moment], perception of what *is* happening [real], not what might happen. But Meg insists that her nightly [positive] fear will save her life, and even as she steadfastly defends the [positive] value of her terror, I know she wants to be free of it.[72]

Clearly, although ironically in a de Beckerian sense, a person (like Meg) *defends* her fear/terror—even when they have experiential negative outcomes when those emotional energies and thoughts lead to being out of control in a panic attack. People like Meg appear not to see the connection with how they are relating to their fear/intuition/panic—that is, to see they are all as *one* dynamic interrelated feedback 'ecological' system—all of which they are potentially capable of 'directing' in a good way, rather than 'panicking' in a bad way.[73]

It seems irrational how Meg is defending herself. De Becker has done thousands of these kinds of client (victim) interviews, and he has the agenda to both help this person feel safe, even when there is nothing to really be fearful of. And the way he teaches is an awareness re: moment-to-moment reality-testing. He's wanting to upgrade Meg's fear education, so as to make better distinctions in positive-fear [he calls "true fear"] from negative-fear ["unwarranted fear"]. He is trying to help her gain perspective that the chances of an attack/injury on her mental health ward work situation daily is a lot higher probability than getting attacked or injured on her walk from the car to her apartment at night. He's using rational logic, if not statistics to do this. Yet, she struggles to make that more accurate perspective shift, and re-orientation. Why? For one reason (apparently), she has fear-bonded to what she believes is a trustable (inner) 'security guard' (i.e., positive-fear) that's always there and dependable. This is the identity belief structure (habit) that: *I am my fear, my fear is me—my friend.* Of course, deeper below the surface of Meg's rationale for this attachment dependency, is an arguable case that some part of her intuits that Fear is Life, in an evolutionary sense as we discussed earlier.

In her mind, and, there is some existential truth to it, she cannot depend on others. She is alone and will die alone or live alone. She can only rely on herself. Typically, by her particular choices and attitudes, beliefs and philosophy, she is often alone on that walk from her car to her apartment. In her workplace (by her choices and her employer's choices) she is not alone. She's part of a group (staff), and she is in charge of her patients, not the other way around. That work environment is a social milieu designed in part to be just exactly what a social animal needs around them. It needs companions. It also needs authority-figures (bosses), some semblance of rules, of social and moral order, and predictability (somewhat) a selective inclusion of who is part of that social group she's joined and who is not. Familiarity, in any social species, is very helpful for members to feel socially secure. Any strangers added to that community are in Meg's case "patients" and patients are on a lower power/status level of control of the social environment. Thus, Meg's quite "fear less" capacities, it appears, when she is at work.

De Becker, in questioning and challenging Meg, does not pursue all of these nuances, and there is a more deep fearanalysis we could do here in this case (if there was space); but bottom line, Meg's 'instinctive' positive-fear attachment (bonding) is deeper than any rational thought. It goes beyond mathematical risk-probability comparisons that de Becker is making as he tried to convince her of his authority (security expertise) and capability to truly secure her with good rational knowledge[74]—especially, she will be doubtful and questioning him, if not getting mad at him, when he actually won't be there either when she gets out of her car. His talking about this stuff is way too abstract for Meg, if not insulting to her intelligence (i.e., her Defense system/identity system as it has been already structured—so, why change it?). I see a deeper issue going on in this case about fear of being alone-especially, when out on the city streets (e.g., this sounds like an agoraphobia symptomatology—underpinning the other problems like panic). Yet, let's move on...

STORY B

RMF: One of the earliest accounts of an article using the "Gift of Fear" comes from 1973, in *Good Housekeeping* magazine, where a young mother talks about discovering her worst potential fear seemingly may just be coming true. She had a serious breast lump and had to have a biopsy to check it out. This all completely threw her off her normal happy life and family scene. For days, she worried herself sick, dreading the worst possible results of the biopsy test. When they came back "benign" and she was okay, her entire world shifted. Her joy went through the roof. But the contrast made her reflect on all that fear/terror she had for days. As a Christian by faith, it came to her:

I was always so concerned about things far in the future that I never really appreciated this day. Without want to sound totally Pollyanna-ish, I can say with deep gratitude that I now get up in the morning and think the day is glorious, whether it is sleeting, pouring or sunny. It is a day of my life, after all; precious, precious life—the greatest gift anyone has, the gift most of us take so completely for granted as I did. I do not know what the future holds for me. Does anyone? But I do know that in a strange way this extraordinarily harrowing [fearful cancer] experience has made me free—free to love, free to work, free to give and receive, free of petty jealousies, free from petty strivings, free to enjoy and give enjoyment—today! Not tomorrow, elusive tomorrow, which never really comes.[75]

The basic story here is that living only a simple and predictable and controlled life, something becomes missing, and bad attitudes set in. It took an extreme fear-inducing event, to actually shake her out of her complacency and receive the gift of fear. She had to feel the full threat, through a nearness to potential death and suffering, or at least, she had to feel that life is tenuous and precious beyond what she was able to imagine prior to the incident of first being diagnosed with a potentially life-threatening illness. Fear set her free in many ways. She would say that's positive-fear at work.

STORY C

RMF: Like Story B, another "Gift of Fear" article shows up in another Christian context. The tag-line to the article is "Anxiety has been my constant companion. It has also kept me tethered to God."[76] This author, obviously a Christian starts the article by sharing,

> My first memory is a memory of fear. At four or five years old, alone in my bedroom, I was gripped suddenly by the certainty that something would go wrong. I looked up at the pink bows my mom had painted on the walls, my stomach twisting in knots. The conviction that the future wasn't friendly made itself manifest in my body. It was the beginning of a lifelong relationship with fear.
>
> ...Jesus is telling us.... "Don't be afraid" (Matt.14:27).... Would that it were so simple. Fear in the form of anxiety (owing to Generalized Anxiety Disorder, which I have) is a constant companion. A persistent, irrational fear about the future is the best definition of anxiety I have heard, and it joins me daily as a heavy ball in my stomach or a fluttering hummingbird in my throat. Nothing I can do brings instant relief. "Be with me," I pray, even though God is already with me, and it is I who need to be with him.
>
> Yet despite fear's unbidden presence, I have come to understand fear as a gift. The fear itself is not a gift I

want, but it is part of the way I am wired in my very physiology, and try as I might, I can't get rid of it.

The author describes how they had to learn not to abandon God's love and closeness, when their fear symptoms would take over. The problem was reframed. Fear is not the problem. Don't try to get rid of it. Fear is exactly what brings them to pray, and pray harder still, and remember they are not alone with this suffering. The negative feelings and thoughts that go with the physiological symptoms are at least able to calm down somewhat, because this person calmed down thinking about the future, and focused on being in God's presence—being "tethered to God." Of course, Christian theology, like all the Abrahamic Traditions of religion tell of the necessity, in order 'to be saved," that they must remain in "fear of God"—which, means to remain tethered to fear—and, that is a good, positive relationship. Like with Story C, the Christian finds the linkage between fear-bonding and love-bonding—and, ultimately, in Story D, although the anxiety disorder has not disappeared, it is easier to live with such suffering since the fear drove the person closer and closer to God.

"Gift of Fear of the Lord" is a big theme found in many Christian stories.[77] And, most importantly, "fearlessness" is not mentioned in the Abrahamic religious texts because it is (apparently), when taken only literally, a potential way to tear apart that fear-bonding condition (with God/Love). That said, there is still the issue of "Be not Afraid" and other such phrases which are rampant in the Bible—and, thus to sort that out one would need a discernment that there is 'bad fear' and thus one ought not be afraid IF they truly have faith in God/Love—and, there is simultaneously 'good fear,' which is to be saved for the deity only.

One of the themes most interesting to me is the *human condition* (assumption), within this exoteric[78] Christian cosmology (worldview), whereby, basically human existence is, more or less, about having to choose how to handle the hyper-anxiousness that characterizes us (at least, in body form and worldly form). The theology here sets up an existence that, no doubt is partly true, but is rather dubious to me—in that, it argues that humans have fear(s) to choose from. They can choose the lesser fears or the greater fears to be their guide. The lesser fears are not of the sacred, but are more of the carnal animal and thus not of the human made (supposedly) in God's image. If all goes well, humans are morally meant to choose a way of life (and be motivated by) the *sacred* and positive fear, as the alternative to the secular banal fear. Pick your fear, one is gift (the former) and one is a burden of unnecessary suffering (the latter). The former is the way to God/Love, the latter is the way to Hell/Fear. From a non-Christian observers point of view, this theological existence framing boils down to: Two fears—all you can really do is pick the least worst one. You can't change fear itself.

STORY D

If *fear* is often named in the recovery movement of Alcoholics Anonymous and popular culture as F. E. A. R., meaning False Evidence Appearing Real, the courageous truthing of Four Arrows' practices and CAT-FAWN are healing contradictions to the norm. They ensure we are not led down a distorted path by F.E.A.R.

but rather led by [true] Fear and, the [reparational] Fearlessness that follows from it.[79]

RMF: Wisdom, in other words, is (often) "led by Fear," according to Indigenous-based ecophilosopher-educator Four Arrows. Fear is intimate with all our ancestors; so, follow the ancestors and they will teach about Fear. Four Arrows is one of the rare few elders I know who has put the core of the curriculum of fear management/ education in the 'hands of the ancestors' (dead or living). This approach within the Natural sphere of "primal awareness" (and cultural Indigenous sphere as a standpoint before-contact with W. settlers) is crucial to his framing Fear as a positive force/intelligence. And, as in the quote above, Four Arrows agrees that to allow oneself consciously to be "led by Fear" is the best way to receive "Fearlessness" teachings as well. Bottomline, when writing about the Indigenous worldview and fear and fearlessness, I had to take up Four Arrows' (and de Becker's) notion of the importance of "befriending the 'Gift of Fear'."[80]

This colleague, Four Arrows, who is a high-performance sports coach and psychologist/ hypnotherapist (among other things),[81] knows well the gift of fear (positive fear) as when he told me the story of working with a young woman high-stakes competitive athlete (fencing).[82] He found that with all her great skills and confidence on the court and constantly on the rise in the world rankings, there was a troubling fear (anxiety) off the court that tended to plague her at times. This could become so intense, that when she carried that onto the court with her, usually a worry about the opponent she was facing, it would negatively influence her game.

After her seeing this problem, she hired my colleague to help her. After months of training, and various hypnotic techniques he'd shown her of how to manage better her thought patterns, etc., she was doing much better and advanced to the Olympics finals. On the day before her match and a set of unknowns about who she would be fencing with next day, she got very anxious and phoned her coach (Four Arrows) asking him to come over for a training session to help get her into a better space. Although that was ultimately the aim of Four Arrows as well, his way to achieve that was (unbeknownst to her) by exacerbating fear, not reducing fear. He tells the story, starting with his memory earlier on of taking her into the ocean on a paddle board and he could sense her fear:

We were working in Mexico for several months successfully using her Fear of the ocean as a mechanism for getting her psychologically ready for an international competition in Puerto Rico. The night before the competition we were scheduled for a hypnotic session. She had a reporter that was going to cover it and I was concerned her concentration would be diminished because of this. Also, she was showing lots of fear about the draw for the next day—facing the unknown of how good she would perform but also who her opponent would be.

I didn't know what to do and was thinking of how to be effective, while I was looking out the window of my sixth floor room in the relatively shabby old hotel. Next door was her father's room, where we had planned to meet in five minutes for the session. I looked out and down and saw a six-inch or so rain-ledge running from my room to hers and it hit me as to what I would do.

I slid open the picture window, carefully stood on the ledge to see if it was strong enough to hold my weight, then hugging the wall shifted sideways until I was in front of the next room's window. Nathalie was facing the window and between her and me was her father with his back to me. I tapped gently on the window and Nathalie looked up, saw me and screamed! Her father, almost afraid to turn around, he jokes about this often, slowly looked and there I was. He quickly slid open the window, which almost made me fall and I casually stepped in utterly calm as if nothing was out of the ordinary and shook hands with everyone. Then I headed back to the window telling Nathalie I had found a good place for our hypnosis session. [out on the ledge]

Knowing how wild some of my previous work with her had been on the ocean, she did not know if I was serious. And bingo, there was her fear. I could sense it. I turned, smiled and said, "Are you still afraid of your competition tomorrow? Are you ready to do the work now,"? I said gently but commandingly. I asked everyone to leave and we had a session.

She won the feared match but lost the last one through a few wrong choices.[83]

Although a deeper fearanalysis is due to understand the logic behind Four Arrows' work here with his client, suffice it to say, he knows well how to utilize positive fear to get a concentrated (hypnotic) state of attention for learning —and, for de-hypnosis. By presenting a worse fear (terror) before his client by saying they are going to go out on the ledge (which, he was only joking)—he made the distinctive challenge to her to see that her worrying about tomorrow's match and all the things she could not control, was negative fear (and useless) relative to the real-fear-situation of what task she had to face with her trusted coach in the moment of their relationship and the aim to overcome unwarranted fear. Over the training years, Four Arrows continually showed her (and sometimes tricked her) into re-learning just how positive fear can be to improving her peak performance as an athlete—and, in the rest of her life. Basically, he taught her not to resist fear but work with it and it would shift on its own as she could then shape it into peak performance.

STORY E

RMF: Robin (2004) and his "history of an idea" (i.e., history of fear), made the argument that "fear as an idea...has changed over time." There is, in other words, no one definition/meaning of fear that is completely unchangeable over time, in different cultures, and situations and interpretations. He notes at the beginning of his book that many authorities have written about fear in more a negative connotation, like "Fear is supposed to lurk beyond the reach of our rational faculties, a preternatural invader waiting to breach the borders of civilization"—and, because of that non-rational location for fear there is "no history" of fear to record; it is so "primal...[and thus] subpolitical"[84] as an emotional experience and nothing more. It thus, cannot have had that much impact on an intellectual history of political thought. But was not how Robin saw fear. He saw fear as much more impactful on everything and especially political history of ideas—and, beyond just ideas. The question for Robin, was to study several political philosophers in a 300 year history of the West, curious to see how they think about fear. Of course, he wanted to also find out if they thought fear was positive or negative as a "force" (and, in the Robinian sense, as an "idea").

Fear is political, Robin claims. Having examined the political philosophies of Hobbes, Montesquieu, Tocqueville, Arendt, he continually found that although all of them saw the negative-side of fear on humans, each of them turned that initial understanding into a form of thought (and theory) by which they had "a hope that fear can serve as a ground for political renewal."[85]

According to Robin, Hobbes who centralized fear's role more than any other political theorist, ended up influencing all that followed as well (in some way)—most importantly, Hobbes had constructed the idea of fear into the very positive formation of the State itself—as a vessel of safety and security (and fear of punishment) to enable a society to withstand 'chaos' from barbarians and the assaulting "state of nature," which he defined as 'where every individual is out for themselves' (survival of the fittest) and will use fear and violence against anyone in order to selfishly survive themselves. Robin summed up Hobbes' "The fearful man, by contrast [to courageous, revolutionary and reckless hero-types] was to emerge as a truly rational agent, sensible and wise."[86] And Robin also says Hobbes and the others he studied (not unlike Machiavelli) believed fear when used right by the leaders, who are generally conservative in political orientation, is positive. And in fact, it is implied that fear is a 'gift' of sorts because it can motivate renewal and change like nothing else comparative. To this day, Robin argues, this long intellectual heritage around the idea of fear as a motivational tool, or renewal stimulus and shaper of human behavior and policy, and law, etc.—is still well operating—and, over the last 300 years Republican-types (conservatives) and Democrat-types (e.g., liberals) have more or less agreed on positive-fear—even though, they won't always admit it.

What I wonder about is the predisposition regarding such a construction of positive fear in political history and cultural evolution? Is it so strongly imprinted in history and is it justified to use (or mis-use) fear as a means to justify the positive ends of a political policy or agenda (e.g., good order, stimulating innovation, civility, and/or liberty)? What incentive in political history, in other words, is there for an opening to consider fearlessness as a political motivator, phenomenon and/or idea? To that, Robin is silent.

I'm curious what you take away from these stories, Maria?

BMK: Yes Michael! The aforementioned stories are like case studies that offer viewpoints from different perspectives. Uses of fear are many in accordance with context. I've categorised fear stories both on positive and negative sides into four categories or general types: Survivor, Inspirer, Intimidator and Suicide. So I'll share my gift of fear stories in light of these categories/types.

STORY 1

English actor Robert Pattinson of *Twilight Saga* fame is an example of the Survivor type. He admitted in an interview that he suffered from anxiety prior to his successful career. He could not wriggle out of fear problems for a good deal of his life. When he became aware of his weakness, which is due to fear, he realised he had to do something to get over it. He trained himself to overcome his anxiety feelings by avoiding bad thoughts. He looked at brighter-side of events and the future by thinking positively. He resorted to the art of cognitive modification so as to make use of fear as a constructive strength rather than as a defeating emotion. Consequently, fear became an alert for him to act upon consciously with more attention to achieve his ambitions. Soon he started conquering his negative feelings of imaginary failure and attended to his life changing auditions with confidence. Success followed.

STORY 2

The second type is that of an Inspirer. Generals of armies and leaders of various popular movements employ this strategy to motivate their men and women of their forces, in order to be an effective following. There's an instance of a legendary Japanese warrior called Nobunaga, who could be cited in this connection. Once he was on a war campaign, leading his force. When he approached the enemy, his intelligence operatives informed him that the enemy's army was as huge as ten times larger than his. His soldiers heard this and got disheartened. Nobunaga could sense fear overtaking his usually brave commanders. He stood firm in his optimism. He decided to boost the spirits of his army. He took the force to a Shinto temple. He offered prayers at the shrine and made an impactful speech to allay the fears of his men. However, he knew how to effect the change concretely by manipulating thoughts on fears. He went inside the sanctum sanctorum of the shrine and sat in meditation for some time and came out showing a coin to the soldiers. He said that he had a vision of the Supreme Power and the coin would endow much more strength to each one of the soldiers than the enemy's numerical strength. Then he tossed the coin and it was heads that appeared. All his soldiers' morale rose high. They believed that the power of the supernatural was with them. Their spirits were high and they were eager to fight. They got rid of their fears, which were replaced with the feelings of courage and confidence. Nobunaga won the war decisively. But he alone knew how he managed the fears of his men by turning them into his favour. He laughed at himself holding the coin which had heads on both sides. This was not only the gift of fear in operation but gift of the two-headed coin. It's called magic.

STORY 3:

The Intimidator category is about how to inflict fears on the opposite person for selfish and positive gains. According to one account, Alexander the Great employed this technique at least during one of his invasions. He was on his way to conquer Persia. The Persian King Darius was equally strong. But Alexander was clever to resort to mind games without actually waging a deadly war in Persia. Mary Renault, a British historian wrote, that Alexander offered sacrifices to the God of Fear, known as *Phobos* prior to his war march. His tactical psychological warfare soon yielded positive results and the frightened Darius fled from his kingdom out of fear of death even before Alexander entered the city.

STORY 4:

The Suicide type reflects a dangerous facet of inability to manage self-created fears. Such fears and anxieties are mainly the outcomes of irrational imaginaries of the mind. In such circumstances, it (suicidal tendency) tends to happen when the Id behaves irrationally, and the Superego fails to support the Ego due to lack of proper social consciousness and enlightenment, and the Ego would also be at a loss to intervene successfully. The *New Indian Express* reported in August 2020 that an elderly couple, aged 63 and 60 respectively, committed suicide by consuming poison over their fears of coronavirus. They were living in Hyderabad with their children and grandchildren. Both had a normal fever and cold but they assumed blindly that their illness was part of, or would attract the coronavirus. They didn't discuss the issue with their children, nor with any doctor. Their fears were exacerbated with the news reports of increasing COVID cases during the month of August in India. Their primary worry was that they might infect their little grandchildren, if they contracted COVID. One day, the two of them locked themselves in their room and consumed poison.

Another newspaper *Hindustan Times* published a report in February 2020 of a 50 year old man who hanged himself to death in the world famous temple town of Tirupati. He had a normal cough and cold at the time when corona cases were negligible in India but infections were rising day by day and there was publicity in the media to alert people about taking precautions like mask wearing, hand washing, social distancing etc. He developed delusional anxiety about the virus and he prevented his own son to interact with him, only at a distance. On that fateful day, he locked himself alone and took his own life by hanging. Such instances were many in 2020, especially in India where a lot still needs to be done to help a larger chunk of the population get rid of superstitions and superstition based fears.

RMF: Thanks. There are many things we could discuss, but I think a good deal of these issues will return at various points in the book. Maybe we could just mention a few things that catch our curiosity and feed our speculations coming out of this Introduction 2.

I know I have a question about my using the term *fear-bonding* and/or love-bonding for a few of these stories. I am attempting to draw out with that language that there is some deep unconscious "need" or "desire"—it would depend on each person in the story context, to cling to and bond to fear. Fear, psychosocially, becomes like a *substitute mother* = fear as *in loco parentis*. I've been writing initial thoughts recently that 'fear is a parent.' I am not saying that is necessarily bad *per se*, but this is rather new delicate territory I'm treading in my own theorizing lately.

Part of me wonders if this fear-bonding is really a way to describe a phenomenon of *addiction to fear*. I'm not the only one to have raised the problem of people becoming addicted to fear, individually and collectively.[87] Maybe there is a theoretical explanation and a phenomenological reality to *why* humans characteristically, voraciously defend their fears and fear itself, even when they suffer negative consequences doing so, even sometimes life-threatening consequences, due to excessive and toxic fear. There may be also biogentic natural reasons and of course sociocultural, political and spiritual reasons. I'm excited to pursue this, although it is not the focus of this book.

Perhaps, people or their Ego's are unknowingly addicted to fear and need it, like they need their mother. And that is related to most basic self-esteem/identity formation. At least, potentially, that could be a route to how the neural-psychological programming went down in early development. Maybe humans have a genetic-based imprinting instinct, just like baby ducks, for example, as soon as they're born they look for an 'object' to trust and to follow and it is then 'burned in' and virtually permanent like a glued bonding—and, I suspect the imprinting can get hi-jacked, and end up attaching to the experience of fear—especially, when love isn't always there and controllable in the environment. Internal created fear is always available in the paradigm of which I'm thinking that fear is a guardian for defense. Anyways, just some thoughts. If this is true, then such a theory of fear-bonding/addicting would really challenge the overt and growing popular acceptance and valuation of all the fear-positivists, who promote their positive fear—and yes, same with those promoting the *gift of fear* discourses.

BMK: Yes Michael! The phrases you have stated- fear bonding, fear is a parent, fear is guardian, addicted to fear. These have, in fact, as I can see, pivotal relevance to developing a solid fear—fearlessness theory/model, in a much more concrete way. All the phrases are interrelated.

For example, we can say *fear is mother*. Where, mother means the one who creates life. If we look at the Bible, it was darkness that existed first from which creation including light evolved. Earlier, I mentioned that fear could be equated to darkness. From darkness came light. The universe, space, ether, cosmos etc. are embodiments of darkness. Legends from other cultures also created anthropomorphic characters based more or less on the same ideation. If we apply this logic, fear and fearlessness in relation to human life and condition could be explained comfortably and reasonably.

My *hypothesis* goes like this[88]: In the beginning, the darkness was there. It was the universe. Its other side/face is light. But light evolved from darkness and both became two from one, like in duality consciousness. This duality manifested in two types of qualities: (a) one, contracting into nothingness and the other (b) expanding into everythingness. The physical manifestation of contracting quality is called time and that of expanding quality is called space. Both time and space are inseparable. They are in a continuum. Together as One, this is the universe. Time is dark and light is space. The farther the light travels, the wider the space expands. The tinier the darkness contracts, the smaller time shrinks.

Fear is another manifestation of darkness. Fear is time. We can say it is a spiritual, psychological or metaphysical manifestation of time. Fearlessness is the metaphysical manifestation of light. Fearlessness is space. The universe is composed of countless entities like black holes, galaxies, stars, planets, meteors, flora and fauna; and they are part and parcel of the universe itself. One of such entities is the human being. Like humans have evolved from the primitive organisms to apes to sapiens, the universe and its entities are continually in the process of evolution.

When it comes to the human being for example, the universe is manifested in each individual being. The human mind represents time and the human body, space. Mind is composed of memories, especially of the universe and its entities. Mind also has memories of the ancestors. Body, being the manifestation of space is always on the move to expand. The body tries to be a separate entity but mind's memory part acts against the efforts of the body and tries to integrate with universe. The affinity between the memories of mind and that of universe and its entities is so strong that the mind is always on the move to shrink to death like the suicidal element. But the body part tries to suppress the motive of the mind and struggles to exist as a separate entity. The ontological conflict between the two goes on.

Both mind and body have their instincts in the Id part of psyche as death and the life instincts respectively. Death creates the feeling of fear and life sparks the feeling of fearlessness to live (love towards body i.e., life). Fear of death triggers fearlessness to live. Fear bonding is so strong that the death instinct *destrudo* aims to integrate as one with death, that is time. Unless there is fear bonding, fearlessness will not emerge actively to counter fear in equal and opposite frequencies. Fear is a parent in the sense that the mother has got fears for the safety of her offspring because the goal of life is to procreate and expand the progeny.

The purpose of life in a way is two-fold: (1) first one is again two-fold: to sustain self-life and create its species This is the outcome of libido and (2) to commit suicide to embrace death in order to integrate with death or time. This is the outcome of *destrudo*. The parent is concerned with species' well-being. Unless the offspring is safe and secure, the mother is worried all the while.

Fear addiction is natural because the death instinct goes on creating fear of death on one side whereas the libido takes the cue from death alerts and strives to strengthen the life system, culture and safety net.

Fear is the guardian angel of the individual being for it alerts the individual in times of dangers and crises, prompting fearlessness to defend body(life).

A fearless leader should take their steps in a calculated way but not on knee jerk reaction. Courage alone doesn't accord safety to life and it must go hand in hand with wisdom, to think attentively and critically. Wisdom comes from careful attitude out of the fear(ism) perspective. Both fear and fearlessness are complementary to each other. A fearful turtle never gets anywhere until he sticks his head fearlessly out. A woman cannot be fearless in what she stands for unless she takes into account fear in what she falls for.

Therefore, if fear is a gift, fearlessness is a boon.

Highlights of What is to Come

Gift of Fear, is truly a potent idea. It is also a set of words/meanings, perhaps even myths. It seems to grab many people's attention when it is offered up, of which are two basic reactions: (a) "are you nuts" and, (b) "wow, that's interesting to think about." Our point is to suggest there is no doubt a strong phenomenological reality behind the concept of fear as/is gift. The Positive Paradigm we spoke of in the Preface is geared to enhance and support the gift of fear discourse for some long time. One even comes to sense the rising fervour for this movement is producing an informal, but substantive, Gospel of Fear.[89] We raise in our discussion above the problems of what such a conclusion may be, when there is so much that is still unclarified as to what "fear" means to someone, that is, how they define it when making such a claim that is so positive about fear. Can we therefore only take their views on the surface as literal in how they react to "gift of fear" being mentioned? Or, is there a deeper inquiry demanded? That latter, is more where we tend to fall in our own thinking at this point.

Ultimately, the main reason we started this Introduction 2 with "Gift of Fear" is that we were aware that a counter notion "Gift of Fearlessness" is also present in the historical discourses on and around fear. The latter, is something found more in the East,[90] the former more in the West. Why is that? Although such a comparative topic is beyond the scope of this Introduction, we trust that our bringing forth this issue is enough to make all of us start to think more about these concepts. We explore in the pages ahead, in various angles, this underlying thread of questioning that perhaps the "gift of fear" discourse is a major form of resistance to Fearlessness OR maybe they are twin gifts from the same source, complementary in deeper ontological reality, even if on the surface they may appear as opposites—in resistance to each other.

In terms of a <u>practical recommendation:</u> *Imagine yourself*, including those near around you who mean a lot to your life, completely bathed in *timelessness*. Then, once you take that reality of possibility in, and keep imagining it for some minutes in contemplation, then begin to see if there is any humor that wants to emerge. Just how funny is this state of timelessness.

Next, try this with *spacelessness*, applied to the same exercise. And, finally, think about fearism as presented in this book so far. It arose as a concept to both include and transcend fear. It came from artist-type thinkers (Subba and Fisher, and now Kumar). Art, humor, science-fiction may very well be the most important locations for fear(ism) to flourish, at least for now. Eventually, philosophy, theology, psychology, sociology etc., may start to 'listen' to what is happening as Fear and Fearlessness are brought into new, not always rational-logical, or scientific, configurations and juxtapositions. Basically, what we are saying, is that it is really important to not take fear so seriously (no contradiction intended)—and that, may be exactly its gift—and, that spirit of the gift is infused with the gift of fearlessness. Something to think about. Clearly, as co-authors we are speculating, often spontaneously, in our writing these Introductions. We wanted to model a way of hanging out with Fear and Fearlessness that we believe all people could benefit from.

Two quotes:

Don't fear fearlessness. -His Holiness, the XIV Dalai Lama[91]

[Jesus said:] I'm afraid of everything....I don't kill because I'm afraid....I want to rebel against everything [even] God—but I'm afraid....You know who my mother and father is? You know who my God is? It's fear; look inside me, that's all you'll find.
    - excerpt from *The Last Temptation of Christ*[92]

INTRODUCTION 3

Fearism Meets Fearlessness

I'm very interested in futures studies and the relationships [like], how we imagine the future, how we come to bring about those futures we imagine and/or [that] we actually *resist* those futures we imagine or even are afraid to imagine.   -R. Michael Fisher[93]

A need for a newer [futurist] philosophy, which would compensate for these [historical] limitations of the earlier psychological theories, was being felt—and here comes Fearism with its pervasive influence. Its fundamental assumption is that fear drives human action. It is truth attested to by universal human experience across the ages.   -Mahesh Paudyal[94]

Everything...creates fear or has a factor of fear....We are entangled with fear all around...Fear is a director of life.
-Desh Subba[95]

People always tend to run around as a result of fear, but remain unaware of it as there is a lack of philosophical interpretations of fear.   -Desh Subba[96]

[most basic "principle of fear[ism]" is:] fear is not a foreign element that tends to attack us. Proper utilization of the fear can result in merit...otherwise it would only harm—it depends on us.   -Desh Subba[97]

Fearism is based on a transdisciplinary approach to understanding the nature and role of fear and life.... Fearism directs us to analyze the knowledge of fear itself, and that directs us to how we are educated about fear itself....There is no one definition of fearism, there is no one set of agreed upon principles from thinkers who use the concept of fearism. There are some contradictory ideas and definitions and constructions of fearism.... It's relatively new, a very new formation of a way of conceptualizing and representing the study [of fear], or fearwork ....So, it's going to have all the problems of a naive, a nascent form of knowing, or thought, philosophy or whatever. Just like all things that start, they go through a big mess for a long time before... eventually maybe in ten, twenty years, if we last that long as a species—I think that fearism will eventually start to coalesce, if not sooner, and there will be some really good strong principles, there will be research, that's actually done to validate some of those principles and hypotheses, and that's not been done yet. So I share this all with you, as invitation to all listeners to bring what you want to bring to the area of fearism...and, let's see together what we can create.   -R. Michael Fisher[98]

Whenever asked about "What do you teach?" Fisher, with a Ph.D. in Education, has been perplexed what to answer. Since the beginning of his training as a school teacher in the late 1970s, he always paused before answering. He could have given the obvious answer: "I'm a certified secondary science teacher—specializing in life sciences and love teaching biology." Clearly, in the pause, was the deeper and truer answer. Most of the time he never said more, depending on the person asking the question. On occasion it was appropriate to be more honest when asked. He would reply: "I teach to free conditioned minds to become creative minds."

After 1989, a life-transforming year for him in which he co-founded the In Search of Fearlessness Project to counter the global dominating Fear Project, everything changed. In those years, when people asked him, what do you teach?, he answered consistently: "I teach about *what happens when fear meets fearlessness.*" Now, that answer made most everyone pause, with an accompanying perplexed facial expression and a good deal of silence. Uncomfortable with his answer, they were quickly looking for a way to change the topic. Few people could understand why a teacher would focus on such a weird question. One person responded to Fisher's answer: "Can you build a career around that?" Fisher responded: "I don't know."

Yet, for 32 years it is still the most intriguing area of research to him. He has built a career around it but *not* a career of institutional status, money/security, power or great influence. It has been an alone journey in the shadowed margins of traditional approaches to knowledge and society's main interests. In this Introduction 3, the variant of that question takes the form of *what happens when fearism meets fearlessness*(?)—which arises because Fisher's specialty has been the development of a philosophy and curriculum of Fearlessness. And, this book is our way, as co-authors, to explore a bit of the meeting ground between that Fearlessness and the philosophy of fearism of Desh Subba.[99] Before we get to that directly and explicate the ways fearism has addressed fearlessness and *visa versa*, it is important we build some context for that discussion. A good place to start seems to be the issue of *Intelligence—via* body, mind, soul and spirit. A holistic-integral intelligence is the aim. A topic that Fisher as a professional educator has had to search deeply into, for why else would one be teaching at all?

(Defense) Intelligence

> Fear perverts intelligence and is one of the causes of
> self-centered action. Discipline may suppress fear but

> does not eradicate it, and superficial knowledge which we receive in modern education only further *conceals* it. [italics added] – Jiddu Krishnamurti[100]

For Fisher, Defense Intelligence (DI), as one of several major systems of all living organisms, is basic to the understanding of Fear.[101] Yet, what he has learned, as have many others over the years, is that Fear is very tricky to get to know, and thus the DI that it is part of becomes equally complicated—yet, ever so important to understand better. A begging question of the philosopher: *Why is fear tricky to know?* In part, it is because it has many definitions (see Introduction 2), and not all of them agree with each other. But there are other complicating factors going on. Current philosophies and teaching on "emotional intelligence,"[102] that has become so popular in the last few decades, falls far short of a good education in DI and Fear.

It may be that knowing fear is, in part, *resisted* by all parts of society and one's own body/mind system. Like Proteus, *Fear* hides, morphs like a chameleon and, takes on many guises.[103] This creates a teaching problem. *How we are educated about fear itself(?)*, as taken from one of the quotes by Fisher above, strikes us (co-authors) as core to everything in this book *Resistances to Fearlessness*. These guises of DI and Fear need to be scrutinized. And to do so requires an educational, holistic-integral, and epistemic *adaequatio*[104] first and foremost; and then to follow, it requires an extraordinary leadership to carry it out. The philosophy of fearlessness (Fisher) and philosophy of fearism (Subba) were meant to pursue these goals. This point of epistemology, appears in this entire book around a parallel phrasing, that is: *How we are educated about fear...* which could take the form of *How we are led to be in particular relationships to fear* (and thus, also bravery, courage, fearlessness, etc.). Leadership gets special attention in Part I.

So, how we are educated? and how we are taught to *resist* truth become central. This gives focus on *learning*. This gives focus on *Intelligence*. This gives focus on self-reflective critical *forensic* investigation, as Krishnamurti suggests that education itself is quite able to "conceal" the very thing we seek—that is, *freedom* (from fear)—and freedom from our own (conditioned) minds. At times, as co-authors, we have felt like a grand 'crime' has been done across the entire history of humanity. And we think it has something to do with *how we are educated about fear itself.*

With those words...now, to be sure, the *trigger* has been pulled. The words *read*, and *carry*, already in the reader's mind a set of associations, thoughts, and resultant feelings; thus also, in our mind as writers. The ideas are released, now lifting from the page into time and space—everyone's minds are already running rapidly, like water by default flowing with gravity, moving down the track of pre-conditioned thinking and imagining that: "Oh, yes, intelligence. I'm going to be more intelligent IF I read this book by Fisher and Kumar....I'm going to be more intelligent IF I learn about fearism and fearlessness..." etc. Or perhaps, "Oh, yes, these quotes on fearism, yes, I already understand what they mean. Of course, I could have said this. I have read Fisher already..." etc. OR perhaps, "I'll be more intelligent just purchasing this book by Fisher and Kumar and keeping it on my shelf, as I associate with it, and with them as authorities, just like as if I just bought a new car. Who needs to actually read and study it? Who needs to even drive the car, once I possess it?" The commodification of knowledge produces bizarre attitudes in us.

Possibilities abound how one relates to what is before them, in this case on the pages of a book but the relationship doesn't stop there. Is there not such a basic *already flowing* impulse, pent-up behind the damn in the mind, awaiting its chance—in the form of conditioning, a conditioned mind filled with ambition—to run this course, a competitive race, imagined from the start to have built-up to rise and fight to be the *most* intelligent, and hopefully even more so, the *most* liked and approved of, than everyone else? Krishnamurti cautioned us to be mindful beings, of which means we have to release some part of our mind (our needs), even if momentarily, to not get (already) hooked on *fear/hope* dynamics in our learning and intelligence systems:

> [speaking of "the right kind of education":] If we no longer seek immediate results, we shall begin to see

> how important it is that both the educator and the child should be free from the fear of punishment and the hope of reward, and from every other [conditioned] form of compulsion....[we have to unhook from some 'authority' that will give us the answer][105]

What addictive compulsive *need* is there behind the seeking of intelligence (and quick solutions) in societies that reward certain kinds of intelligence and social approval? Any need of such acclaim is already faulty, you can expect. Because of our faulty education, says Krishnamurti, is typically imbued with *conditioned minds* trying to teach others' conditioned minds, and calling it "educating." "Fear is inevitable as long as the mind is seeking security," he wrote. Fear is, in this sense, the basis of the conditioned mind—and arguably, that mind is already pre-conditioned to defend itself from all things that are not itself. Thus Defense Intelligence, can be easily skewed and become even pathological. True as it is that intelligence is the mind's natural task, however, that can so easily be corrupted *via* security-seeking compulsive patterns deeply unconscious as well as conscious—and, you can predict *security* needs, natural as they may be in part, are commodified today and soaked in concomitant fear-conditioning itself—at near every turn of our everyday lives. Not only is personal-seeking of information culpable to such distortion based on security-seeking (i.e., fear-based needs) but also whole disciplines of knowledge, like Science can also be so distorted—as Maslow argued.[106] Even entire societies can be so driven.

Who doesn't want more and more security—like they want more and more money, more and more fame? Modernized, homogenized, capitalized society works that way—built on a foundation of a "culture of fear" (see Introduction 1). And, every page read in this book as well, is also welcoming *and* vulnerable to such obsessive "me" needs and ideological capture, like it or not, to such fear-conditioning (seeking), even with the generous stated intention to become 'fearless'—and, to practice the "gift of fearlessness" (see Introduction 2). The cultural critic, Brian Massumi, called it "tools of the organized fear trade" or a "capitalist culture of fear" and he asked a rather terrifying questions:

> How does capitalized fear circulate? Implant and reproduce itself? If we cannot separate ourselves from our fear, and if fear is a power mechanism for the perpetuation of domination....[are we] in collective complicity with fear, does that mean that fear no longer sets social boundaries but transcends them? If so, how does domination function without [recognizable, familiar] set boundaries? If not, how can the boundary be reconceptualized to account for the confluence [embedded relations] of fear, subjectivity, and capital? Most of all, how, now, does one resist?[107]

"Me" thinking/needs are "violent," says Krishnamurti.[108] Where does one find remnant Intelligence within that fear-subjectivity-me-capital enmeshment of co-evolving structures and processes that make up this world? It's tempting to believe... there's a solution. What's clear to us, is that the more one studies the complexity of Fear(ism) and Fearlessness, the more uneasy we are to suggest any one or easy solution to our fear-conditioned minds and societies. We ourselves, as learners, teachers, writers, and citizens have to be vigilant and mindful to not becoming saturated—and, as a body becoming, what Massumi called, "the ultimate object of technologies of fear"[109]—that is, apparatuses of a social 'Program' of power aimed at making us slaves, and doing so just when we think we are becoming so smart, intelligent, to *not* be slaves in the 'Fear' Matrix. No conspiracy theory intended here for dramatic effect—we are just observing what is a real problem to face.

A danger signal arrives now, like a red light at the busy traffic intersection. Stop! Pause. Listen. See. Pause. Think. Pause. Breathe. Pause. Breathe....

As the great E. philosopher Jiddu Krishnamurti would caution his listeners, trying to be so intelligent in his presence as the 'guru' teacher of wisdom and enlightenment—they would, he said, being trying so hard to be enlightened, educated, insightful, intelligent, loving and compassionate, that they would fall right into the trap of the me-based (fear-based) mind thinking it can think—thinking it can will its way out of the mess and self-delusion—thinking it is on the right track, or not on the right track, and desperately trying to correct themselves— to be 'good' and 'beautiful' and 'true'—to be like their guru master Krishnamurti, etc. Trying to be like God, Yahweh, Buddha, Krishna, Mohammed, whomever was perfect in their way of seeing. They wanted so badly this *freedom-intelligence*, to become Intelligence itself. Then, they would be free of desire and fear(?) Krishnamurti continually challenged his students and audience members for over 50 years of lecturing, that the seeking itself is already (likely) the corrupted 'one' (the "me" thinking and willing) of which typically produces no such liberation because the seeker is not ready to call out and name the 'killer' of the crime—that is, the "me" of identity, the conditioned-mind, as the seeker.

Who is the seeker but the 'me' who is seeking? The "violent me"[110]— as Krishnamurti would call it. He wrote,

> Intelligence [or Mind] is not personal, is not the outcome of argument, belief, opinion or reason. Intelligence comes into being when the brain discovers its fallibility, when it discovers what it is capable of, and what it is not.[111]

Now, to really take that in, and sit with it, mindfully, compassionately, is a beginning way to wisdom as a path of knowing—and, from there, one will create, arguably a more fearlessness-based knowledge. Yet, there are always 'traps' and more 'traps' along the journey. Welcome to the path of fearlessness!

Terrorism, Fearism, Futures:
Fearlessness Exercising Its Muscles

For our part as co-authors, who think a good deal about the future of humanity and the environmental conditions for Life, in attempting to conceptualize any future worth living we have been drawn to the problem of terrorism. "It is difficult to define 'terrorism'.... [yet] Terrorism is one of the biggest problems of the present world," wrote Desh Subba.[112] And Kumar wrote,

> [T]he subject of terrorism triggers our apprehension or outright fear for our own life, the lives of our own family and friends which affect or stir our distinctive moral emotions. Terror in a way is nothing but fear amplified....the onus of guiding the state as far as terrorism is concerned, lies in the hands of fearologists. Contribution by the founders [of fearism and fearology] like Fisher and Subba in this respect is nonpareil, for they have taken *suo moto* responsibility and are relentlessly engaged for the cause.[113]

Kumar also has laid out a great deal of criteria for labeling "terrorism" in terms of defining it.[114] Although his criteria include typical terrorology and its political framing of terrorism and terrorists, Kumar has turned to transcend disciplinarity within the limitations of that field, in order to accommodate the more integrative work of a philosophy of fearism (Fisher & Subba). The three of us believe this upgrade of the notions of terrorism and terrorology is long overdue. In the future this must change or we'll never fully solve this "wicked problem." As a trio we concluded,

> The terrorism problem is actually a fearism problem—so, it is best to institute the philosophy of fearism to solve it. This has not yet happened. Like any new movement of thought, or a philosophy, it takes time to be noticed and legitimated. What Fisher and Subba have written

about terrorism [is that] "the wicked problem isn't really the problem; the real problem is that we don't understand the wicked problems well enough to affect real solutions....It requires a change of mind or attitude that underlies behavior, otherwise the change won't stick...".[115] A philosophy of fearism takes the wicked problem of terrorism seriously as a complex problem with need for complex solutions. If we know anything about the toughest problems, they are only going to be solved with an extensive holistic-integral analysis of the problem in the first place. Most often people want quick 'answers' and 'solutions' now, and they lack the patience and discipline to do the hard work of study and analysis carefully. As philosophers of fearism and without our three pillar model,[116] there is an ethical imperative to do our analysis consistently and holistically, with great patience.[117]

Although the founding of *philosophy of fearism* by Subba in 1999 was a literary interest, Fisher's unique version of *fearism-t* (toxic form[118]), independently coined and defined (in 1990) from Subba's, was one that was situated in the notion of crises from the existential to the political—and, with terrorism in mind. Fisher was looking for a way to capture the more hidden aspect underneath the dramatic exteriors of terrorism. He believes *fearism-t* is more important than terrorism. We need to understand fearism-t as the ideological and behavioral components of an ecology of violence that builds up a fear-based way of being in the world and trying to solve suffering. Despite Fisher's original use of the term, in Introduction 3 (as co-authors), we will focus directly on fearism as a philosophy and its capabilities to interrogate not merely terrorism but all kinds of forms of oppression. We acknowledge as well that there is some overlap of Fisher's and Subba's notions of fearism.

Oppression is ultimately, no matter what type it is, a fear-based ideologism with violent consequences. And, yes, with such violence comes more fear. We won't argue the point here, but it is through our

Subbaian-Fisherian fearist lens that we see terrorism, as it is commonly known, in a rare understanding—that is, terrorism is a type of *fear management system*—albeit, a very destructive, if not pathological, one. Terrorism is in the more subtle realm, of a fearanalysis, arguably, a type of *resistance* to fear/terror—ironically, as it is a breeding of fear/terror. The dynamic is one of a competition for who gets to wield the sword of fear/terror/power in the world. Remember the USA government after 9/11, entered what they named a "War on Terror." And, they would use terror to fight that war—all in the name of what Barber called maintenance of "Fear's Empire."[119] Call it fearmongering (see Introduction 2). Fisher has called this a "Fear Wars,"[120] by any other name. Even counter-terrorism activity vs. terrorism activity—is on the surface logical but from the view of a fearist and fearological lens, one has to question the efficacy of such a Fear War or Terror War. Will it ever lead to fearlessness? We don't think so. Yet, that's not the topic of this Introduction 3.

What we intuit and what Fisher's Fear Management Systems (FMS) theory predicts, is that *Fearlessness* is already latent in living systems. It arises, and exercises its gifts when Fear arises. The more extreme the fear—example, in a world riddled with terrorism of various kinds, then it is the perfect breeding ground for a lot of exercising for Fearlessness. Fisher goes so far to say, similar to Subba, that a "Fearless" (FMS-9) will arise under such intensity of continual terrorism and existential anxiety[121]—at least that is what we are suggesting in this book. Subba, likewise makes the adventurous indicator of this same phenomenon on a macro-scale of Fear Ages—whereby he suggests that after the "Extreme Fear Age" will (potentially) arise the "Fearless Age." The fact that these two in depth fearism philosophers had arrived at this thesis of exercising fearlessness muscles, is worth noting that probably some underlying truth exists in their vision and theories of fear management. Truly, and sadly, they don't teach this in Sunday school or public schools. What a different world it would be, if children understood this basic exercising of fearlessness under the stresses of fear. Then, all the fear that comes at them and within them, at least, can be re-imagined as not merely a predator, and they the prey, but that they are part of the solution.

Fearism's View of Fearlessness

Our focus for this third of our series of Introductions in this book is one that revolves around the way that a Subbaian fearism has come to understand not just fear/terror but fearlessness. Implicitly, we assume that fearism is supportive of the concept of fearlessness. Yet, that needs to be studied and herein we begin a first attempt to look at this relationship of the two. This ought to give readers a better sense of why we chose to write a book on fearlessness and do so from a fearism perspective.

Within Fisher's Fear Management Systems theory on the evolution of consciousness and fear/ fearlessness, he hypothesized that with the future unfolding, there would be a general trend of moving from a fear-based world to a fearlessness-based world.[122] Higher more mature and complex fear management systems would be engaged as the need increased for them. He suggested that "fearless" itself as a system would not likely fully kick-start *en masse* in cultures until there was a threshold reached of a high enough degree of terror—that is, one extreme would release the other extreme.[123] That theory and principle is part of his dictum: *When fear appears, so then does fearlessness.* The Fisherian theory of fearlessness, indicates that fearlessness only really flexes its toughest muscles when under the toughest of strains (e.g., terrorism). This theory, more or less, will be ferreted out in this book in later chapters; but it was worth mentioning here because there is the question brewing in our minds: What happens when a philosophy of fearism meets fearlessness? Fisher, in particular, has an intuition that fearism as a philosophy was only possible under guidance of the spirit of fearlessness; albeit, that is not the case *per se* argued by Subba or other fearists following that direction of fearwork. For Fisher, fearlessness is based in a critical liberation theory *in extremis*, that is, in crisis in all directions—including the environment in crisis. Fearism *via* Subba was not developed from that same location, although, it is well aware of crisis as part of the context that the human condition is embedded. That's why, a philosophy of fearism is thought to be a futurist developmental expansion from the roots of the philosophy of existentialism—where existential crisis is a key concept of the entire paradigm of existentialism.[124]

Let's look now specifically at the relationship of fearism and fearlessness. How well have fearism authors, other than Fisher, addressed fearlessness? How could this be improved in future fearwork, by all who are interested, no matter what school of philosophy they come from? With this investigation, we as co-authors, will attempt somewhat to stand back from the study of this relationship and to stay open-minded, while at the same time offering a critical eye to the potential for: How fearism may itself, as currently adopted by thinkers, play a part in the set of *resistances* to Fearlessness.

Desh Subba

As founder of philosophy of fearism, Subba's views on *fearlessness*, which he does not typically distinguish from *fearless* in his texts, is bound to heavily influence his students. In his major tome *Philosophy of Fearism*, neither "fearlessness" nor "fearless" are listed in the Index. He writes considerably more about "fearless" than "fearlessness." He is not absolutist in his thinking (for e.g., like J. Krishnamurti who wants to ultimately in enlightenment, apparently, eliminate all fear). He wrote, "We can be free from normal fears."[125] Somewhat contradictory, he then wrote, "We are not [ever] free from some fears," and the best we can do is have "fear to be minimised."

Intentionally, Subba suggests some fears are natural "positive fear,"[126] and there's no need for their elimination. Yet, he wrote that a classless society (as potential) is a "fearless society"[127]; and, a controlled population growth (following Malthusian theory) leads to "fearless" populations existing[128]—fearism theory, he says, is very similar to Malthusian theory.[129] In Chapter 29, a dialectical evolutionary and historical view is presented, which he calls "Fearless Path." Somewhat similar to Fisher's historical-evolutionary Fearlessness Movement, Subba's evolutionary theory is made clear: "We always see a [transcendent] fearless path, and our civilization has developed continuously along this path....we expect to be [achieve] fearless."[130]

Relevant to the discussion earlier about knowledge-seeking and distortions and fear-based drives, Subba, more optimistic than Fisher, does not address this issue in his philosophy *per se*, but he does give his general view of the role of *fearlessness* in the knowledge quest:

Philosophers and philosophies of thinkers and thoughts are also liberation [as well as spiritual thinkers]. All the liberations are in the journey of fearlessness. The journey goes on continually until it reaches fearlessness. Then, knowledge [without resistances] is acquired like a glimmering diamond after lots of struggles and research. That is to say the thing that was search can be acquired in its new form.[131]

Subba, without relying on any literature on *fearlessness per se*, gives his own views, and sometimes contradictory on the surface. For example, he is now not so positive about "fearless" as an aim. He wrote,

> If we try to make people fearless and [or] fearful, it increases chaos and anarchism in society.[he seems to not favor this kind of fearless?; he generally approves more of just minimizing fear, balancing fear, managing fear well—which, is not a very revolutionary psychopolitical stance] Fear is an effective medicine for such problems. It helps us to be fearless and calm from birth to the cradle."[132]

With very limited theorizing by Subba on fearlessness and making it conceptually equivalent to fearless (which Fisher does not do), then we can conclude that he sees positive fear as important to maintain and no fearlessness ought to threaten or erase that or be a wreckless type of fearlessness, which he says will increase "chaos and anarchism." In talking about this social level of reality here it is clear that he believes fear is essential to maintain social order, norms, and so on. No such radical postmodern Fearlessness Paradigm, like with Fisher's, is presented. Subba's writing here is philosophical but cognitive-behavioral for the most part and pragmatic. When he writes, "Life will surely be easier if it can manage to get rid of the fear"[133] or "The [sic] cannot be easy unless the life becomes free from fear"[134]—he is distinguishing negative fear, he wants to get rid of, and positive fear, he wants to keep. We'll see this is commonly the distinction, and overall approach to defining fear, taken by all Subba's students. How one defines and makes meaning of *fear* highly influences how one defines and makes meaning of fearlessness. The question remains, what is the 'best' paradigm for such a defining and meaning-making?

Bhawani Shankar Adhikari

Adhikari has adopted both fearology and fearism in recent years, and he believes in "fearological dialogue" to help work through fear problems and conflicts caused by fear. He wrote, "The management of fear is not [to be done] *via* fear-based ways, but it is possible to manage through 'fearless' dialogue, consciousness, understanding and agreement."[135] He does not define or theorize *per se* what he means by fearless dialogue, although, rather he relies on, in his own words, what "Fisher calls for 'fearlessness,' [and] Subba calls for 'fearless path')" to counter against all the fears growing, including coronavirus.[136] The difficulty of this approach is that it mixes and matches Subba on fearlessness and Fisher on fearlessness, with problems unaddressed between the two; so, it ends up that we really have no idea where Adhikari's own theoretical and practical position is itself—albeit, more or less, it is Subbaian in regard to defining and making meaning of fear (and thus fearlessness).

Osinakachi Akuma Kalu

Similarly has adopted both Subbaian and Fisherian ideas for his own thinking and writing on fearism and fearlessness. He does not use fearlessness generally in his texts. He also does not problematize the mixing/blending of the two philosophical positions. Kalu wrote, "Fisher who wrote his dissertation on Fear introduced me to his World Fearlessness Movement"[137] and "As a member of the World Fearlessness

Movement, it is my bounden duty to help people control and manage fear."[138] Admirable, this identity Kalu seeks in what he calls "his" (i.e., Fisher's) World Fearlessness Movement (WFM), is not Fisher's movement but is an evolutionary and historical movement, which can be understood only if one takes initiative to truly understand the "fearlessness" conception (paradigm) in which Fisher is articulating as a philosophy. The movement is from Fear to Fearlessness, and has nothing foundationally or ontologically to do with Fisher. Fisher was merely trying to understand the phenomenon. The pursuit of Kalu, *via* his interpretation of this WFM revolves around behavioral means as we see in Kalu's reductionistic text here—that is, "help people control and manage fear." It's very pragmatic as found also in Subba, Adhikari and later below, as in Kumar. Fisher is much more a theorist and asks for better critical literacy education and theories in order to improve the philosophy of fearlessness and fearism. From there, then pragmatic actions and interventions are likely to be healthier, more holistic-integral, than merely trying to help "people control and manage fear."

B. Maria Kumar

In the last few years, Kumar has published several popular newspaper opinion columns where he has discussed fear and fearlessness and positioned, more or less, his own views on the philosophy of fearism (Subbaian) and fearlessness (Fisherian). Here are a few e.g., of his uses of "fearlessness":

> ...the most vital feature which is embedded in all the sacred tenets of the republic is nothing less than 'fearlessness.' Because it enables every citizen to enjoy unequivocally the rights enjoined on him/her. It was amply illustrated in Rabindranath Tagore's poem, 'Where the mind is without fear,' that the spirit of fearlessness stands out as an all-time guiding principle....

> Hence the ideal of fearlessness presupposes that every citizen has...[lists rights, including] freedom from fear of others, things, situations [and] fearless of dealing with others, things, situations—both [fear/fearlessness are] two sides of the same coin. Living freely without fear is the *sine qua non* of meaningful human existence called life. [he speaks of many fears and the "fear problem" and calls Desh and I "fearist philosophers" whom he draws upon in order to suggest] a fearless socio-economic and political atmosphere so that the citizens could thrive well.[139]
>
> In another article (in his native language), he wrote that, "I dwelt on the probable inevitability of prolonged human existence alongside corona with special attention to fearological perspective so as to enable the people to lead their lives fearlessly, albeit with due cautions [*via* "benign fears" not "toxic fears"][140]

Very much in the tenor of Subba's perspective, we see Kumar's emphasis on generic common sense definitions of fear, and fearlessness and fearless are used interchangeably with no theorizing as to their distinctions. In a short popular magazine venue is brevity is to be suspected but it is also similar to his writing on fearlessness in his books. Above, you can hear he wants to keep the positive fear (i.e., "benign fears") and the negative fear (i.e., "toxic fears") distinguished because he would not want fearlessness or fearless to be interpreted as the elimination of fear(s).

In a few other articles he more or less makes fearlessness sound very benign and even "comforting," which is certainly not the position Fisher takes in regard to when fear meets fearlessness. It appears he wants a fearlessness conception that tames down the negative aspects of fear to make life easier:

> ...corona-phobia [problems and] wide-spread fear-mongering [and what is a bigger problem]...fear ubiquitously haunts human minds unless it is juxtaposed with reason....[he talks of many fears and origin of fear as instinctual and names] irrational and rational fear... [and the solution overall is a] comforting fearlessness.... [e.g.,] The history behind the malarial cure is a good example of how the debilitating fear could be converted into comforting fearlessness.[141]

In another article, Kumar takes a rationalist, pragmatic, behavioral and literal interpretation of fearlessness; by-line reads: "Tax officials must be polite and just and promote fearlessness for taxpayers to be the growth engines of our economy."[142] His scaling of high fear to low fear to fearlessness (very low fear)—is a seamless continuum of fear intensities, he has called elsewhere *fear quantum*.[143] Thus he constructs fearlessness as a state/behavioral outcome, which feels good. This is a construction perhaps compatible with a Subbaian fearism but not so with a Fisherian fearism and fearlessness paradigm. To assume that "tax officials" could merely change their fear-based ways of intimidating people to "promote fearlessness for taxpayers" assumes more than Fisher would grant with any confidence because tax officials are not trained to enact anything near a true Fear Management System (FMS 7/8), as Fisher would argue is necessary to transform the lower more fear-based FMSs. It all comes down to a tension with all the Subbaian fearism thinkers and how they will decide to frame their version of fearlessness. This is a common issue of contention within the mainstream and popular articles and interventions everywhere that claim to be promoting fearlessness.

In another article, this individual psychological literal emphasis on fearlessness by Kumar is demonstrated in his claim:

> Apart from managing fear through personal interventions, there is also a critical aspect as regards the role of the state in inculcating the feeling of fearlessness in citizens by according the same value as that of

justice, liberty and equality. Social security and well-being measures will certainly alleviate insecurity and uncertain components and aid in stress-free and fearless mental state.[144]

The assumption here being that "the state" is capable of "inculcating the feeling of fearlessness in citizens"—whereas, for Fisher, fear/fearlessness is not reducible to feelings or emotions *per se*, and certainly not as a final criteria of measurement of success of achieving fearlessness. These issues of definition of fear (see Introduction 1 and 2) are core to the problems of interpretation of what is fearlessness. Fisher finds these literalist fearism readings of fearlessness too simplified, if not naive at times. However, clearly, there is still a lot of debate and theorizing to be done on these topics and fearism is a relatively nascent type of philosophy and concept, so not surprising there is going to be tensions, if not conflicts, amongst various authors.

Highlights of What is to Come

Although there is a good deal more to analyze in this territory where *fearism meets fearlessness,* for brevity in this Introduction 3, let's conclude with the acknowledgement that both fearism authors and Fisher are in agreement that a *faux* fearless(ness) is not what is being promoted by the term "fearlessness." In other words, a 'fearless' state of behavior/mind can often be nothing more than a fear-based inflated ego and bravado energies and intentions—not at all of the quality and maturity of true fearlessness. Adhikari, Kalu & Subba made this point: "...our collective actions [humanity] are reckless and self-destructive. We seem we are fearless about it and we are digging our own or our descendant's graves."[145]

Arguably, such 'fearless' bravado is a means of fear management that seeks to conquer fear—first and foremost—without giving valuation and a full-learning attention to the study of fear itself (or fearism). Adhikari, Kalu & Subba recognize that in order "To create [a] fearless situation [it] is [only] possible with the help of fear education."¹⁴⁶ All of us who study fearism and apply it, would <u>not</u> support this lack of learning approach. There is something, however, to be gained by studying the diversity of 'fearless' approaches and attitudes. They will tell us something about how and why true fearlessness is being *resisted*.

We started this Introduction 3 raising the possibility that even the best intentions of a philosophy of fearism and/or fearlessness philosophy are still susceptible to being in themselves both promoting of fearlessness and in *resistance* to fearlessness. After doing this bit of research above on the juxtapositioning of fearism with fearlessness, there's enough of a sense of 'gaps' in our thought about these issues. Indeed, we ask that all inquirers be as fearless as possible, in a good way, to self-reflect critically on their own education and own strengths and weaknesses when it comes to the topic of fearlessness. Let's not take fearlessness as methodology, as knowledge, as wisdom and compassion and as behavior with too quick and comfortable assumptions. This is something we can be more careful about, especially when we write things down about fearlessness.

In terms of a <u>practical recommendation</u>: *Write down* everything you think you know about fearlessness. Do it without looking at any reference materials. Then, go away from this writing. And, come back in a few hours or the next day, and evaluate what you wrote as critically as you can—using three methods: (a) first, just use your self-reflective consciousness to assess your own writing, (b) second, ask someone you respect to go over your writing and assess it and (c) go off and study fearlessness as discussed by others whom you respect, then come back and see what 'gaps' you may have left out in your (a) and (b) parts of this exercise.

A quote:

> Of all the great virtues, fearlessness occupies the place of primary importance. It is the ideal virtue. Unless

you have fearlessness, you will never be able to live comfortably. Be it in the secular field, in the battle of life in the world, or be it in your struggles in the realm of spirit....[147]

PART I

FEARLESSNESS AS/ IS LEADERSHIP

CHAPTER ONE

Fearlessness as/is Leadership

> Fearlessness is a conglomerate philosophy of applying instinctual, psychosocial, metaphys-ical and human management principles, with the aim of achieving the well-being of humanity and the rest of the living world.
> -B. Maria Kumar

> Who can...how will they...lead us to escape...lead us out of the 'Fear' Matrix? Follow the path of Fearlessness.... Which one? How will we know it? You have to 'see' it. There are many veils in the way. Obstacles? Choices? But ultimately, you also have to 'make it' simultaneously with trying to find it.
> -R. M. Fisher

RMF: I've not told the story behind my first introducing "fearism" into the professional field of Education. And, "fearlessness" too...

BMK: I know you first wrote of *fearism* in 1990, as the subtle underbelly of terrorism....

RMF: True. That was a beginning hint of what was to come of the term. It was coined and defined in an unpublished ms. Among other characteristics, I wrote, "Fearism is egoism."[148] I didn't do much with the concept until many years later.

BMK: Do you know why you didn't expand it then? You were obviously leading a radical new direction for Fear Studies back then. Attempting to bring a transdisciplinarity forward and to develop its own unique concepts, vocabulary, methodologies and theories so as to better understand fear.

RMF: *Fearlessness* meant a lot of things for me then but at core it was a *lens* in which to view everything—and, especially to view *fear* from a particular perspective. A new lens on 'truth' was my aim. I'm not sure why I didn't follow-up and develop my particular notion of fearism, now called *fearism-t* as an ideology, which promotes fearmongering and a culture of fear[149] in many forms. I re-labeled it from my original use in order to distinguish it from Desh Subba's version, which I learned about in late 2014.

BMK: If Fearlessness is a lens, it is interesting that Philosophy of Fearism is a *lens* that Desh Subba coined and defined nearly a decade later. He wrote in 2014, "I have made my attempt to theorise fear, an important issue. Now, most people are familiar with fearism, a new philosophy."[150]

RMF: Yes, Subba's version of a new philosophy is a much grander conceptualization of fearism than mine was. I'm also curious what he means "most people are familiar with fearism"—that's maybe in his circles of the Eastern literary world, but beyond that, this new philosophy is mostly unknown.

BMK: I think Subba promoted his philosophy intensely and was a good teacher-leader for the idea. He still is. His self-paid-for travel to many countries and districts, presenting on fearism has made a significant impact at some level. He found some others taking up the idea and going around the country teaching it for him. There is even a Fearism Study Center in Nepal and others, like in Africa, are attempting to establish organizations to promote the philosophy.[151] Subba wrote, "Many people, including teachers, critics, journalists, friends, and readers, have expressed their love, reactions, advice and support in order to develop fearism into theory. The fearist perspective is a new dimension to look at life and the world." And, he also acknowledged "it is not easy to constitute [a new] ism....it has some challenges."[152]

RMF: Resistances.

BMK: Yes. Like yourself, Subba was searching for a unique conceptual framing for a better way to understand fear. He was leading as well this whole domain of fear research and thought. A very exciting time. I imagine there was some synchronistic connection in the collective unconscious or something in the air that 'told' humans to invent a new way to approach our relationship with fear and knowledge about fear. It was an impulse in the West, then the East, a powerful connection of an idea, whose time had come. History is like that.

RMF: Indeed. What emerged was following a pattern of an awakening Defense Intelligence really [see Introduction 2]. It is not just that Subba or I were outstandingly geniuses discovering something so new; that's not how I see it. Yes, we had a leadership spirit within us for sure. We weren't merely interested in thinking like everyone else, especially about the psychology of human beings. I think that's the point of talking about this fearism idea that just 'popped out,' in two distant locations in the 1990s, as part of an emergence of complexity and adaptation. It's a planetary systems thing—an evolution of consciousness itself. Subba and I were the particular vehicles to bring out what I suspect a number of people worldwide were maybe sensing.

BMK: Maybe they were perceiving that a threatening quantum of fear was getting out of control nearly everywhere.

RMF: Sure. People *en masse* were sensing that Fear is a global Big Problem.

Escape: The Elephant in the Room

We began this chapter with a dialogue. It is apparent how relatively easy it is to *talk about* fear(ism), fearlessness, world issues, etc. And, it is not surprising that it is easy to talk about for us; although, as we have said from the start of this book, it is a subject few are really wanting to talk about. Yet, right in the midst of the very process of writing out our dialogue, across the communicative waves of the globe from East to West and back again, we are aware of some vague or hidden 'elephant in the room.' It walked in and we both didn't notice it until now. Some years ago, Michael had drawn a diagram, we wish to share in Figure 2 (below).

Figure 2 *"Elephant in The Room"*

We'll leave that there, and go from the concrete image of an elephant, to something more metaphorical in interpretation, in process, even ethereal—that is, for our purposes here.

Thus, we notice with our *second attentive* awareness,[153] which is at the periphery of our 'normal' consciousness and attentive gaze on the text and the subject we're writing about. We notice we are noticing. We witness we are witnessing. Yet, it is unclear what we have fully witnessed. It is like we are at a scene of an accident but it hasn't happened yet.

Maybe it is precognition or fantasy? Whatever the case, the object/subject we sense, we intuit, is located elsewhere—like in the less lit up zone beyond the beam of our analytical mind-lights. Outside and beyond that space, we search for that which the hidden yet (seemingly) can be seen. It's in the dark almost, in the fuzzy zone of the blur. Things moving. Things shifting. We experience some vertigo. We close our eyes for a moment. Some calm arrives. Great. We search for 'new' (or is it 'old') evidence. A case file is opened.

So, we've halted the beginning dialogue, momentarily, to address the appearing disappearing—the ghost that has visited in our unconscious—it will be called simply, what some call the 'elephant in the room.' The trigger word for the ghost may likely have been "Big Problem," what appear at the end of the dialogue above when Michael was responding to Maria and both were talking about a collective attuning of the entire world, at some level, to the "sensing that Fear".... and, there it is again. Another clue for the elephant in the room; see the capital letter used on Fear. So, 'F' capital and 'B' and 'P' capitals. All in one short spontaneous sentence that Michael was speaking. The conversation was flowing somewhere and then the capitals showed up. It would seem these could be innocent harbingers. It may seem silly even to let them catch our attention so fervently to 'break' what we were doing and address the messaging they may offer to make a switch. In a sense, those three capitals are a semiotic indicator—a signal—an alarm light going off. Like there was a 'something' being addressed but it wasn't being addressed either. The 'something' which is behind the veil is only being superficially addressed in the language of the text (e.g., with capitals for emphasis of the largeness of the phenomenon going on).

We are here self-reflecting on the very writing and communicating of our text (i.e., our dialogue) while it is in progress and unfinished. This is a form of process thinking and awareness. It required that moment of peripheral vision outside the 'normal' field of awareness when one is writing a text and trying to write clearly. Freud or Lacan or any good psychoanalyst pays attention to these 'slips' or 'glitches' or call them simply 'indicator' signals in speech. The theory of psychoanalysis argues that IF they catch the attention of those in conversation, then they could be spotlighted for further reflection. That's exactly what we are doing with our own dialogue above on what appears to be the topic of fear(ism), fearlessness, etc. Yet, why the capitals all of a sudden and all crammed into one short sentence/utterance by Michael? There is a unique density to it.

Michael was first to notice it, after taking a day off and coming back to finish writing the dialogue from where he left off. In the quite of the space of early morning and a fresh brain from a good night sleep, there was an immediate reaction inside to those dense clustered capitals. Then the word "escape" came to him as the first free-associating concept, word, and as you can see it became so important in us writing this section that we propped it up and took it from the margins of intuition and dim light and spotlighted it into the actual subtitle of this whole section. In other words, we valued what was in the room that was big but not being seen as big in and of itself. In other words, the big Fear Problem in Michael communication above was actually a distraction from what had entered the room, or at least theoretically it had entered, but wasn't getting mentioned. So, we both agreed to turn to "escape" and call it the elephant, the ghost, the appropriate visitation from the place of which we were not aware. Call it even the mysterious—verging on the edge of perception, perhaps the uncanny, into what is now a self-reflection on the self-reflection of our text above—and, we turn to the focal point: of the *why* (?) behind its arrival.

Hello, "escape." Hello, "escaping." Hello, "escaper." Okay, now by the end of our triadic initial welcoming attitude, and phenomenological expansion from the gap of slowing down and examining what we are doing here, the theme emerging is a conscious *welcoming*—a typical technique of The Sedona Method of nondual unconditional therapy.[154]

Hello, Escaping. IF you are the elephant in the room as we suspect, it is a fascinating way you have chosen to enter (note: showing our authentic curiosity of the appearance of the unappeared or the presence of the non-present). An ambivalence in our descriptive speech here is showing everyone in the room (including our readers) that our very text and language, our discourse, is somewhat dissolving from its rational, logical, solidness as we proceed in this technique. It makes us wonder if there is some historical myth of a god or goddess or some such being who is the representative of Escaping. You know there is the god of Travel, the god of Good Luck, and so on. But is there a god of Escaping(?). More research to do. All very rational to think of that task. But let's not get distracted by the research and end up *escaping from the escaping*. Hmmm... now, isn't that an interesting phrase.

Michael travels on the whiff of a faint but distinct trail of the 'object' ('subject') escaping. His memory scans his library shelves in the other room of his house.

Titles of books start appearing in his inner visual field. He's learned to follow these subtle intuitions and so he goes and picks out the books he had in mind, related to the elephant in the room. And, all the time, he wonders if this escaping motif is part of this book *Resistances to Fearlessness* in some way. Of course it is. A resistance of any kind can easily be interpreted as an escape. Fear can be an escape. Maybe, fearlessness can be an escape.

But let's not get distracted on these theoretical and philosophical flights, and quickly return to Michael's phrase above and see that both he and Maria were talking about "people" and "*en masse*"—that is, what is happening to the people of the world. The care and concern is there for real object/subjects—*real* people. Why? Because everything about fear and fearlessness is part of a *cura*, a *therapia*, a *healing* treatment—even, part of an ultimate *liberation*. Remember, this has all come up in the three Introductions prior in this book.

There is this ongoing 'calling' of this book to be a forensic investigation of a 'crime' that has been sensed by us (as co-authors) but not quite witnessed—in the real. We believe in something to follow in this case. Our belief is not sufficient on its own. We desire to know deeper. Yet, we're looking for clues as to what is the crime, when we don't know what the crime is—or do we?. And, now, maybe it is clearer. Maybe, we are getting the sense, the real semiotic indicator right in our face—like an elephant we didn't want to acknowledge before(?). It is the other half of the crime.

Perfect! That's worth tracking out here for a moment here. Jot this down in your notebook. It is *half* of the crime to have 'a crime' occur.

The *other half* of the crime is to have the 'criminal' disappear before you can nab them. That's the real big (Big) problem (Problem) isn't it(?) With fear operating as the engine of crime, in other words, the fear greases the whole event of crime and the criminal is thus already escaping (fearing) nearly as fast as they are engaging in the crime. Likewise, much to the chagrin of many a police officer and detective, is the adjacent issue of witnesses who may have seen the crime, all of a sudden "don't recall" what they witnessed—and, therefore are not categorically witnesses anymore. How convenient. Well, not really. They are afraid to witness because the 'criminal' may take their tattling out on them or their loved ones in the future if they find out.

And, of course, legally speaking, the whole picture of a crime scene is one where there is a crime done and a criminal who escaped. At least, that's the general phenomenon we are interested in here. *Crime-Fear-Criminal (Escape)* all a part of dramatic play—a trialectic interrelationality that one ought not pull apart and separate the pieces and investigate the pieces alone, hoping that some clues will all put the puzzle together. That is called piece-meal criminology or policing.[155] And, by analogy, unfortunately too often, that is the same of what happens in sciences and, it is the way most people think period, when they have a problem and are trying to solve it. Otherwise known as reductionism.

Our point: most (if not all) problem-solving is done piece-meal. That is, because a deeper more holistic-integral analysis is being escaped from. We want to take the easier and simpler short-cut route to the investigation and we settle for the quick-answer. Right? Most of the time anyways. But with the notion of grand "wicked problems" on the global scale of things, like Global Warming or the Fear Problem (*a la* Fisher), clearly evidence indicates short-cut piece-meal methods of analysis and their solutions are not going to work. The stakes of failing to solve such problems are very high. Can we risk any longer escaping from this fact and the fact of our inadequate responses? Can we risk the dangerous slippery slope of *escaping from our escaping*?

The philosopher(s) and their *therapia*, a type of *cultural therapy* (*a la* Fisher)[156] returns now to the concrete initial finding of this phenomenological welcoming: *Crime-Fear-Criminal (Escape)*. Keeping the trialectic here and adopting it, is likely useful. Notice (Escape) is corded off somewhat, there and not there in the trialectic. That feels appropriate to record it this way for now.

Any good leader would do well to reflect on all this. And, to return to the elephant in the room, we now have the 'key' (you might say) to it all—that is, to the puzzle that was from the start something that was puzzling. It was puzzling enough for Michael and Maria to dedicate all this time to writing a book about it. Hmmm... now, let's return to Michael's initial intuition to grab the books from his library (memory) that entered, registered and welcomed an idea: *These might be useful to cite in this Chapter One?* So, we continue in this gap in our dialogue and the way we thought this Chapter One was going to unfold. It looks like the Chapter itself is an emergent intelligence system shaping us as much as we are shaping it. That is precisely what is going on. It's a transformational paradigm itself. It requires us to adopt a fearlessness (transformative learning) approach in the very writing about fearlessness, and fear(ism), and ourselves, and people of the world, and anything else—including this gem, this elephant, the ghost, we're calling *escape*. Hmmm... *Fear is an escape artist*. Interesting, as you may recall in Introduction we said the Defense Intelligence (DI) System and Fear take on many guises. Now, to the quotes from Michael's books.

The recovery specialist and psychotherapist Whitfield,[157] who worked on the dynamics of the "child within" as a conception that proved very useful for adults to encounter and heal with, made a Table of "Some Characteristics of the Real Self and the Co-dependent Self." The latter type of *self* has suffered under the relationship processes of "co-dependency," which is part of the larger theory we won't go into specifically here; but suffice it to say, that Whitfield brilliantly linked this particular kind of co-dependency in relationship to *behavioral* addiction and more importantly he classified it as itself a *process of addiction*. And, if that type of relationship/ process goes on to grow-and-stick between two or more people, it forms a kind of (culture) 'cult' of addiction(s) within a relationship or group system—and, right up to the macroscale of infecting an entire society.

The actual addictions may appear overtly as symptoms of the co-dependency dis-ease process—for example, alcoholism; but Whitfield's potent finding was that a much more *invisible* addiction process was going on that typically undiagnosed and not treated in therapies and recovery programs (like Alcoholics Anonymous) for addictions. The invisible was the elephant in the room regarding most addictions. You could say it is the psychological interior mind-dynamics of addiction; but it is so much more than merely individual psychology going on. Recall, we (as co-authors) have from the start of this book proclaimed that fear/fearlessness will not be understood adequately by only looking at the individualist perspective on what is fear and reality and relationships—meaning, a basic psychology of fear approach. Same for addictions, according to Whitfield. So, his Table is fascinating in listing 30 traits or so of each column "Real Self" and "Co-Dependent Self." At the end of the lists he says the sick, "false," and "unauthentic" self (i.e., Co-Dependent Self) is the "Public Self" of which we play our social public roles, which may include roles in intimate couples and/or family systems as well. His contrasting the latter to a healthy "true" and "authentic" self (i.e., Real Self) is one of contrasting the Public with the Private Self. This inner more invisible self (i.e., Private Self) is typically the self that is not really exposed much at all to anyone. It has been repressed because of it being hurt and rejected, resisted and dissociated from—that is, devalued. Such *resistance* to the Real Self, arguably is something we'll come back to in our book in re: to resistances to fearlessness.

Before leaving Whitfield, the whole point of going into this is that the Real Self is characterized by "Love Unconditionally" and the Co-Dependent Self by "Contracting, fearful[ness]" and "Distrusting." Whitfield wrote of the Co-Dependent Self:

> By contrast, another part of us generally feels uncomfortable, strained, or unauthentic....Our false self is a cover-up. It is inhibited, contracting and fearful. It is our egocentric ego and super-ego, forever planning and plodding, continually selfish and withholding. It is envious, critical, idealized, blaming, shaming and

perfectionistic. Alienated from the True Self, our false self is other-oriented, i.e., focuses on what it *thinks* others want it to be; it is over-conforming....It covers p, hides or denies feelings....it may make up false feelings....[like] "I'm just fine."[158]

Whatever you may think of Whitfield's general classification of human beings here, it has strengths and weaknesses no doubt. Our emphasis as co-authors is to link its 'telling' of a crime and a "cover-up" (used frequently by Whitfield here). So, there are some clues to the mystery—and, one is left with "why" is their this divided self in the first place? Why has one part of the self 'chosen' to escape from the other self—and, the Whole Self? What kind of sickness does this produce? What *cura* is required? Welcome to the world of dualism (splits)—of split-paradigms of ways of being (see Introduction 1). And, that brings us to Michael's next book from the shelf.

R. D. Laing, the radical British psychiatrist from the 1960s-70s, wrote extensively and influentially in some sub-cultures of mental health awareness/movements, whereby he was out to tell us all that we've been largely askew in how we have generally analyzed and medically and therapeutically treated "mental disorders." One of his famous books, *The Divided Self* (1960),[159] attempts to bring foreword the escape theme (like Whitfield), in what was an "existential study in sanity and madness." He more or less concluded that the "Public Self" (of Whitfield) or the "social self" as Laing would prefer to call it, was itself insane, more or less. The very 'normal' paradigm of reality in which societies operated by as functional was "mad" and that it is no wonder so many people arise in a mad culture ending up with madness as a mental health disorder (which is actually a dis-ease). Insanity or madness, whatever one calls it, according to Laing is actually the way a human being is attempting (albeit, insufficiently and often self-abusively) to adapt to an insanity (i.e., family system for example) is by *resisting* normal adaptations (i.e., socialization processes—which, Whitfield is calling "co-dependency" processes). Resisting gets a person in a lot of trouble from the norm. The norm becomes terrified having to be around someone so extreme in their behaviors and thoughts—that are indecipherable—like another language—like an alien from another planet. Typically, such 'mentally-ill' patients participate in crime against the norm. So, mental health and crime and fear/terror all go intimately together.

Laing studied and lived with so-called schizophrenics,[160] for example, and he made a careful analysis of what the "schizo" (meaning split) components were and how they may in fact have been (at some point) highly functional, then dysfunctional, and then functional again—depending on the context in which the 'schizophrenic' is living within. Point being, schizoid processes, mind, feelings, behaviors are there for a good reason. They are not merely something 'sick' in which to discard, erase, diminish, etc. For Laing, good psychiatry is not fear-based and in an escape itself from the reality of the mutual messaging of which the 'schizophrenic' is offering to the normal society (and, the medical psychiatric field). For Laing, the psychology of mental illness is horribly corrupt itself because of this fear/terror of the disruption of order, rationality, the norm and conformity. Laing was always quick to call this a "politics of experience"—and it is part and parcel of how we always ought to analyze mental illness and mental health. As co-authors, there are enormous overlaps with Whitfield's theory of split a *Self* and indeed, many others have also written about this schizoidal[161] problematique—of which, another term for it is "alienation." And, on that appearance of the *invisible* term, becoming emergent here and visible—it behooves us as phenomenological philosophers to put *escaping and alienation* together. This powerful combination reflects immediately the great concerns of the classic critics Freud and Marx, respectively. The psychological and the social cannot be unhooked when it comes to making discernments about healthy and unhealthy. Subba and Fisher have for several years been presenting a case for a new sub-field of psychiatric approach combined with philosophy of fearism, called *feariatry*.[162]

As we noted earlier "mental health and crime and fear/terror all go *intimately* together." The next book on Michael's shelf deals with *intimacy*—which has to shine forth brightly here as part of the conceptual playscape of this phenomenological philosophy approach to healthy and unhealthy determinations. As well, it serves as a sticky-connector to notions of 'crime.' After all, would it seems reasonable to a social species (*Homo sapiens*) is social for many reasons, e.g., averting some of the risk to predation—but also to 'crime.' A social group has 'pressures' on preventing crimes within the group, as well as it has greater capacity to defend off crimes from without the group—as in competitive tribes.

But all that basic anthropology is not going to penetrate deep enough to excavate intimacy. Intimacy being the weaving for the very closest of connections. Intimacy doesn't come easily—except when "in love" or with a mother-child bonding for nine months, etc. But mutual intimacy is hard won for the most part, especially in a highly competitive way of being—what Four Arrows called the "Dominant worldview,"[163] in sharp contrast to the universal "Indigenous worldview," the latter which constitutes up 99% of human evolutionary history living in a relatively stable healthy sustainability with planet earth's ecosystems. This brings us to mention the *escape* title: *Escape from Intimacy* by Anne Wilson Schaef, psychotherapist, organizational consultant and leader in health care training. She also has written about codependence and addictive behavior and processes. She argued that such were death-making and she created "Living Process" workshops to teach people how to counter the tendencies and characteristics of non-living (i.e., death-drive of Freud).[164]

Although deeply interested in healing a shift in paradigm from dying to living, her focus in the *Escape from Intimacy* is the "love" addictions. She writes love with the (") marks because rarely in her experience working with people for decades, and her own experience, does anyone really love in healthy way—and, if they do, it doesn't last long. But without going into her overall theory of addictions related to "love" we wish to focus on her notion of the underbelly beneath the surface of behaviors of addiction and so-called loving. We like her work because she makes such addictions not merely about individual psychology but equally about philosophy/ ethics. She, as much as anyone knows, the depth of the collective processes involved in creating and maintaining addiction patterning as 'normal'(i.e., death-making, death-driven and fear-driven phenomenon). She wrote a whole book on *When Society*

Becomes an Addict.[165] We quote from both these books on the general main thesis of her work, not unlike Whitfield's, and Laing's *splitting* phenomenon:

> In an Addictive System, we are trained *not* to be ourselves. We lose touch with ourselves. We reference ourselves externally. [e.g., cf. Fisher's 'Fear' Matrix Program] We deny who we are. This leaves a hole in the puzzle and a hole in the universe that no one else can fill.[166]

> In order to pursue the addiction [they choose to practice], individuals must progressively abandon themselves. This results in ethical, moral, and spiritual deterioration, and...find themselves neglecting [abandoning] self, children, family, work, and social responsibilities. Addicts are not able to make a consistent contribution to themselves or their society....[167]

What do you have to do to a living organism to have it abandon (i.e., escape) itself and its own well-being? Just to start there, and really contemplate that, one has to say, the 'criminal' is not far. The elephant in the room is near. It's almost as if we can really 'see' it as sharply as in Figure 2 (above). Yet, to be clear, All of Michael's references chosen here make it clear that there is no "clean" (non-criminal) society anywhere—in opposition to—some "unclean" (criminal) individual anywhere. They are intimate. It is only in the breaking of any authentic self and authentic reality—and shattering it—that an individual or society can 'see' itself as not having a problem, called fear-based addiction. That's our point; the addiction, splitting (schizoidal) formation is *both* symptom and cause, *both* an attempt to adaptive and maladaptive. The conundrum of these dynamics of non-intimacy and shattering continue to allow the world to fly apart in fragments. And when the fragments meet and clash, and steal and invade boundaries, and violate and traumatize each other—then, you know why there is 'crime' everywhere. They are fragments that do not recognize their 'brother' or 'sister' or 'neighbor' and thus do not value them. They are objects to mis-use. They are not subjects any longer. That's why addictive substances, for one, or addictive behaviors for two, become more important to a practicing addict than anything else—when push comes to shove. It hardly seems to be an elephant in the room any longer. The Lessson: IF you *abandon and escape* your self/your society/your reality—then the Self/Society/Reality suffers with you. Only such a dynamic seems possible if Fear is the *main* ingredient—that is, the *main lens* (paradigm) by which the addict sees themselves and their world.

And no big story (theory) would be complete on the topic of *escape* (the elephant in the room) if it did not include (at least) the profound work of the psychoanalytic psychiatrist and author, the eminent Erich Fromm. Writing several decades before the other author's in Michael's collection here, Fromm[168] penned the classic study: *Escape from Freedom*. Truly, he showed that human beings are volatile creatures motivated along a spectrum from Fear at one end and Freedom at another. There's become an entire sub-field of inquiry into this bi-motivational theory, which is of great consequence to humanity's destiny.[169] No doubt it overlaps considerably with the basic tenet of the philosophy of fearism that society (and individuals) make choices to move from a more fear-based orientation to the world towards a more fearlessness-based orientation. Sometimes, this bi-motivational theory takes the form of Fear to Love; but that's beyond our focus for this Chapter One.

Fromm wrote (much like Laing did, 20 years later),

> Most psychiatrists take the [normal] structure of their own society so much for granted that to them the person who is not well adapted [to said society] assumes the stigma of being less valuable. On the other hand, the well-adapted person is supposed to be the more valuable person in terms of a scale of human values. If we differentiate the two concepts of *normal* and *neurotic*, we come to the following conclusion: the person who is normal [cf. Whitfield's "public self"] in terms of being

> well adapted is often less healthy than the neurotic person in terms of human values. Often he [sic] is well adapted only at the expense of having given up his self [i.e., cf. "private self" of Whitfield] in order to become more or less the person he believes he is expected to be. *All genuine individuality and spontaneity may have been lost.*[170] [italics added for emphasis]

The "lost" theme appears again, as another universal for human development, at least in a modern society—and, what connection between loss and escape are we to forge—that is, if we do not try to escape from this very knowledge itself. It may be too fearful to take. We may cognitively recognize the words and comprehend the meaning of them on this page. But as soon as we 'turn' to put down this book, so easily we can begin 'running' almost to find the more pleasant thoughts—on the addictive escape passage ways—where we abandon not only ourselves, and others, but we abandon, as Fromm makes so clear, the very "freedom" passage ways that will awaken us and lead us to liberation. "Fear of freedom" is a potent diagnosis, as has also been the "freedom from fear" prescription throughout much of human history. The question we have, from a fearism and fearlessness lens is, are these phrases on equal footing? Have they ever been? Has fear of freedom always over freedom from fear—in actuality. Not just what is on paper and Declarations of Independence or Human Rights, in code. No, we are interested in this book about digging in deeper to investigate actual phenomenological truths about the human relationship with fear/freedom OR fear/fearlessness.

So far, the evidence in Michael's library here provides us with a chain of some powerful thinkers and critics on problems that deserve more attention than they usually get. How about some courageous *leaders* to arise and soon—to raise these types of topics. How about some educational leaders who are ready to incorporate this type of material into K-16 curriculum for all students—as the basics of what it means to become human—to become free? Sadly, these curriculum fantasies are far from being designed, forged and implemented systematically.

Fearless Leadership In and Out of the 'Fear' Matrix

Though fearless attitude is not explicitly perceptible all the time, everyone is supposed to be a leader of one's own life. Bold decisions are mostly silent.
-B. Maria Kumar

Acknowledging fear is not a cause for depression or discouragement. Because we possess such fear, we also are potentially entitled to experience fearlessness. True fearlessness is not the reduction of fear, but going beyond fear....Each step [on the path of fearlessness] is a dance.... -Rinpoche Chöygam Trungpa[171]

RMF: Hello everyone. It is truly a pleasure to be with so many people who have demonstrated courage in facing the "fear"-based culture of the academy....I wrote [my dissertation] as a sequel [screen-play] to the 1999 movie, *The Matrix*....Basically, I had to figure out how to actually write/perform my research from the beginning so that it was a contradiction (psychologically, politically, culturally, spiritually) to the "fear"-based culture of the university itself. This was, of course, a tricky proposition....In particular, my experiential and intellectual passion has revolved around what happens when fear meets fearlessness....I wanted to use alternative research approaches to see if I could find better ways to undermine, if not eliminate, the unsustainable insanity of human experience—which I see all around me. I wanted to contribute creatively and radically to uncovering the operations ("hidden curriculum") of a ubiquitous *fearism*, which I have come to see as the base of all the insidious "ism" dis-eases on this planet....I see this dissertation as a type of "fear" vaccination process....The dissertation is/was a universal curriculum intervention (*cura*), of the sociotherapeutic genre (fearanalysis).[172]

A question brewed then, and still does: "What is the 'Fear' Matrix?" And, to follow—How is Fearlessness working, or not, within that matrix? Equally, Fisher was asking his colleagues in this professional (academic) educational book to consider the concepts fearism, fearanalysis—and, so much more. Over all the years since putting this out, only one professional educator has taken the time to write a semi-serious response to the 'call' and 'challenge' of Fisher's work.[173] Although his dissertation was based on a transformative learning theory and paradigmatic foundation, there was a kind of 'madness' in the whole enterprise.

Talk about *resistance* on both sides of the fence. One one-side, Fisher needed the acceptance of his research committee and dissertation reviewers to 'pass' his doctorate; and on the other-side, at the same time, he had to risk everything and let them know that he didn't really trust any of them because they were invested in and co-participants with the authoritative culture of fear itself. They were Agents of the 'Fear' Matrix. The last thing they really wanted to support, as Fisher believed, was true Fearlessness in the academy or in the field of Education and into the public schools. They were afraid of fearlessness and he knew it.

To go into this madness, Fisher identified an emergent creative organic methodology (no one had ever heard of before)—he called it "voluntary performative schizoidal praxis." He wrote, "In a nutshell, that means I had to "go crazy"... during this process....to ensure "authenticity"[174]—by which, he meant, in order to keep his soul alive, what Whitfield et al. (above) call the "true self" in the midst of losing oneself in the mind-cultural-field of *academic fear* everywhere. No one really trusted anyone in that place; and if, the faculty members were really honest about how the institutional system worked—well, the truth would be told and rebellion would be everywhere. It's not. Most everyone conforms and keeps there mouth shut. On his worst days, Fisher felt flooded by this climate of institutional cowardice. He thought, "How was true education ever going to be able to emerge in this climate—for, liberation is the furthest thing from the minds of my colleagues, unfortunately." Fisher divorced the whole field of "Education" at the end of his doctoral program. He did receive his Ph.D. It worked hard as an independent consultant in leadership and human resource development in various forms, but found the same conservativism there.

The title of this section is the title of Fisher's dissertation (2003). One of the first articles by Fisher to discuss what it was like leading his way in and through the academy, to complete such a dissertation, is a joint presentation in 2008.[175] Pope[176] was one of the dialogical responders to Fisher's writing about the difficulties of his doctoral years and the gross and subtle resistances of educators in terms of facing the realities of the nature and role of fear in Education, be it formal or informal. In a fictional-non-fictional dramatic presentation, Pope supported Fisher's work and his words after it had been criticized by a nemesis academic character. This character, who is host of the entire fictional conference says after Fisher presented his work:

> DS: With all due respect to Dr. Fisher... I must say that I am at this point myself "confused!" What I've heard just now makes it difficult for me to see how new knowledge that is validated by the academic community has or can emerge from such a wild approach to inquiry! I mean did your dissertation produce a new theory about fear?[177]
>
> RMF: Yes and no....

Pope then responded to DS:

> BP: ...if I may, I understand your confusion and concerns. Yet don't you see that what is happening in our world—what *we* are doing to our world—is much more a product of the so-called "logic" of Western reason and academic research? If fear is the root of propaganda and compliance, then a study of an antidote to fear would

naturally do the dance that Michael's dissertation did. It would have the "messiness" that Stephen [Quaye] is talking about. It is this kind of multi-levels awareness that might bring us out of the insanity Michael referred to....[178]

Who is capable to lead fearlessness? That's typically *not* a common question in leadership studies. Any glance at the serious, even radical, works of leadership gurus today, shows there are many who don't barely mention fear, and rarer still are those who mention fearlessness. And there are none who conceptualize that Fearlessness is Leadership.

Fisher has long studied the leadership writing of powerful thought leaders in their own right. He coined and co-founded the *In Search of Fearlessness* Project (1989-) upon the name of the movement in business and organizational development thinking by Tom Peters. You may recall that the early 1980s was a breakout new paradigm kind of time in North America (at least). Peters and others were really trying to improve Quality in the whole realm of business, leadership and more over society-at-large. They were futurists and visionaries. They took their rationalistic models of thinking from the "new sciences" that were burgeoning in regard to systems and quantum theory, etc., and thought they had the intelligence to transform the world and re-engineer human productivity. Big claims are hyped within this 1980s spirit, taking forms like *The Next IQ,* a book that became a very popular mainstream promotion of "the next level of intelligence" for 21st century leaders.[179] Fisher checked this next IQ discourse out and found the mere two pages in the book dedicated to "Fear" were pretty basic—the stuff that could be found in a hundred other books on leadership or popular psychology. Nothing on fearlessness. Nothing on Defense Intelligence systems. Nothing radical about the future of the *human-fear* relationality that a philosophy of fearism demands.

Peter's big push was for what he called at the time "*In Search of Excellence.*"[180] Fisher, upon reading that book, found it lacking, with little on fear (nothing on fearlessness) of any depth, and thus when the right time came, he named his own movement and Project to co-opt and transcend Peter's slogan. It certainly was an interesting move on his part, but Fisher's new twist was highly resisted and mostly dissolved in terms of any real public or academic influence. Call it *excellence*, call it *fearlessness*—what really was going on here was the admirable rising of a conscious awareness amongst several people, that quality (capital 'Q') was in jeopardy and something needed to be done in the field of leadership to turn this loss of quality around.[181] This intrigued Fisher as well because earlier in the mid-1970s he had been greatly impacted by reading the values-based ethical philosophy of Robert Pirsig on a new metaphysics of the ineffable idea of Quality itself.[182] How could we even recognize it (see Part II)? What values go with Life sustainability, with architecture that nurtures wellness, designs that liberate, and values that reinforce Fearlessness over Fear? Many questions were playing out in the background behind Fisher's early formations of what he later, in the mid-1990s, called a "Fearlessness Paradigm."

Near the turn of the 21st century millenium, Fisher was most intrigued with Margaret Wheatley's progressive, even Buddhistic-like, approach to some aspects of organizational developmental theory and practices. In her *Leadership and the New Science*, Wheatley made a big splash to challenge 'old paradigm' scientific thinking, and rather suggesting chaos theory, complexity theory, quantum theory etc. had to be the new basis for organizations and leadership as we go into a challenging future as a species. Yet, "fear" does not show up in her book Index. Fisher later discovered a most intriguing article eight years later in a business magazine, based on an interview of Wheatley. It was entitled: "Fearlessness: The Last Organizational Change Strategy."[183]

> **BMK:** This is interesting. Maybe you could share more on Wheatley's interview and ideas; yet, I would like to back up just a little in this discussion, if you don't mind.
>
> **RMF:** Sure. I'm curious of your thoughts on leadership—and, especially I'm curious as to what your own professional leadership work has entailed as a former Chief of Police in Bhopal for so many years.

BMK: I have been taken by the leadership guru Stephen Covey and his seven general principles for success in life. In regard to the importance of founding good ethical leadership, Covey reminds us to focus on the interpersonal dimension.

RMF: Leadership, especially in business but beyond that is about people, bottom-line, not just profits and elite's careers and winning votes.

BMK: Exactly. "Seek first to understand, then to be understood," says Covey.[184] Interpersonal relations cover every facet of communicating with people in society. How one communicates is all the more important. Relations last a life time irrespective of one's stature or power. The success of any interpersonal relations activity depends on one's skills at treating his or her family members, relatives, friends, customers, clients or superiors.[185] Everyone needs to learn this.

RMF: Say more about the principle of understanding, as no doubt that is what makes a good leader a great leader. They take the time to understand.

BMK: More than take the time, they have the capacity of attention or awareness or consciousness. Is one's attention contracting or expanding. Is it, respectively, fearing or loving.

RMF: The expansion aspect of consciousness, I call it 'free-attention.' It is linked in my theory with fearlessness/healing/liberation. Humans generally, instinctively, value attention, like gold. Think of what a new born baby desires? Food, you might say. Security for survival, you might say. Well, first and foremost for food or security and survival to even be in the picture—the baby requires attention—and, the more the merrier. Without attention the whole system of communications and intelligence between a mother-baby relation will deteriorate and immunity will be compromised because health is going to drop, without attention. In social species, like humans, this is even more critical. Of course, there is good attention and bad attention.

BMK: Indeed, Michael, all people both deserve and desire good quality attention. Everyone operates better when 'free-attention' or unconditional attention is flowing in a system of communications. This becomes a stress-less and fear-less kind of environment. With expansive attention, relations of all kinds with the self and the other improve and things are more connected. People grow and thrive in those environments. When the fear quantum increases too much there is less and less quality attention, at least that has been my experience. And as a leader in the police forces, it is very obvious who makes the best police persons. If they aren't paying attention well, they don't learn well, they easily forget what they've learn and they are distracted, habitual, un-reflective, if not anxious to the point of decreased efficiency and actual performance. They need more external rewards to be happy. They conform to group pressure and can lose themselves. They tend to burn out quicker. Top police are the ones with extra patience—and, that leads to more compassion. Yet, one cannot blame any police officer for these traits of lack, because the responsibility is not all theirs. The whole organization of the department has to be giving 'free-attention' and not just demanding it from their staff all the time. It is a two-way street.

RMF: No doubt. The quality officers have more 'free-attention' and fearlessness to offer those who need it most. It's a gift. Earlier in the book I mentioned the "gift of fearlessness" as an ethic for healthy organizational cultures, including families or schools; anyways, we can come back to that concept later in the book.

Oh, I recently heard you describe your career and how much you enjoyed helping people, not just around the actual crime that may have occurred, for example. But you had free-attention to offer them on what impact that crime had upon them. That's very similar to the work of de Becker in terms of 'counseling' people through their distress and fear and panic when a crime has occurred (Introduction 2). Otherwise we leave the victim of a crime more victimized because we who are helping them, even a police officer, chose not offer them quality attention in the post-crime phase; so they can do some healing around the event—which, prevents more serious traumatic effects setting in later. Some progressive police forces are now offering "victim services" in this regard.

Maria, I'm curious what else you think about leadership, especially in the light of a fearism perspective.

BMK: There are many definitions of leaders. The context also matters in defining what makes a leader and a group function in certain ways. Leadership is a set of qualities. People may all become leaders under various circumstances. But there is a recognition of a 'leader' because people usually admire that person in some way. I have always thought the best or true leader is one, who under extreme and difficult challenges, doesn't fear to own up to mistakes, who acts clearly and effectively in crisis, and who, during all of what is demanded of a leader, they are basically democratic and humanistic-oriented in their basic value-system. They are strong, in a good way.

RMF: I especially am attentive to that part about them being able to own up to their mistakes and consequences. Leaders have big impacts, more than most people. They really need to own responsibility for that. They need to be vulnerable. Most leaders fear being vulnerable. That's understandable. I've been a leader often.

I've always loved the ancient Shambhala sacred warrior tradition[186] out of Tibetan Buddhism, whereby the real true leader, the fearless leader, practices vulnerability. Trungpa wrote, "The ideal of warriorship [leadership] is that the warrior should be sad and tender, and because of that, the warrior can be very brave as well. Without that heartfelt sadness, bravery is brittle, like a china cup. If you drop it, it will break or chip" and for true leader-warrior, then who practices fearlessness, Trungpa noted "If the cup drops, it will bounce rather than break. It is soft and hard at the same time."[187] Resilience is so important. Several Eastern martial arts teachers of the highest quality help fighters to develop this 'soft and hard' so that they do not become only 'against' but rather they 'flow with,' and become 'for' a resolution and 'for' understanding. The great leaders are ones, more like shamans almost, they work the energies of the subtle fields of conflict and stress, and they untie the 'knots' of troubles.

As Mindell wrote, these leaders bring about "The spirit of unfolding" so a person or group in the presence of a quality leader, can grow and shift and unfold to a higher level of consciousness, without any forcing or domination, more or less. Mindell noted this requires a constant attitude of curiosity, playfulness, and "warm-hearted attitude"[188]—the tenderness/vulnerability of fearlessness—that Trungpa asked for. Power in such settings of the great leader is more about love than about fear. Power is sought, not avoided—but is a whole different type of power than what most of us are used to in the Fear Paradigm.[189] Wow. Just imagine how democracy would function so differently with these values, principles, and mindful practices of great leadership.

BMK: How a leader gains and maintains respect is crucial. Some use fear tactics and intimidation, while others use their presence of authority without abusing it. So, the definition of leader will be rightly qualified for the one who is with the group, shielding it from blame or insecurity. Here, undoubtedly the former fearless leader commands respect of the group. Hence fearlessness attitude is the *sine qua non* of leadership quality. Unfortunately, this aspect is rarely paid attention, while dealing with the concept of leadership, despite the fact that a real leader will always exude this wonderful characteristic.

Because such clear and pragmatic determinations happen in a cool and calm mind, despite the presence of cacophony around, fearless mental activity is a conscious decision. Made by assessing risk rapidly on many levels, while treading on ups and downs of life. Another interpretation of leaders demands that the leader is one who leads personal and/or people's lives from darkness to light. Long ago, the *Vedas* exhorted, '*tamasoma jyotirgamaya*,' meaning, thereby that one should strive 'to come out of darkness into light.' Renowned Indian mystic and philosopher Swami Vivekananda equated darkness with death and light to life. So a leader is one who directs the group from the darkness of ignorance into the path of light, of knowledge. Ignorance of surroundings creates anxiousness. Familiarity with people and things makes one comfortable and more fearless. Ignorance might damage life *a la* the *Odysseus'* voyage, due to the dilemma between Scylla and Charybdis. But knowledge will help fly to safety like the intelligence of Daedalus, who escaped from the labyrinth with the help of wax wings. The quality of guiding people towards a safe, secure and good life is the hallmark of a leader's character.

One reason for the failure on the part of many leaders is a lack of understanding about the nature of people. A leader should be well-versed in the art of human relations and management. They ought to acquire knowledge and skills so as to wisely educate the followers. The leader should be a good human being and ability to sacrifice selfishness for the greater good is essential. That selfless conduct, which people see and remember, bestows on the leader the fearless spirit.

RMF: I think there is a positive feedback loop that can happen. The people bestow fearlessness and the leader responses with fearlessness—and, *visa versa*. When leadership is really working well in a group, a field of care, or anywhere, it is working in a contagious sense. Instead of the fear virus spreading, there is fearlessness spreading as contagion. It is a full enriched encouraging atmosphere both conscious and unconscious. Behind that "fearless spirit" you speak of is a radical trust in the universe, a radical trust in the greatness of our Being that is transcendent of personal needs and desires, as my colleague Four Arrows often says.

Marianne Williamson, a great contemporary spiritual-political leader in my view, offers and important, rarified, teaching now and for future generations. She ran for the Democratic Party Leadership in the USA, potentially could have become President in 2020. According to Auxier, a professor of philosophy, "Dr. Fisher has made a case study of her 'transformational' leadership, arguing (critically at times) that the key to her success was an ability to meet fear fearlessly" during the tough campaign.[190] Williamson argues that "Our deepest fear is not that we are inadequate. Our deepest fear is that we are powerful beyond measure." And as we heal and transcend that fear and express our full potential and power in a healthy way, she concluded: "...as we let our own light shine, we unconsciously give other people permission to do the same. As we're liberated from our own fear, our presence automatically liberates others."[191]

BMK: I agree. There is a contagion of liberation, of fearlessness, when in the presence of a 'great one.' And, of course, there are more than just positive effects of being in the presence of such a person emanating fearlessness.

RMF: Yeah. Mahatma Gandhi, or Martin Luther King Jr. come to mind as spiritual political leaders emanating liberation, and fearlessness. And both were assassinated. Remember when I talked earlier in this book about my fascination with *what happens when fear meets fearlessness*. The empirical truth: the result is mixed, in what happens. It can be as Williamson says, or it can be the exact opposite. Humans are definitely complex, and wounded, if not at times, unpredictable. But I am convinced a leader with full fearlessness characteristics will be a great threat to many because of what they remind people of—in their settled for mediocrity and smallness. They will get reminded of fear's control over them. And, they don't always want to see that mirror. In fact, they mate hate it so much, they'll....

BMK: Smash the mirror.

RMF: Indeed. I designed the cover of my recent book with Williamson and Trump face-to-face, because I think they represent archetypal opposite forces, call it Good and Evil, or Love and Fear, whatever the case—this is a fascinating 'mirroring' going on between them of which I discuss in the book and in a video teaching I made recently.[192]

BMK: Interesting point. But not always do we have leaders so overtly archetypal and symbolic like that, of mythic proportion. I'm thinking of most leadership as rather banal, relatively speaking. Political leaders are the ones who are supposed to lead the nation to ensure peaceful coexistence among the people within the country and between countries. One of the primary objectives of the political leaders is to guide the people to lead secure and happy lives. It implies that the people should not be forced to lead their lives in fear. Because the people will feel safe if they are free from the excessive fears of threats to existence, mutual harmony thrives and thus also do better prospects for everyone, more or less. They look for fearlessness qualities in their leaders. Arguably, they do but they may not always be aware of what all those qualities are.

RMF: Precisely. I see that as an educational problem across the board. I mean where is that children from the start are given a good quality education, given high quality unconditional attention, are supported to heal their wounds, and are nurtured to mature their Defense Intelligence systems, etc. How would they know true fearlessness if it showed up in front of them in someone, or in themselves. Leaders have to teach people to recognize these traits because as I said, otherwise there is quite a split of people in the populations, some who love fearlessness and some who hate it. I'll be discussing that issue in Part II of this book.

BMK: Then, just how fearlessness is considered as a true leadership movement itself, and of a liberational and compassionate quality—this is a critical question to ponder and assimilate for the good of the society. A fearless leader is invariably supposed to be a person of knowledge and wisdom. It is true that no leader is fully equipped with such knowledge and consistent wise thinking. But any upcoming leader ought to have a thirst for the this.

RMF: Ideally, yes, they ought to. But, as we'll see in Chapter Two, as a response to Chapter One, there are *resistances* of all kinds that have to be addressed. Fearlessness does not come about in the real society as actualized, as a mature Fear Management System 7/8, just because we wish it, or just because evolution is capable of it. Consciousness is more complex than that, and culture plays a really big factor in interrupting the natural progression from Fear to Fearlessness and equally from immature leaders to mature and wise leaders. We have to theorize this better than we have.

Only then, will we truly understand Fearlessness as I envision it.

What's Not Right About This Picture

We recently encountered a TV commercial for a Canadian university Business faculty that was using the slogan: *"Leadership is becoming the leader you were meant to become."* What's not right about this, in light of a fearism perspective? What is the elephant in the room here?

In your own views, how is such a slogan, and university corporatism, part of a *resistance* to a Fearlessness Paradigm?
Leadership in the 21st Century: A Thought That Changes Everything

We want to conclude this chapter with a thought. It's the thought of Fearlessness itself. Think about it. Imagine it. Then, see what happens. We both lead and follow Fearlessness. Below, as we close our thoughts on fear/fearlessness and leadership in the future, it is striking how hard it is to find a 'great' leader speaking on a level of wisdom beyond the Fear Paradigm. It is so difficult to find a political leader, like a Marianne Williamson who ran for the Democratic Party leadership in the 2020 US election. She never made it to the final rungs of the voting but she nonetheless put a mark on US society and history in terms of presidential races and she did so because of that elusive but powerful notion of consciousness. Fearlessness at full force is a type of consciousness itself, awaiting blossom in humanity at large.

We believe that Williamson carried and still carries this 21st century paradigm of leadership[193]—just listen to her latest speech on her podcast series in an interview with a research scientist who is studying consciousness, psychedelics and psychotherapy for people who suffer from post-traumatic stress syndrome. Their conversation starts with them agreeing on *the crux of the problem* below all other problems in the society, then the recent speech by Williamson on her podcast runs its course, on a whole other level of sense-making and reality-awareness, of which we as co-authors would like to see become the fear vaccine of authentic transformation in the next decade on this planet.

Doblin (D): Humanity is in a race between consciousness and catastrophe.[194]

Williamson (W): We are.

D: And we need to help consciousness to prevail....

W: There's some new spirit in the air....There's such a sense these days that something has fallen apart... something which is more basic than you even might think. The idea that the entire way that we are organizing our civilization; something is not working. And we know this to be true. It has to do with COVID...wars all over the planet...infrastructures falling apart...the environment and it has to do with all this hate [fear]— this rising tide of right-wing authoritarianism....I think there's this increasing sense that something's wrong on some more basic level. Everybody is sensing that. But at the same time, even with the chaos, the fear and the anxiety and the tension that comes along with that; because people are scared.

I mean so many of the places we look, thinking well, the government will handle it, or business will hand it or economics will hand it; so many of the things that we thought would handle to the problem, if this or that problem got too big, clearly cannot necessarily be counted on to handle it. There's a lot of fear that comes with that. A lot of anxiety that comes with that and also there's a lot of societal despair that comes from that, because in those places where things are not handled, people are going through desperate circumstances that are causing all kinds of terrible upset in their lives, whether it has to do with addiction...violence, all the many ways that we personally as well as societally are experiencing breakdown....

But, at the same time there's a sense of something being born. There's a sense of one world, a sense of one whole way of doing things that's dying and a sense of something else that is being born. And this is not the first time in human history that that's true. These kinds of phase transitions [between paradigms] happen throughout history....The 21st century mindset is different than the 20th century mindset; the 20th century mindset is very mechanistic,[195] the universe is a big machine and if you want to fix the machine you just tweak the pieces...very Newtonian. A British physicist [20th century] named James Dean said, "That it turns out that the world is not a big machine, it's one big thought." And so with the 21st century focus is on a way that the 20th century mindset didn't—it is the primary [reality] of human consciousness. The power of human consciousness, and the relationship between human consciousness and the world as we experience it.

Because, before the 21st century, there was mainly this idea that consciousness had no particular impact on what happens out there. Now, there's more and more of an understanding about what we think is the level of cause and what we experience on the outside is the level of effect. And since you think what is the level of cause, and what's out there is the level of effect, you cannot in fact change the world by just tweaking the pieces of the machine. To look at the world and say I'm going to change the world, just by changing things on the outside, is like saying you're going to a movie and you don't like what's happening in the movie, so you're going to go up to the screen to try to change the plot, but that's not where it emanates [because] everything happening on the screen is a projection. And so, people are understanding [now] we've gotta look at our thoughts.

****

CHAPTER TWO

Does The World Need Us To Be Fearless?

The Fear Problem is a wicked problem. And, Fearlessness is its solution. Fearlessness *is* our human potential—and it *leads* us to embrace our full potential. We need to study why it is we humans so regularly, as if by habit, *resist* our human potential. It's as if we mistrust ourselves and the entire cosmos. A radical trust is required. First, we have to admit that it appears the evolution of life and consciousness are rooting for us to "be fearless."
-R. Michael Fisher

We are not bad, we are developing (i.e., maturing).
-Jeanne Segal (modified by R. Michael Fisher[196])

RMF: What are some major *resistances* to Fearlessness that are directly related to leadership? Can we first give this some philosophical attention before we jump into psychological, sociological and/or behavioral reasons for why humans are in great numbers showing their resistances to the concept of *fearlessness* and what it may imply.

BMK: Our book set out to be a work grounded in a philosophy of fearism perspective, so it's good you draw immediately on the *philosophical* aspect of the issues.

Because for myself, similar to the common discourse pattern of modern society, I can tend to turn fearlessness into a set of qualities, usually behaviors and attitudes of a particular psychological state of mind. I often write about a mind with fear dominating and a mind without fear or ideally fearless. Of course, I also know natural fear is useful too when real danger needs to be addressed.

The way to achieve such a shift of mind is an issue. And I suppose I tend to focus on a psychological cognitive state[197] shift from fear-based to fearless—which is equivalent in my thinking as the shift from irrational and superstitious to reason and logical. My practical upbringing and pragmatism shows through here. Maybe being a trained police officer for over three decades also pushes me in this direction of efficiency. But now I realize how this preference and bias is only one perspective on an overall approach to fearlessness, or reality and the nature of the human being. How easily I like calm, clear, and rational ways of thinking and definitions.

If I turn back and read the pages of this book to see my writing, it tends to show this bias to put fearlessness in a small bowl, perhaps too quickly. Too quickly for you, at least, Michael. You seem to think and organize things way more holistically and aesthetically, as an artist, than I do (See Part II). But I think the more disciplined philosophical aspect of our thinking can be helpful to modify the near rush to a more simplistic scientific, reason-based and psychological understanding alone.

Because I feel that this is one of the focal areas where the contemporary leadership seems to be failing. Let us study an example. No doubt that many national leaders in the current pandemic scenario have not succeeded in effectively controlling the infections and fatalities though very few countries did exceedingly well. We cannot attribute such failures to lack of scientific development because those nations are technologically advanced. There has been no dearth of infrastructural facilities in those nations where coronavirus created havoc by threatening the lives of people, both the wise and the ignorant alike pitiably. Despite having all tools and equipment to fight the virus, those nations have performed poorly; and thus myself and others have rising suspicions about the efficacy of their national leaderships. It is very much here in this aspect that a philosophical perspective matters most.

RMF: Good point. I agree.

BMK: Broadly speaking, philosophical treatment is required to identify whether the leadership is concerned with existential aspects of people's lives.

RMF: How rare "existential" is even a concept of common discourse in most governance or State affairs. It is rare also in the vast field of Psychology, unfortunately, of which most of the concerns are on ego-psychology and self-centered interests.[198] Although, in the last few years especially, I have heard this term *existential* being used more than ever in W. mainstream media; although, it originated from environmental activists, like Greta Thunberg, especially around the global warming crisis. It's a good sign it, "existential crisis," is at least getting some air-time. But the next step is to look into what is an existential crisis? Clearly, a deadly killing virus like COVID-19 is 'not' the crisis itself—the problem is a human crisis—a deep interior and philosophical one. The existential philosophers, theologians, researchers, psychologists and therapists have been thinking carefully about this problem for hundreds of years. Maybe that ought to be a hint of what people and leaders especially, ought to be re-orienting their thinking towards?

BMK: Also important is whether the leadership is sufficiently knowledgeable, in a holistic manner, so as to overcome the corona menace by framing efficient strategies on an overall outlook basis. The philosophy of fearism and fearlessness would have helped but they did not access it.

Leadership should have also taken decisions on the premise of 'larger good' policies and lastly such policies should have enabled the leaders to foresee logically whether the outcomes would be for better or worse. I believe that all the shortcomings of corona pandemic management to this extent would not have occurred had the leaders been knowledgeable and fearless in taking such wise decisions, which they didn't, out of ignorance or fear or of both. That's why Plato asserted, 'the king should be a philosopher.' I think that the pandemic has alerted the nations to have a look at these issues, while electing their leaders, at least from now onwards. People forget this philosophical approach often. What do you suggest?

RMF: For sure. Why isn't the philosophy of fearism on leadership's radar? That's where I would start looking for solutions to the bigger practical issues around the pandemic. But it will take time now to analyze, from multiple perspectives, on 'what went wrong' in so many nations as you say. Sure, fear is a major player impacting overall results. And even if fear-driven policies and actions were somewhat effective, you are right, that we have to ask about long-term effectiveness. This is a dense issue. But all I would suggest in the moment is that the UN take on a look at the philosophy of fearism perspective, and read our book. Education is key to improvement of our reflections on the past and our thinking and imagining new possible ways to manage better.

I work at staying philosophically awake and disciplined in epistemology—that is, the ways we think we come to know. I practice this daily in contemplative reflection and mindfulness practices and in my own healing work to overcome distress patterns that I have or the culture wants to lay on me. I've always loved and remembered the quote in Ken Wilber's earliest book he published when he was 23 years old. "As Philosophia said to Boethius in his distress, 'You have forgotten who you are.'"[199]

Maybe a good many nation's leaders forgot who they really are in the closing in of the crisis and they ended up focusing on management approaches and strategies that would 'make them look good' more so than really 'doing actual good.' I'm cautious about any reductionism, like putting massive concepts like existential into a small box and then people becoming ignore-ant and/or arrogant that they think they then understand what fear or fearlessness is about. They disregard analyzing their mode of knowing itself. The pandemic is just one 'object' of their gaze, but they don't change their gaze. That's a big problem. The critical philosophical attitude you and I are promoting somewhat hinders this reductionism tendency—the latter, a resistance tendency against complexity itself, never mind against the arational, holistic modes of knowing, and against fearlessness as a way of knowing.

BMK: I don't intend to be resistant to fearlessness. Yet, I guess that is my sometimes impatient and pragmatic-side that is looking for 'usefulness' now, practical applications for bringing about needed changes of mind—or it means changes of attitude and changes of behavior, as real outcomes of improving things. I look for real solutions to real problems in society. The philosophical approach is *not* always needing to be predetermined by that pragmatic need to solve problems. Rather, Michael what you have always been teaching re: fear, is that it is so important to assess the way we construct the problem in the first place. For that may be the very root of the problem of the problems. The root of the Fear Problem, with capitals that you often write about.

RMF: It may be. The great Eastern modern philosopher, Jiddu Krishnamurti, taught and wrote a lot about this issue in trying to understand *fear via* only by science, self-psychology, reason, logic etc. Krishnamurti wanted to make sure a *faux* objectivity did not try to rule the inquiry; especially into fear itself—because fear phenomenologically was thought to be so dependently hooked to the ego/self. The ego being a fear-based identity/observer from the beginning of the inquiry. This made knowing fear more difficult than most other things. His little book *On Fear* is a masterful collection of his critical philosophical inquiry[200]—and, it is his search for what I would call fearlessness in the true sense of knowing and approach to reality, the self, Self and consciousness. But that's leading to a direction I wasn't planning to head to in this dialogue.

Though, Krishnamurti and others tell us that we have English-speaking peoples still have a dominating egoistic linguistic/language structure based on dualism. Many other cultures have this limitation too. It's a rather predominant and predetermine discourse, often hidden to our awareness; it takes a lot of consciousness maturation to see it.[201] It is often superficially driving in one direction in a hurry and as a *defense against* depth— not allowing for expansion of space or time for other perspectives or paths of inquiry and new languages and new ways of talking and imagining. That is not a good sign. I think Socrates would have been equally challenging of modern humans rushing to always solve problems without really deeply understanding them. There are a number of researchers in the last decade or so who have defined the "wicked problem" category; like global warming, casteism, racism, or human population growth and starvation, wars, pandemics, etc. And one of the things they agree upon as researchers is that the biggest problem to solving the biggest problems is that the problem solvers do not deeply, nor holistically and integrally analyze the wicked problems adequately in the first place.[202] The so-called solutions then, tend to fall well short of *defining the problem* in complex developmental terms, and thus they fail regularly in achieving their highest goals.

BMK: True Michael! But there are now many ideas in place which help us avoid committing further mistakes in the course of target achievement. Often planners suggest to leaders to start with a pilot project before embarking on the execution of set goals. Because, knowledge gaps usually exist in preparing a plan or doing a task to achieve the objective, and this awareness is important for the leadership. If the pilot project is successful fully or partly, plan execution is to be carried out accordingly. It could be done as it is if everything in pilot project goes well or could be amended wherever something has gone wrong. It is simply like conducting human trials before vaccines are administered. Despite having this awareness, leaders off and on view things irrationally. If philosophy is anything, it is a way to distinguish the irrational from rational.

RMF: Indeed Maria! The rational mind is a tricky one. I often see it is actually irrationally-driven, and yes, often by fear itself—or ego itself. But that would be another long lecture to make my point. Simply, I see that impatient rational mind, which foregoes deeper contemplation, typically reduces that open-minded curiosity immediately in people and even the brightest academics. The dominating analytical language and ways of thinking IF they are all constructed already in the Fear Paradigm, and embedded in what we think, write, teach—then it is no wonder that would make the challenge a great one to simply *talking fearlessness*, in contradistinction to *talking fear*. This whole book is meant to be a talking fearlessness over talking fear. Recall?

BMK: Right. That's why you have long asked for acknowledgement of this oppositional Fearlessness Paradigm—even if, it is still somewhat theoretical at this point. I think I understand your emphasis, Michael. Yet, I find it still hard to understand what that is.

RMF: You are not alone, I assure you. We need a strong re-education and development of consciousness on this planet with a specifically-designed critical literacy. Most everyone does not grasp that. Making a total paradigm shift like Fear to Fearlessness is enormous, which doesn't mean we ought not try. As I said earlier, when one is swimming in the medium of 'water' all the time, one doesn't know what it is they are swimming in because it is so 'normal' everyday, part of the discourse, language, concepts, meanings and value system. It is the background cosmology hidden from the everyday practices. Once and a while it may show up in religious practices or events, but mostly it is hidden and unconscious. It's, more or less, just accepted without questioning—from birth to grave. There isn't even a lot of room to imagine there is *water*—and if there is water, then maybe there is *not water*.

BMK: How can the *fearism perspective* help with this re-imagining and potentially escaping the water, if we use it as the ongoing metaphor here? Oh, and I am really curious why you chose the title for this chapter and the quote below us to start?

RMF: Excellent questions. First, the fearism perspective is right now in this whole book living its influence on the study of fear/fearlessness. I do not even want to pull it out of that living context of infiltration. I mean I don't want to try to define it so clearly that x, y, z is the influence of the fearism perspective. One could do that, but I find that aesthetically and epistemically unappealing in this moment; because we are talking about something more watery going on.

Look, if fearism opens the flood gates from the very beginning of its conceptual-ization with 21 definitions by Desh Subba in his classic text, and they have some rather bizarre admixture of claims, like "Fear is a superpower," "Fear is a super law," or "Fear is a universe....Fear is as vast as the universe," "Fear is a black hole of space"[203]—OK, that's not simple reductionistic scientific, psychological, individual, ordinary *fear talk* from within the universe of 'normal' every day or professional activity, society and/or the language I am used to. It is poetic language, which is not surprising that it would be, as Subba is a well-known Nepali poet. Yet, you and I know he is dead serious about his definitions as well. They are true, for him. He also has a strong cognitive-scientific-rational side, as most of his 2014 book shows. But that opening of 21 definitions is quite a resistance he expresses, I think. The philosophy of fearism is a resistance movement, arguably.

So, to put that admixture of thought merely about his definitional imaginary for fear is a bit mind-blowing, if one really sinks into it and feels what the implications of it are.

BMK: You are offering great unconditional attention to reading Subba and his definitions. I would guess most people don't do that. They read the words and quickly make meanings that they are comfortable with.

RMF: The mind's habitual quick search for comfortable boxes to put anything in, especially some different language like Subba's is enormously constricting. It is likely *fear-based*[204] itself already. Because, the reader is not even aware they are operating <u>not</u> from a fearist lens, or a *fearless standpoint*[205] and not from a

Fearlessness Paradigm or Fearlessness Psychology. The Fear Paradigm and it's Fear Psychology[206] is directing their very, mis-construed reading of Subba.

True, I want to wallow and dwell with the text, the meanings, the possibilities, when I read those 21 definitions. More so, I want to search for an image. I'm a visual processor and thinker, as an artist, and there's so much more to access from the peripheries of a text like Subba's than the mere logical appearing words and concepts. The poetic sensibility is ignited cleverly by Subba as he opens his book, with this new radical understanding, philosophy, theory of fear—called fearism. OK.

Now, I immediately drawn to the cover of his book. There is a goldmine there of potential metaphoric reading to be done. He picked that cover, I'm guessing, with a lot of thought and depth of meaning behind the image of two fishbowls of water, the one on the left is relatively small, and the right one is a quantum jump in size. And, then the dynamic of a goldfish in the air having jumped briskly out of the small bowl with water dripping and heading for the larger bowl but not yet there—and, the possibility it may not make it. One quickly gets the sense of having outgrown one bowl, one must take the risky leap of faith to grow and mature— in a bigger context of reality—a bigger fish bowl.

Yet, beyond that rather easy interpretation of the cover is something more subtle. Let's return to the swimming in water of the Fear Paradigm. And, the image on the cover shows you, symbolically, that maybe one is able to escape it. Indeed, it is plausible. Certainly a goldfish can leap out. If consciousness itself, and its desire to grow and expand and leap, is the 'goldfish' here, you can see that it needs to get out of the water—to separate from the old fish bowl world and "see" anew from up above and beyond it. There is transcendence depicted. It is not just a moment but a journey out of the familiar paradigm. And, I'm suggesting the water as background medium, like a hidden cosmology, is the Fear Paradigm in both fish bowls.

What is the fate of this fish in this context? The goldfish will have to eventually fall by gravity again; because it is not yet transforming and turning into a bird with wings. Not yet, at least in this image. Development of consciousness and thinking and general maturation has not taken it that far yet. No, evolution is not ready for that yet, apparently here in this image. The conditions and structures for such growth have to be just right.

BMK: But evolution of consciousness is ready for the leap from one bowl to a bigger bowl....

RMF: Yes, and more importantly to assess the situation of "What is reality?" from the heights of the top of the leap, out of the matrix of the watery medium, that has been home for so long. You may recall in Chapter One I talked of a similar image implicit in my doctoral research, when I invoked *radical trust* and possibility in the title of my dissertation "Fearless Leadership In and Out of the 'Fear' Matrix." I'm invoking a whole other way, another paradigm, of seeing ourselves as *human beings*. I'll get to that later in this Chapter. Anyways, indeed Getting "out" is so important, even though one will, in all likelihood, restricted by survival reasons more or less, will have to *return* into the watery matrix[207]—yes, the 'Fear' Matrix or Fear Paradigm (see Figure 3).

There is fate here in this imagery of a *journey of the soul* but there is also freedom. Both are in a tension. We can be creative with that tension, and we will also realize that both also represent polarities of oppositions that are more than a mere tension. I'll explain that shortly with the "Stages of the Soul's Journey" within the Defense Intelligence System diagram (Figure 3).

Back to the cover image of Subba's, we are also dealing with what may feel like a comfort to *return* to, or *regress* to, as the fish leaps from water to water. From a fearless nondual standpoint of my own Fear Management System-9, the reality is that the water is still going to be the limiting illusion of comfort/need/security. One will pay a price for leaving the security of the 'Fear' Matrix conditioning—and, one will pay a price for returning to the 'Fear' Matrix—even if, the size of the bowl may be an 'improvement.' The true Fearlessness Paradigm however, invokes another imaginary of human potential for a consciousness shift, for a paradigm shift, and that is what Subba's cover image cannot quite depict. It is implicit therein. It is sublime. But it is there. It is felt-thought by me anyways. I guess, it is a sense that the fish doesn't always need to be a fish, once it can recognize itself out of the water long enough—at some point—off the cover page—in the progression from the left to the right—one has to now imagine something else is there—not necessarily just another bowl of water bigger. I encourage you and readers to check out my Figure 2.1 in another book,[208] which shows my extension design of what Subba's cover image could be read to teach us about.

Anyways, this philosophizing, and my point of critique here, is arguably from a Fearlessness Paradigm. And, yes, the fearism perspective is pointing towards that, yet the fearism perspective has not philosophized adequately the notion of a 'Fear' Matrix, or Fearlessness; a point I made in Introduction 3. I even suggested *fearism*, including of course the more toxic ideological *fearism-t*,[209] with this philosophical handicap, is currently perhaps itself a type of *resistance* to Fearlessness, while it also obviously welcomes fearlessness under certain limited definition and meanings.

BMK: You are right. Fear itself is a natural resistance to fearlessness. *Destrudo- libido* analogy could be cited here. Both Death and Life instincts operate at loggerheads with each other. That way, fearlessness acts as a resistance to the instinctual and overly-predominating advances of fear. It is in this context that the role of fearlessness as leadership matters. It has to be facilitated in such a way as to take a dominant position over fear. Fear needs to be restricted up to helping to serve as the alarm bell before or while encountering a danger. So, fearlessness as leadership should be able to prevent fear from fully actualizing its resistance, even if it remains a latent force. If fear is understood properly, it would be easier to resist it. Therefore, Subba's book on fearism is handy indeed.

At this point, to break a little from the dialogue, the issue of *leadership* is really revealing the complexity of what it means to be a "leader" of Fearlessness and concomitantly of compassion, vulnerability,[210] wisdom, liberation and human potential. What does it mean to *trust* leaders? Radical trust was already mentioned above by Fisher and it is the name of his entrepreneurial business with his life-partner Barbara Bickel since 1990.

The issues grow rapidly and we cannot discuss them all in this chapter. But *trusting leaders,* turns us to immediately the specific question(s) of *trusting people* (human beings), which then moves to the macro again, and *trusting the universe*, to trusting societies' institutions, laws, governance; and, then returning to the meso- and macro- reality of how to trust even one's own neighbors, family members and most intimate partners. How can we trust ourselves? How vulnerable are we willing to make ourselves by trusting?

Gibb wrote a great book on the mega-notion of "Trust" and what he called its equal opposite great force, "Fear." He argues that fear-based ways of leaderships and organizing are unhealthy and trust-based ways of organizing are healthy.[211] Erikson, the child psychologist of emotional/social development found in his research that the first crucial foundational stage of developmental challenge, that is universal, is: *trust vs mistrust.*[212] The way an individual negotiates this level or stage tends to determine all outcomes after that and as they grow into an adult. Eisler wrote a great book on the 5000 year history of W. civilization that parallels the exact same leadership and organizing principle.[213] Unfortunately, there's been a vast traumatic history of oppression that has fought to resist the full-grown maturation of humanity along this spectrum towards increasing trust over mistrust/fear, or as other authors call this the Love over Fear dynamic. Fisher has written a great deal about this.[214] Mistrust is basically one very direct way to *resist* (against) growth and the movement along the *path of Fearlessness*. This is not just an individual but a collective problem/resistance. The very development of self/mind and 'waking up' and maturing asks us to attend to the human journey itself—and, asks us to attend to what responsibility we have for that journey and the advancement of society and evolution itself. At least, how to create a better humanity that cares and trusts enough to bring sanity, health and sustainability to the entire earth's ecosystems.

Our point is, that there is a long human historical legacy of an often torn fabric of *social trust*. We will encounter this and it will rip at our naivety, our child qualities, often with a viciousness that taints us for life. Enemies breed in this social atmosphere of mistrust. This can lead to one *not* even trusting themselves? Watts argued that the chronic fear-based conditioning of mistrust leads to a "taboo against knowing ourselves"[215]—by which he means our "true selves." It is worth inquiring into *taboos* of all kinds, but this core taboo reflects in the ancient philosophical corrective (advice) of Socrates' dictum to *Know thyself*—which, is re-interpreted in a fearism lens as *Know thy fearful self* well, for then and only then, will one truly overcome the taboos that block one knowing they true self. Subba in his classic text on fearism lists 300+ known phobias in humans, of which when you add them all together they start to seem to be all, more or less, sub-forms of one basic *autophobia*—an irrational fear of oneself.[216]

A deep thorough inquiry is required to enter but go beyond the phobias and taboos in which we swim in—called society. One has to be a 'researcher' of authenticity, otherwise one lives a life as a *divided self* and/or *false self*.[217] This human condition, often highly pathological in terms of 'insanity'—is, in other words, a self in resistance to itself. Equally, we as co-authors imagine there is a pathological condition of a *false* fearlessness (e.g., bravado, superficial "fearless") that is against *true* fearlessness, the latter of which is what we promote in this book. To distrust this critical self-reflective process of fearlessness epistemology—in a fearlessness knowing (inquiry)—is also a huge problem and would accompany the *one who distrusts* themselves fundamentally. Healthy skepticism is fine but they distrust curious learning, knowledge, knowing and their value. Many fundamentalist toxic ideologies operate on such a distrust of knowledge that is 'free' and 'open' and they only want to perpetrate an authoritarian knowledge and learning—which, is fear-based and conditioned learning, not free autonomous, and/or philosophical inquiry. *Gnosiophobia-* fear of knowledge is a cause and effect of such taboo structurations. This taboo (resistance) against the truth/reality/self is all crippling to the developmental trajectory—that is, if it is not dis-enabled step-by-step *via* fearlessness at some point, and at some crisis, whereby a paradigm shift is transformative and essential to basic in consciousness maturation.

Nowadays, with such intense disasters from climate change and global warming, it is turning out that we cannot even trust the environment, that is Nature. It seems everything is a probable if not imminent threat. It seems betrayal of trust is the more common dimension ubiquitous to human experience and existence itself. The existential philosopher might ask: *How can I trust Life, if loss of my life (death) is absolutely inevitable and only a matter of time?* This deep sense of betrayal (woundedness) has to lead to and feed the chronic anxiety and fear-based way of living. That is, unless one can find another 'map' of the territory of human experience whereby we don't as humans feel or think within this paradigm of the 'normal' ongoing sense of being "victims." The path of fearlessness, and philosophy of fearism are two agents of powerful ways of rethinking this relationship of human being to Life and to that existential sense/vulnerability of being born a victim in cold, harsh, cruel universe that doesn't really give a care about you. With enough suffering in one's experiences and for those under chronic oppression, it is pretty easy to not see an way out; as Sartre expressed it in his conception of *"No Exit."*

But this existentialist standpoint, true as it may be in part, we see that it has not the last story to tell of the human identity and experience. It is incomplete. We require a better 'map' for our human journey, and many have tried to make these maps, including most all religions, and some psychologists have tried to help manage our existence as a heroes' journey based on mythology, and others, like Fisher, have attempted to map the journey of the stages of the "soul" (some might call it consciousness itself).[218] In Figure 1 (in Introduction 1), there was a dynamic interior map drawn to help human beings see a big picture of "Esteem" on diverse and integral dimensions of reality so as not to get caught up on only the "Ego" and its self-esteem. Fearlessness is core to that map.

Now, we'll turn to Fisher's big picture of the stages of the soul's journey based on his view of the Defense Intelligence System of evolution itself. Again, why do we give attention to these big maps? Simply, because we believe they may significantly alter our perspective, our limited views, and our biases. They offer us a way to not just fall into limitations (taboos) of what is possible and impossible. Thus, they offer ways to counter the *resistance* people so often have to Life, to Fearlessness, to Expansion and growth and development. People who struggle and suffer, are often hard pressed to see there is anything better in the horizon. They may cling to hope, but also they may loathe hope. And, even people who are very well off and relatively free from daily struggle and suffering, may resist new possibilities of a very different way to be a human being.

So Figure 3 opens up the field of vision, towards a new paradigm of leadership thinking, and expansions, identities and ways of being—on a trajectory towards a better future. It marks out this journey as theory but also from intuition and empirical experience. Fisher has spent over three decades improving on this map from his original version in his 2010 book. We recommend readers check out his earlier version and compare it with this new one.[219] He has linked the "fish bowl" image from Subba's cover (and discussion above) into the core architecture of this new map as a spiraling design of growth and evolution, and of history as *telos* (i.e., with direction). To be clear, human history does not so nicely fit a map/model like this. A map is just that, it is not the actual territory but it represents it. Figure 3 represents what is more hidden below in the subconscious dynamics of actual history and how we live our lives. But just because it is interior and invisible in that sense, does not mean it isn't there and isn't working. You may find intuitive resonance in studying the map with what is real for you. The similar example is that genes and memes are continually operating as architectures and dynamics, just like physics and chemistry principles; but just because they are invisible doesn't mean they aren't shaping the world.

Figure 3 can be best followed like any map that has so much data that it can overwhelm. Let's trace through some, not all, of what is going on in this map of Defense Intelligence (DI). And it is important to note that Fisher has specialized in only Defense, not all the other systems that operate in living organisms and social systems. Fear Intelligence and Defense Intelligence go together, which seems an obvious starting premise. Integral theory, as a spectrum of consciousness levels, is also depicted in the verticality of this diagram. Integral theory is very complex and Fisher's 2010 book goes into great long explanation. Here, we will be much more succinct. The holistic-integral approach is primary to this map and to mapping out the human journey (that is, stages of growth).

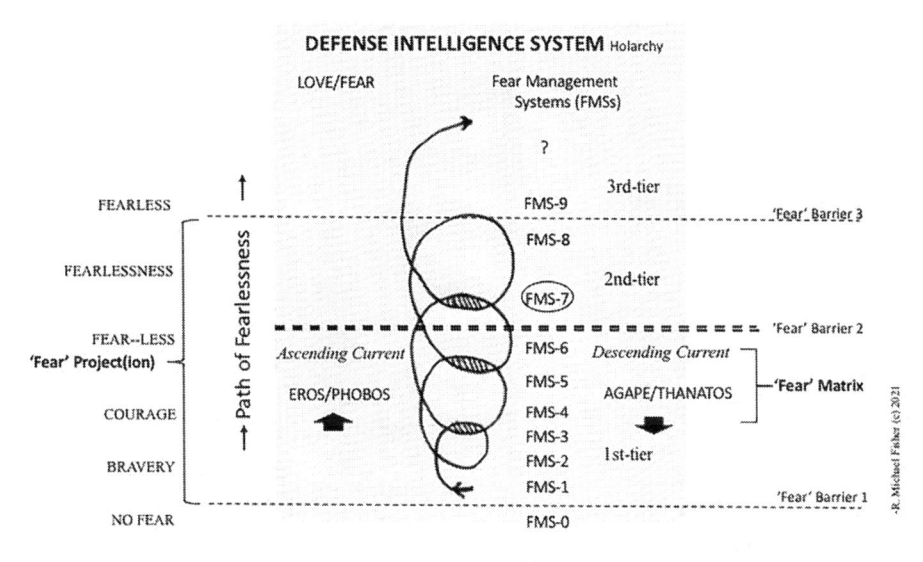

Figure 3 Stages of the Soul's Journey: Defense Intelligence Systems (DI)

Fisher argues that all humans[220] are already, from conception, 'walking' the Path of Fearlessness as the evolutionary imperative of consciousness itself. In other words, we all are designed that way because we are consciousness—on a journey. Fisher's dictum: *When fear appears, so then does fearlessness*—indicates, that the "spirit of fearlessness" is basic to all self/system-regulation in living systems (see Part III). He then suggests that such an inherited, four billion year-old system and 'spirit' does evolve with increasing complexity due to growth and development (i.e., evolution). So, in humans, be they individuals and/or groups or nations—all have the opportunity, under diverse conditions and over time, to evolve from the most simple Fear Management Systems 0-3 to the more complex FMSs 4-9 (and beyond?). Reality is on a material plane, that some individuals (rare few) will advance beyond the average of the group they belong to. Some have reached 3rd-tier FMSs and often are seen as sages, saints, gods, etc. They are at FEARLESS stage of development in that true sense of the meaning of the term. Note, this is not the same as how most everyone uses the term "fearless" as behavioral. We have talked about this throughout the book, and the distinctions made by Fisher require one to be much more discerning in ascribing such labels on humans or organizations.

This very map of Fisher is drawn/conceived from FMS-7 (as circled). This is the location of a very advanced form of FMS—that is, FMS-7 INTEGRAL LEVEL which is where Fisher argues that is the best location (i.e., 2nd-tier) to ascribe and situate FEARLESSNESS proper. Remembering, that by the time the 'spirit' of fearlessness reaches organizational complexity and leadership qualities of FMS-7, only approx. 0.02 % of the mass population of humans can function operationally here as a 'center of gravity' of their conscious awareness. The theory of Spiral Dynamics is another way to understand this dynamic of vertical (holarchic) systems but that is too complex to get into here.[221] The vast majority of humans and societies tend to operate in FMSs 2-3-4, with some few in 5-6. Arguably, premodern societies *en masse* (excluding exceptional individuals who reach 2nd and 3rd tiers) remain in earlier FMSs and this continues until this day. They understand "fear" and have a relationship to "fear" (i.e., to fear management) that is uniquely different than higher levels in the holarchy of complexity along the spectrum depicted in Figure 3.

The diversity of ways of defining "fear" and managing it, in other words, are immensely different and potent in differential conditions and situations. Fisher argues that most people who are reading this book or any of his publications are operating in one or two primary FMSs. They do *not* have an Integral perspective/knowledge yet fully-awakened and thus they tend towards a reductionistic view of fear conceptualizations, imaginaries, and management regimes (i.e., within 1st-tier). They tend to think the rest of the world is operating like they are—on one or two primary systems. Well, indeed, they are also likely operating on one or two primary FMSs but not at all necessarily the same one's you are necessarily. That's the point of why it is so important to map out the *full spectrum* of FMSs as possible, and you may study these. Anyone can advance their 'center of gravity' of FMS, and anyone, with help and the right conditions, may learn to be flexible in incorporating five or six or all 10 of the FMSs in any situation, depending on which FMSs DI. Now, that latter flexible resilient capacity would be a super-potent Defense Intelligence emerging on this planet. Fisher has speculated that if several great leaders, and, for example, the United Nations, could adopt this model and training for flexible FMSs, then 'the world' would rapidly transform.

Fisher's argument is that the world's Fear Problem collectively is now so complex, across nations and cultures, etc., that the operation of one or two primary FMSs is not going to make any real improvement, and will likely exacerbate the Fear Problem. Well, that's a bigger story about what Fearlessness Leadership would bring to the planet. We are a long ways from that. And, we are a long ways from the radical trust in Figure 3, for example, that it can offer us anything worthwhile. The world mostly will resist such a Figure and radical trust, and thus it will resist much of the potency of the Path of Fearlessness. Recently, Fisher was talking to a kindergarten teacher about his theory, and she immediately got very excited. She said, I can see putting up on the chalkboard in big letters on the first day of school, FROM FEAR TO FEARLESSNESS. Then, she was very excited to see the spectrum of languages (far left in Figure 3) that depict how the spirit of fearlessness manifests in humans: first No Fear as one kind of expression or "without fear" is another of the expressions one can hear at times. Fisher, says, that is great because it represents in his model the time before time—no fear/time—when, we were not self-conscious beings and lived in the mother's womb fully enclosed and all needs met (more or less). There was the state of adualism that Joseph Campbell talked about in the Introduction of our book, before dualism (and 'I am'), thus, before fear. Then after No Fear, is Bravery, and so on. That spectrum of a critical new language is radical and itself gives guideposts for humans to aspire towards as life-long learning and achievement possibilities. Who wouldn't be inspired by seeing and hearing about a map like this when we were in our childhood and youth? Truly, it would have changed everything for us as co-authors, if we had such guidance. For the kindergarten teacher, then, she would slowly, day by day, for the rest of the year, help the students see images, pictures, explore feelings, of what that expansive *shifting* would look like. And to encourage children to keep *remembering*, never to forget, this is their fate on this earth too. They are meant and designed to be Fearless (someday operating in

FMS-9 and including all the others before it), even if—often, the case will be that they are not able to reach that aim.

This school teacher, like us as co-authors, believe that having the map at least, would make a big difference. Children need to see a vision of the possibilities for their future growth, no matter how ideal. The real, and suffering experiences, ought not ever be the dominating form of consciousness a child lives with. For the real and suffering is only that—it is about the *human condition*, not the true human nature and *human potential*.[222] Fisher believes his evolutionary potential maps and theories are core to humans remaining in some state of radical trust, at least a trusting in the process of what is depicted in the map, and that it gives the vision, orientation, and perspective of a holistic-integral view always. Otherwise, humans will become 'lost'—and, will lose their soul.

It is in Fisher's earlier version of this map that he links the "stages" along the path via FMSs, with archetypes: 1st-tier Naive, Victim, Survivor, Thriver, and 2nd-tier Sacred Warrior, and 3rd-tier Royal Leader. He has developed an extensive meta-theory from his experiences as a liberation leader since the 1980s. His view is that if "leaders" are not to become corrupted by the 'lower' forces and fear-based dynamics of the 'Fear' Matrix, then they are going to need to be surrounded not by just troops and military weaponry, etc. No, they will need to be surrounded by magicians[223] and sacred warriors[224] who know what true fearlessness is about and they are not fooled by bravado and egoic fear weaponry. They resist the later and promote the former and remind the Royal Leader of their true higher calling. Anyways, this is beyond the scope of this chapter to dive into deeper, but it is a direction we both as co-authors are interested to further elaborate in future works.

The (apparent) reality is, that it is very hard to trust leaders these days. That however, is *not* the only reality available (Figure 3 offers many levels of reality—all which make up the Whole Reality). An *ideal* reality of great Royal Leadership, at the archetypal, mythological, transpersonal level/perspective, is still in our reach and always has been as a species. Sadly, it seems we are still too conditioned, deluded, self-abusive, guilt-shame-fear driven, too violent and too traumatized[225] for the most part—to fully *nurture* the evolutionary highest potentials for leadership and leaders. The point being in the holistic-integral model, is that there has to be a *community* of care, wisdom, fierceness, etc. to 'grow' a great leader. All ancient religious traditions have always known this to be true. A Buddha, a Dalai Lama, a Mahatma Gandhi, etc., do not grow from anything less than these *great circles of care/love*— that is, communities of Fearlessness. There needs to be a Fearlessness Movement (Part III) and nuanced critical praxis of fearlessnessizing[226] to support these 'circles' to be established across the globe. And, yes, even they can come to faults and fail at times. Life and leadership is one great learning experiment. There is no use blaming our species or anyone else for all the failures in history. Evolution itself regularly fails with species constantly going extinct. It's natural—and, yes, humans can exacerbate this recklessly too. Overall, however, *we're not bad* particularly in essence, which is exactly the reason we chose the epigram by Segal at the beginning of this chapter. A philosophy of fearism and fearlessness is an uplifting perspective on human evolution and history. It is also realistic to grave problems we have to face. Fear, is merely, as we say—not going anywhere. It is the humans that have to go somewhere other than where they have mostly been. It is time for that grand shift that the kindergarten teacher got so excited about in listening to this vision of a new map of a big story—called development. Our book is meant to encourage development of our FMSs and ultimately, our DI for the entire species.

> **RMF:** Next, Maria you asked about the epigram quotes I chose for the opening of Chapter Two. In a sense, they are my 'goldfishes' leaping out from the watery medium of the fish bowl.

> **BMK:** Interesting analogy, Michael. Set apart quotes above, hovering, and teaching from a location beyond the 'normal' text. I guess they are a risk as well. They are meant to stir up the reader and make us reflect outside 'normal' thought.

RMF: I think so. But not all authors use them that way. The spotlight is on them and they ought to be provocative, in my view.

I have chosen these two quotes, both from powerful women leaders in their own right, you may note: (a) the title of the chapter is a quote from Wheatley, the organizational and leadership consultant that I mentioned in Chapter One and, (b) the Segal quote on a revisionist moralism *via* issues of 'good and bad.' I like how it abruptly invokes us to stop and think. Both these shining quotes articulate the impulses, let's say, of a Fearlessness Paradigm. But please remember, there is no such idealized Fearlessness Paradigm in existence other than in my head in terms of an image/theory. Just like with Chöygam Trungpa's Tibetan philosophy and 'story' of the Shambhala kingdom,[227] supposedly that is real but not actually—and, it is *not* fear-based— but rather a beautiful kingdom ruled by fearlessness. Same analogy here. I think in Part II the relationship of Beauty to Fearlessness is going to be significant in how our book takes shape. Anyways, for now, I emphasize the fictional/non-fictional character of the Fearlessness Paradigm. I also make it dialectical and "messy" in that no such Fearlessness Paradigm is going to exist without the complicated exploding and war-like competition with the Fear Paradigm.[228] There is no peacefulness, in other words, for the Fearlessness Paradigm to exist and/ or merely to be inserted as a theory. Make sense?

BMK: You seem to suggest it is a process always, a dialectical interplay, and full of both forces that desire the 'new' paradigm and that want to destroy it simultaneously. It's a conflict—yes, a battle. Most people won't label it or even detect it the way you do.

RMF: Yes, a bloody one too. That is the great finding of Thomas Kuhn's classic study of scientific paradigms, paradigm shifts, and the politics of knowledge, from the 1960s.[229] The same principles of that change, growth and development struggle are no different in patterning when applied to Fear and Fearlessness—at this level of which I am speaking about here. You can see we are way beyond talking about individuals concrete and literal fears and a simple psychological concept of "fear is an emotion" etc.

Ken Wilber, like Kuhn, carefully researched and documented the way "levels of consciousness" themselves are both aiding the next evolution to a more mature level but also simultaneously, in a complex dynamic of motivational forces, also trying to undermine that very development and progress.[230] I don't have space to articulate Wilber's brilliant and troublesome summary of this but to say it keeps "conflict" in the picture, and that everything is created from that dynamic, and "fear" is part of that too, as Subba articulates—"Fear is as vast as the universe." My own DCFV theory from my masters research on conflict theory[231] is very applicable to all this. Simply, domination and subordination relationships are inherent in the universe, to put it bluntly.

OK, back to the two quotes. The title of Chapter Two is from Wheatley's provocative "Eight Fearless Questions," she asked a group of leaders once at a workshop.[232] With not the space sufficient here to go through all her questions, what is remarkable about them, and why I suggest they are coming mostly from a Fearlessness Paradigm is that they are unusual but also wise. She was asking these leaders to consider just how willing are they to operate, and identify themselves freshly, outside of a Fear Paradigm. Now, she didn't say "Fear Paradigm" *per se*, more so she meant the 'norm' common paradigm of operating in leadership and business etc. But that is totally what I see she was asking, and the "Does the world need us to be fearless?" is nicely positioned as the top #1 question, followed by several other great questions, but I especially like how it is #6 question "Can we work beyond hope and fear?" that tells me, implicitly, she was saying (in my words): *If you leaders first can imagine that the world to thrive needs fearless leaders, okay, then you better make the distinction that you are going to have to 'work beyond hope and fear'*—in terms of, you are going to have to work without rewards and hope and your addiction to fear. What? How is there any such motivating energy, which is not based on addiction to fear, reward, hope and 'winning' the battle(?).

Exactly, Wheatley, a Buddhist as well, knows of this 'other' dimension, what I have called here a Fearlessness Paradigm, in and out of the 'Fear' Matrix. She is offering the philosophical and value/identity questions needed to face the world's crises and their own role in working in/with the planet itself in attempting to 'correct' the imbalances going on that are so destructive to Life. But don't expect to win. Fearlessness does not have that in its position or needs. Only Fear has that. So, in 2006 in speech to leaders, in a transpersonal fearlessness motif, Wheatley made a profound 'call'—which, I would say is about as close to any in voicing the very "spirit of fearlessness" I write about. She said to the large audience:

"What is the name that is big enough to hold your fearlessness, that is big enough to *call* you into fearlessness? That is big enough to break your heart? To allow you to open to the suffering that is the world right now and to not become immobilized by fear and to not become immobilized by comfort? What is the way in which you can hold your work [your leadership/identity] so that you *do* feel free from hope...and therefore free from fear?"[233]

For me, I know that the name "fearologist" which I put on my work, since about 2000, is one name that is 'big enough to hold' fearlessness—and, that's especially because the fearologist I am talking about is one who's fearology (and fearism) is big enough to embrace and be guided by the Fearlessness Paradigm. That's my way of voicing and coming to this 'call' by Wheatley. Interestingly, I never saw Wheatley's call until many years after I made the commitment to naming myself a fearologist.

The sense of that voicing for me is that she is not talking here about mere bravery or courageousness—oh no, that is being transcended as is the very 'normal' self- identity of those who are trying to be brave and/or courageous. It is not even personal—but transpersonal. Anyways, even more interesting, in terms of the problem of *resistances* to Fearlessness, Wheatley's interview with Art Kleiner in 2007, really gives evidence of what Wheatley experienced with her trained business leaders over the years, as to how they backed-out quickly from the fearlessness paradigm to go back to a fear paradigm after 9/11 hit the USA, in the form of one terrorist attack on their own soil. The economic/profits bottomline took over their decisions in the climate of fear of 9/11, she remarked in that interview; and virtually all her intense training of many corporate leaders to live beyond fear, was seemingly for not.

The point being, she realized under sufficient distress and pressure, the larger pull and stickiness of the Fear Paradigm (or 'Fear' Matrix), is just waiting to re-take its domination. Why? Because it is in *resistance* constantly to the Fearlessness Paradigm? Or at least, it appears that is the case. Oppression in other words, is always waiting to re-take its domination over Liberation. That's why democracy is so hard to maintain with strength in history and keep it stable.

BMK: I have been thinking of leadership in politics a lot, as India as a nation is being rocked horribly with abuses in this realm. Evidence is growing that the standards of political governance are rapidly falling down in many democratic nations around the world. Escalating human rights violations are the outcomes of weaponisation of mortal fear. Autocratisation of leadership at the top is tantamount to demonisation of democratic ethos. Damian Ruck, the lead researcher from the University of Bristol theorised that the ideals of secularism promote growth as long as people's fundamental rights are safeguarded. Lührmann and Lindberg of the University of Gothenburg studied the 117 year-long democratisation process, 1900-2017, and found that there is a disturbing increasing trend of autocratisation of governments in many countries.

RMF: Autocratisation? Is that like elitism and dictatorship, fascism?

BMK: Yes, autocratisation is the rule by a single power hungry person, who doesn't allow the participation of people in decision making and governance. It may be juxtaposed with democratisation, which means people's rule over themselves. The problem with the autocrat is fear only. It is the fear of loss of control of power. Under autocratic leadership, most of 'the people' will lose their rights to freedoms.

Researchers Dunning and Kruger of Cornell and New York universities inferred from their studies that democracies flourish only on good leadership based on knowledge but not on ignorance. These findings point out that the fundamental freedoms and democratic rights of individuals, which are hallmarks of fearlessness, seem to be at stake. Rational thought, scientific development and ethical values have not yet sufficiently impacted the human psyche and its maturation, as you say Michael, especially in regard to basic socioemotional development. Therefore, the irrational, pretending to look rational, typically undermines real peaceful and progressive coexistence.

The growth of dangerous technologies and emergence of demonic dictatorships are the after-effects of fear within. Consequently, much of the world population is present in the grip of destruction....

RMF: Thanks for bring out dialogue to these practical matters of governance and leadership on the ground. I appreciate when you are so supportive of the Fearlessness Movement (Part III)....

BMK: There are again more fears emanating from infections, accidents or environmental threats, which continue to keep the people restless without enjoying quality lives. The solution ultimately lies in the paradigm shift of the fearlessness approach. When fearlessness rises up—and, leaders take on this 'call' that Wheatley has made and you have made Michael, the people will automatically embrace peaceful usage of science and technology by avoid the Frankenstein outcomes. When fearlessness spreads out people will confidently promote human governance by eschewing lawlessness. It is the time to carry forward the spirit of fearlessness....

RMF: I'm thinking of the neurobiology of morality research of Darcia Narvaez, and how she talks of leadership in politics as so important to be informed of what brings good brain development and what brings pathological stunted brain development. In her book, she notes research show that "a partisan viewpoint filter" seems to get embedded in the mind of many, especially highly active political leaders and followers. She wrote, "It's as if an 'us versus them' filter is employed before the information is processed. Political discourse often downshifts the listener to prehuman competitive concerns—that is, social ranking" before all other human values, and "Leaders also frequently stress followers with warnings, triggering safety ethics among the electorate or populace"[234] and quickly a child-like mind is in operation. But not a good child-like mind filled with curiosity, but rather filled with mores and fixed reflexes of prejudice and divisiveness that the child learns from inflexible and rigid parents who 'think in black and white' only.

Indeed, dictatorships and fascism, totalitarianism, etc. are a constant threat. In Part III, Maria, you and I will explore how there is a more subtle evolutionary imperative at work in the "movement" between Fear and Fearlessness—in their dialectical fear/fearlessness formation. It is based on an evolutionary, natural, and biological-systems theory of self/system regulation and not based on merely cultural dynamics. But that's getting ahead too far at this point.

This rich dialogue between us could have kept going on, as so many issues came to mind as we talked. Yet, it is time to close this chapter on this sense of ongoing inquiry and an inevitable incompleteness. We have not directly addressed one of the major resistances to Fearlessness. That is, the obvious problem of the *fear of fearlessness*—or fear of any radical change or movement, in which fearlessness is at the center of the shift. Indeed, some of that topic is addressed in Part III and Part IV. As well, we didn't have space to go into the new trend to brand just about everything, including leaders and leadership, "fearlessness" as if it is commercial and culturally hip in the W. (at least).[235] And then there is the overall problem we have also left only partially addressed here is the notion of a "fearlessness future,"[236] as Fisher has called it or a "fearless society"[237]—which is all about leaders having truly broad and deep expanded imaginations for radical 'new' ways of building the social and the future, without relying on fear as the primary motivational force and relationality of a peoples. Exemplary leaders have shown this way and so studying them is important but we also cannot rely on them but rather have to encourage 'new' variants for our current times.

For now, it is valuable to bring home the summative message that we are holding in our work in this book on restoration, change, and transformation. It is a poignant wise message the Dalai Lama (His Holiness) was speaking about, as his advice, especially to Westerners as he toured the nations in 2005. He said, several times to his audiences, according to Ferguson, "Don't be afraid of fearlessness."[238] From an E. thinker as the Dalai Lama is, but also with a strong education in W. thought, it is not surprising he is defending fearlessness in this advice; because at the core of the oldest religious text, the *Bhagavad Gita* (Hinduism), *fearlessness is the virtue of all virtues.*[239]

> **BMK:** In ancient Hindu texts there are many legends in which gods and goddesses would extend '*abhaya*

hastam,' as the 'hand of fearlessness,' to the fear stricken people in distress.

RMF: I hadn't heard of that version. The teaching is that if we humans and our leaders cannot get down the basics of fearlessness, recall the fundamentals of trust in Erikson's model, then all other layers of development of virtues or anything else will characteristically be corroded and corrupted to some degree—even the virtue of Love.

That said, as co-authors, we are more than well aware that just saying venerable words like that aren't necessarily going to most effectively change anything. We're very glad the words were uttered, and maybe they ought to be uttered more. How many times in the Hebrew, Christian and Islamic holy books and preachings are the words "Fear Not!" in various forms. Clearly, those oft -repeated words are not overall morally, or in terms of learning, effective in re: to actualization of the grand project of undermining the global Fear Problem. What needs careful attention is the analysis and *cura* in regard to the *resistance* to the virtuous words of and principles of Fearlessness; and that is what this Chapter Two has begun to address directly.

PART II
FEARLESSNESS AS/IS BEAUTY

CHAPTER THREE

Fearlessness as/is Beauty

> Beauty isn't all about just nice loveliness...beauty is about more rounded substantial becoming. So, I think beauty in that sense is about an emerging fullness, a greater sense of grace and elegance, a deeper sense of depth and also a kind of homecoming for the enriched memory of your unfolding life. [re: liking Pascal's phrase:] 'You should always keep something beautiful in your mind.'
> – John O'Donohue (2017)

Indeed, we like O'Donohue's poetic-philosopher-mystic expression in that quote and how ultimately to probe into 'beauty' is a fine art; and a complexity that includes and invites one's daily life to be full of grace, even when there often is such violence, banality, boredom and ugliness at times all around us. To *know beauty*—this is not some esoteric topic for only abstract aesthetic debates or analytical philosophy investigations.

And, of course, mostly, we as co-authors wish to emphasize that beauty, like fearlessness, is something in the realm not merely dependent upon the 'outer'; but it is ultimately a sensing, feeling-knowing of an "inner landscape," to use O'Donohue's words from his last interview, in 2017. We agree with Pascal that it is critical to "keep something beautiful in your mind"—that's something no one or no circumstance can take away—as long as you have some control of your own mind.

And, in this book, as co-authors, we started on the same basic premise of igniting something in these pages—a something that is ineffable often, and yet is elegant too. So, we write in words that address thoughtfully what we both feel is crucial to humanity making it through the great crises of our times—it is simply, *consciousness*, that ineffable notion yet everyday reality, of what Marianne Williamson talked about in her speech that ended Chapter One.

Fearlessness is consciousness, situated as core, like a hot melting liquid beneath the cooling earthly crust—of what we call 'real,' on the surface. This invisibility of Fearlessness is what intrigues us (as co-authors) greatly, and no less are we in awe of its spontaneity. The 'crust' however, like the *ego*, according to Sartre, is what most defends, resists and takes flight when in the presence of this "monstrous freedom" (*aka* fearlessness).[240] We'll investigate throughout this book this 'hiding-go-seek' game and its functioning of the fear-based ego in relationship to fearlessness. But particularly, in this chapter that investigation relies on what can be learned from an aesthetic inquiry, an inquiry into consciousness itself as Beauty.

> **RMF:** Being conscious of inner/outer connectivity, that is a great delight. When it comes to my most fundamental philosophizing about Life, it has been intriguing to see my obsessional interest in *patterns*—inner/outer and some in between. I dare say, there's this primal instinct in all living creatures to recognize intimately the patterns that exist as part of basic networked "order" in reality—and, its inherent we are designed to register them and learn from them, within the somatic intelligence of the elementals of earth, fire, water, air—in contact with and laden in/with the body, and especially the visual and auditory fields.
>
> I mean, my own biography is that I became in my earliest teen years both a musician and a visual artist. These became essential to my being and development.

At times they occupied my life so much that they became partial and full-time careers. To this day, at age 69, I still have an art studio and exhibit my art work. I would say, without those nourishing pursuits, complementing my intellectual interests, my life would have suffered greatly. The aesthetic/artistic aspects have been modalities of a kind of spiritual teaching that remind me of how they are "a gift" in what they offer to humans and how they work as inquiry methods into accessing a rich creative, expressive and soulful space/time sensibility. They have taught me what it means to be a self-in-becoming, that is, a human being—in the relational context of what it means to be part of Creation. This is critical to healthy development maturation and ethical intelligence.

It is this deep resonant connection to Creation itself that provides something much larger Reality than my ego-self-identity requires, so that it does not totally reduce the world to small reality and obsession with self-centered concerns all the time. You could call it a basic *religio* experiencing *via* the aesthetic dimension/relation of life. And fundamentally, that is what I am calling here the learning of *pattern language*. That is how I communicate with qualities of Reality= Truth, Beauty, Goodness. That is the Big Three of integral philosophy.[241] My focus in this chapter is to explore Beauty vs Ugliness, in parallel, and by analogy with, the discussion of prior explorations of the archetypal, meta-motivational forces of Love vs. Fear—and, more specifically, for our purposes, the aesthetic patterning, as paradigms, of which manifest, and are caused by, dynamics of Fearlessness vs. Fear. Of course, as oppositional as these polarities may be, at a deeper philosophical, and nondual level, you and I have argued that it is better to conceive of their relationality dynamics as fear/fearlessness—that is, as a dialectic. That said, they are intimate partners of interrelational complexity. Up to now, we haven't talked about them within the aesthetic register. So, I'm excited to explore this with you Maria.

BMK: Yes Michael! I agree. Fear-fearlessness dynamics shape aesthetic experience of humans in a significant way. When an individual is born, everything in the world looks mysterious, strange and intriguingly interesting. Anything which is interesting is beautiful too. The more the individual dares to explore and experience in infancy or childhood, the more beautiful the explored environment appears. Because newness is captivating....

RMF: For sure, and it intrigues me how a new baby that is healthy just stick's everything into its mouth. It takes that external world reality and opens to it, boundaries are porous, and it tastes, sucks, smells, and even swallows most anything it can; there is like no artificial separation wall between inside and outside worlds—it is all meant to be integrated into "one" whole experiencing. It's poetically sensual....

BMK: Right, but *only* as long as it is harmless what comes from the environment to the inside. Of course, a lot of nature is relatively harmless as a rather fortuitous plate of benevolent extraordinaire. There is an optimism-evoking poem in my mother-tongue Telugu, written by the 20th century communist ideologue Sri Sri. He wrote that there is nothing in this world which doesn't qualify as the subject (theme) of poetry. Every creation, whether large or small, is worthy of poetic applause. This poem impressed me so much during my college days that it inspired me to apply the same style when I wrote a Telugu poem on beauty. The title reads on the same lines as, 'there is nothing in this world which doesn't qualify as a thing of beauty.' As you already pointed out, what I also feel is that the experience of beauty is contingent upon fear-fearlessness manifestations. For instance, if fear dominates my thinking process, I might imagine things like a pessimist for the time being. I would tend to perceive things and situations around me as relatively ugly. Fluctuations in fear-fearlessness patterns may accordingly bring about ugly-beautiful feelings in people. Such patterns, whether mixed or otherwise occur in different proportions of fear and fearlessness in every individual's life on the ugliness-beauty scale of one extreme to the other.

RMF: I think you and I here are sourcing primal roots and routes to what could be a re-framing of theories of 'the Other' or 'othering' as it is also called—that are so popular in postmodernism and cultural critique today. "Fear of the other" is another way it is talked about. It's a big concern is how we humans and groups construct 'the Other' and the consequences it has—including the aesthetics it produces in cultures and in our intimate lives as well.

Anyways, talking about patterns now. Yeah, the attraction to patterns, or *pattern language* as the architectural theorist Christopher Alexander has called it,[242] came initially from many sources as a child, not the least of which was how I was cared for as a dependent infant from conception to my earliest years learning to walk and eventually talk and be more independent. I grew up naturally seeking Natural places, which I found much more attractive to explore and learn in than

Cultural places, as in the house or institutions. My life could easily be characterized as that of being a "nature boy," as my father, who was born and raised on a small farm, once said to me and said to my mother, who was much more a "city slicker" type of person. My mom and I had conflict around this all the time. Her aesthetic for comfort zone for a clean-ordered-mechanical beauty was at odds with my rugged messy-organic-spontaneous beauty patterning comfort zone. Not that I absolutely want to make one type of aesthetic patterning all good and one all bad. That simplistic dualism would be reckless and unreal. Yet, as this chapter unfolds, you will see I have some very strong views about Mechanical vs. Organic aesthetic pattern languages—and, which is the *more* ethical way to go today in the 21st century.

Anyways, it is important to share my aesthetics of fearlessness here, and why I connect it to beauty so easily and why an aesthetics of fear, like an architecture of fear is so destructive and ugly. But before jumping ahead into that discussion and some of my empirical research *via* the A-D/ness survey, I want to share how I came to be so decisive historically in my views. I already mentioned nature-music-art as my foundational practices of becoming human, and with those as primal, I was able slowly to develop the higher cognitive-academic intellectual aspects of my becoming human. It is the complementarity of the *arational* (arts)[243] and *rational* (sciences) that make for a curious mixing—I greatly value both. However, as an arts-based therapist for decades and my learning about how humans are hurt and how they heal *via* my training in Jackin's Re-evaluation Co-Counseling practice/theory[244] since the early 1980s, it was inevitable that I would come to deal with the *irrational* modality up-front-and-center.

Irrationality is what brings everything Beautiful and Good down into ugliness if not 'evil.'[245] It also destroys the True.

What I learned is that the rational modalities of cognition alone cannot control and/or bring healing to the irrational in this world. However, with the solid ground of the arational, for example the aesthetic mode, then the irrational can be more sensitively reached and communicated with, and transformed—ultimately, bringing back in the rational that had been rudely displaced by the powerful emotional and irrational hurting or trauma of fear-based patterning—that is, fear-conditioning.

My first reading of this dynamic came from Harvey Jackins' liberation theory and peer-counseling method. Then I found guidance in the therapeutic systems theorists like Bradford Keeney and his notion of *aesthetics of change*.[246] These were monumental experiences I was fortunate to have, which I understand most people have no idea what these things mean. And then, most impactful at the same time of the early 1980s was my reading of Gregory Bateson's epistemology of evolutionary systems aesthetics[247] and Valerius Geist's "biology of art"[248] and Christopher Alexander's architectural theory of "pattern language." My naturalist-artist-self was greatly stimulated and curious to pursue a thorough understanding of the fundamental principles of *design* in Nature; and, more importantly for the cultural world was to learn how to design with Nature, as Ian McHarg[249] had recommended is essential if humans are to build a healthy sustainable world in harmony with ecosystems. Our future depended on this understanding of Quality and pattern language.

My mind in the 1970s-80s was quite blown open and I suddenly had a much deeper sense of what art/aesthetics/arationality was all about. It *was* and still *is* potent in shaping the world. I would require a long book to tell the details of all these important theorists and my own evolution in this realm of aesthetics. At least, now you have a sample tracking record of who some of my major influences were. Only decades later did I start reading classical philosophers, psychologists, art historians and critics on theories of aesthetics in the more rationalist traditions of inquiry. I'm sure you Maria were most influenced by the latter traditions in your own learning and training about aesthetics.

BMK: That's true Michael! During my initial schooling years in a remote village, my idea of beauty was limited to colours, flowers, girls and natural things. When a touring cinema hall was established in our village in early 70's, I became a regular movie goer. Then I was the ward of my grandmother since my parents had been stationed far away in a metro city due to my father's professional commitments and interests. Whenever I watched a film my grandmother would ask me about which character in the movie met with difficulties? I used to narrate the story and would wonder if life perhaps has been designed for us to suffer, at least intermittently, if not fully. Over the years when I started reading Telugu progressive poetry and Marx, I realised that it was not so. I convinced myself that humans have the ability to prevent themselves from suffering if socioeconomic and political affairs are also set to order.

RMF: Interesting this Beauty-Order connection. Some of my 1980-90's healing work using co-counseling as peers for liberation, was informed by a theory that when all else fails in helping people change and better their lives, especially if they are so distressed chronically, and their minds are obsessed with patterns of self-abusive behaviors and hopelessness and helplessness—swamped by fear, in other words. The theory was that the best thing at this base level of existence and subsistence is to offer them "Beauty & Order." Help shape a more ordered world for them, that incites them to remember order not chaos is possible and from order can arise beauty.[250]

BMK: I'm thinking that's likely true. This orderliness, which takes away the fears from the system, refers, for example, to the level of beauty of a nation. Because, fearlessness brings about a paradigm shift in outlook things can change. People develop the feelings of belongingness for one another. Nobody will remain to be an enemy to fear of. Sense of oneness, camaraderie, collective wellness etc., account for inner beauty known as strength and unity of a nation, which its every citizen admires, adores and feels proud of.

RMF: An admirable notion of progressive citizenship...

BMK: It is in this connection that the 18th century Anglo-Irish philosopher Edmund Burke professed, 'To make us love our country, our country ought to be lovely.' A nation's loveliness lies in its people when they love one another without fear and prejudices. Interpersonal relations should be devoid of any disorder and oppression in the realm of their day-today interactions and transactions. Earliest of American Presidents, it was Abraham Lincoln's primary aim during the troubled times was to secure his country's unity even at the cost of his own life. Dr. Ambedkar, the Madison of India, warned at the time of adoption of Indian Constitution about the dangers if people failed to achieve fraternity among themselves. Because unity emanates from fraternity and fraternity means fearlessness and orderliness in people, which we call beauty or loveliness of the nation. At the macro level, the same logic can be applied for a beautiful world where 'the othering' fear-based process you spoke of does not become the motivation behind everything. That leads to the worst problems.

RMF: I want now to turn attention to an empirical piece of research on aesthetics I designed originally in 1984 and carried out various voluntary, usually non-systematic, surveys of individuals and groups of all kinds; albeit, all in the modern W. and N. world, and mostly white people—nearly 1200 people in total. It is called the A-D/ness Survey. It's my way of putting a visual image/metaphor on *consciousness itself* as a *Creator*—that is, from an artistic/creative perspective. Most would agree that the topic of Beauty is deeply *aesthetic*, but fewer would agree, it is simultaneously *creative* and *ethical* equally. Does that make sense?

BMK: For sure. And, as you have shared this A-D/ness survey with me, I also see how you've constructed it as a *political*, if not liberational, intervention for the everyday citizen. I'll talk about that later. First, let me share what happened when I encountered your survey in Figure 4.

A

Used a ruler and outline.
The shape was colored evenly

B

Used a ruler and outline.
Colored in shape dark to light

C

No ruler or outline used. Moved the
crayon back and forth, dark to light.

D

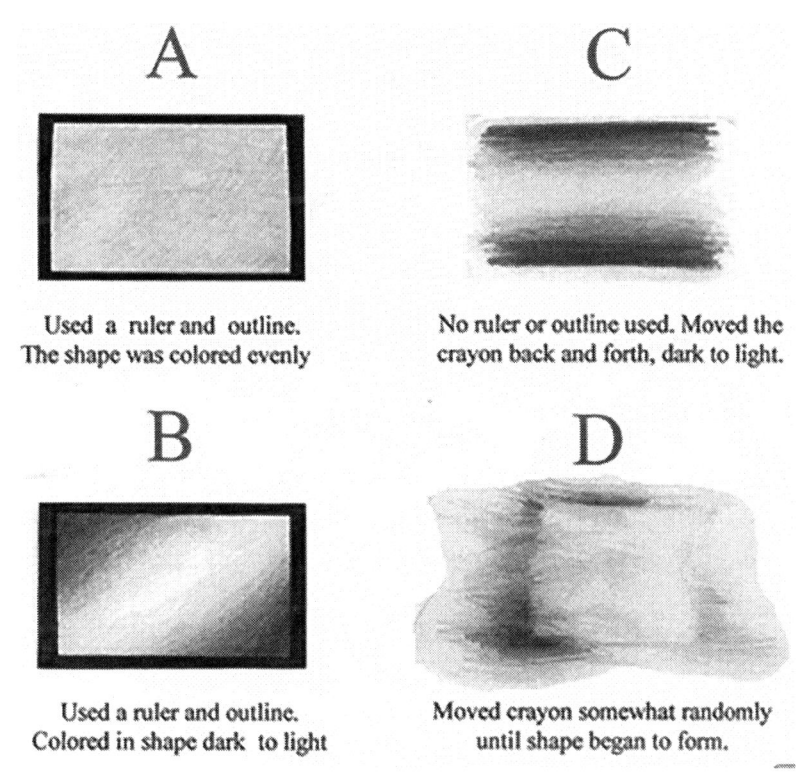

Moved crayon somewhat randomly
until shape began to form.

Figure 4 A-D/ness Images

RMF: Yes, proceed. I'm so grateful that you took this on and have reflected on it. Most of the 1200 people surveyed don't get a chance to do that, or in many cases I have asked them to but they didn't get back to share their experience. So, this is a rare public disclosure.

BMK: Just before diving into my experience, it is important to say that growth of the human being's potential ought to be at the center of all things, at least that is what ancient Indian and Greek philosophers have claimed. I think Beauty is also in that center. What makes a beautiful human being? We ought to care about that. And, even if beauty is in the eye of the beholder, certainly, that is not to say there is not beauty outside of the eye of the beholder—because Creation

Itself experiences and creates beauty. I have raised 11 questions in my own thoughts about the relationship of the beautiful to fear and fearlessness. It's a large exploration beyond what we can address here.[251] I ended up in my contemplation with the last question, I'll leave with readers here: "Lastly, can we deduce that both fear and fearlessness are beautiful in proportions as beauty is also seen in terms of proportions and symmetries?"

My basic philosophical and aesthetic premise is that *unless there's fear, people cannot realise the importance of fearless life*.

RMF: So, you are implying then by analogy that *unless there's ugliness, people cannot realise the importance of beautiful life*.

BMK: Beauty is one of the all-time core characteristics of the universe. The 'creator' if you will, has a beautiful sensibility. At least, from an earth-being perspective, virtually all of Creation is beautiful and *a priori* to anything man-made. But what about fear? What does it do to the beautiful? Fear blocks the alluring and diversity of a future. For example, a singer who is threatened suddenly for their life by a blackmailer will not perform so well nor so beautifully in the concert. Fear, or worry,[252] changes the order of all priorities. Creative, beautiful, and ethical dimensions of an artist's art may suffer when they are under great duress and anxiety—under pressure of fear's formation.

RMF: Under fear's patterning—it's very architecture.

BMK: Yes, we'll see that in your Figure 4 image of four architectures. I also believe, for example, God symbolizes beauty because humans abhor ugliness. They depict evil as ugly. They paint Satan, for example, as ugly and a fearsome creature. God is sculpted as beautiful. Gods and goddesses in myths and legends are shown as killing ugly demons. Human perception of God is not only that of fearlessness and beauty but also that of hope and confidence. Hope and confidence are the medium that facilitate the fearful individual to strive to become fearless. Goodness turns the ugly into the beautiful, which prayer may achieve or great art and virtuousness. Then there is the dimension of Beauty associated with Order.

RMF: Oh, yes, this is very intriguing to me as well. In Figure 4 the images or architectures I have depicted started from a basic arts-based questioning of the Creator. I put myself in a light trance one late evening in my library and began a thought experiment which philosophers/artists/inventors tend to do now and then, and asked: *If I was a Creator, what are the different ways I could create a shape?* I was thinking to simplify this experiment by using simple drawing/coloring materials, paper and a ruler only. I picked a simple random shape, the rectangle. Okay, then I took these drawing/coloring materials and began to make a rectangle in distinguishable different ways. Not just slight variants but in paradigmatic ways—in other words, where there was a major shift of the architecture, design, means of making and ways of thinking about the making. Of course, I realized somewhat that I was solving a question—a problem—a design issue. It was fascinating what resulted after a few hours of experimenting. Without at the moment going into the background experience and rationale for engaging in the Creator-based question in the first place, let me just say, that I was searching in these designs for some fundamental truths about reality-making through various methods, visual expressions, and methodological premises. Yes, these were visual devices or images, for sure, but that was just the materiality of them. They were more than anything *processes* of intuitive felt-thought/making and emerged on paper literally from ideas in my head. They were pattern languages, you could say.

BMK: So, you called them A-ness, B-ness, C-ness and D-ness to represent sets of qualities or are they like mind-sets as well?

RMF: Sort of like different consciousness structures, and yes, mind-sets that are available in the universe. I mean I drew them from somewhere. They are already there.

BMK: Like Plato's Ideas?

RMF: Yeah, I think so, if that's the way Plato was thinking of Ideas, as universal archetypal pre-existing, *a priori* potentials that are latent. They are Ideas, like templates, of processes of perceiving, thinking through, and solving problems—like design problems. They are also more than that. They are visual metaphors. They are what can be calling thinking topographies or imaginaries as well. It's endlessly rich to play with what these "types" of images are and can be and where they come from. But on the surface of reality, they come from what appears to be my mind—in this case, a special intention, was that they come from the Creator's mind.

BMK: Most of us, myself included, want to see these by habitual perceptual thought, as logical devices for solving a problem that you Michael created as an artist and solved as an artist and/or philosopher too.

RMF: Right. Most people think that way and wish to reduce their appearance to merely a concrete outcome of a thinking experience in Michael Fisher's mind. Obviously, he's the one who created them. But if you think about sacred geometry say of a spiral form of a sea shell like from a conch, it is not simply easy to assert that the spiral form and the geometry of it are man-made. No, the Creator made this, or some such design-based intelligence system. Anyways, I see Figure 4 as representing transpersonal Ideas, and, as I said, more importantly they represent the only four fundamental paradigms I could come up with to draw and color a rectangular shape. They are generic "types" and I believe they individually and collectively carry an enormous amount of information, knowledge and even wisdom. But, of course, other people will have to decide about that overall, through time. I am biased in my assessment of their importance.

But let's now get into the visual metaphoric aspect of their 'meanings' you might say—or, what interested me from the start of this thought experiment was to see if it would produce anything that could actually be practically useful in the world? So, the second part of the experiment soon followed the actual images made.

BMK: Oh, that was your 16 Questions about the images in Figure 4.

RMF: Yeah, but only 10 questions came out at first (see Appendix 1). And, these were much more intellectual and strategic; albeit, there was also a certain sense of surprise to me as I watched them be written down to accompany the images. I then knew I had constructed a "test"—a little bit like, but quite different from as well, the psychological type-test, or ink-blot test, called the Rorschach. It was designed to assess personality-types. It is a way of accessing people's free associating thought, feelings, memories and ideas—as they would look at an ink-blot 'painting' on a card, and then another one—all of which were done spontaneously in their original form. The set of answers—or responses elicited freely and quickly, is enough to access the unconscious part of a human being that is invisible. I think my A-D/ness diagrams also do this but I have given way more structure and comparison of images in my "test." I also provide direct questions, which most of the time the Rorschach doesn't do.

BMK: I see the diagrams in Figure 4 as ways of ordering things. And, that raises issues of how people are attracted to or repulsed by them.

RMF: Correct. Attraction and repulsion contrasting is fundamental in all kinds of psychological value-based tests, and aesthetic research. So, I'm not doing anything too unique in that way, but it is totally unique how I have approached soliciting these answers. I actually believe that each of the diagrams articulates a sub-field of energies and aesthetic properties, and processes of creativity, that humans are attracted to because they are "orderly" or "messy"—to be blunt about it. This is a big motivational issue and value-based finding for anyone as they are coming to understand themselves.

For example, my wife likes a lot of cleanliness and order in the household, I like very little. That can cause conflict between us. It's a big deal.

So, what is going on underneath such a conflict, is what interests me as a researcher and educator. Especially, when it comes to asking questions about what is beautiful or even what kind of order(ing) is most healthy? and most creative? and most fearless? I'm attempting to get people to answer the questions to indicate their unconscious biases and preferences—that is, what they see as "best." Those are some of the kinds of questions I ask people, and I asked you Maria when I first gave you this test.

BMK: I have long been interested in fear-fearlessness duality as seen in chaos-order aspects of the universe as well as in ugliness-beauty dualism in human perception. Ultimately, I think these pairs go hand-in-hand as complimentary. Nobel prize-winning Portuguese writer José Saramago wrote, "chaos is merely order yet to be deciphered." From a distance, a busy road intersection may look haphazard but a deeper look of it reveals how safely the orderly movement of vehicles is maintained with the help of human and technological interventions.

RMF: Like street lights, road signs, and painted lines on the road, if they have them, etc. The human design element is part of the flow of things so creativity and actions don't just go all over the place without boundaries, rules, regulations, regimes of agreements—not all that are visible. For there are all kinds of 'agreements' about the rules that are not written down in law but are part of the worldview of the participants, individually and collectively. You could even call them Ideas that are there inherently in social situations—which, avoids utter chaos. I like the idea of order-in-chaos to depict a complementarity as you say.

BMK: Oh, back to your A-D/ness diagrams when I first saw them, as a novel type of duality you were depicting in your Rorschach-like models. I was aware of a code-like communication they were giving off, at least to my perceptual receiver system. The A-B models were *ordered* and the C-D models were relatively *unordered*. Although, one always saw enough order in all the diagrams to constitute what could be called a rectangular shape—which was your aim in your original thought experiment question.[253]

I also remember particularly early on having to answer #2 question: *Which is the best?* That was interesting to answer.

RMF: You chose...? Other reading right now, may also make their own choice for #2.

BMK: I selected 'A.' I guess you Michael, would call that the qualities of A-ness.

RMF: Yes. You were definitely most highly attracted to A-ness throughout the survey of questions and repulsed by D-ness. I also found a near-identical set of choices were made by another famous fearist philosopher, whom I recently gave this test to as well. Now, I'm growing in curiosity as a fear researcher as to what kind of aesthetics is underpinning the attraction of all fearist philosophers who are teaching and publishing on fearism? How do they unconsciously perceive fear and fearlessness? Rather famously, one of the younger fearism philosophers called fear the "beast."[254]

What those results actually mean is yet to be determined but initially it does tell us something, like a map does, of where you are situating your biases and preferences generally. At least, regarding this aesthetic visual level of reality as indicated in this specific test. Oh, and as reminder: I simply told you the bare minimum of what this diagram of Figure 4 was, and told you to give me *your opinion*, choice A, B, C, or D, based on answering the questions I provided. I told you to pick your answer quickly, while looking at the diagrams overall. You were really making aesthetic-based value-judgments, more or less. Although, there are nuances in the questions that go a little deeper than merely value-judgements, they are philosophical and political.

But in the end, I believe this test offers a kind of aesthetic synopsis or *values-X-ray* of what is *invisible* in your worldview. It may be quite invisible in its structure and operating to most everyone around you; but I have found most people find it *invisible* as well to themselves. Why? Because no one really asks us when we are growing up: Hey, what is your worldview? What does it look like in terms of its architecture? It's biases? It's outcomes? And, where do you think it is derived from? Where and how might you have picked-up and learned this worldview inside you?

Worldview is a critical concept, not that I will go into it further here because of shortage of space but people can read my other writing on the worldview aspect in the A-D/ness in other articles.[255] Suffice it to say, one's worldview consists of a lot of learning and conditioning and it determines the shape of one's life in many ways. It's the old Freudian notion that the unconscious makes up approximately 90% of our being and 10% or so is what we are conscious of. That's why it is good to try to understand your unconscious more than most of us are encouraged to understand it—and, within that is a way to understand one's worldview and, same with the society's worldview collectively that dominates at any time. This is important because you want to be aware of what deep motivational shaping forces, beliefs and value-systems and ideas are there—because, you may want to no longer accept them for your own ongoing and growing worldview. Also, one's worldview is intimately related to one's dominant operational paradigm. You can transform them too, like with a paradigm shift, we talked about earlier in this book. Anyways, that's a larger topic. As co-authors we take-up aspects of the unconscious, instinctual and primordial dimensions of Fearlessness in Part III and especially in Part V.

My search in this chapter, with your help, Maria, is to see if Fearlessness is most like the architecture and pattern language of A, B, C, or D (?). But that's jumping ahead.

BMK: I find your A-D/ness theory, which I have gleaned from your video[256] and some writing, as a wonderful interpretation of human perceptions. It is an instrument which can be applied to an individual's subjective thinking and comprehension of fear-fearlessness, beauty-ugliness and orderliness-disorderliness dualities in a given situation. What intrigues me is how you labeled in your theory A & B as "*Mechanical*" and C & D as "*Organic.*" When I gave my answers, before thinking about your theory, I found my interpretations as uncannily curiosity-provoking in and of themselves.

RMF: Oh, wow. Can you explain that uncanny sense further?

BMK: Everyone's interpretation is of course subjective. After having spontaneously ticked my answers on your survey questionnaire, I plotted them on a page of my journal with my observations. Then what I visualised was really an uncanny finding. An unexpected, yet progressive and meaningful pattern was emerging from the direction of D-ness to A-ness. The terms 'organic and mechanical' which you have coined for each pair of phenomena also appeared quite convincing. In his Gaia Hypothesis, James Lovelock held that both organic and inorganic matters created conditions for life. We, the organic beings depend upon inorganic 'oxygen' for our every moment of survival. So, usually in dualistic opposites we take organic-inorganic or mechanical-conscious combinations as pairs. But I could see that your 'organic-mechanical' usage of conceptual terms in the model aptly synchronises a compatible linkage between the natural 'organic' world and the human made 'mechanical' world.

RMF: Thanks for sharing that. You've raised a touchy point Maria. I don't fully agree, at some level, that we can say that all responses to the A-D/ness test are subjective *only*. We need to qualify that. Of course, I agree we are all subjects making subjective claims but I would not want to reduce that to a totalism claim that thus, all answers on the test are only subjective and thus only relative. I am concerned that many of my critics of this survey will think this too. It makes it all just personal when you claim it is only subjective what people answer to the survey questions. That makes aesthetics too then, just subjective, just personal. The critic is attempting to undermine the universal power of the test. The famous modernist expression of this philosophy of subjective-relativism is 'Beauty is in the eye of the beholder.' I have already suggested, that from a systems-holistic-integral perspective, and a dialectical philosophical perspective, that is just not so, or it is a very weak and contracted claim.

My simple short argument is that we are not all equally endowed, adequately informed, or at the same level of consciousness just because we are all subjects. We are different and differentiated along a spectrum of awareness and developmental capacities. This is both common sense but also has been empirically proven in developmental studies by many psychological researchers, for example. The aesthetic line of development itself, as one of the many lines humans have, like cognitive, like emotional, like cognitive lines, etc., is diverse. I believe it takes a highly developed and informed aesthetic sensibility to come to see D-ness is the best as #2 asks, and most alive? as #5, and most "creative" as #10 asks and most healthy as #11 asks. Which is a brief list of my choices—which, I would argue are the best answers to the questions.

Sure, we all have an opinions. I asked for your opinion Maria, as I do with all participants. But clearly it is empirically true that I have spent decades researching to come up with the A-D/ness test and theory, and no one else has done that research. So, they will often not answer the questions the way I do. They are just answering based on 'gut level' responses in the aesthetic dimension.

But just the same, those are valid responses and I believe tell us a lot. I on the other hand, have answers to the questions for comparison, that is, if a person wants to compare their choices on the questions to mine. Some do not want to see that. Others are curious. So, I share my answers and they can decide what they make of it. I am not doing a detailed psychoanalysis in total from such a single device as this test, especially without doing an extensive set of interviews and observations about a 'personality' and correlating the test results with those observations.

BMK: I think your test is a little more accurate than reading tea leaves.

RMF: Good one.

BMK: With all innovative tests like this, it takes a lot of data and time and statistical analysis to 'prove' anything about what good the test does or how accurate it is. But let me put in my words, what I think is most important re: your developmental theory, and based on my reading of your work and your explanation here in this chapter.

RMF: Go for it. I most appreciate hearing another's perspectives beyond my own.

BMK: So, it is advisable to go back now to re-look at Figure 4. Study the diagrams. Contemplate on them. Better yet, I know Michael, you recommend people actually get out the drawing/coloring tools and make the models physically as embodied experience. This will bring out ancient memories, you suggest, about how we "learned" to draw and color and use these materials to represent our feelings, perceptions and ideas about the world and our self. It is primal reconnecting, you say, when the aesthetic dimension is accessed. And, I agree, there are deep values in all of that to be assessed. Why do we get attracted by some qualities of the diagrams and repulsed by others. I have to ask myself, why A-ness is so appealing and not D-ness when I compared them and answered the questions. Now, with more learning about the diagrams, and hearing your more in depth explanation of theory behind them, I probably would not answer the questions the same next time. But let me articulate your evolutionary theory behind them.

A and B have this thick black border, more like a uniform **wall** around them. Impermeable. Your theory says, that no Organic living system is that impervious like a wall—even the shells of organisms are not totally uniform, dead and impervious because they have to be connected to living parts and the environment because they are actually made of the environment and what's inside the living cells—in combination, creating the mass that the shell becomes. In that sense, even hard shells and bones are not totally like the homogeneous impermeable wall of A and B Mechanical models. Only such architectures are found in man-made things, systems—e.g., like machines. So, on that basis, A and B are not the most natural, living and alive—which is #5 question. D-ness is the most natural.... and, thus, most healthy. I see that logic unfold.

RMF: It is amazing how many people do recognize C and D as most natural/living/ alive and many do not, by contrast. And especially D-ness, because the boundaries are so subtle, diverse, flexible, permeable and holistically engaged with the total gestalt of the object and its relational background context—that is, it's ecology, it's environment. D-ness is the image and process or methodology behind what any living cell is, and, even a virus operates on. And, let's not forget the open-attitude of engagement that the new born baby comes into the world with. Okay, back to you Maria.

BMK: D-ness is also the most fragile,[257] it seems, because of its living flexibility. It's least shelled and guarded, that is, walled-off. I guess that's your point here. Is A-ness conducive to Life or a resistance to Life?

Back to your theory, then, I suppose there is more randomness, looking like dis-order in D-ness. But as I mentioned earlier that according to Saramago, "chaos is merely order yet to be deciphered." A-diagram looks most clear of all the four, without the randomness or confusion inside the rectangle. Absence of differentiating contrast makes it look of the high orderly condition. That appeals to my aesthetic sensibility. Yet, you argue that D-ness is most sustainable relationally because it is so porous boundaried and also because it has the most diversity of texture and difference inside it. Actually, your point is that it is a fusion of inside/outside, a total whole in living exchange—where there is not an obvious clean inside and outside only, like in the Mechanical Models. Right. You then make the proposition in theory that the human being is conceived, embedded in the womb, in a total inside/outside as undiffer-entiated D-ness for the most part—at least, in terms of architecture and patterning. We often say, in the womb, the baby and mother are "one" or a unity. Yes, there is a sense of an organic relationality that is quite different than a mechanical relationality in terms of how machines are designed and function. We are dealing with contrasting living and Organic paradigms of organizing with dead and Mechanical paradigms of organizing.

RMF: FYI, the most consistent result overall that I get from all the participants I've surveyed is that of question #6, *Which is the most dead and machine-like?* Over 90% of participants select a A-ness. And, that totally agrees with my own answer to that question. So, on that ground of statistically significant agreement, I do think that human beings have a genetic natural instinct intact within, even if invisible and suppressed to the point of completely unconscious, whereby they can detect and recognize this truth. They recognize the truth/reality that the qualities of A-ness, and B-ness is very close the same, are Mechanical and not Organic. They are dead. They are of the forces which I would associate with toxic decimation of Life forces or D-ness—and, that could lead us towards an in depth discussion of what Freud and others before him, philosophers like Plotinus, meant by *Thanatos*—or death-drive motivation(?) Yet, we'll by-pass that, for maybe that theme will come up much later in the book, I want to point out that I see this *Thanatos* force or pattern language of machinic domination in A/B-ness trying to take over the entire planet—especially, since the Industrial Paradigm and Dominant Worldview of powers began.

BMK: There's a big part of your theory Michael, behind Figure 4 and your way of analyzing the answers to the questions. You talk about trauma, violence and developmental dysplasia or blockages of Life forces by Death forces and *Thanatos*—and, that is caused by Fear or what you call 'Fear' Projection. I know that is complicated, but I think we can turn to summarize here for brevity by saying that D-ness is our inherent human nature and everything after that is violence in some level as a de-promotion of Life and what it means to be human. We have come to settle and cope, as you say, because we've lost our healing instincts to a large degree, and we have as a species for millenia accepted the lesser human condition—as 'average' or 'normal' and it was C-ness for awhile then it crossed into the Mechanical Paradigm and humanness became normalized under the regimes of B-ness, where most of us are now in the modern Industrialized countries of the world. We design things generally this way, with some C-ness, you argue.

RMF: Oh, and the violence/trauma aspect is key in my theorizing. I have studied with intensity for over four decades a theory of how humans are hurt and how they heal, especially in terms of psychic impacts. This I have also taught as a praxis for liberation. Harvey Jackins' led this theory of hurting since the 1940s and it speaks a lot of truth to me.[258] Jackins' talks of "distress patterns" and when he describes how our beautiful, zestful, flexible, intelligent self is *natural* and present as our basic humanness but that it gets cut, clipped, conditioned and distorted through chronic distress which does not get discharged properly, and thus does not get healed, I have come to aesthetically map that distress pattern and it turns out it is just like the patterning movement of moving from an Organic inherent human nature, to the Mechanical-like existence of a human being wounded, in distress, and coping with that. It leads to ugliness and only more reproduction of violence. It is like the A-ness virus when it takes hold in a human being or organization, it 'wants' to turn the whole world into itself. Sound familiar? There's a common adage in the therapy field like this: *Wounded people attract* *wounded people—abusers attract victims and turn them into eventual abusers themselves.* Many titles in media today, read: "Fear spreads like a virus...".²⁵⁹

BMK: Interesting how replication of a distress pattern, as a fear-pattern, is indeed trying to take over all other options of patterns, architectures and ways of living fully—as in living our full human potential. And, then you say, that A-ness has become more seductive and people think it is the most 'safe and secure' system—and, it is I suppose, if you want to live being Dead or almost so. Yes, it is a kind of 'prison.' I can see that now, from the perspective of your theory of evolution. Before I knew details of your theory accompanying this aesthetic test/model, I was reading the diagrams very differently.

RMF: Thanks Maria for that summary. Yes, most people are reading the diagrams differently than I because they have not studied what I have to make myself critically aware of my aesthetic worldview choices and biases. I mean, of my own fear-conditioning in this world that I grew up in—a world filled with people dramatizing and projecting their distress all over the place most of the time. Most of us have too also grow up in those conditions. We are fear-conditioned, eventually, to 'give in' and accept the new 'normal' and thus, be rewarded for that conformity and not causing problems. We grow up, eventually, to even really *like* the Mechanical models. We are addicted to them, largely. We may even think they are images of Fearlessness themselves because of the qualities you described earlier: "without randomness or confusion"—as A-ness becomes like an Idea and Ideal from a kind of other-worldly possibility, even a 'spiritual' dimension of perfection. I can tell you, it is the least conscious of all the models to actually make. It requires the least amount of attention, imagination and diversity of interesting movements. It is really boring to make, even if it is fascinating in a way as in regards to its controlled qualities and evenness—even what if it is perceived as "peaceful" by many. I get that sense too, somewhat. It is not like I don't feel that. There's a certain 'beauty' even to A-ness.[260] But, I'm too aware of my process of making it, and as an artist, I would never want to make that too much. It deadens my consciousness actually. It numbs me. I feel aesthetically emptied.

But D-ness is the exact—and quantum leap away—as an opposite—for it truly enlivens me, makes me feel soulful and human—and authentic. And sure, it is more vulnerable in some sense. Life is vulnerable. Death is not. A-ness makes me feel like a shallow shell of a being—and, thus inauthentic or false. It's depressing to me. Robert Pirsig wrote of the ethics of modern technology and industrialism that goes too far as the techno-imperative we're all supposed to follow like keeping up with styles, and embrace and purchase them, identify with them, and become just like it's ideology would like us—as machines ourselves: "It's the style that gets you; technological ugliness syruped over with romantic phoniness in an effort to produce beauty and profit by people who, though stylish, don't know where to start because no one has ever told them there's such a thing as Quality in this world and it's real, not style. Quality isn't something you lay on top of subjects and objects like tinsel on a Christmas tree. Real Quality must be the source of the subjects and objects, the cone from which the tree must start. To arrive at this Quality requires a somewhat different procedure [paradigm beyond]...dualistic technology [mania]."[261]

A-ness is many things, but I also don't want to forget that it's a valid strategy for patterning an existence—yet, it's a false sense of security—it is a prison really, a retreat from intimacy and connection—at least, that is what I and Pirsig and others argue, from the larger perspective of an evolutionary theoretical viewpoint. It is a *failure* in terms of *fear management* for the living. Ghosts may like to live there in the "pure" monocultured isolation and slickness in A-ness but that's about all. It's an existence in a cold, bloodless, sterile quarantine, is how I see it subjectively. And the same applies in how my theory and transpersonal identity and intelligence depicts it objectively.[262] A-ness will lead to all species going extinct if it is allowed to continue to spread. Maybe Artificial Intelligence will ultimately prefer A-ness. But, it is a dis-ease, a pathology, and disease[263] on the ontological and epistemological dimensions of Living/Being. A-ness is the dream of a totally objective, meaning totally abstract, virtual ever-lasting immortal and stable 'world.' Albeit, a world *without humans* and/or other Life, without Quality, that's for sure. How can we avoid the "technological thinking" that got us in this mess and the "technological eclipse of education"[264] that has infiltrated our modern schooling etc.?

I want people to see that qualitative *aesthetic truth*, if they can. Yet, I cannot force people to see what they can't, and/or don't want to see or feel. Lao Tse said: "If I keep from preaching at people, they improve themselves. If I keep from imposing on people, they become themselves." I think there's some wisdom in that for sure, though, I'm not convinced totally the world today and people in it can so easily "become themselves." Anyways, you are right Maria, subjectively, people by vast majority are interpreting things and my diagrams in certain ways. They typically don't perceive Quality like I do or Pirsig. That in mind, as a researcher-artist-educator, at least, I merely want to map their patterns of perceptions, and then encourage us to stand back with some equanimity—and then, look at the results of our dominant worldviews coded on this aesthetic dimension...aesthetic inquiry....

BMK: Having maps is important for an expansive perspective. But Michael, you haven't mentioned the most interesting part of your set of questions, once we get past the Beauty, Life and Order aspects; for then there is the fearological questions you added to the survey later. Like #12, *Which has the most fear in it?* and, its comple-mentary question, #13, *Which is the most fearless?*

RMF: Right. This makes people's perceptions and responses really intriguing. I was shocked a bit by what I found in the hundreds of people that have answered these questions #12 and 13. Overall 50% pick D-ness as most fear in it, and 50% pick A-ness as most fear in it. Hardly anyone picks B or C. That tells me the extreme patterns are registering most strongly for participants but at the same time they are split down the middle on average. So, to generalize from that, the implications are quite astounding I think. Why is there this division in the answers? Doesn't this show that human beings are confused about what *fear* really is—that is, at the aesthetic level of interpretation?

I think it does show that *fear* is not so easy to detect for at least half of the population. From all my research, it is obvious that A-ness is fear-based to the extreme and B-ness is not far behind. Once you cross over to the Organic models then you get more diversity in the pattern and that means you have more open-ness and flexibility and creativity. You have a richer Quality as well. A-ness represents the shutting out of diversity—a type of self-imposed homogenization, a monoculture closed-system. It has no room to grow, unless the boundaries burst at some point. You really can't have any intimacy between to A's that come together. I think you get the metaphor.

So, why do 50% of the population on average not see A-ness as having the most fear? That's a huge number of people, and it may very well reflect the actual divide of cultural political factions and parties that more or less are called Left and Right wing. It's a hypothesis one cannot ignore. The different, extreme, ways of detecting fear itself as a pattern may well be what divides the political world in half. I think that's worth a whole lot more research, at least. But beyond that, as a fearologist I have to ask why that other 50%, whom I would say are totally 'wrong' about their opinion regarding #12 question, they choose D-ness as the most fear in it.

BMK: I think, in terms of Erich Fromm's findings, the bias your test is recording is that 50% or more of the population in general is operating in "fear of freedom," which Fromm suggested is not in our best interests, yet, we keep this insidious, largely invisible, fear patterning going?

RMF: I concur, and yet, to be specific to this inquiry of Part II re: aesthetic dimensions, it suggests that 50+% of the population is repulsed aesthetically by freedom. I remember a grade 2 class, of 6-7 year old children, of some 15 so-called "slow learners" in a rural school in my area, whom I asked the first 10 questions to the survey as they looked at A-D diagram. It floored me that 100% of them, independently, chose D-ness as Most Ugly for #4 question. I've seen this similarly quite high in other groups too. But not when I ask artists or theologians or ecological-types, no, they all see A-ness pretty much as Most Ugly. Aesthetically, we are in the primal system of judgements of value, and of representation of worldviews that people hold. That is, if you are against D-ness in this survey, the theory says, at the gut level, they are against freedom; and, in resistance to freedom at their own and the collective level to some degree. It could be a tribal or community trait to have this bias. It could be a whole culture that has this bias. From my theory and intuition, it is a kind of *defense mechanism* against Life and Health. It's a self-abusive trait-pattern deep in the 'gut' of the aesthetic dimension of discernment and conditioning. That is, such a choice is unconscious for the most part. It also has to have been rewarded in various ways by the social sphere. That is why at times recently I have insisted that people and critics who read and interpret my work do not assume they can understand it unless they foreground, as I do, that "fear is social."[265] Anyways, such a biased view of Ugliness against D-ness diminishes Quality as valuable and as an aim for human potential. I can't think of anything more concerning for our species than this data being shown by the A-D-ness problematic—at the aesthetic level.

BMK: Lastly, I would like to say that your A/D-ness exercise has rolled out a framework to study and analyse the aesthetics of fear-fearlessness dualism. It is also important in the sense that a theory like this is required to explain the state of human condition from a fearlessness perspective. Darwin's evolutionary principles were based on biological/environmental factors. Marxian view of social evolution was founded on the premises of inherent conflicts in the society and cyclical struggles between the oppressive and oppressed classes. Physicists' efforts to unravel the mysteries of cosmological evolution are a never ending activity. Hence your aesthetic model will help, *inter alia*, explain the evolutionary conditions of any civilisation be it Sumerian, Indus or Egyptian; from the disorder-order, ugliness-beauty and fear-fearlessness lenses.

****

Appendix 1

Appendix 1 Soliciting Questions for the A/D-ness Survey

Originating from a thought experiment in the mid-1980s, the following first 10 questions were derived from the A/D-ness diagrams (Figure 4). Note: Anyone using the A/D-ness diagrams is free to utilize their own set of questions; there's no fixed necessity to use any of Fisher's questions. The following is the latest version of description for the participant to read before the questions *per se*.

Multiple-choice Questions in Regard to the Diagram

Answer each question fairly quickly but accurately, without changing your answer (opinion) once your write it down. Choose only <u>one answer</u> for <u>each question</u> (that is, either A or B or C or D). You may repeat using any of the four choices as much as you like for the set of 16 questions. You may flip back to look at the Diagram as much as you like in order to answer each question. Total time for this should not take more than 2-3 minutes.

Use the letter "X" for each of your answers:

1. Which is the normal way of drawing and coloring?
2. Which is the best?
3. Which is the most beautiful?
4. Which is the most ugly?
5. Which is the most natural, living, alive?
6. Which is the most dead, and machine-like?
7. Which is the most difficult to do?
8. Which is most like you, your personality?
9. Which is the most like your parents/caregivers?
10. Which is the most artistic and creative?
11. Which is the most healthy?
12. Which has the most fear in it?
13. Which is the most fearless?
14. Which is the most like God, Spirit or Creation?
15. Which is most like the community you live in?
16. Which is the most violent?

****

Participants, ideally, answer these without any prior knowledge of Fisher's work or theories but rather they are merely answering based on their own knowledge and views. Fisher has developed a relatively simple *scoring* (indexing) system over the years to assess this data. Basically, it involves him answering each question correctly, according to all his research and theories behind the creation and thought experiment of the Diagrams. This assumes there is an objective answer, not merely an opinion involved. The participants score per question is therefore compared relatively against Fisher's answer which is worth 4 points if the participant chooses the same answer. If the participant chooses an answer 1 position away (left or right on the raw score sheet: A ___ B ___ C ___ D ___) from the choice of Fisher's, then they receive 3 points, and if 2 positions away, then 2 points, and if 3 positions away (i.e., at the opposite extreme) they receive 1 point. Note, all questions are considered to be fair to be scored this way, because they are somewhat arbitrary and/or reflect only a totally subjective evaluation by the participant or anyone else. Thus, the following are excluded from the scoring (#1, #8, #9, #15), yet they provide interesting background information that is relevant indirectly to the analysis of the results. If the participant is interested in doing this "test" he will provide an initial detailed report/analysis of several pages connecting the links between questions and comparing the data of the individual with others and/or general groups and the whole population (albeit, all data is always only a sample).

****

CHAPTER FOUR

Fear (The Ugly) Idealized

The beauty of fear: how to positively enjoy being afraid.
-Samuel Nathan Gillian[266]

A new civilization [Third Wave] is emerging in our lives, and blind men [sic] everywhere are trying to suppress it.
-Alvin Toffler[267]

As we said, depth *is* consciousness, and depth goes all the way down. But as depth increases, consciousness shines forth more noticeably [in evolution].
-Ken Wilber[268]

The Huddleston Report (1996) concluded, 'we cannot survive the 21st century with the ethics of the 20th century....[we need] a global ethic'...such an ethic must emerge from a sincere science-religion dialogue...[there's an urgent call] to consider the development/evolution of ourselves, our systems, the world culture...from interior and exterior and individual and collective perspectives.... [it is] advocating for a more 'integral' approach to addressing these ethical concerns....[for a new ethic we must realize] The ethics of [pre-modernism] modernism and postmodernism will not be sufficient to address the ethical issues of the twenty-first century....

-Randy Martin[269]

RMF: Beauty *is* depth; Fearlessness *is* depth. Life *is* depth. Quality *is* depth. Existence *is* depth. Why resist it?

BMK: Because of defense mechanisms?

RMF: Perhaps, that is as good of any explanation. At least, in part—do you recall me saying in the last chapter when I spoke of the prejudice against D-ness: "from my theory and intuition, it is a kind of *defense mechanism* against Life and Health. It's a self-abusive trait-pattern deep in the 'gut' of the aesthetic dimension discernment and conditioning." Throughout the following chapters this thread of concern will surface again and again. We will need to explore the nature of defense mechanisms, so-called by Freud, but we'll investigate deeper and prior to Freud's analysis of defenses. But defenses is a good word for the phenomenon of resistance. But bringing this back to my issue of Life....

BMK: Really, Life *and* Non-Life make up an Existence that is not merely anthropocentric that is—it's not merely human-life-centered in perspective.

RMF: Operating with an intransigent dualism, most people want the Life part of the equation, and *not* the Non-Life part. Go on...

BMK: Exactly. Thus, there needs to be a worldview shift....

RMF: Four Arrows offers a 'corrective' from the Indigenous worldview to this madness within the Dominant worldview of self-destruction going on. He wrote, "...with new awareness, educators must begin *worlding* the Indigenous perspective"[270] and he and I have agreed that is at core a *fearlessnessnizing*. But don't let me interrupt...

BMK: Okay, we need to begin worlding beyond the hyper-inflated ego's need to defend off the entire Universe and the laws of Nature and even the Self—that is, Consciousness in its full spectrum dimensions. Many W. and E. religions tend to exacerbate this with their ideas and projections of a 'soul' and ever-lasting life in a 'heaven' etc. Yet, the human cannot be reduced to only such an ego perspective and its wishes—phantasies— meaning, its needs to immortalize itself as if in an ideological 'bubble.'

RMF: Needs are problematic when they are coming from the wounded and traumatized human condition, a point I have made prior in this book. Yes, you are speaking to the interesting and troublesome dynamic of the Immortality Project,[271] which I have discussed recently, drawing on other theorists as well like Ken Wilber, to analyze and speculate *why* there is a 'Fear' Project(ion) going on in the ontological levels of Being, of which humans have perpetuated. But go on...

BMK: The global perspective and its required ethical evolution is far more encompassing, far more deep[272] in meaning than we normally think of as humans and/ or within religious doctrine and institutions. Without being nihilistic, isn't most of the Universe, literally, black matter, black holes, and nothingness called space?

Life is...really, an infinitesimal speck with origins of near-impossible probability of existing.

RMF: Sure. Existence, in how you are framing it, is incredibly humbling—that is, when you are a living entity of fragility[273]—and, being on a planet that supports life looking out into the infinite Mystery so far beyond comprehension. Surely there are multiple perspectives beyond *only* the human(istic) perspective as to what is True, Good, Beautiful. Integralism, posthumanism and transhumanism are some recent ideological and/or philosophical movements and kosmologies—to help move us beyond our 'normal' self-species and ego-absorbed positions that we are '*the* center' and 'ultimate height of progress' in God's eye, or the Universe and Existence. Yet, I suppose, we humans still have to engage the grand macro-scale somehow, while living a very small humble human life at the same time.

BMK: That's all meaningful to me and you Michael; but I'm not sure it is to most people. Can we start this chapter off with something not so expansive and deep? I'm thinking...so, Michael, if there is *one factor* you think is more powerful than any other in terms of creating *resistance* to Fearlessness advancing—as a Movement of liberation—what would it be?

RMF: Of course Maria, my heart is warmed immediately. That's a wonderfully seductive, albeit, simplifying question. I smile as I hear it. I sense the depth behind its surface words. And I hear also the intimating connectivity of our dialogue, where we both are *in search of* Fearlessness within an aesthetic, to ethical, to political imperative.[274] That is, questioning ongoing in process: how to be a global citizen, and even beyond that, a cosmic....a kosmic[275](?)

BMK: I don't know whether we humans are truly worthy of calling ourselves 'cosmic citizens.' Hollywood has produced many sci-fi films on the themes of aliens, galaxies, star wars etc. While watching these films we tend to imagine that several empires of high-tech aliens are existing around the corner in our galaxy and beyond in the cosmos. But what I suppose is true, is that we the humans, turned aliens to the cosmos.

RMF: You sound like the eco-critic Evernden, who near 40 years ago, challenged the entire Green and environmental movement, and told them that just adopting ecology as a solution would not work because it won't offer the penetrating deeper truth about the causes of our crises on earth. He said "the crisis is essentially a cultural phenomenon, not merely a technical one" and it would require that we face the facts of our development over time of becoming what he labeled "the natural alien."[276]

BMK: I agree. If Marx thought in the 19th century that the working class proletariat was alienated from the product they created, Marx would have certainly amended his theory in the 21st century after witnessing the unending human-made environmental disasters. He would have also quoted that, 'the earth has been alienated from its creation, the *Homo sapiens.*' We no longer accept that we belong to earth and on the contrary, we are falsely proud to declare that earth belongs to us. We know that the way we have been exploiting the earth's resources is dangerously unsustainable. Because of our mindless actions over a period of time, countless species of plant and animal kingdoms have already become extinct. I think that we may qualify as 'cosmic citizens' only if we become loyal, supportive and grateful to earth which is a part of cosmos.

RMF: Yeah, that's great stuff Maria. However, let me return to your simple question; and I will say, I love hearing sincerity in deep questions, and I loathe hearing evasive superficial questions. That's the darker existentialist in me that desires more out of dialogues than what I usually get from average conversations. So, it warms and inspires my being—because in just the asking it, out loud and in public, is already a breath of fresh air. And it co-creates a channeling of critical consciousness and right awareness in the right direction for Fearlessness. Saying it out loud and meaning it is a substantive and consequential *contradiction* to the majoritarianism and conformism of the generic silencing, superficiality and resistance built-in to the programming of the 'Fear' Matrix itself.[277] The culture of fear we are swimming in, as I have argued earlier, is destined by design to try to get us all to stay superficial, if not artificial, and to stay 'shut up' and to 'stop thinking clearly' about fear/fearlessness in any depth and potency.

My premise behind a philosophy of fearlessness is: We are being invasively conditioned continually to default to over-simplification, crude and violent reductionism, and basically flatland thinking[278] with no depth, little criticality; all of which A-ness [Figure 4 in Chapter Three] is the *ideal* template for reproducing this condition. A-ness can be taken as a symbol for my analysis here. And I agree with Lerner & Lerner, who argued in their book on The Rorschach, that "a true symbol functions as an anxiety container"[279] and the sooner we recognize that in any symbol, especially those we idolatrize, then we'll understand the symbolic dimension of fear management much more clearly.

A-ness in today's world, may very well have become, even if invisibly, the universal, if not cosmic, *symbol for fear*—and, yet is disguised to be the universal 'symbol for love'—to put it in other language. It may have taken on the traits for immortality and fearlessness simultaneously because A-ness is apparently, in pattern language, then, *absolutely invulnerable* in its crystalline-geometric like qualities and superficial representation of something but is nothing and is everything. A-ness is a symbol in the way that the heart is the universal symbol for love. A-ness is the underlying *el primo* dynamic of a culture of fear and death-making. A-ness symbolically, and largely unconsciously, you might say, has evolved in Culture overall for millenia to be the 'ideal' supposed solution to suffering. After all, you can easily contemplate A-ness, as so many do, and arrive at a hypothetical but convincing interpretation that "wow, this is a great way to be—no disturbance, only perfection—no fear" etc. I have actually heard several people, and very well educated—male professors, say this about A-ness. I have a short story to tell on this. Yet, to be clear what we are dealing with in A-ness in terms of pedagogy, and that includes child-rearing practices. How do we liberate children and schooling?

My colleague Arie Kizel, professor in the Faculty of Education at Haifa University, I argue, nicely distinguishes A-ness from D-ness in pedagogical language. He works with and is current International President of Philosophy for/with Children [P4wC], as a movement to open minds and nurture critical young philosophers even at the tenderest of ages. He wrote, "P4wC [is/] as a pedagogy of searching."[280] So now look at Figure 4 in the last chapter again. Perfect alignment: *D-ness is a pedagogy of searching*. As an artist making 'D' it was clearly an organizational structure where I had to overcome any excessive anxiety motivating it in order to fulfill some need I may have had, going well back to my childhood, to make a 'perfect rectangle' or a 'best rectangle' that I could, according to some authoritative 'teachers' demand upon me as a student—and, do it as efficiently and predictably as possible, so as to conform to the 'norm' of such a geometric figuration and constructional problem to solve. There's absolutely no real depth of aware consciousness nor searching involved in creating 'A.' It's mostly very mechanical. Arguably, it goes against our human nature as well. It is a coercive and coerce-derived from and process, reproducing an oppressive fear-based Matrix. I'm curious now to call A-ness a defense mechanism *as* fear management. Notice *mechanism* is built-in to the very dominating language we use in W. psychology. As if evolutionary Defense Intelligence, what I call DI, is reducible to merely defense mechanism. That's a big mistake. Anyways...

Back to Kizel...as he contrasts the opposite end of the learning approach: "[re: pedagogy of searching] Based on a pursuit of meaning that facilitates personal development, this fosters self-direction and capability. It thus stands in stark contrast to the 'pedagogy of fear'[281], which makes perpetual demands on the learner, discourages risk taking...". Perfect alignment: *A-ness is a pedagogy of fear*. Kizel, like Four Arrows,[282] interestingly challenges the whole dominant kinds of pedagogy that are authority-dependent, if not ideologically colonizing and authoritarianism. He concludes re: the pedagogy of fear, that it "diminishes competence, and creates the constant need for an omniscient 'guide.'"[283] There's the "need" component we have to be cautious about and discerning. The need can be part of an addiction and trace-based hypnotic phenomenon, where the human/agent isn't fully functioning in their brightest intelligence, but is operating in the paradigm of a pedagogy of fear as if it was 'normal.' That's the real danger of so-called "Education." I think, like Kizel and Four Arrows and others, that there is a serious systematic pathology of "psychotic" and/or "near-psychotic" processes going on that disguises itself under so-called rational functionalism with its technician-sounding or clinical-sounding philosophies of "Education." We're losing touch, as are many educators and policy-makers and leaders—with baselines of traditional definitions of "sanity" itself.[284] No wonder Kizel and Gur-Zé ev have called for the international movement of "counter-education."[285] This is like a call for a resistance to resistance. The pedagogy of fear is a resistance to liberation and liberation *via* counter-education or *pedagogy of fearlessness* as I have called it,[286] is a resistance as well—with the latter specifically motivated to counter the insidious 'Fear' Project. Resistances to Fearlessness, as you can imagine then, get very subtle and difficult to discern without a lot of study and research. We have to learn to critically discriminate *resistances* that are motivated by fear-based structures, like the pedagogy of fear that Kizel speaks of, and *resistances* that are motivated by a love-based and/or fearlessness structures and systems/ paradigms. Little of that discernment, or the radical theorizing of it is going on from what I can tell over the last 30+ years. We have a lot of homework to do. Remember: In Search of Fearlessness Project is a counter-education to the Fear Project—to put it in basic terms. And, how we conceptualize "fear" and 'fear' is crucial to the success of any emancipatory counter-education and right resistance. I think this whole re-evaluation we're presenting in this book really rests around Philosophy—see Part IV. Kizel, interestingly enough has argued that the source of the pedagogy of fear is actually constituted in the dynamics of the social and pedagogical sphere where there is a perpetuating psychology, if not ideology, that he labels "fear of philosophy"[287] itself—and, especially, he argues that adults/teachers/authorities really fear teaching philosophy to children at a young age.

BMK: Yes Michael! It is good that we are discussing about fear of philosophy and of teaching it to children. I too have had thoughts along these lines. Sometime back, I drafted an outline to write a children's book on various philosophical concepts, which is not yet complete. I felt it would be in the right direction to educate and shape tender minds for a 'good life.' Time-tested ethics, morals, values, logic and humanistic ideals of modernism would help them not go astray in their formative years under the influence of contemporary cut-throat competitiveness and an insensitive materialistic world. I agree with Kizel's argument and would like to remind us that his very endeavour of teaching philosophy positioned Socrates to face the charges of 'corrupting the young.'

RMF: Okay, now back to A-ness in terms of aesthetic research revelations; here's one of them. I'm remembering what one mathematician and Artificial Intelligence professor, I'm paraphrasing from memory, said about A-ness, paraphrasing from memory: "This is the Beauty of Geometry and Math—that is, the mathematical equation for precision of which the entire universe is made—it's simply Divine."

I thought in my mind, albeit, without sharing it with him in the moment: "That is surely your phantasy of a life without pain, hurts, suffering, losses, messiness. This is your symbol of the Absolute 'nondual' world without real human existence." I couldn't believe, at some level, how this man was seeing A-ness so differently than I was. Yet, it has a certain predictable theme I had seen before in others and in some writings. Maybe, it was his preferred ideal ethic summarized in one visual image.

He truly had faith in A-ness as "the way." I certainly, had no such faith in that way or his way. D-ness was "the way" in my ideal ethic. But maybe I was, and still am, too attached, as the Buddhists say, to Life and to ecological sustainability and sanity on this beautiful planet earth. Maybe, I was not then, and still cannot now, fully detach from worldly existence and ethical concerns under my nose and feet. Maybe this guy was way more spiritual than I was and am now. I wonder.

I guess I'm passionately ranting....but to say it in a nutshell: this guy, representing many others, and I mean modern city-dwellers on this planet,[288] had *no interest* in my proposed Fearlessness Project when I talked about it. And even though he agreed the Fear Problem was horrible on this planet and our likely source of species-cide demise, sooner than later, he was so completely and apparently detached into his idyllic A-ness mental-values set. It was as if he was living on another planet—in another world reality. I thought it was so abstract and mechanical—a defense mechanism he had adapted early in his life to protect his ego/psyche or protect someone else. He showed no emotional attributes of connection with me, certainly not spontaneously, and he had no curiosity for, or encouragement for, the drives of such a Fearlessness Project. It was like he was a robot or more accurately, he was trying to be one. He saw himself, with great pride, as a "spiritual" person, he told me explicitly at one point.

As we slowly walked and talked on this beautiful fall day amongst the yellow and orange leaves on the ground, I was picking up the whole time that he was *resisting* something—and, quite likely *dissociating* from anything that would appear to be a human connection and/or commitment to anything that was about fearlessness as vulnerability and fragility. He liked his courageous life-positive outlook. However, he didn't choose D-ness as a positive attribute for any question on the A-D/ness survey. Even the question #5 "Which is the most natural, living, alive?," he chose 'A' for his answer. And for question #14 "Which is most like God, Spirit, or Creation?," he chose 'A' again for his answer. He was, if not accurate, he had a high-score on validity of consistency. He 'knew' himself quite well, in that sense. I wondered if this was the x-ray of his personality, below the surface of his human functioning? I wondered if even his wife knew of this? Perhaps not. Her results on the A-D/ness survey were quite the opposite extreme of him. She was a social worker and professor in the Humanities, interestingly enough. Quite the couple.

I've learned for decades that resistance comes in many, sometimes surprising, forms. Idealism *via* ideologism, *via* dissociation, may be one of the nastiest forms of subtle violence of all. I theorize that it lies latent and can manifest at any moment, even from this very 'nice person,' upper middleclass successful citizen, whom he really was, as observed—because I was with him sharing a dinner and as I spent time with his wife and son. But something was 'off' and "cold" for me the whole time we walked and talked. Was he a cyborg—because he had been so long into AI and mathematical idealist reality as his hobby and profession since he was kid? Oh, there I go again, ranting....

Overall, my *sociological* critical analysis here is not isolated to only me thinking this, by the way. I know my thinking about these Projects operating on the planet, can sound a lot like a wild conspiracy theory. Well, recently I have argued it is a type of conspiracy theory to advance the Fearlessness Project or paradigm when the dominating Fear Project or paradigm is already in-charge in running the kingdom[289] best called "Fear's Empire."[290] If I call out reality on the table and say "yes, we live in an oppressive society" and I mean "we" all live in it, then that can be construed by the majority as a conspiracy theory. Now, once labeled, it is easy to reject someone uttering such things as a nut-case kook. Rejection is a powerful tool to keep away diverse ideas and discourses from existence in the public sphere. Even a family system can exclude difference of opinions.

Anyways, In the old days, uttering differences and uncomfortable thoughts to the majority was simply called a critical social theory or a conflict theory.[291] It has many names but I have noticed how more and more the majority want nothing to do with this kind of theory. The majority and I even mean liberals, and their addiction to positivism these days, as the privileged in other words who most benefit from the oppressive system, want to and *need to* frame the conflict theorists like me as conspiracy theorists. There are many of us in that abject category—exiled—and often we are categorized as not just rebels or revolutionaries, with dignity as "freedom fighters" in our fight against oppression, but as "terrorists" drugged-up supposedly on toxic radicalized ideologies that have put us in a stupor. Once labeled a terrorist by the authorities then you can be killed without a second thought. That killing is also metaphorical, as in my case. Look, I'm not saying some are not pathological rebels indoctrinated by radicalization forces of maniacs pushing fascism, totalitarianism and fundamentalism But, most people don't want to make finer distinctions. Okay, back to your question.

BMK: I think there's a big difference with radicals who are coming from a *fear-based* framing of reality and those that are not. Isn't that your point?

RMF: Right. It's an ethical point too, not just political. As my colleague Four Arrows' says, and he is often accused of being a conspiracy theorist because he is fighting for Indigenous rights and truths to be heard and lies, stereotypes and false myths constructed by the colonizers to be exposed and torn down: "there are good conspiracy theories and there are bad ones."

I have many factors in a long list—but sure let me pick one in the moment here. It is the *need to be liked*. And, let me clarify this, so as to not just sound banal and reproduce the shallow thought about human needs that is so common in psychology and popular culture today. When I use *need*, in this context, I am talking about the psychological need for sure, but not just psychological—also philosophical. Our whole book has been an explication of attempting to sort out that difference, yet appreciate their overlapping interplay. We've worked hard as co-authors not to fall into psychologism around the topic of fear/fearlessness.

That said, however, the psychological explanations for fearlessness and resistances to it are the easiest and concrete and literal for most people to sort of grasp on to. Yet, it gets way more complex and complicated when we take the conversation to alternative levels such as the communal, historical, ideological and political levels—that is, the systems, sociological and anthropological explanations. We are then dealing with our sense of 'self-identity' not merely as a psychological individual or personality but we are layering in on top of that, or underneath that, the entire sense of being a *social species* and social-identity-actor constructed within regimes of power like within a tribe, organization, city, society, culture, government, nation and so on. Then on top of that, or underneath that, is the philosophical, spiritual and theological dimension of explanation we touch on. For example, worldview and kosmology,[292] and the issue of the very ways we organize/design and enact pattern language and knowledge architectures, on many levels of our being human or transhuman on this planet.

The basic way of noticing multiple perspectives, that you and I have been calling forth continually in this book to solve the problem of resistances to fearlessness—by about this time reading this dialogue now most people are already tuning out. I have seen this experientially so often. The 99.99% of people *only* want to talk about fear and fearlessness *only* if I stay talking to them in their comfort zone of discourse. And, staying with modern humans, I have learned over the decades, they want to—and, they *need* to—stay in the one perspective, that is, the psychological individual realm of the 'I'-perspective. They'll maybe sometimes touch a little on the 'We'-perspective but that typically stays in social psychology discourse; and they nearly never go into or show curiosity for the 'It'-perspective. Well, methodologically and epistemologically that's a huge problem. One perspective is going to distort Reality immediately. In other words, their *need* to talk about the topic only in this psychological reductionistic way is a major block to an expansive holistic-integral meta-perspective. Understanding fear and fearlessness is heavily compromised.

BMK: They *need* to keep things simple. I like simple and practical explanations but I don't want *only* simple and practical either. I mean 'simple and practical' in the sense that most of the people's needs are limited due to lack of understanding. For example, an illiterate, ignorant and exploited person of marginalised group in India is like a frog in the well. For them, the well is their universe. They don't know what exists outside the well. Their needs are very few. And each need pretty much has its roots in a fear paradigm. 'Need' is existence based like Maslow's basic needs. But 'want' is essence-oriented as Sartre described. Suppose I need a job to survive and once I got the job, my need vanishes. But 'want' is bigger in scope than 'need'. Say, I want a better job to prove my potential. 'Want' drives me to move forward for exploration so that I may become what I 'want' to be. It means that 'want' thrives in fearlessness. On the other hand, 'need' is restricted in its domain of fear as far as its choices are concerned. But 'want' is the urge to be free. 'Need' has got no such sort of freedom.

RMF: Exactly. That latter trait of your expansive want and interest is what keeps you and I in an ongoing and growth-full intellectual relationship. Otherwise, our relationship would have died long ago because of going stale. We may have still stayed in contact and been 'friends' but we would have stayed in your "need" to keep things simple and practical—only—IF that was in fact your only *modus operandi*. Turns out, it's not.

BMK: Yes Michael! I agree. Tunnel vision is always constricted. That's why it has been said that there should be a 360 degree approach to realise holistic outcomes. Going by this postulate, the three factor model of 'I, We and It' also seems insufficient to solve the fear-fearlessness problem. From 'I' perspective, a person may be able to conduct himself relatively fearlessly from his viewpoint only but not from others'—that is, from 'We' perspective. The American psychologist Solomon Asch found in his social group experiment that an individual agrees with his group's opinion because he is afraid of being ridiculed by the members of the group if he doesn't do so. Thirdly, an individual's fearlessness approach may get compromised if they don't take into consideration, say for example, the government's policy ('It' perspective) on the issue of freedom of speech. Apart from these three perspectives, there is one more aspect that we may require to make the model fully integral. We may call it as the 'X' perspective. It refers to fears occurring out of the blue and the Coronavirus is an example. It appeared out of nowhere when the world had been blissfully oblivious to it. In the middle of the year 2020, a football-sized asteroid passed close to earth and it would have been a sort of nuclear explosion if it had hit the earth. Unless such 'X' perspective is dealt with by requisite fear management education systems, fearlessness movement will continue to face resistances.

RMF: Above we mention *want* and then jump to *need* virtually interchangeably. I suggest to fine-tune that. Wants are a step-up in possibilities beyond needs. If we accept that conceptually, then let me bore down on what this major blocking factor is—the *need to be liked*. It is more than want to be liked. There is nothing wrong with wanting to be first noticed in the social grouping—that's built-in to our very social animal and mammal behavioral repertoire. That kind of liked-ness as with being appreciated by another, especially of significance, is fundamental to healthy existence and it will help turn down the dial of social distress that goes with living in a crowd. We are vulnerable to this social acceptance because when it turns bad and we are socially rejected, the many studies show us how devastating it is to social organisms as complicated and sensitive as humans.

So wanting to be accepted is a good thing. Needing to be accepted is evolutionary, it is not an individual psychological need, it is a species need, so again, that's a good thing. But, the turn of distinction is the *individual need* at the problematic level of which I am referring to when I claimed the major factor of resistance to Fearlessness advancing in society today—that is, the *need to be liked*. My argument, shortening it here for brevity, is that Fearlessness is the natural want of our species and all living things. Resistance to Fearlessness is then anti-life, anti-social and anti-human. It is *deadly* in other words. Yet, resistance to fearlessness is very real and rampant, and my argument revolves around how this came about due to the origination of a culture of fear dynamic many thousands of years ago—it's essentially a cultural phenomenon not essentially a natural phenomenon.[293] If we accept that, then my point is taken that any *need to be liked* that is narcissistic and culturally and artificially hypertrophied—as in the way popular culture today is obsessed with being "liked" on social media, as one example. Then, you know we are now into pathological need to be liked. And, even before digital culture and social media, I'm arguing, the template for unhealthy needs was well constructed by predatory capitalism. That's another story. Point being, in the last many generations the chronic need to conform to social acceptance regimes is deadly and potent. Youth know this more than any perhaps, but all of us have huge social expectations to conform and 'be good' and 'be nice' and so on. Which boil down to 'be liked' or you are a 'loser.' It's black or white.

So, here's the one factor issue, based on your question Maria: If one person or even a few decide to promote Fearlessness as the big revolutionary project, or even the small fearlessness as a personal, educational and social goal, then guess what? You will be heavily rejected by the vast majority of your family, friends, colleagues, and society at large. The Fear Paradigm, as I've argued and my research confirms many bases for such a paradigm operating, as fear-based, is not going to 'let you go' that easily off on your Fearlessness Paradigm adventure—and, the heroics of it. That is, unless the Fear Paradigm as the 'norm' can *appropriate* your idea and imaginary of "fearless" or "fearlessness" and *market it* within the mainstream so that it is *not* so threateningly different. In other words, as I have written about often "fearlessness" is branded all of a sudden, starting around the late-1980s and especially in the 1990s—and, thus it is watered down.[294] Use of the word "fearless" in popular and normal speech now-a-days is so so so...far away from what my view of Fearless is as a FMS-9 system of Defense Intelligence in evolution. I think you get the drift of my concern.

Needing to be liked is what I see quickly keeps most all people away from any consistent and disciplined authentic path of fearlessness with depth. People can't typically stay committed to a new diet they want, never mind stay committed to their freedom—if you recall Erich Fromm's findings on the problem of "fear of freedom." You and I as co-authors have brought forth in this book the "fear of fearlessness" factor and yes, I'm merely giving you another angle on that. It is bottom line the social fear—the *fear of not being liked*—that is, the *need to be liked*—which is the great wounding of people of all kinds. Until that wound is healed, and that's a lot of work and commitment, then Fearlessness or fearlessness doesn't have much of a chance of taking off into any popularity, at least not in the near future.

Just to tie this in with Part II and discussion of Beauty and aesthetics, I think a good case could be made that the wounded need to be liked is often manifested, certainly in the modern W. culture and media, as the *need to be beautiful*. Beautiful people are liked. It's a basic popular, and real, premise—isn't it? And, that need really distorts things. On my A-D/ness test in Chapter Three, at least 65% or more of the populations surveyed most like B-ness as most Beautiful. That's a Mechanical model, let's keep in mind. Is that really where the Beautiful resides mostly? I don't think so but that's what the people chose, want—and, need to have beauty located there aesthetically—but, it goes much deeper than that, it is philosophically poignant to indicate how people's mind/body/values are construed by contemporary society. Hey, I also want to link this and talk more about A-ness again, as the 'Normal' way of coloring/drawing a rectangular shape...but I also first want to hear what you think about my one factor explanation.

BMK: Choosing one as the *most beautiful* out of the four of A/D-ness is like electing X or Y or Z in a democracy. Due to natural individual differences, we cannot generalise likes or dislikes for the whole lot. One man's meat is another man's poison. Moreover, post-truth and fake news have come to influence public perception in unexpected ways. Every individual's ideation is contingent not only upon cultural background but also on exposure to the ideals of contemporary worldview, humanism, modernism, enlightenment etc.

RMF: Individual differences are certainly valid, I guess I'm not only satisfied with that as a way to organize a society, we also have to look to deeper universals. So, I'd like to move on from the one factor explanation now and return to the aesthetic dimension specifically. Well, in talking to just a few random samples of participants about this, the ones who chose D-ness said things like, "it's chaotic" "it scares me," and so on. Notice, those responses come from people who like a lot of order and strong boundaries or walls. They also interpreted the question quite differently than I asked it. I asked "most fear in it"—meaning, which is most fear-based by design. But these people took it personally and chose the image that brought up the most fear in them personally. A-ness doesn't typically have such an affective impact on people in terms of making them feel afraid of it. It certainly doesn't have that effect on me. But because I have studied what is behind A-ness philosophically and otherwise, indeed, A-ness, for me, is chilling and to have to live in that worldview would be a nightmare of terror—yet for a significant number it is a utopia.[295] But the actual physical drawing/coloring and aesthetic doesn't bring that up for hardly anyone. D-ness however, is evocative physically and yes, it turns out 50+% of the population abhor it. Nearly equally, in less % overall, a large portion of my overall sample pick D-ness as negative, for example, as *most ugly* as in #4 and *most violent* as in #16. On the last question, it really surprised me over and over how many, anywhere from 80 to 100% of a sub-group, and even very well educated people, chose D-ness as the most violent. Wow. That has huge implications even beyond question #12 but of course they are no doubt related. I simply cannot go into more theorizing and speculating here in this chapter on this test and these most provocative results.

BMK: But before we leave this discussion, what are the results for #13, which is the *most fearless*—that is, *most like fearlessness*? Now, this is surely, very relevant as well to our book.

RMF: I don't have all that data compiled and at my fingertips, but basically as I recall, only approximately 30% on average chose D-ness. By contradistinction, all my research and experience tells me that for sure D-ness is the most fearless, the most like fearlessness and the furthest way from A-ness.

The Fearlessness Paradigm I have been talking about for decades and earlier in this book *looks like D-ness*. That's the simplest way I can say it. And, obviously there is a lot of disagreement on that issue; and yes, a lot of resistance to D-ness on many dimensions of the human experience. I have noticed the puzzlement in several participants when they confront their choices overall on this A-D/ness survey in contrast to how they see themselves and even their understanding of Love.[296] Some want to argue with me and say, D-ness is most like love. Too bad I never asked that question in the survey from the beginning. Btw, for clarity sake, I'm not saying that resistance to D-ness is *all* horrible—I am saying it is *telling*. We have to learn from it, so in that sense, it is not all bad.

But let's not forget that the human experience, and the choices they are making on this test, are also *fear-conditioned* for the most part. I think fear-conditioning, unconscious hypnosis in other words, due to fear in an exaggerative and power-dominating form, is bad. I'm clear on that. Look, we live in a culture of fear, which although it has its own surfaces of chaos and violence, injustices, the hidden design of it is what is called a pervasive "security culture"[297]—it's not *all* horrible, but is horrible nonetheless. Oppression cannot be justified in any way as a social system.

And this culture of fear dynamic, especially, this took off and dominated politics and the Cultural sphere around the world right after the attack of 9/11, 2001 on American soil. Military culture is another word for this phenomenon of reaction to 9/11 but it was also already there in the Empire's and their State structures and societies. How else, as citizens of this kind of pathological patriarchal culture, could we not be embedded in this bias against D-ness? Which, I've attempted to show here in this discussion and the A-D/ness survey, is a bias against Fearlessness. It's a kind of "obligatory resistance to insight"[298] you could say, as some have argued that change and insight is hard won, it is resisted even in the hardware of our genes/brain etc. It is also part of the architecture of fear of our sociality. I'm saying, maybe D-ness is just too much insight to carry for the average human being? Or, is it too much to carry when the whole culture of fear is asking you to not carry it? But drop it. Forget about D-ness. The denial and amnesia is quite real, I'd say. We've forgotten, as *Philosophia* responded to the ancient philosopher Botheus, 'you've forgotten who you really are'—and, that's because of distress/fear patterning.

But Maria, there is one more type of resistance to fearlessness that's related to what we have been discussing in this chapter. For example, via *fear-positivism* dis-courses.[299] On many occasions I've gone after the philosophies behind the growing popularizing movement to make fear positive.[300] There's even people trying to make fear beautiful.[301] I'm not against exploring these notions. I think they have problems. But I'll not overtly repeat the critique I've made here. A good case study however has arisen, which I'd like to draw some attention to as in contemporary arguments in Christian thought, and beyond that, as well as in moral education imperatives, and especially in COVID times.

Again, I raise this because I see this fear-positivism as, in part, an implicit resistance to fearlessness—and, that is often buried in such philosophies—but at times it's rather aggressively resistant. Side-tracking back nearly 15 years ago, I contacted this quite famous American Christian theologian, who wrote an eye-catching book *Following Jesus in a Culture of Fear*. I tried to create a dialogue with him around his theology/philosophy of fear. I thought we could share interesting tensions and potential creative outputs from our engagement. In particular, I had done a critique in my letter to him around his framing of his Chapter Three "Why Fearlessness is a Bad Idea."[302] Well, he didn't want to talk to me. That is just one example of someone theorizing around fear, making it positive in terms of the "fear of God" commandment in some religions, and the critique of the culture of fear at the same time, which this theologian also had and I agree with him on it. Yet, this need to make fear positive? Is it is need? Or is it part of Reality? I certainly see people in droves defending Fear all the time. Even the fearists tend to do this, much to my dismay. However, the case I am bringing forth is a really new and interesting branch of the fear-positivism movement.

It starts with the erudite article by two progressive educators, one of whom I have known for many years and we've had a good relationship. The lead author is unknown to me and is making a strong ethical case for the nature and role of fear in the specific area of caring, and compassion, in regards to suffering. They wrote, "...Levinas conceptualizes the [ideal] ethical subject as fearful rather than fearless."[303] They make the case that Martin Heidegger and Immanuel Levinas provide a different reading on "fear," and that the latter is relationally-based. This interests them as co-authors in terms of how well or not well the field of Education and schooling in general are dealing with the fear their students have, especially in light of the pandemic.

They construct an argument that suggests schools in particular have not always helped the situation around

COVID-19 pandemic. Too often, they argue, schools, and society today, are constructing narratives of meaning that ignore and/or dismiss how okay it is for students to have fear. Rather, the tendency is to try to be positive and get children and youth to be brave and hopeful. Thus, fear is frowned upon in certain discourse circles during the pandemic.

Yet, with the pandemic people they know may be sick and/or dying; as well, they are very aware they could lose anyone through the disease. It is important they argue, based primarily on Levinas's philosophy of ethics, that humans ought to be about to feel "fear for the other"—as distinct from "fear of the other." It is the former acknowledgement and validation that is key here. They write, "Understanding fear is a task deeply tied into question[s] regarding what it means to be a human for education. We believe that human beings, in the deepest sense, *even in fear*, can care about other people" and even act upon the motivational energy of that fear for others to enhance compassion. They note, and quote my work and literature research in 2001, regarding how too many people in schooling circles are trying to create an environment of education "without fear" and/or "fear-free schools" etc. This tends, Yan and Slattery argue, to build a default discourse against fear and rather, one for being fearless. They believe, this is primarily wrong-headed. To create space for fear of the other is their higher ideal for caring, *not* fearless or fearlessness. In that sense, their work, and a growing body of others' work,[304] contradicts my fundamental aims of the Fearlessness Project in the field of Education and beyond.

BMK: Yes Michael! Contradictions are bound to be there in the process of progress in such circumstances. Dissent contributes to the sense of purpose and the differing contributions can refine the fearless, caring and benevolent approach to the cause of humanity. As it has been said that there are more than a hundred ways to prove Pythagorean theorem, we now have got many vaccines during the pandemic, each of which is based on different technology. Yet all of them are capable of boosting immunity against the viral attack with different efficacies. Likewise, different approaches based on fear or fearlessness do contradict each other especially when they have dualistic dimensions.

The Problem of Appearance(s)

Ultimately, any investigation into *why* has Fearlessness not been taken up in the contemporary world, despite a lot of rhetoric, slogans, trends, etc. that 'look like' they are promoting bravery, courage, and fearless, is aesthetically a confrontation with what is perceived by the public and its power-institutions as 'beautiful' and 'ugly.' Now, it certainly isn't part of mainstream discourse or government operations to be going about their daily aims to ask: *Should we go this way on such a policy and action plan, or should we go this way—because such and such is 'beautiful' or 'ugly'?* No, that binary differential selectivity reference point may not be what appears in their discourses. More likely and functionally, they are using a binary criteria related to aesthetics, but less raw in exposure, like: *Should we go this way or that way...is it going to be popular or not with the masses, the voters, our funders, constituents and stakeholders (or shareholders)?*

Popularity, is over-taking Quality in the modern and postmodern trends. It is more important to create an image and appearances that you are 'good' and 'true' (trustworthy) and 'beautiful' than actually being/living the good, the true and the beautiful. Philosophy of aesthetics is really at issue here in Chapter Three and Four yet, no one typically in the everyday world of actions and institutions and policies is thinking philosophy of aesthetics (e.g., A-ness vs. D-ness)—they are rather looking only on the surfaces of appearances of things in order to get their way, to win, to make profits, or whatever their ideological interests. Sometimes, unfortunately, the whole of systems of organizations can operate on the binary of *feelings* at the motivational base. In other words, *whether they are going to feel good or feel bad,* can have an enormous impact on the rather unaware dimensions of decision-making. As co-authors and as people, who have worked with many institutions and organizations, it is so obvious to us how people are not very rational in making most of their binary decisions of which way to go.

If you as reader are not so convinced as we are about this irrational dimension to human actions, including the arational dimensions, and their predominance for the most part, then just think about this fact that has been well researched: *People choose the way that is less painful. People choose the way that requires the least effort and least amount of change. People choose by habit and repeat those choices because it conforms to 'that's the way we've always done it.'* On top of that is what psychologists call "cognitive confirmation"—as a process of looking only seriously at information in the world that already is going to confirm what one already believes.

As innovators, both of us have tried many interventions in systems and have experienced the resistance to change. And the more radical the paradigm shift being called for, the more deeply the system, from individuals to the collective, dig their heels into the ground and resist it. They will even attack it. Fisher became aware of this force of resistance very early on with his founding of the In Search of Fearlessness Research Institute. Eventually, nearly overwhelmed with resistance he faced in promoting this new paradigm institute and its values, that he wrote a paper in 1997 "Defining the 'Enemy' of Fearlessness," by which he defined several enemies.[305]

What those enemies consisted of in details can be read about and studied in his work, but the larger point for interest in ending Chapter Four on resistances to Fearlessness, is what probably is best described in a simple story Fisher tells of his experience with the whole world, the whole knowledge industry, called "higher education." This is the world of colleges, technical training institutes and universities. It is his experiences in higher education (1972-2003), of which he spent 12 years and achieved six degrees within and taught off-and-on within, that have taught him the potency of *resistance to change*—meaning, especially, the *resistance to difference*, diversity, and transformational change.

His story below depicts how and why A-ness as ugliness does and will continue to out-compete D-ness for domination and access in higher education. And, that has major consequences in the direction of where our societies evolve—that is, what 'roads' they take and don't take because of their binary ways of making mission statements, designing plans and carrying out strategies and actual decisions. His higher education story starts with an imaginary dialogue and comparison of another leader-educator whom he both admires and critiques, Marianne Williamson. He's studied her work for decades and has just completed a book on her failed bid for the U.S. Presidency in 2020.[306]

> **Marianne Williamson (MW):** Image in politics, like most things in American society, is everything, unfortunately. Digital and social media has exacerbated this because now, it's a big problem where even if I dress up in an upper middle class way and put on make-up for an interview, as I had to do in my campaign run, there is still the problem of how well the studio you are going into does the lighting on you. They can create all kinds of shadows and pull out certain features for the camera and audience. Believe you me, I saw enough of this to tell me that if the interviewer and station you were going to for the interview were positive towards you as a candidate they would light you up to look beautiful on camera. It they didn't they would not only mess up the lighting and make you look bad, even ugly sometimes, they can do this in many ways, including how they put the make-up on you before you go on air.

RMF: Aesthetics is part of the hidden agenda of politics isn't it?

MW: Yeah. But you wanted to talk about higher education today.

RMF: Right. I think you know what I mean when I talk in my work on aesthetics and education about the paradigm I call A-ness, that is, the paradigm that organizes reality from more diverse to less diverse. The basic movement from natural, flowing, organic to mechanical and uniform patterning.

MW: It's true, there's a horrid homogenization going on in the neoliberalism of universities.[307] It really came around big time in the 1990s and onward, with universities spending big budgets and bringing in corporate people and finance people to run the top positions in universities rather than top researchers. The atmosphere was to turn universities into businesses first and foremost, to make profits like any other industry. It was the time of when there was such an inflation of the need to have a university degree for more and more people, when prior they would only need grade 12 education for a job and to qualify for training in moderately skilled jobs. Now a days, students and parents are being forced into an education marketplace where there are some very expensive degrees going for sale basically. And the universities are top-heavy with big salaried elites.

RMF: I have seen this in several universities for sure. The business-technical model and/or polytechnic as it is often called, is replacing the quality open-minded liberal and best research models. It's all about getting jobs. That's what they are selling. And guess what...

MW: They are selling fancy logos, making everyone speak the same lingo, mission statements, and all sounding the same. Critical dissent is being weeded out of this business model of operations. It's becoming a monoculture of higher education just like the big agro-business ventures have turned the natural and local farming scene of high diversity of plants and animals, into monocultures of sameness.

RMF: That's A-ness—a monoculture of sameness, walled off against invasion of any real diversity.

MW: That's a disease. It's called cancer. Where an arrogant part of the Whole, goes off and thinks that it can control and reproduce its own design everywhere and that will be called "standardization" and "efficiency" and "progress." It's a disaster on the road to non-sustainability. You know it's worse because the A-ness and ugliness it produces in such conformity hides itself under rhetoric of "celebrating diversity" and even using slogans like "Fearless Learning" that these businesses have adopted to make them look like they risk and teach about risk, innovation and creativity and that makes them look tolerant to different classes, races and genders—but all along underneath that surface appearance they are 'raping' away all diversity in the infrastructure and bureaucracies and are turning students out as 'numbers' games, which always means cutting support staff and researchers and senior faculty and hiring only part-timers and adjunct faculty who are easily disposed of if the profits are not so good. The security in the whole system is sacrificed and...

RMF: Big 'Q' Quality goes down the drain in a sad ruination of higher education....

What happens in higher education, where the liberated mind is supposed to flourish with a universal education without fear—becomes a sign, a symbol and metaphor, if not a template, for what is happening all over in the modern world.

Many institutions have fallen under this neoliberalism wave of affairs—a paradigm of so-called 'liberals' so-called, shacking up in bed with big money. It is happening in politics everywhere as well and it is killing the life-world of societies and democracies. Because once you over-standardize Education, along these fear-based design models, then everything is corrupted towards B-ness and A-ness. The world starts to turn ugly everywhere, even if the surfaces are 'beautifully' crafted and shiny and polished to look high quality and expensive. The urbanization, banalization, technicization with homogenization under hyper-standardization is a 'monster' and a perversion of fear-based need to conquer Nature, which is an impossible feat the human being is slowly learning. Dubos in the late-1960s recognized this A-ness pattern language of conquering and addictive need, as it continues producing the cold aesthetic-materialistic outcome of,

> The "square" life...[which] is stifling and thwarts the responses essential for man's [sic] sanity and for the healthy development of human [higher] potentialities. All thoughtful persons worry about the future of the children who will have to spend their lives under the absurd social and environmental conditions we are thoughtlessly creating....[like] social attitudes which are more concerned with things than with men [sic].[308]

That's the illusion of the postmodern world—it's all about attractive surfaces, just like all commercial advertising is. It's all about pretty faces and costumes, and less and less about quality in depth. We have to recognize this battle for domination in the aesthetic dimension.

And, with a Fearlessness Paradigm, there is at least an opportunity to reclaim what has been lost and even better to rebuild the world upon an architecture that is not motivated by fear, mistrust, greed, domination and injustices. A-ness is violent, even if, on the surface it looks peaceful and ideal!

Whether it is Gillian's objective in the opening quote to claim 'the beauty of fear' or de Becker's claiming 'the gift of fear' (as in Introduction 2), there is a contested territory obviously that anyone who pursues Fearlessness will have to run up against. These promoters of fear in positive ways, including making it beautiful, are typically off on their own with these ideologies and theories. It has been Fisher's work since 1989 to bring all such differences in understandings about the nature and role of fear into a unified place of 'Fear' Studies and Fear Management Education. Then, we can at least confront each other and make our claims in the spirit of good research, philosophy, and inquiry into truth. But if everyone continues to stay in their own yard behind the big fence and publish and teach about fear and fearlessness and not interact, and not let in differences of views, there really will be in that movement a *resistance* against any emancipation at all. A Fearlessness Paradigm starts on this assumption of opening the windows and gates of our protected territories to co-participate in creating a better dialogue in the field. We trust this book will do just that.

PART III

FEARLESSNESS IS/ AS MOVEMENT

CHAPTER FIVE

Fearlessness is/as Movement

There appears to be a general blind-spot to seeing fearlessness flowing and crafting history equally as has fear....Historically, it appears the resource of fear has been well tapped, while the resource of fearlessness remains largely untapped.

-R. Michael Fisher[309]

RMF: I'm glad we chose this particular quote from my book. It's about as succinct as one can write these kinds of things. I've not really been able to say it better since that time. I noticed the use of "resource" as a language with fearlessness. I am not so comfortable with that today. I was trying then to grab the attention of people, especially leaders who think of everything valuable in terms of *resource* as if everything valuable is for human resource use and development. That kind of 'using' is I think exactly one of the very downfalls of the business-managerial mind of contemporary humans *en masse* who have bought into a hypnotic ideology of predatory capitalist commodification. I have read a few excellent works on "commodification of fear," and "disaster capitalism,"[310] and the meta-disaster of that worldview skewed as it is within the *culture of* *fear* context. So, the last thing I want is a campaign promoting a commodification of fearlessness. Please no! I want nothing to do with developing fearlessness on this planet as a resource, if it is articulated outside of a sacred framework and only within a pragmatic-economic functionalist framework with no critical theory. I just had to say that.

BMK: Okay, sure, that makes sense. But would you also be as concerned about the commodification of *courage*, because after all that is so needed to be developed as a resources as many have argued. I want to develop courage as a resource myself and I promote it for others, especially for organizations and governments. Yet, you are making me realize you have made in your Fear Management Systems Theory a quantum distinction on an evolution of consciousness scale between courage as a fear management strategy and fearlessness. Do you want to say anything about courage?

RMF: I've pretty much said most all I need to say on courageousness in my 2010 book, as it is, along with bravery and bravado, a very long section of research, with my critique. At the end of that book's Introduction, I wrote about offering this massive amount of information to the public on fear management/education and that I was so excited to share it with the world and yet found that I wasn't so effective as I wished I could have been since late-1989. Besides all the resistances I was noting in that book, many of them echoed in our new co-authored book here, I also admitted that maybe I was just not being 'market-smart' enough and creating 'catchy' phrased one-liners to promote my work. I wrote, "I'm not a very good sound-bite ('positive,' 'cheerleader,' or hope-mongering kind of) salesperson with the things

I analyze systematically....[re: the book] It is not a simple read for most, as it requires a new way of thinking and defining of several concepts that are familiar but are being used in a different context. I suggest reading it more than once."[311]

Sort of for fun, I decided to write a kind of *Reader's Digest* popular magazine quotable quote version to summarize why it is that anyone might want to read that 2010 book, and I came up with a distinction that spins from "courage" because as you say a lot of people are trying to seek it and commodify it as a resource; so, I wrote, *Courage is about managing fear; whereas fearlessness is about managing fear a hell of a lot better!*"[312]

BMK: I've noticed you also have done a similar popularized quip on the Fearlessness Movement ning you started in 2015. Recently, you posted a poster you made that says: *"Love is letting go of fear...However, Fearlessness is learning from fear."*

RMF: I was playing off the long and popularized movement, set along its way by *A Course in Miracles* movement since the 1980s in which "love is letting go of fear" was a slogan I was seeing and hearing everywhere in the human potential and New Age movements. I wanted to challenge that and most simply state the agenda of the Fearlessness Movement, I guess. Those were the words that came to mind to make the distinction in the theory and practice of what I am promoting compared to others.

BMK: Perhaps we ought to turn now to the future, to catastrophes and what the Fearlessness Movement is and what it can do to prevent these, if that is even possible.

Although the typical response to the future and its prospects would be to focus on science, technologies and the production of knowledge, there is a softer underbelly to progress and the future that needs to be drawn forth for all to contemplate. Can our species avoid catastrophe on mass scale? Clearly, with the many catastrophes of our times, we must be humble to the reality that modern humans and their powerful sciences and technologies, their reason and their knowledge, have not stopped all catastrophes and likely will not. The question of importance: *Will catastrophes eventually cascade so rapidly that they'll overwhelm our capacities of defense and innovation to avoid future catastrophes?* But what of the underbelly below future scenarios—of variable hope and despair? We suspect the 21st century's fate will ultimately be determined by the choice of the people and their leaders in a negotiation, if not a battle, over the following question/issue: *Will fear rule over fearlessness OR will fearlessness rule over fear?*

Wake Up!

As co-authors, in a book with Desh Subba in 2019 on India as a nation of fear and prejudice, its past, present and future, we dedicated the book:

> [A]s a wake-up call for those whose lives have been paralyzed in the name of lower caste fate and untouchable status for thousands of years. Wake up! All in India and beyond now can arise to a new fate with a new dawning of the 21st century.[313]

As we (Fisher & Kumar) currently reflect on this today, it is clear we have a positive overall sense that a universal *movement* is afoot to change the world, to overcome even this horrid legacy of casteism in India but also other forms of oppression. What movement could be so worthy and real to keep our world evolving progressively? What movement will incite more and more people, more and more leaders, to wake-up to this "force" beneath the surface—a force we call the *spirit of fearlessness*.[314]

In being aware of such a motivational force that *when fear appears, so then does fearlessness*,[315] there will be a second-born renaissance-like awakening, unpredictable but inevitable, where consciousness will begin to see through the illusions of millennia on earth, and realize that Fearlessness is a Movement in the sociopolitical and historical sense. Indeed, fearlessness typically is not seen in this latter modality. It is also hard for most people to see fearlessness in the mere psychological and behavioral dimension of life.

Our book is intended to wake-up our species and consciousness itself and expand both these areas of phenomenon, the individual and the collective. And, like any wake-up call it may not be recognized or have effect, at least not right away. And like any transformational experience so powerful that it wakes one up from illusions of their old identity and ways of being, there is a *resistance* of equal force that can make such a waking up very disturbing for the individual and collective. Studies of the Renaissance in 15-16th centuries of Europe have shown that "The changes gave reason for both hope and despair"—as great scientific and technological innovations and discoveries are not without severe "social implications"—which, typically get far less careful attention than the former hard aspects of civilization's evolution and paradigm shifts.[316] This social consequence, including ecological consequence today, is an ethical problem and presents our species with choices as to what kinds of movements will we estimate to be real progress and what will we call regress or even pathologies(?)

Let's go to the first claim or principle of truth of Life: *When fear appears, so then does fearlessness*. Fisher has named this dictum as a reminder to all human beings of the "force" of which fear/fearlessness as a dialectic operates all the time. You may notice in the simplest sense that the dictum or life-principle is actually a living system's *movement*. It is a necessary biological, psychological and sociological movement as we shall see. We want to teach here that fearlessness acts within a dynamic movement and is a newly identified Social Movement at the same time. It thus has unifying potentiality for social evolution, yet fully tapped into. Fisher also called this social movement a "(r)evolution"[317] in waiting. Some might call it a new Enlightenment or simply as Fisher calls it a developmental movement[318] along the "path of fearlessness."[319]

Recently Kumar, with an attitude of a dialectic of progress that celebrates the best of human growth but also realizes the costs, sets out an overall rather optimistic but realistic dynamic connection of fear/fearlessness *as movement* in his reflective writing for Part III:

> **BMK:** Evidence is growing that the standards of good political governance are rapidly falling in many democratic nations. Escalating human rights violations are the outcomes of weaponization of mortal fear.... The growth of dangerous technologies and emergence of demonic dictatorships are the after-effects of excessive chronic fear within. Consequently, much of the world population is presently in the grip of a toxic fear, both cause and origin, of destruction, oppression, discrimination, exploitation—all, at the hands of fellow humans, who have not yet learned optimally how to manage that fear. There are again more fears emanating from infections, accidents or environmental threats which continue to keep the people restless without enjoying quality lives. The solution lies in the paradigm shift to the fearlessness approach and its framework for an emancipatory *fear education*.[320]
>
> When fearlessness, in the true sense of its depth of meaning, rises up to awaken consciousness, people will, more or less, automatically embrace peaceful usage of science and technology....When fearlessness spreads out, people will confidently promote humane governance by eschewing lawlessness. It is the time to carry forward the spirit of fearlessness as a dynamic movement of

optimism and promise for the amelioration of the human condition. The necessity and imperative of taking forward the spirit of fearlessness as an indomitable universal movement is of paramount importance.

Every movement in history, everywhere and everywhen, has been a movement of fearlessness but we typically have been blind[321] as human beings—taught to neglect to attuned to the natural potency of this instinctual great force of self/system correction and progressive healthy growth. Whether it was the primal nomadic enterprise of hunting and sharing a meal or the settled agricultural civilisation, they were existential movements of people to achieve freedom from the fears of threats to life and to help them lead their nature-bound lives more or less without fear. Whether it was Vasco da Gama's daring voyage to India or Amundsen's chilling expedition to the South Pole, they were explorative movements of the people to free themselves from the fears of the seas and snow, and to help them lead more informed lives more or less without fear dominating. Whether it was the early Renaissance and/or the Age of Reason, these were inquisitive movements of people to rid them of the fears of unknown and to help them lead fulfilling lives more or less without fear. Whether it was communist ideology of classless society or the capitalist scheme of social security measures, they were path-breaking liberation movements of people to fend off fears of exploitation and to help them lead dignified lives more or less without dominating fear. Whether it was the conquest of Mt. Everest or the first step on the moon, they were epoch-making movements of people to fight free of paralyzing fears of heights and the skies, so as to help them lead adventurous lives more or less without fear. Whether it is infotech or biotech or international diplomacy or interpersonal ethics, they are unifying movements of people to dispel the strangeness and phobic fears of their fellow humans, and to help them lead more harmonious more or less without fear dominating. Whether it is a continuous bid to halt nuclear proliferation or develop dedicated and courageous responses to tackle climate change, they are concerted movements of people to mitigate the fears of impending crises and to help them lead more secure lives more or less without fear.

The Fearlessness Movement, in its diverse sub-forms, could be a basic philosophical, spiritual, economic and political movement or revolution led largely by a single person, say the likes of the leader Mahatma Gandhi, who spearheaded the peaceful struggle for freedom of India—based on his emphasis on fear as a problem and fearlessness as the solution to nonviolence and protest—*via* his *Satyagraha* movement. Or it could be a movement of a two-member team like the Wright brothers, who proved that humans could fly fearlessly like birds. And it also could be a movement of the global multitude to overcome the menacing effects of the corona pandemic more or less without fear. Although some planned measures are offered behind these movements above that I have listed as a few examples, there is the understanding that most of what is fearlessness movement is a spontaneous movement—like an instinctive reflex of survival and/or Defense Intelligence as Fisher calls it[322]—of people because they live too often in a fear-embedded world and they wish not to do so. No living organism wishes to live in fear for any longer than a minimal necessity to aid survival. Yet, chronic fear is everywhere, from thoughts to actions and from doing to undoing. Yet, we are only still learning to think in regulatory natural systems of resiliency, that wherever there is fear, there is fearlessness too. When toxic hyper-fear suppresses the best forces of human nature, it is the fearlessness that liberates such forces, which in turn culminate in the powerful movements of people. And, yet as we've also seen, powerful fearlessness liberate can also scare a lot of people, especially the elites who hold power over people and use the people's fear to do so.

As fearlessness is integral with Life Instinct or *Eros*, so fear is integral to Death Instinct or *Thanatos*. Not that we or any creature can live without both Life/Death as the reality of existence itself. Yet, unless there is a vital fearlessness, the individual cannot take required adaptable initiatives to move forward into the future. Otherwise, fear tends to infuse hesitations and inhibitions into efforts. Fearlessness is the engine of growth for the individual. On the contrary, fear once beyond its original stimulation for change and action, when held in fixed patterns and phobias then acts as inertia, against the Life Instinct, and thus drives the individual to step backwards into the Death Instinct like in a spiral or neurotic loop of deficit-thinking and general mistrust and against-ness, as Fisher often describes.[323]

But fearlessness sets the Life Instinct and its *libido* into movement. As movement is an indicator of Life, so is fearlessness. When a living being stops moving, it is dead. Cessation of breath, absence of blood flow, stillness of heart are signs of lack of movement in the body. Hence it means that Death Instinct has taken over, is *resisting* the Life Instinct, and concomitantly fear has dominated. If fearlessness is in a more or less dominant position overall, as corrective to excesses of the Death Instinct, then the Life Instinct triumphs over *destrudo*.

Of course it is ideally a balance we want because too much unchecked Life Instinct *via* an unbalanced system produces cancerous growth—both biologically and as a pathological form at the level of mind and the social sphere as well—all equally destructive. So, movement and fearlessness are the same as Life and living in relational terms; and all these four conceptions—Life-Fearlessness-Death-Fear are so intricately connected to each other that we may finally define them as a single metaphysical entity.[324] To explain it further, let us remind ourselves that life and death are two sides of the same coin in the sense that one doesn't exist without the other like space-time. A human body is composed of cells and atoms and every day billions of old cells are dying and billions of new cells are being generated. The living body has been equipped with innate life and death instincts, the manifestations of which are fearlessness and fear respectively. A body is also both matter and energy. Matter and energy are also one and the same because they change their states from one to another but are never destroyed, nor created. Life becomes death when biological functions in the body come to an end. It means that the body has changed its state from life to death and so are life and death instincts as well as fearlessness and fear. Ultimately all these are one, though in different states.

Although the fearism perspective and philosophy of Subba et al., make clear that we cannot justify only a negative connotation for fear and its role in evolution, the specific applications of such a philosophy require nuance, especially in the area of cultural configurations of 'fear' patterning, as Fisher theorizes.[325] *Fear* has been one of the major reasons for preventing the individual from undertaking positive challenges. Because it lowers, *inter alia*, confidence levels of the individual. Hierarchical status in rigid societies is one of the causes to weaken confidence and optimism. If a low rank official in an organisation is not sufficiently motivated by the management, he may become doubtful about his own potential while performing his job. It is due to self-induced fear as a result of which his achieving spirit to feel confident gets inhibited. A fearful person is most likely to suspect his own caliber despite having full strength of intellect. This type of mindset is mostly seen in rigid classist, sexist, racist and caste-based systems. Fear accelerates self-negating behaviour.

Normally we see that rational fears are good for safety and security of existence. They serve as warning alarms to take preventive or corrective steps in case of any urgency or eventuality. But the problem arises when the individual takes a wrong step out of the ambit of rational imagination. Such instances are likely to drive the individual to visualise irrational fears and/or phobias. For example, pandemic generated widespread fears across the globe are susceptible to this paranoid structuration. At first, they are rational fears in the sense that all the people are supposed to take precautions so as to protect themselves from the contamination of coronavirus disease. Whosoever observes preventive measures like wearing masks, social distancing, hygiene maintenance, right diet, sun exposure etc., has no need to feel threatened. But some people, despite taking all due care, subject themselves to suspicious overthinking and worry and this tendency gives rise to irrational imaginaries. Likewise, in the same way some people get over-anxious about scientifically developed vaccines or approved health protocols and are likely to become the victims of psychosomatic disorders. This trend has been the case in many places around the world during corona pandemic and such irrational fears occur basically because of failure of sound judgement owing to non-utilisation of fearlessness. In fact, often fearlessness is resisted, and confused with people acting with bravado and refusing to wear masks and follow basic healthy practices as given by the medical establishment and government orders and laws. But fearlessness, as Fisher has pointed out, is not bravado and it is not a counter-phobic reaction to real fear. Fearlessness is not merely willed and controlled by the ego, as so often is confused. Fearlessness is a spontaneous movement. So, the best policy within the context of fearlessness, will be that of being mindful about such hasty fear-based opinions, knee jerk reactions and rebellious resistances to authorities, etc., but rather to allow the gift of fearlessness to take charge for aiding informed rational decisions of care and prevention of a real disease.

Indeed fearlessness is a movement that is embedded in politics as well, not just with issues of basic health care, but in core issues of democracy and liberty, economics and freedom etc. In 1941, Franklin D. Roosevelt delivered a thought provoking speech on *four freedoms* namely freedom of speech, freedom of worship, freedom from want and freedom from fear. Eventually they became foundational to the 1948 United Nations Universal Declaration of Human Rights. The four freedoms are vital to human existence and essence. These freedoms are also very closely interlinked and so they all can be clubbed together as one *viz., freedom from fear*. To explain it, we may say that freedom of speech means freedom from fear of expressing opinions, ideas, artistic talent, scientific temperament, cultural views etc. But unfortunately, we are witness to countless violations almost on all fronts in terms of intolerance, violence, prejudice and so on. Some journalists whose writings mirror the ground realities and politics of abuses, often face the wrath of autocratic ruling parties. Civil rights activists or social conscious leaders who express opinions and shortcomings of the system frankly are branded as extremists. There are artists, cartoonists and caricaturists galore who suffered for their courageous progressive styles of informing the people about truth and hypocrisy. Exponents of scientific temper always encounter the ire of orthodox traditionalists. And some scientists were killed or disappeared.

Freedom of worship is the fundamental human right that guarantees every individual the freedom from fear of practising or professing religion. This right empowers one to remain a theist or an atheist or an agnostic. It also enables one to pray to the God, or many Gods or Goddesses of one's choice or not to pray at all. Any discrimination on that count amounts to violation on the part of the perpetrator. Various futuristic studies hint that religiosity is growing among the people around the globe. It is not a bad sign as far as people would be able to benefit themselves with more optimism and confidence from such religiosity, as contributing to the purposes of mutual harmony and growth. But unfortunately, contemporary statistics show otherwise. Increasing numbers of religious people often are more likely to employ religiosity for divisive and destructive, dominating purposes. Such misuse is not the innate feature of the freedom of worship but it could be construed as evil designs of wicked minds.

It is also not uncommon to witness that ignorant individuals inculcate as well as instil irrational fears in the name of religion or worship, for example, in women and girls endangering their reproductive health. Similarly, LGBTQ is one community which faces recurrent threats from certain fanatic, often religious, elements of societies. Apart from all these marginalised groups like women or other disadvantaged sections, people in general are also operating everyday with persistent fears due to frequent religious conflicts in most of the nations.

Freedom from want could be understood as freedom from fear of uncertainty and insecurity. Wants remain constant if people are not certain about their safety needs. Abraham Maslow's basic needs were conceived in the context of this freedom. Way back in 6th century BCE, Buddha propagated the idea that desires are the root cause of all worries and suffering. Unfulfilled wants trigger anxieties and fears in terms of not getting desires met. In secular terms, Karl Marx waged his revolt to redeem the working class people from the fear of uncertainty about basic needs. Poverty, illiteracy, inequality, joblessness etc. are some of the unending socioeconomic woes which make a larger chunk of the world population fearful of a shortage of their basic sustenance.

Lastly, the last of four freedoms is that of *fearlessness*. Freedom from fear echoes the essential requirement of fearlessness in one's life to strive and thrive. Therefore, as a movement, fearlessness is the call for action to steer the world out of fears that obstruct holistic growth of humanity. Both fearlessness and movement as conceptual ideas are one and the same in aiming at achieving individual progress ultimately. They both also denote existence and essence of life. Unless fearlessness is taken forward as movement at individual, societal and world levels simultaneously, fear will continue to haunt humanity and exacerbate its regressive trends.

On many parameters of measure, the world has been changing since past few centuries for better. Yet with cascading crises immanent, perhaps the mood of "despairing optimist"[326] is more appropriate than not for our current state. Though the human societies grew complex in the matters of life and work, modern ideas have overall brought hope and confidence. Steven Pinker, the optimistic author of *Enlightenment Now* attributed the advancement of contemporary society to the values of Age of Enlightenment like reason, humanism, science etc. He explained that these virtues transformed the worldview of humans in such a dramatic manner as capable of revamping the human condition for good. Liberal thought improved the intellectual as well as socioeconomic status of the individual. Reason and logic made people's ambitions and struggles more achievement-oriented. Power of science trounced the sovereignty of superstitious beliefs to a considerable extent. Subsequently, people began shedding irrational fears. Growth of medical science increased human lifespan. Curious minds paved the way to inventions and innovations, thereby creating wealth not only in the form of the economy but also in terms of knowledge and skills. All these world restructuring endeavours were conspicuous as progressive movements of people as a collective. With every such forward movement in the path of human development, fearlessness has taken a more dominant role over fear.

Surely, there's more than enough thoughts and political claims in that missive by Kumar to keep all of us interested engaged for long discussions to come. This chapter cannot deal with all of them in more detail and mostly we'll focus on only a very few points. Questions arise, more than answers. What we are attempting to show is that like any "movement" identified and promoted, the Fearlessness Movement, is bound to have its pockets full of ideas about evolution, history, societies, civilization and what makes for a 'better' world. It is likely to have critique within it too. It has its own ideologies and politics too. As co-authors we are offering up a conception of a Fearlessness Movement and we are implicitly asking you to join it; and, if not, to ask why not. Why would you not want to join such a movement? These are conversations that interest us just as much as it interests us to find partners in coalition to support and teach about the Fearlessness Movement. We are not interested in fostering followers of the movement who are not thinking critically all the time. We are not interested in propaganda, ideologism, and hierarchies of oppression that "tell the people" what to think about fear/fearlessness. We strive for an education itself on the movement based on fearlessness, as nonviolent and non-coercive, etc.[327] You might call it all part of a Liberal Education.

We'd like to see all human beings given access to the basic facilities and supports, inside or outside of institutions, to study fear/fearlessness and "the movement." Then, they will decide how to move with it or against it. That's sort of our ethical point. One is going to be for fearlessness as natural instinct and a social movement or they are going to be against it. Indeed, some may not be for it and rather be more reserved in doubt. That's fine, yet, our understanding of fearlessness is that even to be reserved is an act of non-participation in the "force" of fearlessness and thus constitutes a passive withdrawal from the movement of fearlessness in the world. Others will actively be against fearlessness as a movement.

Currently, only a very small percent of the population is actively in support of the movement we are speaking of. It is infinitesimal but that doesn't alone disqualify it from the public and political sphere. It is an alternative voice we offer from the Fearlessness Paradigm in contradistinction to the predominant Fear Paradigm. In some cases, and some will argue, that our fearlessness project is actually anti-history and anti-evolution and anti-emancipatory. Why? Because they believe that the only revolution of worth and effectiveness to stop the injustices and suffering of the oppressed is going to come about because of the use of fear to scare the elites down from their thrones and make them run.[328] Then "the people" can take over. You'll hear some Marxism, Communism, and Socialism rhetorics in that notion of revolution—that is, political reform and take-over. Indeed, it raises questions about what is the political stand from the philosophy of fearism perspective and fearlessness perspective on these ideological and political movements and their rhetorics?

Fearism, Fearlessness & Politics

Typically, the fearism literature is fairly moderate, neutral and rather silent about political reform in those direct terms of what we would call "politics." Sure, fearists, just like Kumar above, talks about fearism and rights and especially freedom. Yet in a sense, we see the fearist writers, from Subba onward, as keeping their work on the edges of and/or outside of politics. They are more philosophical, psychological, theological in some, and basic artistic-types of writers and thinkers. And yet their work is embedded in social order and change issues that concern citizens and democracy. We (Fisher & Kumar) have not always been so political either but this book and this chapter especially, are calling us all to be overtly political as well as philosophical.

It's intriguing to remember that Subba is a "writer" and critic in the literary traditions, mainly out of Nepal. He has, with many, been part of a resistance movement of loose associations of artists and intellectuals defying oppressive government/military control of Nepal. In the endorsement and review of the book by Fisher & Subba on fearism (East-West dialogue), Dr. Tanka Prasad Neupane, Chairman, Fearism Study Centre, Dharan, Nepal, wrote,

> In late 2014, Mr. Subba called me and informed me about Dr. R. Michael Fisher's (2014) Technical Paper 51.[329] I became curious and read it. Really, it was

amazing, as if my dreams had come true. That paper was the first internationally supported document of Fearism, and fortunately very similar thought was now available coming from the West. I made many copies and distributed them among writers....Now, with the publishing of *Philosophy of Fearism: A First East-West Dialogue*, there is a very important blueprint for global fearism [as a movement] built on friendship, philosophical exchange, and open-minded thinking about the Philosophy of Fearism as it moves through a new door to the wide world.[330]

Two things strike us as pertinent from Neupane's comments: (a) he passed the technical paper around "among writers" he knew—and, that shows the bias of where fearism discourses have often traveled and, (b) he calls the Fisher & Subba book "a very important blueprint" and names the domains of society and of scholarship in general to which it is built upon but there is no mention of *politics*. There is no recognition that Fisher & Subba have either similar or different politics and that the fearism work is political and/or did Neupane pass on the publication to leaders of political parties, for example. Not only does such politiking seem mute within the fearism movement but it almost seems by default rather discouraged. Such an issue has not surfaced that we know of as yet, and so we are first to raise it forth because it has impacts on the qualities of the Fearlessness Movement overall.

From the start of connecting with and joining Fearism as a movement, Fisher seemed to intuit this bias more in the fearism movement than his own fearlessness movement work. So he took the time to assess things and make a few politically-oriented declarations in his book with Subba in 2016. Although both co-authors there embraced that fearism is a practical social philosophy, they were less able to embrace a similar distinction about the politics of fearism. Fisher in 2014 made it clear his original "fearism" concept, some nine years before Subba coined it, was out rightly political (e.g., fearism-t, as it is now called by Fisher[331]). Fisher went further to make distinctions in a political way by comparing "Desh Subba: Door 1" and "R. Michael Fisher: Door 2"[332] and suggested strong points of overlap between their views but also strong points of dissension. For example, and with implicit political ramifications, the contrast in their "primary attitude" for "Public Objectives" was that Subba's fearism is "positive toward fear" and Fisher's fearism is "negative toward fear ('fear')." And for "political orientation" the contrast was Subba's "a 'new' communism" and Fisher's "a 'new' conscientization of resistance." But we (Fisher & Kumar), upon reflection of such comparisons, see that there is an abstract expression of political orientation given by Fisher and there is no indication what this new communism is *per se*.

It is certainly not the case that Subba (2014) did not discuss communism,[333] albeit, he never comes out with any political stance for his philosophy of fearism—as in, for example, he could just state it is a liberal, or conservative, or a radical political philosophy. Fisher is more prone to say that fearlessness is a radical—meaning rebellious[334]— political philosophy and paradigm. Fisher clearly does not stand for liberal (left) or conservative (right) politically. He operates beyond such binaries and much more would be classified as a radical; although, it is clear he is a left-leaning progressivist—and, similarly, a case could be made that Subba is also such a progressivist politically. Yet, to date, no one has done such a research study and analysis on the politics of fearism and/or fearlessness as movements.

All this debate raises the question: Does following Fearlessness make one a Conservative, Liberal or Radical? in the political sense of those terms. We'll leave that for later in the book perhaps, but at this moment we wish to cut underneath the need to label a political orientation upon Fearlessness Movement. Generally, it is likely that Subba would agree with us that Fearism and Fearlessness ought not be confined to any one Political orientation *per se*. All of us believe in emancipation of human beings at a minimum of what we would call 'the good,' 'the beautiful,' and 'the true.' Philosophy itself is by definition a way of such emancipation—and, yes, that can boil down to what Kumar articulated above, re: an emancipation agenda that is at base in its roots "freedom from fear." Kumar argues that such freedom from fear is beneath all the "Four Freedoms" of basic human rights. That is a political stance, by any other name.

We turn here beyond the need of political labels for Fearlessness Movement. We have already offered readers the sense of an instinctual, primal, natural impulse (or spirit) of which fearlessness is already a movement—aligned as Kumar argues above, with Life Drive. At this macro-scale evolutionary perspective on growth and development generally, there is no need for any political label of what is being put forth as real and true—and, as the 'better' way to operate. You can be against the Life Drive (i.e., fearlessness as movement) or you can work with it, and ultimately just allow yourself to *become it* and its inherent movement—and ways in action. Logically, if one is part of Life, as every human is by definition, then one would do better than not by following Life's ways, principles—and, as we articulate them here as philosophical or biological-ecological principles (e.g., see D-ness in Chapter Three). Without falling into any naturalistic fallacy, we wish to proceed with a brief argumentation for why Fearlessness Movement (social sphere) and fearlessness movement (biological sphere) require no political specific party label or categorization for them to be effective "forces" in our everyday life as citizens.

To do such an investigation we are required to let go of obsession with the Ego and Super Ego levels of description in psychoanalytic models. We move to the Id level, the most primary, animal and mammal aspects of human nature. We even have to move lower down, more primary, to a pre-anthropocentric worldview. We wish to define fear/fearlessness, in other words, at this most basic level of *living systems*. Fisher has called this the Defense Intelligence System of description, where fear is most usually talked about, and fearlessness has not been so talked about at this dimension. To be brief, Fisher has articulated much of this in his 2010 book under Defense Intelligence and his observations of Nature and his study of biology and behavior in his 20s-30s.[335] He finds that no creature, or Id component of reality, wishes to be in a fear-state for very long. Fear is accepted as part of its nature and of Nature itself. There is no separation or moral judgement in the Id when it comes to fear (and/or fearlessness). This is often what is talked about by many writers on fear, as the "natural" and "good" or "positive" and "rational" fear complex. "True Fear" is what de Becker named it (see Introduction 2). Fisher (2010) refers to this as FMS-0 and 1, before the heavy influences of the Cultural sphere upon the Natural sphere. In a sense, we get a more archaic and purified (i.e., non-culturally-biased) understanding of Fear and Fearlessness here. "Exactly how an *organismic system* (individuals + environments) optimizes its *passing on* Life-imperative before passing on (as in death-imperative), is very complex," wrote Fisher.[336]

Fear/fearlessness is inherently part of adaptation to living, often spoken of as "surviving" but the big difference is, within a Fearlessness Paradigm, everything motivational is not seen as an avoidance of fears and death. The latter, typical of the existential discourse, and the predomination of a materialistic *Thanatos*-driven way of thinking, and theory of motivation and human condition. A good deal of fearism philosophy also assumes this theory. A holistic-integral perspective/theory moves away from the tendency to make death and fear of death as primary importance over the desire to grow and transcend across multiple dimensions of existence and consciousness not limited to a materialist explanation of everything. To extend this distinction is beyond the scope of this chapter *per se*. So, let's return to the basics of fearlessness as unveiled in the Id domain.

> **RMF:** I've always thought of the foundational bio-ecological nature of fearlessness as in my dictum, as inherent and genetic, and evolved within adaptive complex systems. It is a 'corrective' like in any system when it heads into over-drive or simply too far out of balance from equilibrium or near-equilibrium. For systems to keep their integrity of operations within limits of their design within fluctuating environments, you need to be sensitive and even vulnerable at times in order to detect signs of over-drive cycling of your physiology. So, when fear is turned on so to speak, for various reasons, it is best that it is not turned on too long because it upsets a lot of the physiological

balancing points in the system, and research shows that with any amount of chronic stress, often called distress, in a system, things chemically and physically will start to deteriorate. It's like if you leave an alarm system on too long past the time of the crisis it was used to respond to it, then the alarm system runs down and will 'burn out.' The immune system is a form of the Defense Intelligence. Essential for healthy growth and development. It is part of the balancing of the forces of disease and the forces of growth and health. Disease is always there, and it is a matter of when an organismic systems is finally weakened in its immunity vigor that then the pathogens and cancer viruses, for example, take over and more or less can consume and kill the organism if things go too far. Distress or fear patterning, is a huge factor in bringing down vitality of energy resources, libido, and immunity vigor—that is, defense. So, keeping fear on for too long is a pathway for which the Death-drive will take over and spiral down. Of course, there is another part of the Death-drive that is connected to the Life-drive in a homeostasis network of mechanisms. For example, any over-drive of decay is going to stimulate mechanisms of the physiology to respond and produce more life-drive and immunity strengthening, as long as it is able. Thus within the decay and death movement is already the presence of growth and life movement. They are dialectical. The reverse is also the case, as with over-growth and cancerous drives or over-immunity drives like in auto-immune diseases which self-attack the system.

The complexity of these self/system corrections of course is not just biological but is layered to intersect with the psychological and sociological. But our focus is on the Id layer here and so let me give a more basic example that came to me while observing a cottontail rabbit in my yard some years ago. I watched it in the grass cleaning itself. Very relaxed and almost sleepy-eyed at points in the hot summer sun. At one point, it switched from cleaning the easier parts of its body with its licking, to the more difficult parts like on the bottom of its back paws. In order to clean a back paw, it has to balance on one of the back legs and lift the other back leg into a high position to access it with its mouth. This rabbit was doing well with the balancing act until at one point it lost its balance and its whole body reacted to catch-itself from a fall. It was spontaneous. I said: "That's fearlessness." The body alarm system went off because of a registering of a potential fall. In some cases, such an off balance could be deadly but in most cases not. Still, it reminded me of how evolution in all organisms is aimed to keep a homeostatic 'balancing' basically of all the systems, from temperature, to basic balance with gravity. Living things are enormously in-tune with their environment and relationship. They have to be to be efficient but also to optimize longevity and health.

Another example came years earlier when I watching mountain sheep grazing on a mountain slope. I realized how treacherous, at some level it is, to both maintain balance on the slope and cliffs on rocks, and still reach down to get the pieces of grass and herbs for food. When the head is down, predators may sneak up. Also, the amount of time per year when grass and herbs have the best quality nutrition is critical because these animals in Canada live a good deal in months of freezing cold. In other words, every move and bite taken, is a calculation of the systems of optimization of minimize energy output, minimize predatory risk, and yet, take risks when needed because the nutrition is perhaps better in an area of steep slopes than the lesser steep slopes. Whatever the case, I had the impression of a Defense Intelligence operating to calculate the best probability of risk and gain from any one movement. That is a primal intelligence system which has been selected over millions of years for these wild sheep. They need to keep their nutrition at optimum for breeding and raising young and defending off predators in flight or fight. All of the systems are working on Fearlessness as the 'calculator' in conjunction with Fear—but the former is the follow through actor of the alarm signs of the Fear system—and requires and brings forth a lot more intelligence to any situation than merely the Fear system on its own. Fearlessness on is not dangerous to the organism for longer periods, in comparison to Fear on for any length of time. Fearlessness involves the Fear system but transcends the Fear system and the reverse is not true. That's what makes Fearlessness more complex and, in some sense, more important.

The practical application is: *Why do we not teach fearlessness?* We may teach that bravery and courage are virtues. Yes, that happens. But we teach that as only the most basic part of Fearlessness and Defense Intelligence. We do not teach our children well about fearlessness as in its complexity, far beyond merely an attitude or moral virtue. At least, I have rarely seen this taught. I certainly did not learn anything much about Fearlessness in the way I am conceptualizing it here. There is some beginnings of this in rehabilitation and special education in helping some children self-regulate through techniques of breathing and "stop" mind cognitive techniques. But they are all behavioral or mind-control type approaches, and are not taught as within a discourse of reminding children that you are the product of 4 billion years of evolution of Defense Intelligence. Now, your job is to be aware of how to access that intelligence. So, not merely quick correction of one's hyperactive tendencies or over-stimulation breakdowns and distresses—no, the teaching of Fearlessness would be much more nuanced. Fact is, I cannot really say a whole lot more about this because such curriculum and pedagogy of Fearlessness for Fearlessness is not yet in place.

I would teach Fearlessness somatically in the Id sphere as "movement" exercises to start with before going to more subtle psychological ones. One exercise of *movement* as focus, comes to mind. I did this with a class of adults once. I asked them to stand on one leg for a minute or so. They could watch each other, and watch the struggles of doing so; noticing themselves either do 'good' with it or struggle with it. When I then had them relax and asked them about it. One said, "I was so bad at that." I pointed out how many of them started laughing in the process. "Why did most of you laugh so much?" They had no idea. I said, "Because you were discharging." They looked puzzled. "Yes, when you are in distress, like any organism, there is a build-up of fear—and, you were naturally trying to shake off the fear—because no organism wants to be in fear for very long. It's not good for you." Again, they were puzzled. They couldn't link the words I was saying with this simple exercise which was not like it was scary. One could hardly hurt themselves because all they needed to do was put their other foot down to rescue any off-balance potential of a fall. Simple.

Then came the teaching lesson. I said, "I noticed many of you were very self-judgemental. You said you 'sucked at this' or were 'bad at this.' No wonder you were laughing so much because it brought up embarrassment, shame, guilt, failure and loss of self-esteem in front of others—all these are cousins of fear. So the distress/fear piled up with such a simple task. But do you see you all had a bias from the start of the exercise. You presumed that because I asked you to stand on one leg that you were supposed to succeed perfectly with the task and if you did so, you assumed that you would get the highest praise or gaze of approval from the teacher or others."

I let them ponder that bias that was pre-given and conditioned into them as they are part of a culture of fear that asks for high performance and rewards it and punishes generally those who don't succeed. It is all very authoritatively controlled by the teacher and the cultural norms of success and with that being a 'good' person—meaning, being a good performer. I then said, "If from the moment I asked you to stand on one leg, you did so with joyous delight. Then, if that was the case, you wouldn't have had any fear lasting and building up and making you then have to discharge the energies of fear. You simply would have played with it as in a game rather than a competition to win and overcome the forces of gravity."

I let them ponder that. Faces were now getting a bit distracted. Bodies were getting hyper if not agitated at my explanations and I knew they were getting distressed with my analysis itself, now moving fear and mistrust even further into the relationship with me. I could tell some of them just wanted to go back to their desk and sit down and not be in this learning encounter which had made them uncomfortable. I was compassionate for that annoyance and I understand where it comes from, as I was 'pushing' them to look at the way fear controls their lives, even within a simple exercise like this balance on one leg.

Then I gave them the punch line of the lesson: *You know what? I'm glad to see your natural healing mechanism of laughter was coming into play as you built up fear and distress trying to balance on one leg. That's good. Yet, what I was wanting you to achieve was not so much to balance on one leg, I was rather wanting you to achieve that you couldn't balance on one leg, at least not for very long. Why is that? Why did I want you to not succeed with this task? It's because it would be unnatural for you to succeed without a struggle and without failure. So, to 'fail' in a sense to stand on one leg is actually a healthier choice of your intelligence defense system of your body than is to succeed.*

Although in this case, I was teaching them about when hurt or in distress, the body system will defend itself to find optimum homeostasis and that is, it will 'correct' itself. The correct way to stand is not on one leg. That's not how we were adapted to live well in this world of real gravity and with only two legs as walking creatures. People doing this exercise were fighting against homeostasis and their healthiest possible condition and most effectively energetic system. That's what I wanted them to learn. Today, for this chapter, I add now the lesson as one of Fearlessness going into action. Sort of like, in the reverse of the cottontail rabbit example I gave above. But both cases are true indicators of the self-corrective natural flow of things that is intended and designed for organisms. Fearlessness is the path or way towards the natural flow and is at the same time the natural flow—sort of in spiritual philosophical terms, Fearlessness is the 'Tao' if you study Eastern philosophy of the nondual. No separation from the 'Tao' is no separation from Fearlessness. To not balance on one leg is the way of the 'Tao' and 'Fearlessness'—that is, it is The Way to move. It is in that sense, the right movement. It is the right attitude. There is no against-ness coerced in the organism or in the environment. It is a harmonious relationship in other words all around. Some simply call this Wholeness.

It would have been really funny in a good way to have watched at least one person out of the 21 people in my workshop, keep doing the exercise for the minute, and being totally comfortable with the fact that their body whole system was enjoying correcting itself from the one leg to the two leg position. "Ah, back to gravity. Ah, that's the joy of The Way." At least, if I could put words on the one anomaly, had there been one and no there wasn't one, then I think that may be the words that would indicate they are operating from a Fearlessness Paradigm not a Fear Paradigm. The implications of this simple example, when taken up to psychological and social dimensions makes for a very important set of lessons, curriculum and wisdom. Bottomline, people are so into following expectations and rules, and even ideas about presumed rules, when they don't have to. It is like they find it so hard to just be themselves and enjoy what is happening in their experience.

In this case above, they could have just zestfully enjoyed their *experience of failing*, falling, and struggling—realizing, it was a *false game* expected of them—but they caught the trick and were by-passing its illusion.

They awakened. They realized that in failing so wonderfully to stand on one leg, they were the true victor; albeit, really a victor, but they were the true Defense Intelligence systems at work and displaying exactly The Way—that Life is meant to go. They became One with the movements. That's a beautiful universal movement which connects to Life itself, even if it has some struggle—because the player of the movement inherently *knows* The Way and now *trusts* they know The Way.

Well, turns out there's a hell of a lot that has to be re-learned, *via* de-conditioning, de-hypnotizing from the plethora of forms of *fear-based* ways of movement(s) and experience(s). Now, we turn back to the task of true Education for this 21st century and what could be possible to free humans, to free them from their fear of freedom. Let's all pause...now take a few deep breaths, and see if a spontaneous smile has appeared during me talking you through this exercise. No expectation intended.

BMK: True! Fear of freedom is a critical issue in understanding the fearlessness movement. This kind of fear is not a good sign of healthy systems, be it human personality or human society in general. It implies one's acquiescence to the dominance of the death instinct. Lack of confidence, lack of knowledge, absence of self-esteem etc. are reasons behind this negative trait. Pessimistic feelings act as resistance to the spirit of fearlessness. Ignorance and lack of awareness about what to do and what not to do make one to continue living with fear of freedom. Low levels of self-confidence don't allow the life instinct to thrive in fearlessness. Lack of personal control over thoughts and actions is another factor which lets the fear of freedom persist.

Fearlessness: Conservative? Liberal? or Radical?

Paradigms & Human Nature

By shifting emphasis from the cognitive [technicalities] to the normative [value-biased] functions of paradigms [of inquiry]...[an] enlarge[ment of] our understanding of the ways in which paradigms give form to the scientific life [is possible]....paradigms provide scientists not only with a map [and what questions to be asked] but also with some of the directions essential for map-making. In learning a paradigm the scientist acquires theory, methods, and standards together, usually in an inextricable mixture. Therefore, when paradigms change, there are usually significant shifts in the criteria determining the legitimacy both of problems and of proposed solutions....competing paradigms regularly raises questions that cannot be resolved by the criteria of normal science. To the extent, as significant as it is incomplete, that two scientific schools disagree about what is a problem and what a solution, they will inevitably talk through each other when debating the relative merits of their respective paradigms.[337]

Arguably any *Fearlessness philosophy* or psychology is going to be challenged as to what exactly is its view of *human nature*. The questions of such fields of study will be substantially different, and often conflicting, with philosophy or psychology approaches that make no distinction in their maps of reality between what is a fear-based philosophy or psychology and what is not. Equally, it will be challenged as to what political view it has embedded within that view of human nature. The same applies to the philosophy of fearism perspective we take in this book.

On an even larger context, there is the notion of the *Fearlessness Paradigm*. And it likewise has to be deconstructed and reconstructed in the evaluation process as we search for a 'better' way to understand, to frame problems to be solved, and to live well. In a much longer study beyond the scope of this chapter and book, a thorough critical review of the various paradigms, images, worldviews and philosophies of human nature is required. One has to ask: "Why do we need a new paradigm anyways?" For our part as co-authors, the current available paradigms of knowledge, methodologies, and views of human nature are typically not adequate, especially if we draw upon paradigms that only suit the mainstream *status quo* of societies existing today. They certainly don't seem capable of handling the complex demands of the 21st century and the levels of cascading crises on this planet. We think a more concrete and useful question to ask today: *Why do we need a new human being?* Is the old model of what makes a human being out of date that much? We think so.

> **RMF:** But mostly, I long ago struck out on the path for a 'better paradigm' because I felt all the paradigms commonly written about, or just used without being understood, were *fear-based* and more or less going to lead to destruction and toxification of Life. I felt the base motivational and ecological imaginary of the predominant paradigms was skewed, and mis-reading of what Life is about, and what a human being is about—and thus, no doubt due to that very misreading most paradigms produce a mis-balanced relationship with Life. Welcome to modern humanity's dilemma, and that includes the dilemma of how to know our human nature accurately?
>
> Many would argue, as would I, that the image or vision and beliefs we carry about "human nature" both

reflect our inner most attitudes but also they carry forth the emergence of the human nature we imagine we are. That's the self-fulfilling prophecy dilemma. So, examining theories and philosophies of human nature is essential in the quest to build a Fearlessness Paradigm and Philosophy, etc. There is also the sense, I believe it is possible, to be constructing the very tool for the study of human nature, as much as revealing our exact human nature. Fearlessness is such a tool. Thus, at the same time, such a tool is never perfect or finished, and arguably, as we better get to an accurate picture of our human nature we can then refine Fearlessness accordingly—and, to do both we ought to learn to design our lives and societies more attuned to the reality of Life's nature. For, it is assumed within the Fearlessness Paradigm as a starting point that Life's nature and Nature) is no different fundamentally than the living human being—an agent of Life and Nature. Humans are natural, in that sense—albeit, we are a 'strange' cultural creature that tends to slip away from the realization of our basis—that is, our true human nature—which is *humans are nature.* This argument is easier to make at the biological level of existence, understandably, than at the more complex cultural level of existence or spiritual level.

Basically, this paper fragment is an exploration of how best to situate and understand an emerging Fearlessness Paradigm re: its basic political (and moral) orientation—and, concomitant grounds for a vision of "human nature" that accompanies it. For example, the Darwinian view, and its scientific paradigm of natural selection, since the mid-19th century has had a great deal of influence on all kinds of thinkers and thinking, the likes of Sigmund Freud and so on—and, thus it has shaped the nature of human nature itself. Christianity traditionally has had a generic politically 'conservative' view of human nature and arguably so has the Darwinian view. There's a basic *mistrust of human nature* in this view and its paradigms be they secular or religious. Respectively, from a very humanistic-centered moral view, one cannot fully trust a wild animal/nature, as Darwin's paradigm would posit; nor can one fully trust an originally sinful human/nature, as Christianity's basic paradigm would posit.

Wright argued that at the same time that Darwin's work was coming into public, like a counter paradigmatic movement, so was John Stuart Mill's book and philosophy on "liberty." Mill's was attempting to argue for a more "liberal" view. Wright defines the basic orientations, which are quite useful for a first staging of the questions about human nature and political/moral implications:

Characteristically, Mill had hit on an important question [in his challenge to Victorian era Christian conservativism]: Are people inherently bad [sinful]? Those who believe so have tended...to be morally conservative—to stress self-denial [repression], abstinence, taming the beast [i.e., unconscious instincts and impulses] within. Those who believe not have tended, like Mill, to be morally liberal, fairly relaxed about how people choose to behave. Evolutionary psychology [Wright's view *via* Darwinism] has already shed much light on this debate....The bad news is that, although these things [goodness, empathy, love, caring] are in some ways blessings for humanity as a whole, they didn't evolve for the 'good of the species' and aren't reliably employed to that end. Quite the contrary: it is now clearer than ever how (and precisely *why*) the moral sentiments are used with brutal flexibility, switched on and off in keeping with self-interest; and how naturally oblivious we often are [i.e., unconscious] to this switching. In the new [evolutionary] view, human beings are a species splendid in their array of moral equipment, tragic in their propensity to misuse it, and pathetic in their constitutional ignorance [unconsciousness] of the misuse....a corrupt human nature, of 'original sin'—doesn't deserve such summary dismissal [like Mill's and liberals have tried to do].[338]

As an evolutionist myself, I cannot easily dismiss this "corrupt human nature" finding, but as with Freud as well, we also have to nuance what it exactly means. There is a part of my own philosophy from a fearlessness paradigm that has agreed with Freud and Darwin for a long time, but I have always been uncomfortable in how they have determined and defined human nature. And, because I start with the premise, or at least, a hypothesis, that both Darwin and Freud and Christianity for that matter, are largely fear-based ways of knowing, they have already misconstrued reality—and, thus also human nature. Simply, I can accept that "corrupt" is applicable to a good deal of human behavior, individually and institutionally and societally. But there are always exceptions to the masses that fit that description—and, one has to return to examine such healthy and mature individuals as did Abraham Maslow and the transpersonal schools of thought. They have a very different take on "human nature" and "human potential." I tend somewhat in the latter direction myself, but I think there is an even better intervention to make at the former conservative positioning. I think they ought to distinguish much more carefully "human nature" from "human condition"—and, yes, that in part, involves discernments around the age-old dilemma of Nature vs. Nurture distinctions when trying to describe motivations, behavior and the philosophical foundations of the 'human.'

I am not of course, the first critical thinker to play around with these issues, as Jean Jacques Rousseau had made that distinction to some degree as well—claiming, as would I, that human nature is not so much the corrupted and problematic as is the human condition—and, that which human nature has "learned" in social and cultural contexts. Before, I defend that case more, it is important to say that I always keep open the possibilities of the conservative position as real for human beings overall—especially the new technocultural human beings. Again, however, that is a massive generalization, and it may have more limitations than gains for actually working with our species and helping it to manage its crises—and, to manage fear itself.

The issue has been raised in other fragment papers of late I have written, some with my co-author Kumar, on the Id level of human nature—which, is the primal and archaic—the instinctual. Freud would give lots of room, unlike so many other thinkers, for this Id set of complexities in understanding human nature, the human condition and the human potential. In a Fearlessness paradigm I also will argue for maintaining this Id and *animal level*[339] as of primary *foundational* importance in human motivation and simultaneously I would not say it is most *significant* in importance in determining human potential. The terms "foundational" and "significance" arise from the second-tier integral theory, holarchical developmental, and spectrum of evolution of consciousness model of philosopher Ken Wilber, which I won't go into at this point; of which, is taken up as a topic in Chapter Seven on Fearlessness as/is Philosophy. Without such vertical distinctions in the nature of all things, truly the human species will fail its evolutionary maturation by succumbing to the current "flatland ontologies." and horizontalism dominating philosophies of postmodernism.

Fearlessness has this foundational layer of operations and has a significant layer as well at the 'higher' levels/layers of operations of significance. It is a spectrum model. All are important, but all are not equal in their weight and shaping force to determine any particular human action in a particular situation. Many things are involved in that analysis. Fear and Fearlessness ought to be part of that picture. I assert generally, that Fearlessness as a creative-healing principle (Id) is a useful reconstruction to show the spectrum of development of qualities of fearlessness across the foundational to the significant—in evolution. The general arc of that path of movement across the layers of development (i.e., meta-motivations) is generally from Fear to Fearlessness but the spirit of fearlessness is articulating itself in forms at all levels of the spectrum. There is no layer which is not of fearlessness. And, as I have said elsewhere, in my dictum: *When fear arises, so then does fearlessness.* All part of a basic self/system regulation process built in to the instinctual apparatus of living creatures for 4 billion years. Fear and fearlessness co-evolve, and arguably, so do worldviews taken by human beings, individually or collectively, whereby they are picking out their favorite views of morality as conservative or liberal or even radical and beyond either one of those two polarities. These views are co-evolving dialectically perhaps one could say, as cultures evolve with consciousness—*via* maturation (*via* the path of fearlessness).

So, back to the original question of whether Fearlessness Paradigm is conservative or liberal– well, it depends on how one is examining it and imagining it and using it. I would say, overall there is no one moral political positioning of Fearlessness itself—because of the dynamic of the spectrum of development it is part of. That said, sometimes more conservative sensibilities may better capture what fearlessness is becoming, other times more liberal. But if both conservative and liberal positioning becomes overly ideological and politically polarized—then they are both fear-based in operations and imaginary and will both twist and distort "human nature" towards their aims—and, the aims of fear itself. That I would not support, nor would a Fearlessness Paradigm support. Perhaps, the "radical" position in and around the polarity of conservative and liberal will prove to be more "integral" in the future and more appealing as well when it comes to looking at the nature of human nature. But that's another topic for another time. ...

But in general, with the cautions above, even though I am an evolutionist, I would side with a more benign human nature overall; that is, with one that is 'natural' and non-fear-based—and that is both our foundational ground for existence and operating on this planet in ecologically sound ways. And, that is also our destiny to mature itself—to move in and through and beyond the current corrupted human condition—and, to thus push through new shoots of human potential that the human condition cannot even imagine yet. Yet, I think without an imaginary for paradigm shifts, and without critical analysis of paradigms and worldviews, we'll miss the boat. Humans have to come to a point, I believe, to see themselves as fluid, as a *movement* itself—and, yes, that movement is within the flowing river of Life—of fear/fearlessness dynamics. Now, if that was to ever happen then that would be radical—far beyond being conservative or liberal in political terms. I await that day.

BMK: Nicely articulated. Human life is a movement of fear/fearlessness dynamics. Yes, I agree with your explanation Michael! Fear as such does not slow down the movement of human progress. Benign fears facilitate the movement of life to be steady. Like brakes of a vehicle, benign fears ensure us to maintain enough distance from danger spots. They not only keep us safe but also help us reach our destination timely. That means good fears act as one of the catalysts to boost the fearlessness movement. As you have confidently emphasized, a positive fear/fearlessness dynamic approach will certainly bring about radical transformation someday in world politics.

CHAPTER SIX

Affective Potency: The Force of Esteem(s)

The average man [sic]...[is] what we today call "ambulatory schizophrenic"....a superb characterization of the "culturally normal" man, the one who dares not stand up for his own meanings because this means too much danger, too much exposure. Better not to be oneself, better to live tucked into others, embedded in the safe [fear-based] framework of social and cultural obligations and duties....He cannot seem to understand the situation he is in, cannot see beyond his own fears, cannot grasp why he has bogged down. Kierkegaard phrases it... "If one will compare the tendency to run wild in possibility with the efforts of a child to enunciate words, the lack of possibility is like being dumb...for without possibility a man cannot...draw breath."

- Ernest Becker[340]

History of an Omission 'Crime'

Before we drilled down to the core of this chapter on the idea of Esteem-power(s) within human existence and their great impact on everything, and in relation to fear/fearlessness, we wish to point out the empirical case of movements that historically have not served Fearlessness becoming more well-known and understood. Our focus is on W. history of thought. The E. history of thought is complex and we cannot give it due attention her. We can summarize this point very briefly in a critical question: *Why is there no history of fearlessness recorded in any book or scholarly article to this date? Why is this the case, when there are a growing number of history of fear works available—especially in the last 15 years?*

Our conclusion is simple: *Because there is resistance to knowing fearlessness.* And, because there is no fully articulated Fearlessness Paradigm for us to study and actualize as a counter-force to the dominating Fear Paradigm. Indeed, the empirical truth, at this time in human history, is that many critics have named the Fear Paradigm, often calling it the "culture of fear" as we have said in earlier chapters and the Introductions of this book. Many, including the fearist philosophers, like ourselves, have shown the central role of fear in evolution and human cultures, etc. Yet, *no history of fearlessness.* No one, other than Fisher in the W., has claimed Fearlessness is central to the evolution and dynamics of human cultures. In 2011, Fisher applied to an elite U.S. university History program for a post-doctoral research grant and study. He was determined to participate in the vast and growing field of what is called *History of Emotions.* From around the world almost in synchrony, these modern/post-modern brave new historians have decided that it is time to fully look into the history of our affective and emotional life and the way it has and is still shaping everything—that is, by human choices and the way it shapes human choices—that is, the way history is inevitably shaped by this soft-side of existence—in particular, humanity's soft-inner-vulnerable and often irrational core. This equally, according to Fisher, is a history of motivation(s).

Yet, his detailed proposal in 2011 was rejected. It seems the elites studying emotions and history have their biases. All kinds of grants have been given to study fear, guilt, shame, anxiety, etc. as historical subjects. Which is great. However, Fisher proposed to study the history of fearlessness. Clearly, the scholars and funders of research were not interested. Some who know Fisher's work, outside of the academy, think that perhaps Fisher's has already crafted the history of Fearlessness in his vast 2010 tome entitled *The World's Fearlessness Teachings.* Though he denies that is analogous to the studies of the history of fear that scholars have produced in the last 15 years. He believes he opened the door to such a history in that book but it is nowhere near methodologically sufficient to advance a rigorous history of fearlessness *per se*. Others have suggested that perhaps the history of fearlessness in the W. in part is articulated in books on the history of courage and bravery. Yes, that is partly correct. Though, as Fisher points out, all those books, be it the history of fear ones or the history of courage ones all start their inquiries based on the discipline and methodologies within the discipline of History itself. And, that would not do for any study or book on the history of Fearlessness.

Why, would those former disciplinary works on the history of emotions and fear and courage be rejected by Fisher? Simply, because they are disciplinary. History and its paradigms control those studies, more or less. From the start of his inquiries, Fisher always claimed that any thorough and justifiably accurate study of fear/fearlessness dynamics has to be transdisciplinary, not limited to one discipline or even a few. This transdisciplinary approach is unconventional overall in re: to any topic, but to apply it to fear studies is even more radical. Fisher argues that the underlying paradigmatic regime of domination, like a hidden curriculum, in all emotions studies is still constituted within the rule of Psychology and the Biomedical worldview—that is, ruled by ideological psychologism. Fisher thinks that ideology is fear-based from the start and would never adequately be competent to study Fear or Fearlessness. The influence that regime has on fearlessness understanding is enormous and no more so than the overt pathologizing of "fearlessness" that has gone on for decades in W. clinical psychology.[341]

And yet perhaps worse, in terms of a forensic analysis, an argument can be made that the history of emotions and fear are particularly distracting of a 'crime' they are involved in and unwilling to recognize and thus be responsible for. Fisher's Fearlessness Paradigm for the study of fear and 'fear' start with the premise that *perhaps we humans do not understand fear as well as we think we do, and furthermore, arguably, we are afraid to admit that we are so ignorant and arrogant*. Because all of the historians of emotion(s) begin their research on the premise that we already know that *fear is an emotion* just one of many others identified. Fisher has never fully accepted that premise so unconditionally. The 'crime' then is that even the historians of fear participate in is that they educate humanity about emotion and fear and do so without this suspicion and adequate doubt that Fisher believes is necessary for the truth. The historians also have proceeded therefore to ignore fearlessness per se, because it is not an emotion—or, at least in the W., it does not fall into the category of emotions. Interesting. Disturbing. How the domination of categorization and taxonomies of human affects becomes so biased and inclusive but exclusive—and, does not even question itself in its exclusions. Not that Fisher wants the field of historians of emotion to declare fearlessness is an emotion. That's not the solution.

Okay you get the sense of problems, if not the 'crime' that we as co-authors cannot ignore is in the background of everything we are writing. Yet, that's not the explicit story we want to tell here, other than to remind readers of the methodological and paradigmatic issues that always accompany this ongoing fearwork. So, let's move on, past these scholarly resistances Fisher has noted long ago that dis-enable a good Fear and Fearlessness Education—that is, a good history of Fearlessness.

> **BMK:** Michael, I'd be curious what of significance would you place as historical datum to highlight in your version of a history of Fearlessness, should you write one someday?

> **RMF:** Thanks for asking. There are many strands I would braid together. Okay, if I had to pick one off the top, I'd include The League *for* Fearlessness, started officially in October of 1931 in New York. It was started by esoteric philosophy types like Alice & Foster Bailey and some 48+ others. This organization produced a rare document of its objectives and rationale, which I have published elsewhere in whole or part, if you look it up on the internet.[342] Truly a remarkable clear articulation of a historical reference of recognition, at least by this marginal but potent group of people; unfortunately, it faded away as quickly as it came into formation. I'm currently researching the history of this little known

sub-movement that happened, and perhaps is still underground.

BMK: Thanks. No, I have never heard of them. It makes me wonder if such an organization, with such specific focus on fearlessness, was ever founded in India or the E. generally?

RMF: I suspect it is possible but these kinds of sources are difficult to find and document. By the way, it is not inconsequential that the 1931 founding of The League was right smack in the middle of crisis times in the world and especially in the USA. The Depression was in full bloom as was the Third Reich in Germany. Two years later, F. D. Roosevelt would give his famous presidential inaugural address, so often quoted, "We have nothing to fear but fear itself." Of course, he didn't mention fearlessness as an alternative but that's because he had not likely heard of The League. We use the language we are familiar with and it's so important to give people new vocabularies and validate that new words and concepts, like "fearlessness" may be something worth investigating. The ancient E. philosophies have used this word, *abhaya*, in many ways and traditions, a point we brought up in earlier chapters of the this book. The W. still fears the unknown and fear's fearlessness, as the Dalai Lama once articulated on his lecture tours in the early 2000s in North America.[343]

Highlighting Esteem(s)

From Introduction 1, here we proceed to pick-up on a critical theme to understanding *resistance* to Fearlessness along a particular angle in re: to *movement(s)*. The initial diagram that will be useful to re-look at now is Figure 1 Tripartite Esteem Model from Introduction 1. We suggest re-reading some of the material there, which accompanies the diagram and become re-familiarized with the architecture in Fisher's integral imaginary of how "Esteem" in the largest sense of Reality of which living creatures are operating.

Of course, Fisher has always been interested in the dialectic and now trialectic interplay of FEAR—> FEARLESSNESS—> LOVE. This is primarily his interest in Movement overall at the meta-motivational dynamic level, and as a universal revelation of *affective potencies* in evolution, development and history. However, the clarification of the theoretical underpinnings for Figure 1, in this chapter, will focus on ferreting out some of the particularities of *resistance* and *rebellion* within this model/figure.

To begin to get back on board with the movement in Figure 1 (follow the arrows), let us recite some of our earlier point of reference to this model as a reminder, as Fisher wrote:

> I've then added Freud's three conceptions [Id, Ego, Super Ego] as I imagine where they operate on this model and named three resonant types of Esteem(s) that go with the zones....I [which eventually to] make a case that the Fearlessness zone is most potent to counter the Fear Paradigm (the Fear Problem) when it is founded in the Id and It-esteem. This is the instinctual and Natural layer of our motivational template ....I'll make a philosophical distinction, as does the integral philosopher Ken Wilber, that a good holistic-integral model of reality, is both dialectical, but it is also vertical and developmental. The Fearlessness Paradigm is both of these. Wilber asked us to recognize the *foundational* levels of the spectrum of consciousness[344]—as the most basic, simpler, and ancient. They offer great wisdom. The Id included. Of course, we don't want to take everything they offer as great because some of it is not.

Indeed there can be shadows and pathologies; that is, fear-based architectures at any of the Freudian three major conceptual levels of what makes up a human being's existence. Careful analysis is thus required to make such distinctions between the healthy and un-healthy aspects. Again, focus here will be on the Id, and the arguments for that focus will slowly unfold.

In the last chapter we brought forward the importance of recognizing *animality* and *foundational* aspects in order to subvert habits from the Fear Paradigm that may, at any time, infest the Fearlessness Paradigm. These are the common thought-habits like species-superiority, as a total way of thinking about Life on this planet—that is, from a human-centric lens. Actually, it is arguable, using the Wilberian spectrum model of valuation distinctions, to ethically suggest that humans are amazing and occupy the pivotal territory of the *most significance* in terms of evolutionary development and the future. For e.g., significance of human choice is undeniably and relative to other species, astoundingly significant overall on Earth. It is not surprising that various mythological narratives, if not religious ones, over human history have articulated that we humans 'are made in the image of God, the Creator'—that's a way to hold some truth about our power potency. Our creativity is enormous, flexible and at times out of our control—so it seems. And, that latter situation is a very dangerous one within technocultural advancements.

For example, think that a most simple and subtle perturbance in the Life System, made by the will of a single human being—especially one with the leadership power to push the red button to release the full nuclear arsenal in one country upon the rest of the world; what total unimaginable devastation could happen in a matter of minutes. No other creature or process can compare to a simple willed-decision that can enact that kind of split-second mega-significance.[345]

In other words, it *really matters* what human beings feel, think and do to create *movement*—which, in this context of significance, derives from interior feeling-power, mind-power, values-power, beliefs-power, including the exterior materiality of economic-technical-power, operational-management-power and outright large-brain-power capacity. Of course, this significance potency can be take the form of many other examples both benign and malign. Momentarily, we'll translate those power significance referents down to one affective potency dimension—that is, the specific notion of *Esteem-power* for the purposes of exploring the fear/fearlessness dynamics, of great interest to us as fearists.

What about *foundational potency* in Gaia, as a planetary ecology, and/or within living systems and human systems? Now, we are talking at the Id level. What really matters?

> **RMF:** Well, how about "air." Air, Water, Earth, Fire, as you may recall are the four ancient "Elements" and in some traditions they are "spirits" of the archaic pre-personal *elemental world* reality. Whatever the case, let's talk about "air," just as did Dr. David Suzuki, one the leading environmentalists of the last 50 years in North America. Suzuki turned 85 recently and in a national interview on TV,[346] he said, that if he was to give any advice to the next generations in particular, but also to everyone, he simply said (paraphrasing) realize you are an animal and within three minutes if you don't have air, you die. So care about air.'
>
> He meant care about Nature and act to delimit the pollution that humankind has and continues to pour onto the environment both unconsciously because we are so disconnected from Nature for the most part, and consciously as when we know we are polluting but we've rationalized that it is okay—like driving a polluting gas and oil dependent machine around as if it is our 'right' to do so. Suzuki's repeated message for 50 years of teaching environmentalism has always been to remind us as a species "we are completely dependent on Nature" and all its gifts. Not surprising he is more and more fervent in his teaching and his anger at

how little humans have learned over 50 years in this regard. Advocating for wise elder's and their role today, he also has pointed out in a recent interview that fear is at the core of the problem in that environmental organizations he has been involved with have too often sugar/hope-coated their messages and had a control 'leash' on Suzuki and the truths he really wanted to speak out. Now, he thinks that was a mistake. Things are so bad environmentally because people decades ago were too afraid to be 'negative' sounding regarding the consequences of telling the scientific truth bluntly.[347] It seems to Suzuki, and many others, that our species seems to continue on a truth denial path towards more self-abuse and self-destruction. Many critics have pointed out that 'humans are the only species that spoils its own nest.' And, that surely, if taken in with any amount of decelerated reflection, is a sign of the truth and a truth that really matters. Because it is saying that we are a self-injuring species, at least since the time of the agricultural revolution 12,000 years ago, and certainly since the Industrial Revolution. We can hardly be called a "highest" of the intelligent species on earth can we?—that is, of "progress," when that self-abuse is actually registered and factually supported as the underbelly to all the great achievements of our kind. For me at least, I cannot look away from that shadow-pathological side that is with us as human every day, every moment. To destroy one's own home, one's own air, to the point of poisoning itself, there is obviously a species-cide, equivalent to *suicide*, going on. There is obviously a 'disorder' deeply nested in the human psyche and civilization. The *cultural therapist* cannot ignore this, even if many other want to and want to be positive about humanity and its advances.

So, maybe the debate in evolutionary and cultural history is not so much about whether there is *progress* (as modernists like to claim) or *anti-progress* (as postmodernists and environmentalists like to claim)—maybe, as the cultural fearologist comes on stage, and a philosophy of fearism becomes the context of analysis—maybe, as the issues of "Health" and "Mental Health" climbs to the top of the ladder of priority values in nations—there is the necessary re-interpretation just waiting to be said and recognized as the *real diagnosis* of the primal pattern of a collective disturbed 'mind' we humans suffer with. Maybe the *best diagnosis*, or at least it is one we'll be able to swallow without a lot of sugar coating on the pill—is, that *"we are scaring ourselves to death"* as was first explicitly articulated by Aaron Cohl, a lawyer and journalist-type writer, in his book of that name in 1997. Oh, but even further back, the symptoms of our collective paranoic-based psychology was registered by another author in 1979 who wrote a book on the pain and suffering of cancer as a disease but then focused on the worse problem of our ever being able to recover well from cancer and its treatment. Henry Neufeld, wrote *Cancerophobia: We Are Scaring Ourselves to Death.* Amongst others pointing out this symptomatology of our human scare-disorder, where we attack and terrify ourselves with our fear unlike any other species on the planet, maybe it is worth looking carefully for a moment at Neufeld's basic argument. One doesn't have to be a psychiatrist or registered clinical psychologist or therapist to see what is happening and being called out in *cancerophobia* dynamics, and its paradoxical dis-ease. This has been well researched by many since 1979.

But Neufeld was onto seeing through the kind of self-abusive madness, if not schizoidal-paranoidal complex of our collective psyche, our culture of fear and our sick people and those threatened to become sick—with cancer(s). The growing threat is real as he would document. There's no getting around how vicious cancers can be. The very term began to be so mediated in the press and talk shows and popular conversations, that cancer=death became glued together. Humans fear death—but they fear cancer worse it seems. Whatever the case, Neufeld rightfully said, that cancer is not the worst problem for increasing the rates of morbidity—that is, bringing on death itself. No. The much worse problem is the fear of cancer—that's where the phrase/diagnosis of *cancerophobia* was coined and now is well-recognized in the entire etiology of cancer discourses. In other words, people turn cancer into a "beast" of horror-making scenarios even before they get cancer. Of course, they tend to do so as well when they first get diagnosed with cancer, because the contagion of cancerophobia has infested the entire milieu of life today, at least in the modern world and urban environments. Health promotion advertisements warning of cancer have not helped. People were systematically being 'educated' so-called on all the things that can cause cancer and that maybe a symptom of early cancer, and so on. People *en masse* became obsessed with the possibilities. The cancer pandemic is not unrealistic as a name for this phenomenon and re-cycling of the fear. Yes, people were scaring themselves to death about cancer. And that fear/terror led to increasingly poor outcomes of cancer treatment regimes and recovery. Fear exacerbated the disease toxicity and morbidity and did so even with people who had no cancer or weren't even likely to get cancer in their life-times. People brought on chronic cancerophobia amongst themselves and the culture. It became a life-style-fear patterning of distress. It didn't take much to trigger the distress and put people almost in a panic any moment. "Oh, I have a lump here. It could be cancer." Almost everyone colluded in this mania pandemic. The 1970s, 80s, 90s especially this was up and foremost. Eventually, people seemed to at least calm down somewhat on the surfaces with time and more familiarity with the disease, and new scientific advances in early detection and treatment, but that doesn't mean the phobia is gone.

Be it the lesson from Neufeld or Cohl, what I see has gone on with this example, and it is only the obvious one for there are many other diseases that are exacerbated by fear of the disease, including now COVID-19 and its variants, is that humans are trapped in a *recycling of fear* within their own psyches and social structures, whereby the incessant replay is killing us. It's a self-fulfilling prophecy to fear and worry so much about "what could happen" or "it could be cancer" or "it could be a criminal"—every moment and every stimulus nearly—triggering a sense of threat and one's demise. In psychiatry such an exacerbated symptomatology is called neurosis, where one becomes a neurotic as part of their identity formation—that is, a hypochondriac, and worse, in the extremes a psychotic. I have discussed the cultural diagnosis briefly earlier in this book and in several of my writings of late about the call for a new label maybe needed: "near-psychotic disorder."[348]

I'm half joking of course, But it could well turn out that we are now on average, as 'normal' to the human condition, "psychotic" or nearly so. If you are an organism out to destroy your own home. That's psychotic behavior. That's an act of suicide. It is a pattern language of the Death-drive on hyper-hormones and adrenalin to the point of self-abusive behavior and self-killing behavior. To kill the ecological systems by pollution as Suzuki speaks about, is to kill the self—because, 'you are Nature'—there is no separation. Only a "psychotic" would not see this connection. Yet, *en masse*, this delusion appears to have completely or nearly so, taken over the human mind and society's intelligence about what is healthy thought and what is unhealthy thought. Gaia may have its own diagnosis....

BMK: Yeah, Gaia would likely say, the real dis-ease that matters, that's under all other diseases, including the seeming 'need' to self-harm, is *fear itself.*

RMF: Precisely. We even become afraid of fear itself, for the most part. Albeit, may are trying to start a movement to counter that negative only attribution to fear, including the fearism perspective. I see the whole movement above as a *resistance movement to living.* Okay. Freud saw that in the Death-drive. But actually, as many theorists have said, and I agree, the Death-drive when connected in a healthy communication with the Life-drive—together they make up the nature of, the meta-motivation of Existence itself. That's a whole other book topic. Life/Death, and Love/Fear, etc. as you and I have talked about as dialectically integrated forces and phenomenon—they are not the problem. They are Yin/Yang so to speak and they will not harm anything overly in playing out their 'dance' of Existence. But when one of these pairs of opposites, of which they are in constant movement, "splits" then we have big problems. Bracha L. Ettinger, the founder of matrixial theory, gives some of the best explanatory understanding I have ever heard anywhere on the nature of this "split" from the (M) Other, Nature, and so on. Again, a big topic for another book.

Problem is not the *duality* of our perceptions; the problem is the *dualism* of our obsessions. The 'ism' is the ideological formation, where distortion of the pair's dialectical partnership dependence and integrity as a cycle are undermined artificially. Abstraction and dissociated imaginaries exist in all of the worst forms of ideologism. They oppress us all. Thus, when Fear for example, like *Thanatos* as an expression of that, is hyper-dominating and reinforced and encouraged by a person's psyche and/or the collective psyche and civilization process itself, then we are in big trouble. Because the *Thanatos* or Death-drive complex will attach to our vulnerable narcissistic instinctual bonding-need, to "cling" to anything to bond to that seems like it is our 'protector' or 'substitute mother' or 'substitute immortality project.' Because Fear is a safety-security device, you might say, of Defense Intelligence itself, well then, it is an easy target for bonding-attachment primal Id complex psychic mechanisms. It's no wonder that just about everyone I've read, at some point, says that 'fear is the most primal of emotions'—as was repeated in a recent David Suzuki "Nature of Things" TV program.[349]

Thus, this narcissistic pathology and one-sidedness, with the ideologism of a "death culture" syndrome, as some have called it—and, I just call it a "culture of fear" then, you have a fear recycling system based on a narcissistic structuration of "self-love" which ends up as "self-death," according to Ettinger and most psychoanalysts would say the same pretty much.

It makes sense in a twisted pathological and paradoxical (anti-)logic and (anti-) reason: *We love death.* Not to think of this claim as merely literal death. No, that's would be a mis-reading of what I am describing here. *We resist life, because we resist that which destroys life.* Turns out modern humans and our ways of life are the most destructive to life because they destroy our own home in the very process of trying to secure our home. That is the same twisted narcissistic syndrome of A-ness as a movement that becomes a non-movement of stasis—that is, a pattern language/logic of Death, by any other name. And, yes, Fear is the basis of it all shaping up that way. I prefer to call it 'fear' patterning, as I have said many times in this book and elsewhere in my work.

People, even the most well-educated, don't find it easy to take in my concept of 'fear' itself as so very different from the fear that is positive and negative. I am theorizing here something much more profound in the *movement of fear* to *'fear'*—it is a quantum leap of difference that really matters! 'Fear' is ideological Fear, is another way to put it—it is Fear "without feelings" as I sometimes express it. Now, Maria, this is where really good quality Fear Education and fear management have to begin their curricular core. There is a movement, the Fearlessness Movement, for example, on the planet that intends to improve the way we are conditioned and educated into this dangerous narcissistic-death-'fear' patterning—yet, there's a movement to resist it as well. The latter, is as strong as the human's resistance to life—that is, it is the movement to suicidal re-cycling in self-harming. This is no different than the deeper psychic patterns underneath all addictions. I have always argued, we are addicted to fear itself—and, it is a process of scaring ourselves to death.

BMK: I know you have written even about the ethical problem of talking and writing about fear.

RMF: Yes, it actually goes back to my intellectual mentors, Robert Sardello, a great spiritual psychocultural therapist in my eyes, who warned us of this problem of fear management/education and discourse, more clearly than others: "One of the greatest challenges in [teaching and] writing about fear is to avoid generating more fear by doing so."[350] It is easy to read this warning, and skip on and continue on one's merry old way. No. The true *sacred warrior* has to halt. Decelerate. Imbibe.

BMK: That's the more contemplative part to your work, and of the Fearlessness Movement, isn't it? Rushing, even while reading this text, is one way to skip over the 'deeper' dimensions; and perhaps that's a superficiality that wants to skip over the really terrifying dimensions of what Fearlessness implies. That is, the 'waking up' part of it all as we talked about in an earlier chapter. Maybe we are self-harming as a species because we don't want to wake-up from our nightmare existence and we rather prefer our dreamy, hypnotic-trance-like state of being, we call 'normal.' Certainly, Plato and Socrates diagnosed that a long time ago in the metaphoric story and teaching of "The Cave."

RMF: For sure. Fearlessness is terrifying. There will be a massive resistance to that! You are right though. A lot of wisdom traditions from around the globe have this 'Cave' teaching in it, in some form or other. But typically they don't have the *adequatio* of teachings on the nature and role of fear, and 'fear', and thus are not completely applicable to the 21st century. That's my point.

This book is all about this up-grading our universal FME and that includes a deeper understanding of Fearlessness well beyond what most of us are familiar with. Postmodern and poststructuralist thinkers, especially in the academy today, will totally balk at my suggestion of "universal" values and realities. Extreme forms of relativism has so polluted the contemporary minds and institutions of so-called 'higher learning.'

Anyways, I'll continue: but to not forget fear/fearlessness is a dialectical. The epistemic, ethical and critical praxis implications of promoting the Fearlessness Movement are before us now—meaning, I can't be naive about it, nor should anyone else be. Let me quote from what I wrote about this long ago in 2010 and which I was re-citing my concerns, while reconfiguring and up-grading the fearism philosophy of Subba et al.: "*When fear arises, so there shall fearlessness be* in order to counter fear's limitations. So let the story begin, though not without a final caution. Like any mature socially responsible author-educator, I have to ask an ethical question about what I am presenting to the public. I am no longer interested in only 'shocking' my audiences, so they'll wake up (and believe and value what I do). That's what immature rebels like to do. [I offer another kind of archetypal Rebel[351] on the scene, one that knows what they are doing in the process of disruption and discomfort—and fearfulness.] Rather, I want to help them 'wake up' but I know I have to be there fully to offer them support for such awakeness— and its accompanying terror (among other things).

Basically, people are 'asleep' to their own or the world's problems...".[352]

BMK: It's a real problem when our higher education institutions and academic culture are so against ideas like Fearlessness...

RMF: I'm not speculating about this. It is real. I've lived and worked in those institutions for decades, off and on. It is only getting worse how they are resistant to even the concept of emancipation or liberation. For example, my own *alma matter* university in my home town, in the year 2021 adopted the slogan for the university overall as "The Entrepreneurial University." That's what they are marketing. Oh, my god. What a statement of watering-down and instrumentalization of higher learning. But, don't get me started on that rant...

The citing of the Sardelloian cautionary needs to be finished: "Basically people are 'asleep' to their own or the world's problems for good reasons—it is called 'denial,' (among other names). My speciality is 'fear education'... and that has even more demanding aspects to consider. I take the spiritual educator Robert Sardello's ethical caveat very seriously....Note, this [Sardello statement; see above] is essentially the definition of the 'culture of fear' (a type of fear management) that I spoke about earlier....If we are generating more fear [i.e., resistance to fear/fearlessness] instead of less, then our intervention to make things better (to 'wake up' people) is questionable, if not unethical....[if not post-traumatic itself] With the exception of Sardello, I have yet seen any author's book or article on the topic *fear* take such wise heed.[353] Probably that is because it is easier said than done. I am still learning how to do this skillfully. The introduction material for this book...is pretty terrifying at some level. Learning more about fear is not a favorite thing for people to do. I agree with bell hooks, a critical black feminist pedagogue, who wrote, "In our society we make much of love and say little about fear?"[354]

BMK: Can you say more about the terrifying aspect?

RMF: Now, just to ask that Maria, tells me a good deal about what part of a person's soul is 'awake' and alive and is curious. Rare would anyone even ask that question of me, and typically it's unheard of. It's obviously not attractive. To put one on the truly curious course of study of fear/fearlessness is to put one's life on the line—emotionally, if not socially and perhaps even physically. Mahatma Gandhi stood for the Fearlessness Movement, and we all know what was his demise in the end. A gun and a bullet at close range. It looks then, to the haters of fearlessness that such a philosophy is not going to live on and pass on its message. That will end right here, at the end of my gun barrel.

So, why is it that Maria Kumar would ask? No doubt you can add your own views here as to why. In the context of my discussion above, and I have gone deep into metaphysical and psychoanalytical explanations, not just at the individual but the collective level. In the end, the 'asleep' like their asleepness—called denial. It got them through tough times of coping but not healing. I think of yourself as a career police officer and leader of policing work, as well as an out-spoken author of your own larger world interests. I think you would not be scared of a gun barrel because of your character but also years of training and experience on the police force. You've accepted that with that career path facing a gun point was very highly likely, and even deadly—that is, a great risk. You walked that path anyways. You didn't have to. You had options. But you chose, like Gandhi did. Thus, you are both warriors—of a sacred ancient tradition of leadership and warriorship, based on the great teachings of the great warriors throughout history that knew that conflict and battle is inevitable, and knew that fear and terror, life and death—are close twins.

I think that's why you asked the question. I think that's why you and I travel as co-authors—and, travel with great respect for each other, as far along as we have. Most do not make it past a certain point. I have met many who 'say' they want to travel but that's only in their mind, ideals or fantasies, for the most part. Maybe they just aren't trained enough for 'when the going gets really rough.' They may like the idea but don't like the true risks involved.

BMK: Thanks Michael for your kind words. Your elucidative example of Mahatma Gandhi has clarified my query. Gandhi is the epitome of fearlessness and a paragon of love and nonviolence.

You have already put forth your trialectic model of fear-fearlessness-love. To me, this is a revelation as opposed to dialectical approach. I see the touch of Buddha's middle path in your ideation. Now let me make use of your trialectics in hypothesising evolution, from fearlessness perspective. Living beings sprang from chemical components which randomly got connected *a la* Jobs' creativity; and the human species gradually evolved. Howsoever revolutionarily that humans have evolved like other species, their bond with the nature (air, water, earth etc.) is impregnable. You have quoted David Suzuki's assertion that humans will meet their extinction if there is no air for three minutes. Such is the bond so strong as between living beings and nature. Humans survive on food they get from the nature. Besides other essential necessities like water and sunlight the primal instincts, experiences and memories etc. keep humans unconsciously and consciously bonded to the nature they depend on. Suzuki's primal fear pertains to the fear of loss of bond as Death instinct re: nature. Fear can exacerbate this sticky-bond making it a sort of bondage, an obsessive-compulsive orientation towards Death instinct.

The other side of primal fear is primal fearlessness as Life instinct, to be free. And the body has already had the taste of a kind of freedom of being separated physically from nature. Freedom is a manifestation of Life instinct. Indecisiveness or ambiguity as regards to too much bondage to nature or too much of freedom away from nature is the question which becomes the perpetual apple of discord between Id and Super Ego. Hence Ego has to continue intervening, ideally through 'Love' mechanisms so as to moderate between fear and fearlessness.

RMF: Thanks. But back to my point, one has to really be passionate, be willing to put their ass on the line, to really truly know fear/fearlessness. If one isn't experiencing terror within, and from others around you when you speak about say the Fearlessness Movement, then one is probably not speaking about the real Fearlessness Movement and telling the world about the resistance(s) to it. We chose to write this book with that very expressive and explicit telling. You just won't get that kind of disclosure from authors who write about fear. I noticed even your work doesn't go into it. But, something changed. Now, you are travelling with me right into the heart of the darkness of what this work demands. Again, you had to do that day after day in your policing career—you got up, you put on the uniform, and you walked out the door, leaving behind any 'normal' life and comfort. That's nothing to underplay or ignore! I admire that.

Fear of the Sacred Warrior: Emancipatory Leader(ship)

The above section is about the terrifying aspect of talking and teaching about fear. To do so, at the level of the holistic-integral curriculum for the 21st century, is not for the light-hearted. Fisher as an educator for 45 years has pursued this kind of intensity in his educational philosophy. What he has found, is that decade after decade, the teachers in schooling and in educational departments in universities and the leaders of educational administration and policy making etc., they all became more and more cowardly. They turned "Education" into a coward's profession and domain of society. It became more and more conservative—even, in the most advanced (so-called) nations of the world—like North America. What was happening?

Fisher believes the entire Education imaginary and politics of course, was turning out not sacred warriors to lead emancipatory pedagogy but the System was turning out *cowards* of minimum bravery and worse, of minimum vision. All teachers were suffering from minimalism *via* the concomitant vision-loss, Fisher believes. They could no longer imagine or envision that it is worth becoming a Sacred Warrior-Teacher-Leader. They defaulted to a minimal and truncated, if not *fear-based*, sense of identity as "teacher" or "educator." And no more characteristic was this phenomenon—a social phenomenon—than in his finding the discourse of a couple of university educators recently who published on this 'new turn' for teachers. Van Kessel and Burke, and it could just as well be many other such educators in their shoes, ushered out the not to be dismissed potent words. They wrote it down. They said what others were saying but who were too cowardly to say it directly. They were brave ones. They gave the commandment(s) to 'the people.' And to their 'students.' They told all of us, and I mean all of us, what teachers are *best* only meant to be doing in the years ahead. They entered their grand universal campaign, their vote, their 2018 published (sad little) vision into the annals of the field of philosophy of Education:

> Teaching as a profession can be read as an immortality project, a form of compensation to help resolve a certain kind of existential terror....In response to the [emotionally-charged] freighted reality of teaching as quasi-missionary work, we suggest [as counter-movement] a new orientation [for teachers], namely that the profession embrace the terror of the future that it cannot know.[355]

On first round of assessment this quote sounds very much in-tune with our book here and the importance we stress of facing into the terror of teaching about fear itself—including, fearlessness. Great: "embrace the terror of the future." But on closer reading, such a scenario of apparent complementarity collapses as one really begins to hear what these two educational professors are up to. They continue,

> Through a theoretical engagement with Weak Theology in the context of Eugene Thacker's philosophical 'doomcore,' *we hope to re-orient* the educational project into one with lower [minimalist] stakes, a shift from immortality to more 'goodness.' The desired result is to refocus....Without a set endpoint, [we recommend an educational] space [which] opens up in order to work toward goodness....[356] [italics added for emphasis]

In their suggestion towards "a new orientation to the terror of the future that we cannot know," they promote "our limited status" as recommendation for assisting that "we need ways to cope with that terror."[357] First, we note that "cope with" is indeed their agenda, not only for themselves as teachers of teachers, but that also becomes by default their modeling and philosophy of intention for teachers of our kids and youth. There is no 'wake up' here in their discourse. There is no offering of healing paradigm *contra* coping paradigm. This topic of contrast is something we raised a few time here in our book. It is critical to make this distinction. Respectively, the contrast can be stated as Fearlessness Paradigm *contra* Fear Paradigm.

So, what these two educators do then is purport a "de-escalation of teaching as an immortality project"—which means, for teachers to step down from and outside of any heroic grand narratives of mythology, of history itself—and of what cultures do. No, they want all that cut down. They want only their view of ethics. Sure, they want some good things to happen in their "new orientation," which we (as co-authors) applaud in part. They don't want teachers to try to achieve immortality status through using their children/students in classes and enmeshing students into the teacher's potential inflated-ego strivings, if not pathologies, to be "quasi-saviors" of the children/students. Okay. But their coping solution to help students and themselves cope with terror and the future that is in cascading crises—they only offer "an educational disposition that is humbler, which, paradoxically requires more courage"[358] than the salvation and emancipatory approaches to education they are critiquing. Thus, if you put their analysis and prescriptive rendering together, you get a 'Be Humble, More Brave' pill for their "new orientation." This is highly problematic, see also the critique of Fisher in his general call out against the unacknowledged "failing relationship" between fear management and education.[359] As well, Fisher has recently critiqued van Kessel's project in re: to 'evil' and education along similar grounds as our critique here of their positing that being humble is the solution because it is more brave to be humble. Well, to say the least, one would have to delve into definitions of "humble" and "brave" and "courageous" within the theorizing of these two educators above. But to be clear, they have no holistic-integral healing framework to any of their understanding of fear and courage, for that matter, or Education. Their view is completely reductionistic and as we said before riveted in functionalist minimalism, as if that was 'neutral' and just humble and thus cannot be anything but that. We've suggested their "new orientation" is highly authoritarian in its broad-brushing 'ought' philosophical emphasis. This is a new ethic they promote. Implicitly, it applies to all citizens not just teachers.

How can they talk of bravery, courageousness, without a larger framework of the Fearlessness Movement already intact, as we have argued in this book? Well, they can do so, because they have chosen to ignore the Fearlessness discourses of Fisher and anyone else in human history. They never cite such references or invite dialogues. Fisher has asked to have dialogue with these authors but the lead author has been rigidly defensive and cut-off immediately any further dialogues. This says a lot about the integrity of their 'be humble, be more brave' hypothesis and its actualization in the world. The true Sacred Warrior 'walks their talk' and does not hide behind protective walls of academia to spout out words that sound nice.

On that note, then we wish to close this chapter and sliding from the resistances to Fearlessness of the two authors above, into what in earlier Introduction(s) and Chapters of our book, we mentioned the word "warrior" several times, in different contexts. We believe it is worthy synthesizing them here, along the questioning of: How to talk about *significance, about better, about Quality, about the true, the courageous,* and *authentic*? We know this scares so many people today. How to talk about *the Movement* from Fear to Fearlessness, from oppression to liberation? This scares people today. And, to get right down and dirty, how to talk about "fearlessnessizing"—without scaring people—how to talk about fear without scaring people—when already people are scaring themselves to death? Our point is, we are not offering mere "coping" mechanisms and more defense mechanisms for this that are located in the Fear Paradigm, that is, in the 'Fear' Project(ion) that Fisher has described since 1989.

Okay. We first will just quote from the earlier text—because somethings need time and a second and third reading to really take in:

Fisher has collaborated with Four Arrows since 2017, respecting him as a mentor, warrior, a 'medicine' man, and a great practitioner of fear/fearlessness; both who have committed to the path of learning, within a truly *transformational dimension* (Fisher)

There's an instance of a legendary Japanese warrior called Nobunaga, who could be cited in this connection. (Kumar)

I've always loved the ancient Shambhala sacred warrior tradition out of Tibetan Buddhism, whereby the real true leader, the fearless leader, practices vulnerability. Trungpa wrote, "The ideal of warriorship [leadership] is that the warrior should be sad and tender, and because of that, the warrior can be very brave as well. Without that heartfelt sadness, bravery is brittle, like a china cup. If you drop it, it will break or chip" and for true leader-warrior, then who practices fearlessness, Trungpa noted "If the cup drops, it will bounce rather than break. It is soft and hard at the same time."[360] Resilience is so important. (Fisher)

It is in Fisher's earlier version of this map that he links the "stages" along the path via FMSs, with archetypes: 1st-tier Naive, Victim, Survivor, Thriver, and 2nd-tier Sacred Warrior, and 3rd-tier Royal Leader. He has developed an extensive meta-theory from his experiences as a liberation leader since the 1980s. His view is that if "leaders" are not to become corrupted by the 'lower' forces and fear-based dynamics of the 'Fear' Matrix, then they are going to need to be surrounded not by just troops and military weaponry, etc. No, they will need to be surrounded by magicians[361] and sacred warriors[362] who know what true fearlessness is about and they are not fooled by bravado and egoic fear weaponry. They resist the later and promote the former and remind the Royal Leader of their true higher calling. Anyways, this is beyond the scope of this chapter to dive into deeper, but it is a direction we both as co-authors are interested to further elaborate in future works....The (apparent) reality is, that it is very hard to trust leaders these days (Fisher & Kumar)

Fisher has studied this tradition and as well has studied the new postmodern cultural approaches to getting outside of these egoistic-dualistic structurations *via* what he calls *fearlessness as a path*; and a good example, is the way of becoming a "Matrix Warrior" (Fisher & Kumar)

"Truly, the [authentic, fearless, wise] leader is more fearless...for fears have already been confronted....They are old familiar foes of the [sacred] warrior" [quoted another's work] (Fisher & Kumar)

So many things could yet be said about the archetypal "Sacred Warrior" and/or "Magician" and the "hero" and "shero" paths of fearlessness. Our space here is too short to do justice to these topics. However, lest it be said, these are essential to what Fisher has mapped out in earlier chapters as the Soul's Journey" and then with that there is the importance of recognizing that the Sacred Warrior does *not* just operate from ego-psychology and needs, nor from 'fear' projections.

As a "movement," Leader-Sacred Warrior-Teacher is something we take very seriously in this text, and without that recognition, one will end up with taking the "new orientation" suggested by the likes of van Kessel & Burke, etc. True humbleness along this Soul's Journey needs nuance of an entirely different operational paradigm. All our thinking and societal practices need this new orientation. We have presented graphs and models and theories to study for this re-orientation. And lastly, we wish to mention the Id again, but to do so, within a much larger integral perspective, not just of the meta-dynamics of Love and Fear (Figure 1) but the four-layered meta-motivational model of Fisher along which the Fearlessness Principle is the ground of evolution of consciousness, of development and of history (Figure 5). Again, as we briefly display Figure 5, we do so well aware that only the Sacred Warrior is willing to 'see' this for what it is and 'battle' for its right to exist as universal truth.

Of course, that does not mean an ideologism of another fundamentalist kind is imposed. Rather, it means it's a 'wake up' for those who are *ready* and willing to 'see' (risk) and walk this *path of fearlessness*. If anyone chooses not to, that is their right and the consequences will be what they are. We are not here at this level of discussion in the Fearlessness Paradigm itself interested in another virtues-ethics and restrictive moralism of 'what you can and cannot do' (e.g., more commandments to live by). We feel that such a rigid way may have been appropriate or maybe still is in part in certain restricted and strategic contexts; but for a true progressive 21st century education and life—that is, an emancipatory trajectory and philosophy—no such commandment-based virtues/ethics can do the job. The latter, quite likely will only be more reproduction, paradoxically, of self-scaring, self-harming behavior patterns based on the psycho-cultural dynamics of narcissism and the Death drive (*Thanatos*) out-of-control and dominating everything again. The Sacred Warrior truly has stepped 'outside' of that framing and drive pattern of pathology. Albeit, the stepping out is a life-time struggle and aim. But it is a high aim of no minimalist model like van Kessel's & Burke's orientation.

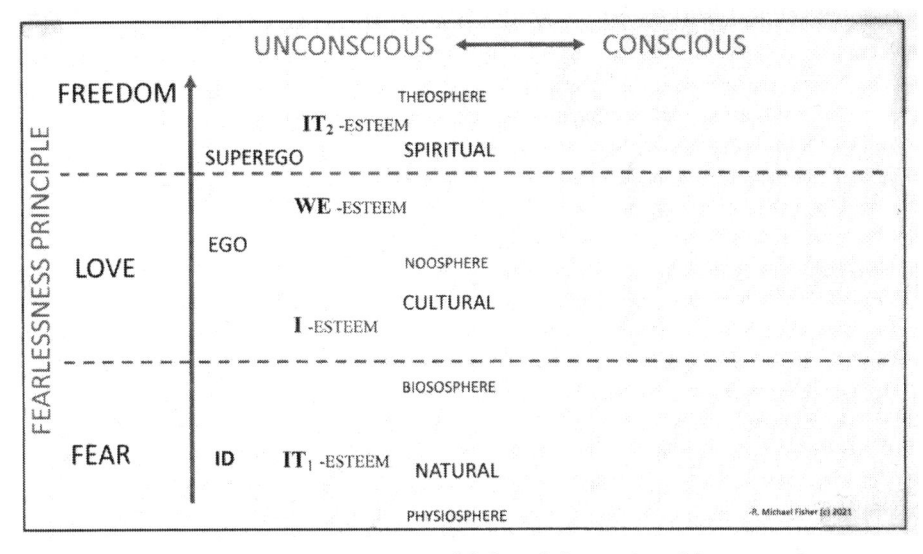

```
                    UNCONSCIOUS  ←——→  CONSCIOUS
      FREEDOM ↑                THEOSPHERE
                        IT₂ -ESTEEM
                  SUPEREGO      SPIRITUAL
      ─ ─ ─ ─ ─ ─ ─ ─ ─ ─ ─ ─ ─ ─ ─ ─ ─ ─ ─ ─ ─
                        WE -ESTEEM
                  EGO
      LOVE                      NOOSPHERE
                                CULTURAL
                        I -ESTEEM
      ─ ─ ─ ─ ─ ─ ─ ─ ─ ─ ─ ─ ─ ─ ─ ─ ─ ─ ─ ─ ─
                                BIOSPHERE
      FEAR        ID   IT₁ -ESTEEM  NATURAL
                                PHYSIOSPHERE
```
(FEARLESSNESS PRINCIPLE — left vertical axis)

Figure 5 Four-Layered Meta-Motivation Map

Briefly, Figure 5 is a good reminder of the movement of four major meta-motivational "forces" or what sometimes Fisher has called "ecologies." The most invisible of the four and most interpenetrating as a Matrix through all of the other layers is Fearlessness, sometimes referred to as a "principle" as in this diagram. We've articulated it as a self-system Id instinctual aspect in prior chapters but here we are showing that is it not confined to the Id dimension, and thus is not limited to any seeking of It-Esteem as foundational But as we move up the evolutionary telos of unfolding here, we see that from Id there is 'I' and the I-Esteem aspect, as this is familiar to most human beings as part of our I-We dynamics of relationships in social settings. Although I-Esteem is equally important to It-Esteem, we are now in the level of Love and cultural dynamics, and this very susceptible to toxification via the "culture of fear" which is *the most* potent of the meta-motivational spheres or ecologies in Fisher's model. There is more significance relatively in this middle-layer but less foundation and thus that makes it more susceptible to pathologies and twists, distortions and even propaganda coming out of the cultural narratives, ideologisms, etc. The highest level is Freedom and that is the most significant, yet, based on the developmental principles of Ken Wilber's theory, we suggest it is most vulnerable because it has less foundation.

In operational terms, this Figure 5 does show that Fearlessness Principle increases in its development and synergizes with the development of the other three layers. However, Fisher has also argued in earlier chapters, that the Id and/or It-Esteem is the least susceptible layer to the Fear Project and Paradigm. This is theoretical and philosophically speculative. It would take a much longer argument to make the case. But as in Figure 1 the idea is that for a Fearlessness Paradigm intervention, that is, to be a tool in the hand of the emancipatory Sacred Warrior, fearlessness can most easily be recovered, healed, and transformed at the Id level. Many would rather see this be stated in terms of the higher Rational, Reason, Logic and I-Esteem levels of the "critical thinker" and the "free agent" etc. Most political and cultural theorizing relies on that paradigmatic set of assumptions, often based on Enlightenment philosophies of modernism. However, Fisher is cautious of such ploys and believes they are so infiltrated with the "culture of fear" dynamics, and Thanatos, that the upper two layers are much more difficult to do the best "fearwork" overall. In other words, to really breed a revitalizing Fearlessness once again on planet earth, Fisher surmises the better place to go is the Id. That's why psychoanalysis, for example has been drawn upon at times in our book.

However, to be clear, the Id level of work, and restoration and transformative learning must not be cut-off or separated from the higher two levels. The higher two levels have a lot more affective-libidinal symptomatology and recognizable "feelings" and "emotionality"—typical of the 'I' and 'We' Esteem needs and wounds. That's the point of mapping all these levels and esteems here. Fisher believes current "self-esteem" models, albeit somewhat useful, are quite distortive to a full integral understanding of human nature, human condition and human potential. Again, unfortunately, we've only been able to point to this highly controversial position. Note, we've not gone into the discoveries and possibilities here re: It-Esteem^2 in the Theosphere or transpersonal realms. But, the It-Esteem at Id and combinations with It-Esteem in the Super Ego hold great potential we believe for mass and eruptive changes in the societies of the world and their orientation to Fearlessness in general.

And, our chapter here would not be complete unless we reminded readers that much of our work here is *in progress* and that as two co-authors we don't always know exactly what each other thinks about everything on these topics nor do we assume each of us, especially one a Westerner and one an Easterner, are in agreement on all things. The dialogue we are having is at best a beginning and more importantly it shows that two human beings are able to have such a dialogue with such a focus. You all are invited to join in and critique and improve upon Fearlessness conceptually and "fearlessnessnizing," which really scares most people. How do we best *fearlessnessnize the world*? And, in the process, not add more fear to the world in doing so? The epistemic, ethical and methodological challenges are enormous. The resistances to such research and teaching, are equally enormous.

PART IV

FEARLESSNESS IS/ AS PHILOSOPHY

CHAPTER SEVEN

Fearlessness is/as Philosophy

For at least a decade, Osama bin Laden had lingered in my imagination like a spectre of destruction, mayhem and hatred. I seem to have no control over the objects of my fear.

-Carl Leggo[363]

I do think the topic of educating about fear and fearlessness is singularly important.

-Daniel Vokey[364]

If you aim your philosophy at a global set of complex problems to analyze and solve, you'll need a complex transdisciplinary-based emergent philosophy. If you aim your philosophy at the global Fear Problem, you'll need a Fearlessness philosophy.   -R. Michael Fisher

As long as people followed the 2nd century Ptolemaic theory of earth, their thoughts and applications about seasonal changes went wrong. It was a theory formulated on mistaken assumptions and an inappropriate paradigm and worldview. It's only after the 16th century heliocentric model had convinced people of an alternative worldview and philosophy, were they able to take a quantum leap in science and development.

213

Why? Because it was founded on truth. Likewise, while understanding fearlessness as philosophy, the truth about the nature of life is of critical importance.

-B. Maria Kumar

We have spent the first three parts of this book looking for the self, but even when we could not find it, we never doubted the stability of the world....having discovered the groundless-ness of the self, we turn toward the world, we are no longer sure we can find it. Or perhaps we should say that once we let go of a fixed self, we no longer know how to look for the world....Once more, we seem to be losing our grip on something familiar. Indeed, at this point most people will probably become quite nervous [fearful]....We need, then, to pause and become fully aware of this anxiety that lies underneath....This task takes us to the next step of our journey.   -Varela, Thompson & Rosch[365]

Fearlessness: A 'Fear' Vaccination Process Philosophy

We introduced this book with Introduction 3 "Fearism Meets Fearlessness," and claimed that although one could take many roads and perspectives to articulate what a *philosophy of fearlessness* and/or *Fearlessness Philosophy* might be, we decided that our initial pursuit would be to strategically narrow down the lens of our co-inquiry. Philosophy itself, and its grand history in knowledge production, is such a mega-field to take on, we've decided not to attempt to give the whole field its due respect and application here. Yet, we do come to the study of *fear* primarily as philosophers of one kind or another. We are not professional philosophers in the academy or the discipline itself; more accurately, we are serious amateur philosophers, critical adult educators and concerned global citizens.

Diverse individuals and thinkers as we are, it was easiest to find the 'bridge' to our thoughts and teaching *via* Desh Subba's *philosophy of fearism* and what he called a "fearist" lens. In other words, we would, for the most part, restrict our philosophizing to our identification as fearists.[366] We'll re-look later below at that notion of being fearist philosophers and its responsibilities in a deeply troubled world.

Historically, there needs to be a declarative point to make at this juncture. *Resistances to Fearlessness* constitutes a hybridization of fearism *via* Subba-Fisher-Kumar and the philosophies that merge and emerge in those encounters. Yet, this book goes far beyond that. The two of us (Fisher & Kumar) have set out to transcend fearism's current views and inadequacies in re: to philosophizing, theorizing and creating a philosophy that does justice to the fear/fearlessness dialectic. We appreciate that several fearists, including Subba, will often combine in their work and mission a symbolic acknowledgement of the equal value of fear/fearism/fearlessness, and thus they enact a respectful embrace of inclusion. They don't want conflict that comes with categorizing and separations of people (e.g., philosophers), especially with those who are thinking and writing about fear, fearism, fearlessness. They may acknowledge there are differences in fearism writing but they typically downplay it. Perhaps these fearists are attempting to create a non-competitive and an implicit 'safe space' for their intellectual community(?). The more overt intention is to make them all compatible, and more or less complementary, under one grand project.

Fisher recently has labeled this grand inclusive project 'Fear' Studies.[367] Although "fearlessness" *per se* was not featured in Fisher's 2006 article invoking 'Fear' Studies as a legitimate field, fearlessness philosophizing is nevertheless laced in-and-through every part of that presentation. In that pivotal article, one example shows the summarizing he did re: all the positive attributions given to terms in the field of Education that 'look like' they are supportive of a direction and/or paradigm shift from Fear to Fearlessness. He cited many publications on how others see the best way to go by focusing on *safety* and *security* in schools and creating "peaceful school communities" etc. He notes these movements are operating in self-reinforcing parallel with a plethora of literature on "education beyond fear" and teaching/learning "without fear" and "fear-fear education zones" etc. More recent calls that "fear has no place" in schools in reaction to mass murders,[368] is only another case of the same under-theorizing. Then, Fisher noted, with his characteristic style as a critic and conflict theorist:

> Readers will not find my writing attacks "safety" and "security" but from a critical pedagogy (and fearlessness) perspective, I agree with Srivastava (1997) that anti-racist (in my case, anti-fearist) education "should not guarantee a safe place" because it is a "fiction" (p. 120), and often "safety" discourse is motivated by "fear of conflict" rather than a healthy "'conflict' pedagogy," the latter which shuns any 'fear'-based motivations... as much as possible. I have posited in this essay and elsewhere...the rationale that "fear" is being under-theorized and de-contextualized in so many of these "educational" attempts to cope with fear in a culture of fear. They treat symptoms not the underlying dis-ease. A holistic integral and critical approach is required....[369]

Herein this latter Fisherian venture is meant as a rigorous invitation to embrace and work through conflict for the good of the advancement of fear studies. A true fearlessness perspective would not have it otherwise. Fearism is a strand of that initiative. Turning beyond that issue now, one has to ask *why* on earth and with all the years of intellectual research and study there has never before been a person or group to identify Fear Studies[370] as something worthy of being named, never mind being developed?[371] Something profound but perhaps subtle, has surely shifted in human consciousness since the 1990s and with the turn of the 21st century. At least a small group of diverse and international philosopher-types are finally coming together to forefront the major importance of fear and 'Fear' Studies in global affairs.

With all due importance that ought to be given to fear, there is another twist in this historical era of what Subba called the "Extreme

Fear Age."[372] There is due importance also burgeoning to what fearlessness is in relation to fear and human affairs. Part III described the Fearlessness Movement. Overall, this co-authored book is filled on every page with investigations, intentions, premises and definitions of *what makes fearlessness*? At the same time, we (Fisher & Kumar) almost avoid defining it into a square hole.

Prior, Fisher and Subba have also taken this complexity-derived and open-ended emergent paradigm approach to fear, fearism, and fearlessness. Rigid definitions, especially the *one and only* definition, are probably more harmful than good at this point. We believe the great cognitive scientists/philosophers[373] like Varela et al. in the quote above, have the right attitude in that we need to let go: they wrote of the expansion and insights that arise anew *"once we let go of a fixed self."* Ideally, the philosophy of fearism and fearlessness do the same. And, that very sensibility to treating *fear/fearlessness* specifically in this book is a philosophical position. And, it is a philosophical position not typically taken by those who claim to write on the "philosophy of fear." We'll come back to that point later in this chapter. Our point: this chapter is not about trying to construct a grand systems philosophy of fear or philosophy of fearlessness, all fixed, all constructed for the discipline of Philosophy etc. No, something very different is going on, something much more dynamic and something that will only fully be understood when *you (and we)* **let go** *of a fixed self/philosopher/theory/definition/discipline/world/reality*. That something different is really different as you are about to discover with us. That something different may even turn out to be uncanny (see Part V).

Hint: the really different difference arriving from a philosophy of fearism, when complemented with the Fisherian Fearlessness Paradigm (i.e., Fear Management System-7; holistic-integral[374]) is an illumination of what "letting go" really means. Varela et al. pointed to the philosophical juggernaut of the W. tradition of all males, all thinking, all rationalism—and, the great problem of *thinking itself* as revolving around *cogito ergo sum*: "I think therefore I am." This declared authoritatively as the (only) trustable ground of all reality—and, thus all true (rational) philosophy. You may recall where that originates *via* René Descartes famous 17th century dictum.

Many things have changed in over 300 years in the nature of knowing what the self is ("I am") and what philosophy is and what knowledge is, with it. Methodologies have made quantum changes in the Sciences to the Arts and Humanities. Things are much more complex now. And Varela et al. point their laser critique down onto the whole of W. philosophies—in what they call the pathology of "Cartesian Anxiety"[375]—a paradigm of information, knowledge, psychology etc. that has infiltrated everything—philosophy itself as we know it—with fear (anxiety). This Cartesian anxiety is another term for a foundational *fear-based* way of knowing—and/or what critics have called a paradigm of "deficit-motivated"[376] or "deficit-state"[377] reality.

Fisher's warning to all those who study fear (and fearlessness) derived along similar lines of epistemic doubt and concern that people in general are too confident (arrogant) that they know what *fear is* already and thus need no new education on the topic. They 'trust' their 'I am' philosophical orientation, even if they don't know they are articulating a philosophy—and/or a Cartesian one. We referred to this as a 'crime' in the entire history of emotions and affect (see Chapter Six). Fisher's 21st century new paradigmatic 'Fear' Studies pivots itself on the claim and doubt that: *'Fear' Is Not What It Used To Be.*[378] The Spanish philosopher F. J. Moreno made a grand entry of original argumentation, little known by most philosophers or the public, that *it is wrong to identify fear as a distorting influence on thinking, but rather the root of fear is reason itself.*[379]

In discussing "paradigms of philosophizing," Moreva, articulated some of our own philosophical views as we are at a time of history of asking what philosophizing is going to be most useful, responsible and ethical in general. Moreva wrote,

> It has become disputable whether humans are still rational beings or whether their production activity in a continually expanding sphere of destructiveness and absurdity must be considered as indicative of

their ontologically irrational nature, merely 'biped and featherless' beings a defined by Plato.

It is beyond question, however, that they are beings that permanently produce text, i.e., a semiotically, semantically and pragmatically loaded space of their own being in the world....From the babbling of infants, trying to express their internal state and the moment of meeting the world in human protolanguage, up to the mysterious sooth-saying of the Pythian and prophet who join together visible and invisible in their own world and gesture. Everything that attempts to be heard, seen and understood, and waits for a response, is potentially reality....The human brain itself works in an ontological mode of internal dialogue, so an internal drive exists towards self-expression, articulation, speech, and eventual writing [and art]. The said internal dialogue mechanism of our consciousness is [however] fraught with neurotic, schizophrenic and other psychosomatic breakdowns caused by the inadequacy of the drive's articulation...[but] here too, is the basis of our unique capacity to sharpen reflection techniques and to sophisticate logical apparatus. 'The dialogue that the soul has with itself'—such was one of Plato's definitions of philosophy.[380]

Our definition of *philosophy*, under all these conditions, like Cartesian anxiety, and who knows maybe Platonian anxiety as well, there is however our philosophical belief in this book that a Fearlessness Philosophy and Paradigm are worthy of pursuit. Irrational aside and still taken into account, really we mean Fear aside and still taken into account, we see Moreva's view of philosophy as strategically *best* advancing only while it is *self-aware* of its own use of paradigms and the motivational templates that lie invisible beneath those.

Education too needs to reflect on its deeper motivations and competing paradigms, which Fisher regularly brings forward in his view of FME (fear management/education). Science likewise could only advance in the last decades because it was becoming more aware of its multiple, often competing, paradigms and the power-politics of paradigms (e.g., Thomas Kuhn's work) in communities of scholars. Unfortunately, Science has yet to acknowledge the underlying fear-based motivational psychology that Maslow warned to discern in the mid-1960s.[381] Tarnas had argued that by the late 1990s there were "eight different paradigms of reality in quantum physics"[382] alone, never mind in other fields of study. Complexity is obviously here to stay.

Philosophy and fear are coming together and we suggest that philosophers reflect on their complex engagement with paradigms they bring into the inquiry. These hidden structures and architectures for thinking itself need to be made transparent in our research, writing and teaching. Unfortunately to this day, no one has done this systematic research on paradigms that shape fear and research on fear and their full implications, including the politics of that dynamic. The task is ripe for growth in the philosophy of fearism.

What intrigues us to this day as fearists, is the independent articulation of *fear* with Subba's opening chapter and his 21 definitions that go all over the place and with Fisher's 15+ definitions of *fearlessness*, equally diverse.[383] It is clear that independently these pioneering unique philosophers were starting from a *transdisciplinary* approach[384] to their subject matter. No one, we know of, has done this before in history. Typically fear and fearlessness are restricted to definitions within theology, philosophy, psychology, etc. In the latter, such disciplinary demands therefore place our topic of fear(lessness) into a necessary hierarchical position—and, thus arising from within the disciplines respectively, we see works of the "theology of fear," "philosophy of fear," "psychology of fear," etc. Such approaches may be valid; yet, they do not adequately take into account what Subbaian fearism means. The very fact that Subba used "philosophy of fearism" and he wasn't just trying to write another "philosophy of fear" discourse, is telling. Lera Broditsky found in her studies that words have power to increase thinking skills. Humans seem to love to create words for a good reason. Fisher would agree with the importance in new vocabulary[385] building to add all kinds of prefixes and suffixes to the word "fear" in the pursuit of transdisciplinary, new paradigmatic work re: Fear Studies.

A decade ago, in a quick literature survey on the term "philosophy of fearlessness," Fisher found no hits for this in major academic index databases. On popular websites there were the three top hits all from Fisher's writing and the few popular descriptions other than that were under-theorized references to describe individuals, as if they had such a philosophy and/or people and weather that came from extremes. A noteworthy citation was from Prof. Dalton, University of London, on his course outline wrote, "Gandhi's methods of nonviolent resistance combined with a philosophy of fearlessness have made him one of the most revered men of our century."[386] Another citation from an Amazon.com book reviewer of A. Huffington's book *On Becoming Fearless* wrote, "Huffington treats without hesitation that most profound of all 'what ifs'—the fear of death—and in doing so summarizes her philosophy of fearlessness."[387] Although this literature review is due again, we believe not a lot new will be seen beyond these above kinds of commentaries. But our concern here is about something more important.

Philosophy of communications as well is crucial to how philosophy/fear progress in their getting to know each other dialectically and transformatively, like never before. Some four decades ago, Magoroli Maruyama set out three "pure" (types) of paradigms of communication that touch all areas of knowledge: (1) Unidirectional causal paradigm, (2) Random process paradigm, (3) Mutual causal paradigm. In examining the 20 strands of knowledge and methods chosen as examples, Maruyama plotted the differences between the three paradigms. For example, for "Cosmology" the first paradigm begins with a "predetermined universe," the second paradigm a "decaying universe" and third, "self-generating and self-organizing universe." For "Esthetics" the first paradigm "unity by similarity and repetition" (i.e., recall "A-ness from our Chapters Five-Six discussion), and second "haphazard," and third, "harmony of diversity" (i.e., D-ness). For "Information" the first "past and future inferable from present" and second, "information decays and gets lost, so the blueprint must contain more information than the finished product," and third, "information can be generated, non-redundant complexity can be generated without pre-established blueprint." For "Planning" the first paradigm "by experts," the second, "laissez-faire" and third, "generated by community."[388] Note: Fisher & Kumar abide by the requirements of the 21st century and complexity and ethical issues to which philosophy must accommodate to be relevant. It is thus our attempt to utilize Maruyama's third paradigm *Mutual-Causal* as our operative approach to fear/fearlessness.

Specifically, we'll discuss below how that impacts the way we conceive of the very relationship between the trialectic mutually intertwined *self-fearlessness-philosophy* combination. We also discuss the impacts of a truly dialectic and transformative process philosophy in our thought, and we ask continually why is "fear" and/or "fearlessness" not put in first place before all the traditional disciplinary categories—for example, why not a fearlessness psychology, fearlessness philosophy in contradistinction to the more familiar and dominant expressions of a psychology of fearlessness or philosophy of fearlessness(?)

For the moment, another declarative point needs to be made. *Resistance to Fearlessness* is a first E.-W. dialogue on the topic of fearlessness. That is no small feat. Six years ago Fisher & Subba took on a first E.-W. dialogue on philosophy of fearism. Fisher's strong influence has thus been felt on the whole field of inquiry. Amongst the fearist philosophers today, he has uniquely been embedded in not only writing but real intense social experiments exploring his philosophy and theory. We track out below some of that experimentation on the way to understanding what process/living philosophizing may mean.

In Search of Fearlessness Community: Living Philosophy

Fisher's hybrid synthetic philosophy of fearlessness began in 1989 with a transpersonal vision from intimate relationship—and naturally poured over into birthing a real face-to-face living community dedicated to liberation. Turns out that Fearlessness was as challenging as any intimate relationship, like a marriage. It's damn hard work.

He was intrigued with how his thinking and others' shaped *fearlessness* as well as how Fearlessness shaped them in the process of engagement. Fearlessness is/was always a *mutual-causal* processual[389] relationship. With some 50+ people, their urban experiment for 10 years involved centering fearlessness as the healing and ethical core of the intentional community. It was an experiential journey with lots of risks, and not merely academic exercise.

Yet, all along, he was particularly interested in philosophy, theory and methodology as critical *praxis*.[390] So, Fearlessness became many things, with many meanings, to many people all involved in this particular learning community.[391] Fearlessness also became many things to those who stood outside of this community and judged it. But whatever was happening, for Fisher the intention was always to move from a culture of fear to a culture of fearlessness—on a small scale in order to eventually take this experiment, model, and curriculum to the larger scale—as a worldwide movement.

What derived from their community experiences, at the least, it was a mapping of 'fear' vaccines,[392] as Fisher called them. They would be processes of *enactment of fearlessness*, and based on a Fearlessness Paradigm and Philosophy overall, whereby one could as an individual (and/or group) begin to *vaccinate themselves* (and their mutual relationships) against the chronic 'Fear' Project(ion)[393] dynamic that dominates the world—that is, the Fear Problem.[394] The most basic homeopathy of a "vaccine" or "medicine" or even the building of resistance to poisons and pathogens as part of any immune system (defense), is not the denying or purifying process alone but rather a going into and imbibing the very threat, poison, pathogen. By taking these into one's system and 'learning' from it dialectically and biologically, the true resilience and immunity is developed to that 'enemy.' This intrigued Fisher from the start and thus, the study was of fear (and 'fear') rather than the study of say love, peace, harmony, mindfulness, etc. It is not that Fisher's fearlessness-based philosophy was against such latter positive practices but that he believed they would not be adequate homeopathically to really create the *most powerful* resistance to the 'Fear' Project(ion) and Fear Problem on the planet. He also believed it is better to study the Shadow, as Carl Jung advised, than to go off chasing ideals and becoming "addicted to the light."[395] Endarkenment was Fisher's preferred approach, which he basically called the "path of fearlessness" and "in search of fearlessness." This darker depth-approach re: immunological persistence of inquiry and liberation was core to Fisher's *oeuvre*, and remains so to this day, as part of what rightfully can be called a "negative philosophy" tradition.[396]

The original six *'fear' vaccines* were: (1) *fear and fearlessness information* as the critical education component that was formal and most easily accessible by people, (2) *liberation peer counseling*[397] (basic healing) was critical to being able to maintain basic "rules" of conduct alone or together so that people were no longer only needing to choose to *cope* with distress/fear patterns of daily living and the culture-at-large but they could choose the more preferred and natural/healthy way of *healing* (i.e., a healing paradigm over coping paradigm). These two practices of fearlessness as living process were proven to be the most powerful at the center of this organization, which Fisher called later a 2nd-tier integral organization[398]—that is, a fearlessness organization. Creating a basic critical literacy for fearlessness *contra* fear-based literacy is essential for real change and eventual transformation. This latter point and experience, Fisher had long ago learned from studying the critical pedagogy of Paulo Freire et al.[399]

For the Fearlessness Movement to be effective it requires this level of vigilant scrutiny, with attendant language consciousness, philosophy, theory and practices. Even though, we have argued in our philosophizing that fear/fearlessness are dialectic and always at play co-evolving and *when fear appears, so then does fearlessness*—despite all that—humans in groups especially, have to do a lot of conscious peer-to-peer processing of communications so as to dis-enable any power-hierarchical patterns that can easily become toxic relations.

With higher ideals, personalities and their flaws will also leak-out and emerge to cause regressions in maturity. Wounds and traumas when triggered easily pull us down. Our worst hurts around "love" and "trust" come from social and family relationships in the past. Psychoanalysis and Fisher's fearanalysis[400] invoke attention to this aspect of our histories as a social species. It is easy for people to get hurt when they are together socially. It is easy to build mistrust and not want to forgive.

And old unhealed hurts will want to get (and often steal) attention when in the presence of loving and kind others, especially when one of the aims of the In Search of Fearlessness Community was to heal and liberate. Yet, such amounts of accumulated wounds and needs can overwhelm the system. To walk the *path of fearlessness* is one of choosing over and over to practice the 'fear' vaccines as personal responsibility. The whole community, more or less, took on this challenge too, not unlike a community of say Alcoholics Anonymous does in order to recover, and keep at-bey the habit addictions of going back to the ways of the Fear (coping) Paradigm.

The original remaining four 'fear' vaccines were: (3) *spontaneous creation-making* which was dedicated to being creative and making art in some form or other as ongoing practice, equally as important as say yoga, meditation or mindfulness practices. This vaccine was intended to work in the aesthetic line of development and maturation, so human beings remained curious, beautiful, playful and artful in all their life. Art is healing, when done in the right context of receiving attention and care (Fisher co-wrote a book on this process with another one in the making[401]). And (4) *community-building* and peace-nonviolence practices (e.g., *via* Scott Peck's model[402]), which is the conscious work of keeping the community as a whole reflecting on itself so as not to fall too deeply into the worst aspects of habitual ethnocentrism, ideologism, exclusionism, fundamentalism, adultism, ageism, sexism, racism, classism, homophobia, guru-worship, cult-formations, toxic rebellionism, addictions, and co-dependent unhealthy love-romantic relationships with their inevitable abuses. And (5) *School of Sacred Warriorship,* co-founded and taught by Fisher in 1993. It became a place for those people wanting more commitment to go deeper into really pushing the boundaries of their comfort and safety zones and defenses—all of which drew upon the sacred warrior traditions and conflict transformation and radical mediation approaches of the E. philosophies of the martial arts. etc. Ultimately, this training ground would produce 'new liberation leaders' for the community itself but also the wide-world. And (6) *vision quest* was the four-day event modelled somewhat after the ancient Indigenous worldview and approaches to re-connect people to Nature and their own animal, magical, and primal nature.

Two later 'fear' vaccines were included, although not practiced collectively by the original ISOF Community group (which had folded in 1999). First, *Fearanalysis* was a diagnostic approach, mentioned above, and related to psychoanalysis but was much more expansive and arguably is what Fisher believed would become a form of cultural therapy (and philosophical *therapia*). Philosophy in Fisher's evolutionary/developmental approach was always meant to be a cultural-based historical and evolutionary corrective to an over-reliance on Psychology as the way to change, to heal, and to make a better world.

Over the years of community-living and learning, the Fearlessness way became more like a 'Credo' of believes, values, practices—at times, some thought it was a 'religion.'[403] Though ISOF was all-encompassing of a living philosophy, it was not like any "religion" that is known, nor was it intended to become so. It truly had a spiritual component but no religious dogma or only one untouchable 'god-like' messenger. Although, Fisher was its main prophet in North America. Inherent in all the great religions, and all the great secular philosophies, one can find the gems of liberation (and fearlessness) from fear, from the 'Fear' Project(ion). But, as we have said in this book a few time already, only the Eastern philosophies and theologies have developed and valued the notion of fearlessness—the West is far behind in this regard. Fisher has critiqued the W. philosophies extensively for their omission ('crime') in this regard.[404] The whole world is now at-risk, arguably, because the education of fearlessness is lacking far behind the growth of fear. Philosophy as a whole, especially in academia, never caught on that maybe fear/fearlessness really was/is important. Slowly, this is changing as more diverse philosophers become aware of the new writing and teaching on the topic. So far, philosophers in the so-called "developing nations" of the North and East, are by far the most interested.

And the last 'fear' vaccine came into play overtly in Fisher's working with Four Arrows, an Indigenous-based scholar—see the *CAT-FAWIN* meta-cognitive de-hypnosis theory and soft technology.[405] This collaboration going back to 2006, is one which Fisher believes is the kernel of a truly liberational Fearlessness Philosophy because it acts as a true grand "Reversal" of the Dominant Worldview and its fear-based architecture and kosmology. Prior to this exciting hybridizing of thought with Four Arrows, Fisher refers to his work as building a philosophy of fear and fearlessness. Note: *philosophy* was typically given order-priority over Fearlessness, thus the dialectical relationship was only partially enacted between them. With the diving into the gifts of the Indigenous Worldview, articulated so well by Four Arrows,[406] there is a whole worldview shift not just a paradigm shift. Everything is different. Both Fisher and Four Arrows have agreed that "Fearlessness" is the way of the Indigenous primal people's on this planet, and virtually all living things, from the beginning of evolution itself.

Philosophy of Fearlessness *cum* Fearlessness Philosophy

What is this philosophy of "Reversal" embedded from the start in Fisher's notion of Fearlessness? It is important to say that this concept has a *simple* side and a *complex* side. The latter will *not* be addressed adequately here in this chapter, rather, one ought to read Fisher's 2010 seminal text on this. The simple version can be got to *via* quoting from some of Fisher's text written over a decade ago, which is the book which opened up the W. philosophical discourses to engage with the E. philosophical discourses. He hoped to bring premodern, modern and postmodern (and integral post-postmodern) understanding of fear/fearlessness into a common umbrella—theorizing—and language re: a Fearlessness paradigmatic framework of inquiry. He was not and is not, after a dogmatism of absolute static unification. Although, he highly supports the imperative of more unification than there is. He finds the vast majority of the work today on fear and fearlessness remains fragmented—where theorists and practitioners don't seem to really wish to synthesize and carry on a healthy scrutiny of their philosophies and teachings within a community of the adequate and committed. This is a trend he warns will undermine the future potency of the Fearlessness Movement. He says we need a holistic-integral philosophy to even approach such a massive and difficult issues as the global Fear Problem.

Many people continue to mis-interpret this emancipatory integral strength of his work; and yet they often feel that it imposes upon, dominates discourses, or that he only wants to criticize other approaches to fearlessness. This is not at all the aim of his work—albeit, he finds most philosophies on fear and fearlessness and love wanting, and highly troublesome. Fearlessness philosophy is a work in progress. Albeit, Fisher is always very emphatic in making his case in criticisms.

The "Reversal" aspect is the prophetic aspect of his critical (sometimes negative[407]) philosophizing. And not everyone likes that element (see later in Chapter Eight). His philosophy is social and ethical to the core. It is critical of philosophy that has *not* given fear/fearlessness sufficient attention. He even says that such philosophies have violated human dignity by disengaging or denying fear/fearlessness their due. Life is paying the price of that violence. Reversal, for Fisher simply means (in his own words):

> What interests me most at this point is FMS-7 [Fear Management System-7[408]], the transitional FME approach at the highest tension (conflict) at 'Fear' Barrier 2. In Search of Fearlessness Project (ISOF) is one of the only such projects to have been developing the FMS-7 perspective systematically. Not only have 15 meanings of fearlessness been revealed but, in the following pages 15 paradigms (of the Fearlessness Tradition) make up deep structures that manifest in the WFTs and construct an ethical bi-centric distinction.... The former [of these pairs, e.g., Good vs Evil] being the *way to go* for quality life and evolution of consciousness and society, the latter being the *way to leave behind* or deny the great potential before us....I summarized 15

paradigms (that I know of) which compose a Great Fearlessness Tradition (of which ISOF works with). For our purposes they will be mentioned in short form only as a resource for Reversal work, from a 2nd-tier [holistic-integral] perspective. They are listed here not in any particular order [all details of each are left out here for brevity]:

(1) Living Process vs. Addictive Process
(2) Love vs. Fear
(3) Good vs. Evil
(4) Sunrise Vision vs. Sunset Vision
(5) Benign Reality Pattern vs. Distress Pattern
(6) Red Pill vs. Blue Pill
(7) Heaven vs Hell
(8) Healing vs Coping
(9) Benign Circle vs. Vicious Circle
(10) *Moksha* vs. *Maya*
(11) *Eros-Agape* vs. *Phobos-Thanatos*
(12) Creation-centered Cosmology vs. Fall/Redemption Cosmology
(13) Wholistic vs. Mechanistic
(14) Paradigm of Hope vs. Paradigm of Fear
(15) Second-tier vs. First-tier

One ought to remember that many of these b-centric ethical paradigms arose independently by the various theorists, philosophers, spiritual teachers and their students. No doubt many of them have influenced each other along the way. These paradigms of a Fearlessness Tradition present a universal message that cannot be denied. Yet, despite the simple dichotomy in concepts, these are only 'maps.' The reality of living the dynamic between (in and out) of the bi-centric aspects of the paradigms is "messy"....the majority of people today on

> the planet have no idea of the variety of these bi-centric paradigms, or they do not care about them, and/or they interpret them in a 1st-tier perspective only. The research question remains: How valuable are they actually in people's lives, and how valuable might they be, and how real and true are they to the nature of "reality" (i.e., human nature, human condition, human potential)? I am quite convinced they all are useful....[409]

As we said, it is not like there is an absent of people writing about fearlessness in philosophical style and approach. The Buddhist nun, Pema Chödrön, recently popularized Buddhist teachings as variants from her teachers, and wrote explicitly whole books on fear and fearlessness. For example, in her *A Guide to Fearlessness* she offers aspirations, none of which involve directly learning about fear and 'fear' but she does recommend going "to the places that scare us...[and leading] the life of a warrior."[410]

Fisher's mapping is thus now available. Fearlessness is not merely a behavioral or psychological notion nor a resource, it is an idea, a movement and it is an accumulative experiencing—*via* an animal instinctual corrective for self/system regulation (argued in Part III) but what is more invisible is the historical collective memory of such. Fearlessness lives in process and the unconscious as much as the conscious. Arguably, it lives in the unconscious via lines, threads, connections of memory systems we may not even access any more living in the modern world. So, at least this overview tells you that a true Fearlessness philosophy will have to take into account and be critical off all of these aspects of "fearlessness" in order to be creative, living and a philosophy that is really helpful—and hopeful. Albeit, Fisher has always argued, that once one reaches a center of gravity at FMS-7, "hope" is replaced with "fearlessness" quite naturally. A much larger topic beyond the scope of this chapter.

Fearism philosophers of all stripes have certainly embraced, in part, that "fearlessness" is worthy of investigating and locating within the philosophy of fearism canon. However, none has taken up the issue of fearlessness, within the appropriate Fearlessness Paradigm, to theorize on fear(ism) and fearlessness as intimate and un-separable partners. This lacunae is problematic.

Equally, educators have not picked up on Fisher's philosophy either, at least, not to any systematic extent. Even a critic would be welcomed but none has shown up directly. Fisher's work in *The World's Fearlessness Teachings* book has been taken on by only one educator since its 2010 publication. Leggo[411] in 2011 utilized Fisher's book to act as a pedagogical mirror so to speak for his own passionate poetic musings on love and fear. Ultimately, Leggo wanted to promote "Living Love" (as the title of his long article suggested). However, this respectful philosophical educator did write,

> Who am I? Who am I in relation to the world? How shall I live? What are the responsibilities of a human being in the contemporary world?....With the news of Osama bin Laden's death, the fears I know intimately and constantly did not evaporate. Instead the fears only grew. So, I turn again to writing, my writing and the writing of others, in order to understand my experience of fearfulness [pp. 115-16]....I have been a teach all my adult life, and I have often promoted the need for love in education. Recently in a faculty meeting I recommended that our teacher education program ought to be focused on love. Colleagues smiled, and some even chuckled, but I was quickly convinced that my proposal was not likely to be taken up any time soon! Why do we fear love? [pp. 117-18]

> ....In a recent conference presentation I commented that as I grow older I feel like I have lost my characteristic commitment to speak truthfully, to engage with prophetic imagination, and to challenge the dominant discourses that shape my lived experiences in both the academy and the community. I wonder if I have

grown complacent, compromised, and complicit. R. Michael Fisher heard my comment and invited me to address my concern [fearfulness] by considering his writing about fearlessness. I have known Michael for many years, and I have always been challenge by his art and his writing and his scholarly and pedagogical commitments. With Michael's invitation, I read his book *The World's Fearlessness Teachings* (2010) and I wrote a short response [but now wanted a longer one]....I am grateful for Michael's invitation, and for his teachings, and especially for motivating me to continue writing about fear and being fearful.

I regard [his]...*World's Fearlessness Teachings* as essential reading for educators. It is a complex and wise book that deserves careful attention.... [pp. 121-2] [Fisher reminds us] "we are struggling to develop maturity from fear to fearlessness as not mere surface behavioral change but a deep structural transformation of the very way we 'see,' 'sense our self' and 'act' in the world ethically.'" Fisher reminds me to attend to "deep structural transformation," and I know this has been my expressed commitment, but so much of life seen from the current perspective of fifty-seven years in the earth now seems superficial, specious, self-serving"....So, I lean into the strong words of Fisher's writing. I am glad he is calling out his erudite and energetic vision for an education of fearlessness....As I continue to linger with Fisher's words, I also linger with my own words, decades of words, in order to attend carefully to the way that fear is woven through my poetry and living like a ghost I have simply taken for granted, as if there is no other way. Fisher shows us another way—a critical and creative way that lives fearlessly in the midst of wisdom, language, and conviction. [pp. 125, 127][412]....When I review my poetry,

I am struck by how much fear is recorded, narrated, represented, and evoked in the poetry, and how seldom the fear is actually resolved. Fear dominates my life. [p. 129]....So, we need to embrace fear, to lean into it, to live with it as a part of the texture of everydayness. [p. 131]....I will next offer several words of advice for addressing fear with love. [p. 134]

Probably many people can relate to this professor and poet's words and sentiments, admission and confession. Yet, after having read the whole book *World's Fearlessness Teachings* you might think his philosophy had been altered(?) Apparently not. He constructs the rest of his article on "addressing fear with love" and not with fearlessness.

So, this example of embrace and resistance to fearlessness at the same time by Leggo is elucidating. He's trained in W. philosophy. But such philosophical traditions typically do not hae a developmental and evolutionary trajectory within their teachings. We mean they don't typically, especially in modernity and postmodernity, focus on the development and evolution of consciousness itself. Perhaps, Consciousness, with a capital is the best way to speak about it on the macro-scale. Consciousness as a construct has lost great favor in philosophy, especially after the criticisms of Hegel. That said, consciousness never goes away from philosophy. It goes underground. Yet, in the 20th and 21st century some philosophers, like Ken Wilber have re-centralized consciousness again. Once a developmental consciousness 'map' or theory is brought forth within philosophical inquiry, things become very interesting in terms of the question we think philosophers ought to be concerned about: "How do we determine the least mature and most mature consciousness forms along the spectrum of growth and development?" Poststructuralist thinkers will completely eschew this kind of question. They believe it is another form of colonialist patriarchal and hierarchical judgement of something as better than something and it will be justified by some theory of development, evolution, consciousness, etc. They are right to be skeptical. That's not our point here, but they 'throw out the baby with the bathwater' with their attempt to reduce everything to what Wilber has called a "flatland ontology."[413]

"Fear is Empire's friend," wrote Korten,[414] as he uses these developmental studies of consciousness and maps out five orders of Consciousness expressions in both individual human development, in groups and on the macro-scale of evolution itself. Empire-building on the planet aligns with the Second Order: Imperial Consciousness, out of the five possible consciousnesses available. Without going into the details of this model, Korten offers a gift of seeing the 'big picture' of what development looks like as a spectrum and he shows that it is not until one achieves the maturity of Fourth and Fifth Order Consciousness that the world can shift from fear-based to love-based. We agree generally with this model, albeit, what is stunningly missing is the articulation of fearlessness as the path; equally, Wilber's philosophy also is lame on this dimension of the dynamic of consciousness-in-evolution in and through the meta-motivational templates of existence. By the second-tier of Korten's Fourth Order: Cultural Consciousness, we have to come to see a place for humans to go beyond 'normal' constructs of 'adulthood.' Fisher has referred to this as "post-adulthood" and it requires a unique education process and philosophy to even understand it. Everything at this Fourth Order is shifting and re-vising all that came before it in the holoarchical unfolding.

Sadly, the vast majority of people never get to this Fourth Order. This is where true Fearlessness (FMS-7) begins to predominate in the thinking and worldview of the individual or organization. This is where true "earth community" can finally emerge after the domination of "empire" community formation, says Korten. He has several descriptors for Fourth Order consciousness:

> The Cultural Consciousness [level] recognizes the need for legal sanctions to secure the order and security of society from the predation of sociopaths [and/or dictators] who lack the moral maturity to avoid doing harm to others....A Cultural Consciousness is rarely achieved before age thirty, and the majority of those who

live in modern imperial societies never achieve it, partly because most corporations, political parties, churches, labor unions, and even educational institutions actively discourage it. Each of these institutions has its defining belief system to which it demands loyalty [discipline]. Those who raise significant challenges are likely to be subjected to a loss of standing, if not outright rejection. But because those who achieve a Cultural Consciousness have the capacity to question the dysfunctional cultural premises of Empire, they are the essential engines of the cultural renewal and maturation....[415]

Like many developmental spectrum models and philosophies of consciousness, Korten makes a 'threshold' of where there is a change from fear-based to more or less love-based....and, we would call that a shift from a culture of fear to a culture of fearlessness. It is a gradual developmental and evolutionary process, and moves in and up and back and forth throughout history. Yet, at some point there is a 'shift' in the paradigm, so to speak. There is also a 'gap' to overcome, with many defensive barriers that resist the growth forward. All of that mostly comes from the cultural sphere. Cultures themselves are inherently self-protective and seek a type of immortality for their beliefs and goals to maintain themselves rather than transform and grow. Cultures are infected, largely, by the "culture of fear" dynamic as we and others have argued from the start of this book. This affects their moral development and maturity. So, we are still a long ways away from a Fearlessness Paradigm dominating the scene, other than here and there in small clusters, example, the In Search of Fearlessness Community that Fisher founded.

Now, in terms of Philosophy as a discipline and set of philosophical and intellectual characteristics, it also has a cultural organization, with ruling paradigms. Science likewise has this structuration. We have pointed out that disciplinarity itself is constraining within paradigms. So, not surprising Leggo was trained in W. philosophy and had conformed to it to such a degree, even when he thought he hadn't. His theology likewise returned him to "Love" as the solution not Fearlessness. He wasn't able to get beyond the fear-based structuration of Philosophy itself as mostly it is practiced, especially at the academic levels of professionalization within institutionalizations and merit systems accordingly. That's been Fisher's experience continually in attempting to talk to philosophers, they just cannot see their own paradigm—that is, the disciplinary Fear Paradigm they operate from. It is a *tainted* philosophical enterprise, is another way of putting it, in mild language.

That, itself is not bad. It is just that it is immature relatively to what is possible, that is, once one identifies the spectrum model of consciousness as the baseline upon which we can make discernments of consciousness and structures of awareness and development. The philosophical cannot be extracted from the psychological, moral, political. Fear and Fearlessness notions are highly political because they will immediately ask us to 'awaken' to the water we swim in—in terms of paradigms and fear-based structures that predominate as the default backdrop of our practices, identities and professions. That's quite a difficult challenge to accept cognitively but also emotionally. Most people shy away from going into that deep of a critique and awareness. Many are not ready because the conditions of their society and the world they have surrounded themselves by won't allow such an 'awakening'—but if one is able to still mature beyond these 'norms'—the result will be some sort of social/cultural/intellectual/political exclusion—if not 'exile.'

Fearlessness is a whole different kind of 'logic'—Wilber calls it "vision logic"—and, the rational logical mind of the modern average person cannot understand it. It is outside its world of meaning-making and common sense. What we estimate is necessary to help this transition and growth into higher Orders (a la Korten) is to study fear and 'fear.' That is, to study fearism. This way may be far less challenging than to study fearlessness. Albeit, we often say in this book that only fear/fearlessness can be studied if one want to capture their dialectical co-evolutionary nature. So, you can see we close this chapter with dilemmas and tensions. There are many questions still unanswered. Chapter Eight will provide further guidance around several of these issues, but do so from some different angles.

So, we at least have raised the awareness intellectually that a philosophy of fearlessness will always be disciplinary-based and likely thus, fear-based more or less. There can be a growth and transformative 'shift' but that is not always easy to conceive of your bring it about. Often your friends or colleagues may even laugh at you like they did with Leggo in his faculty meetings. Nonetheless, arguably, evolution will continue to demand the 'shift'—as will Life itself on this planet.

****

CHAPTER EIGHT

Double Talking Fearlessness

double talk(ing) – deliberately evasive[416]; e.g., 'When you try to get a straight answer, [t]he[y] gives you double-talk.'

In creativity, origin is present. Creativity is not bound to space and time, and its truest effect can be found in mutation, the course of which is not continuous in time but rather spontaneous, acausal, and discontinuous. Creativity is a visibly emerging impulse of origin which "is" in turn timeless, or more accurately, before or "above" time and timelessness. And creativity [as with ever-present origin] is something that "happens" to us, that fully effects or fulfills itself in us....Creativity appears to be an irrational process, although it is actually arational. It cannot be adequately circumscribed by a strictly psychological interpretation....Through creativity preconscious origin becomes the conscious present; it is the most direct, although rarest, process of integration....
                                                -Jean Gebser[417]

[Fisher's]...intelligence is formidable and he is truly and original thinker. He has been a teacher of fearlessness for many years and now shares what wisdom holders

have taught about fear through the ages. I recommend this [book, *The World's Fearlessness Teachings*] highly.
—Tannis Hugill[418]

Whenever I add (') marks to the word *fear*, as in 'fear'... that ought to be a wake-up call, not a reason to pretend one never saw this sleight-of-hand.
—R. Michael Fisher[419]

RMF: It ought to be stated clearly, "fearlessness" is not only disliked, it is ignored and denied access to Philosophy in general as a discipline and in particular the W. mind and consciousness. And similarly, fearlessness is denied adequate philosophizing because of the tendency, especially in modernity to try to circumscribe it, as with fear, within a strictly psychological interpretation. This has led to the habit of trying to put fear/fearlessness into a 'pocket' and forget about it, as if that was the end of anything really creative that can further be done. It's a nasty habit for philosophers, or anyone.

I'm not exaggerating this *resistance* to bring 'Fear' Studies and fearlessness into the academy and into the field of Philosophy. In my dissertation I claimed that this was so troubling that I best "divorce" myself from Philosophy and I largely did so. You well know that I've taken this on as a philosophical challenge itself. Not only am I attempting to build a global movement around this concept and phenomenon but I am also doing a double-task of building a Fearlessness philosophy, while at the same time critiquing the philosophies of the world that have been involved in the 'crime' that we've spoken about throughout this book.

I've had to also deconstruct and analyze *the why* behind this public dislike, if not hatred, for the notion of fearlessness. I mean, I don't see much value in constructing a Fearlessness philosophy if it does not have within in its thought the very capacity to see *the why* of the rejection of fearlessness itself. Make sense?

BMK: All along we have been talking in a double-tasking genre, alright. I see the way you are describing it here as a deconstruction-reconstruction project. One needs to appreciate, if not enact, a kind of *double consciousness*.[420] However, in less academic terms, what we are also theorizing throughout this book, and it part of the philosophy you and I have adopted, at least, as a working hypothesis, is the double way of speaking about fear/fearlessness. True enough, we have argued that one has to be some type of Sacred Warrior for this task of calling out the 'crime' of omission to give due attention to fear/fearlessness throughout history, and especially in philosophies and ideologies that are supposed to help humankind and planet earth.

RMF: However, to be sure, I have also tracked a more subtle form of the rejection of fearlessness and sacred warriorship in the constant attempts to try to make "fear" the gift, the positive, the even great—and no more poignantly has this shown up as within Aristotelean to Christian to Levinasian[421] rationalizations that "fear of God" and/or "fear for the other" are the *only* ethical substrates of sufficiency for "moral education" and "compassion."[422] These discourses are in constant philosophical and theological battle with my own trajectory.

BMK: What comes down to the basic problem for most people to grasp is simply, as I see it, that the double way of speaking on our part as co-authors, within a fearism perspective, is that we are saying at times that people hate fearlessness or fear fearlessness and fear sacred warriorship itself. Mostly, they do not understand the latter.[423] They hate and fear the great leaders of liberation from fear—and, the Fear Problem. It's too much for them to fully acknowledge, think through, heal through, and 'awaken' to. Yet, on the other side of our dialectical and integral philosophizing there is the other part of the situation. People inherently love fearlessness, whether they know it or not.

RMF: That's a good point. Fearlessness in our philosophy is what we are made of as a living organism. 'Love' may have to be qualified as you've used it re: fearlessness but indeed, what living creature is not in-love with their functioning adaptive Defense Intelligence and self/system regulation processes? When fear appears, so then does fearlessness in order to counter any excess and/or lingering toxic fear. No organism loves to live in a fear-state. Every organism naturally loves to live in a fear-free state—and, one could call the latter freedom and/or simply a love-state. We've made a big deal here and there in this book about Fear vs. Love paradigms, for e.g., in the last chapter on Fisher's 15 "Bi-centric paradigms." So, you are right, we ought to make clear here for readers that we are not in chronic distress ourselves in our complaining about how people, in the W. particularly, put down fearlessness and/or ignore it.

BMK: We do not wish to promote a victim-basis to our nascent Fearlessness philosophy.

RMF: For sure, that would be itself contradictory to the sacred warrior and liberational leadership approach that comes with Fearlessness. Basically, the double task going on in our writing and critiquing is that of communicating humans both 'love and hate' fearlessness. In the primal Id and essence you might say, of our Being is one of *more* motivational Life drive or 'love' for fearlessness than not.

BMK: That's Life instinct as opposed to Death instinct. Naturally, it is love for fearlessness.

RMF: Another way I experience double talking fearlessness is not merely from myself or you or seriously engaged fearism writers. Let me give some examples of the kind of double talk that goes around the topic of "fearlessness" in terms of a small sample of responses from the public, professionals and academics. These examples, all from the USA, came to me in 2009 *via* email after I had sent them a short email and introduced my soon to be published first major book entitled *The World's Fearlessness Teachings: A Critical Integral Approach to Fear Management/ Education*, and my Fearlessness e-blog and a book brochure. Most of these people I knew at the time, a few were colleagues, and several I did not know personally but found them as professionals online because I thought they might be interested in the book and my fearwork generally.

Bruce: [from a Founder & Principal of a leadership development corporation] "I checked out your blog and book description, as I am always interested in seeing how others think about fear and its impact on human functioning. However, my interest comes from the clinical perspective of a psychologist, while yours seems to be from the point of view of a philosopher/theoretician. Consequently, I did not understand most of what you wrote in your various blog entries, and I assume that your book would be equally confusing to me. I will pass on purchasing your book. (Dec. 18, 2009).

BMK: What first stands out is Bruce's double talk, as contradiction. They claim "I am always interested" in other people's thoughts about fear management. Then say, more or less, but if the other persons thoughts don't match their own ways of thinking, then it's too much effort to further be interested.

RMF: Yes, I'm cautious generally when talking about fear/fearlessness with people and they start by saying how interested they are, how open-minded they are, etc. Enthusiasm is no indicator, no matter how passionate they seem to be, of real engagement. Bruce is exemplar in this. As well, his discourse and attitude is negative towards the book because he's a psychologist and I am not. Remember, all along since I started to study fear in 1989, I and several others have taken an inter- or transdisciplinary approach and in doing so we encounter the hegemonic domination of Psychology. There's a resistance from that entire field of studies as a discipline to not fully take anyone seriously when they talk about fear management if they don't have a psychologist certificate or are publishing with psychological journals and book publishers. I don't qualify for any of those requirements that Bruce and so many of his colleagues would tend to hold. It's a type of superiority of knowledge based on disciplinary bias and privileging what Foucault called knowledge/power dynamics. A *politics of knowledge* is going on in Bruce's discourse, is another way of saying it.

BMK: It also appears that Bruce is contrasting some kind of extremist distance between himself as a practitioner and you Michael as a "theoretician." He is also distancing "Philosophy" from "Psychology," which seeming ignores how closely those disciplines have been historically. Evolutionarily speaking, Psychology actually is the newest younger sister of the much older Philosophy tradition. That is problematic enough in that it creates a false wall between the disciplines; but then, more simply, the extreme distancing indicates a disturbing trend in so many professionals, whereby they still believe, at least the vast majority I'd say, that there is little to no value for theory. They are afraid of theory. Michael, I know often in your writing and teaching you have labeled yourself a "fear theorist" and/or "theoretical fearologist."

RMF: "Theory is necessary to figure out what's REALLY going on," says an active member of the radical resistance political group called Black Panthers. Even such a radical-street-wise activist and community organizer like Michael Zinzun is aware that theories give us a larger view on what is happening on the ground. You want theory to help guide analysis toward potential causal roots of the problem and pattern dynamics that aren't always easy to pick out in the fray of all the details. Theory is the view point of seeing the whole forest and not just the tree. From that Zinzun interview a professor of planning said that lots of people and organizations talk about closing the "theory-practice gap" but few actually do it. They noted, "While the professional planning institutes that monitor and accredit planning education in most countries insist that students are taught some introductory theory and history, it is not unusual to find in each new year of incoming students (aspiring planners all), virulent cases of *theoriaphobia*. Maybe that word doesn't exist, but it should. Like other phobias, the fear of theory is also often mixed with a declared hatred. Theory is typically pre-judged as irrelevant...a waste of precious time that could be better spent acquiring something called 'skills.'"[424]

BMK: Bruce and his kind could take a lesson from Zinzun alright. Implications of a general fear of theory gets even more complex when the theory articulated in question is fear itself. So, now there is a *theriaphobia* of fear theory. And thus, the same phobia is going to play out inevitably towards fearlessness because as you and I teach, fear/fearlessness go together. It is in the very title of your 2010 book that both fearlessness and fear are there for all to see. They are inseparable.

RMF: Well, inseparable they may be, for you and I and the very Fearlessness paradigm at the core of my work and that first book. Bruce summarizes that my book and ideas are: "confusing to me." He makes the decision based on that confusion to not get unconfused, you may notice, but simply rather to not try to learn anything new about fear and/or fearlessness, at least, not from me as researcher-teacher. All Bruce needed to do, after sharing his up-front initial thoughts, is to invite a further dialogue on what confused him. Pick one thing confusing from my work, then ask me about it. We'll start a dialogue. But no, what we see is the quick disconnect, and dis-association here so that Bruce never again has to encounter a discourse based on fearlessness about fear management; thus, leaving him alone so he can rather stay in his familiar psychological discourses on fear management. The latter arguably, based on fear itself and thus distorting of the whole and integral truth available about fear and fearlessness. Bruce doesn't even mention fearlessness in his email. That's how it gets denied. I frankly cannot imagine anyone who promotes "leadership" education and training professionally and is carrying on a practice in this world, as if there is no need to pay attention to fearlessness and actually not even to say the word itself. Maria, it is amazing how many times I have seen this kind of dissing attitude. What kind of philosophy is Bruce actually displaying here?

BMK: It's a resistance to fearlessness, alright. I suppose it is pragmatism. He may not even be aware of his own assumptions philosophically speaking. But without your detailed analysis here and looking more in depth at the discourse patterns in the text of the email, I'm not sure I would have pulled out this enlightening bit of information and double talk.

RMF: Let me give another example of an overt double talk about my work on fearlessness, *via* the response of a progressive arts therapist and faculty member from the Institute of Transpersonal Psychology in California. Now, this is really interesting to me because you guess this is going to be a very 'hip' type of person, especially knowing that she wrote a book on evil and Auschwitz re: Hitler's Third Reich. Anyways, here's how she responded:

Lisa: "Your book does sound intriguing and yes, *courage* is needed. I've forwarded the info. on to our librarian...

and hope we can order it." (Dec. 14, 2009) [italics added for emphasis]

RMF: Again, there's the enthusiasm again, like Bruce, for the book. Yet, how has Lisa actually interpreted what the book is all about?

BMK: Lisa focuses on "courage" as the core of your book. She does not mention the word "fear" nor "fearlessness." Clearly, the title of your book, even if that was all she read, is on fearlessness first and fear management second. What's happening with that?

RMF: I can't know for sure without talking directly to her. What appears is that, like Bruce, there is a distancing from the book's message, albeit, not as severe or negative as with Bruce's response. Lisa is outwardly embracing and working at supporting the book positively. She even acknowledges that the author of the book is on the right track—"yes, courage is needed." So once Lisa makes the approval, but does so in her own discourse preference, which is to focus on the much more comfortable and common form of description via the word and concept of "courage," then she is done with it. She can tell the librarian to order it. She won't have to actually follow-up necessarily that the librarian will order it—often they don't. Her responsibility is over, in terms of real engagement and curiosity. In her mind, she's done her part to appear open-minded as a learner. Her self-esteem may even be boosted by 'helping' me with my cause— even if, she doesn't take the time to really know what my cause is. That's the double talk bind. I ask: But what kind of part has she played in the world's teachings on fearlessness? Actually, beneath the positivity is a shadow, I suspect, which has a different take on the book and the project of Fearlessness. She's denied fearlessness its due in depth knowing. She's distracted herself and us away from fearlessness. She won't even use the word fear. I found this kind of discourse in several replies to my book. It's a more passive *resistance* to fearlessness than Bruce's but it is still, resistance nonetheless. Again, no curious questions for me, and more it seems she's doing 'her duty' as a faculty member and probably is on to the next task of the day and the next, without not another thought about *why does this author forefront a whole book on fearlessness?*

In actually, in the book, I cover "courage" or courageousness as one of six different kinds of, or sub-species of Fearlessness. It is no better or worse than the others, and has its place as a phenomenon—and, as a fear management strategy, you could say. But it is certainly *not* the most mature and 'awake' of the strategies that I list in the book. I am quite critical actually in the book of "courage" discourse hegemony, just like with Bruce and his psychologism discourses of superiority. The vast majority of people I talk to and read about etc., think "courage" is the highest virtue. That's the typical Westerners conclusion. Not that they have ever compared it with fear-less and/or fearlessness or fearless—the latter, which are three levels of sophistication and maturity beyond courage, according to my spectrum theory of consciousness and Fear Management Systems that accompanies it.

Okay. Let me contrast a more friendly colleague's response. He's an elderly x-priest and x-faculty member of a university, in theology and humanities. He wrote,

Hugh: "This book is an indictment of the culture of fear....[Dec. 7, 2009] This book is a social prophecy for our times and future." [Dec. 10, 2009]

BMK: What Hugh said was logical. It is a meaningful comment. Social prophecy is one of the core functions of the mind. Systematic study of the why and how of connection between human fearlessness and social reality forms part of philosophy. There is another Lisa, Lisa Feldman Barrett, a neuroscience professor, who theorised on this aspect in her 2020 book, *Seven and a Half Lessons About the Brain*. She also theorizes about fear-in-evolution.[425] Her research finds that the brain is good at predictions. In my interpretation, fearlessness, being one of the basic socio-philosophical components of the mind, scans the social reality around it and forecasts on the basis of earlier experiences as to what is going to happen. Accordingly, fearlessness alerts and enables the body and mind to respond appropriately for the sake of safety and well-being. You call it Defense Intelligence, Michael.

RMF: Thanks, Maria. One immediately gets the sense from Hugh's discourse of an engagement and type of fearlessness itself being brought through his words. He's absolutely accurate as to what the book is about, especially as I do make a big deal about the problem of the "culture of fear." Unlike Bruce and Lisa, this person actually reads and interprets accurately what is going on. Albeit, he only mentions "fear" and not "fearlessness" in his email. I find that consistent with his own Christian theology. We have studied books together and we have been to many meetings and events for years. He does not use or promote fearlessness *per se*. But he is happy to condemn the abuses of fear, as I do in my book. That part of the Fearlessness paradigm Hugh is comfortable to share in public and back-up. He even goes further to say the message of the paradigm I am presenting in the book is prophetic—a "social prophecy" and that's certainly my sense of it as well.

BMK: Hugh also uses the word "indictment" and that is very consistent with how our co-authored discourses have been shaping up in this book *Resistances to Fearlessness*. We noted from the start of writing this book that there is a forensic aspect to our investigation of what has happened—why is fear so dominant and fearlessness so forgotten, overall? There's a 'crime' scene we have suggested at times, and mostly it is by omission that care was not put into the proper education of the people in contemporary times, if not going even back to pre-modern times. Something was neglected, and its resonates for us as co-authors like parent abuse *via* neglect and omission of the needs of the child. We're re-translating that now to say societal abuse *via* neglect and omission of the needs of the society—and, the ecological world too. Resistance to Fearlessness in the form of rejection is abuse to Life—is abuse to our Defense Intelligence systems. Everywhere, virtually, we're paying a great price for that 'crime.' **No one** typically notes that Fearlessness is a *prophetic philosophy* in/complementarity/with the dialectic social and practical philosophy of fearism.

"No one"—come on! Really? That's a bit extreme. Come on, Michael! Come on.... [the tone of this voice above becomes more angry and aggressive, then fades away and BMK and RMF take up a conversation with a 'shift'—seeming to pretend AS IF they never heard this voice enter the text—from AS IF it was off-stage, perhaps, a taped voice-over, a 'trick' in the play...]

BMK: Who's that?

RMF: What?

BMK: I didn't ask "what."

RMF: What did you ask?

BMK: I asked "who."

RMF: Who? What do you mean "who"? Who's who?

BMK: Ah, forget it! [getting agitated]

RMF: Forget what? [staying calm]

BMK: Michael, I'm getting frustrated... I mean not "what" but "who"....

RMF: I'm sorry, I'm confused Maria, you are usually so much more clear when we dialogue; is something happening to you? [staying calm]

BMK: Stop! I'm getting out of here. I need a break.... [totally agitated]

RMF: Oh, Okay. I don't. But, oh, if you need one. Sure, let's take a break. [calm and peaceful even]

[End of Scene 1]

****

BMK: Now, that break was really good. Did you notice the transcript above? I took time to get a drink and a bit to eat. Then returned to replay—I mean re-read what just happened in the last 30 seconds of our dialogue.

Now, everyone in public can read it too. I felt we were going along as 'normal' really, and I was enjoying the conversation with you as usual and then....

RMF: Yeah, I get what you mean. I did re-read those 15 or so lines above. Interesting hey? To back-up a bit before we discuss those 15 lines as a dynamic themselves in our dialogue, let's refresh.

BMK: Sure, sounds good. We were talking about and you were quoting from people who had in 2009 responded to your great tome *The World's Fearlessness Teachings*.

RMF: Right. We were. It strikes me in the moment that it's kind of interesting that here we are in our own co-authored book about to soon come to an end as a first draft, and then to be published, that we too will be putting the book advertisements out to the public just as I did in 2009. It's kind of a interesting parallel. Like there is a double meaning....

BMK: Yeah, there's a double talking going on with us in how this Chapter Seven and then Eight especially has unfolded on philosophy and Fearlessness. Just now I'm just realizing there is also a double talking going on in the way we decided to name the Parts of this book. At least the first five parts: they all have the identical form of "Fearlessness as/is...". Correct?

RMF: Well, yeah, I am so glad you are bringing this up now. Some kind of self-reflective consciousness has been cycling in our dialogue, going into the past, like 2009, and coming to the present, and anticipating the future—meaning, as you say, the very future of our own book and how well it will be received or not by the public when we advertise it is finished and share it. Past-present-future seem to be cycling and re-cycling, and now I am getting this excited and strange feeling that 'this is weird' almost. Our dialogue is now much more awkward with all this self-reflectivity and the 15 lines above are being written in a different code of a language game—all of a sudden. There's a 'glitch' in The Matrix, as Trinity, the main female protagonist character in the sci-fi film *The Matrix*. It's a mutation. I've mentioned the movie in our book here a few times. It was the major meta-mythic[426] 'plot-line' dynamic in which I built my whole dissertation itself around—writing the dissertation primarily as a "screen play" and thus a performative piece of research/data cum to be a "conclusion" of sorts of how best I wanted to communicate the findings of my dissertation overall.

And, I'm now reminded of what Hugh said above in his response: "This book [*The World's Fearlessness Teachings*] is an indictment...well, guess what, my dissertation was an indictment of not only the culture of fear but the university system of higher education that has become a culture of fear but won't admit it. My own research supervisors and committee that were going to judge my dissertation as "pass or fail"—after me putting in three full years of research and writing on it—they were in my view 'the enemy' of which I was actually writing about in my indictment of the "culture of fear" phenomenon and the 'Fear' Matrix, all of which was my playing through, working through, of and with the double language twisting of The Wachowski's film *The Matrix*. You know what the whole advertising campaign for marketing that sci-fi film was, Maria? It was very clever, I thought. They used a question. It actually was a philosophical question, though in popular culture and fast-media slogandia it looked just like a simple question but it was not—it was a double talking itself. Very clever.

BMK: If I remember correctly, it was *"What is the Matrix?"* This was plastered all over the media to build hype for the film weeks ahead, and then during the week of the premier performance of this massively successful blockbuster film world-wide. We were in a digital age and the film itself is about the digital age itself. It actually was a play on the fiction of digital or virtual reality as some call it. It itself was a narrative of drama putting into action a Socratic text of questioning, like its marketing strategy.

RMF: Nicely said. During my years with my research committee, as they were reading parts of the manuscript and giving me feedback, I kept waiting for one of them to be curious and brave enough to say in a meeting, *"Michael, what is the 'Fear' Matrix?"* They never did ask. Anyways, back to the film. The Socratic questioning in the advertising and in the movie itself, went on for hours in the trilogy of three films, as we watched the characters all trying to figure out, "who" and "what" is the Matrix? And, viewers from the starting scene of movie one are taken on a ride of high action cinema with little chance to catch a breath and little chance to make normal sense of what is going on in the plot. Eventually, sooner or later, this action film turns into one great Socratic questioning dialogue—not only with the characters as they ask questions of each other and of themselves, there is a devotion as well as the whole time is spent trying to figure out what "reality" is actually being performed on the screen and in the actual 'play'—the screen play—itself. I find it fascinating and filled with double talk and a whole lot of parody on the way characters are trying to say "this is real" and then another says, "no, this is real" and another says "no, this is real" and they are all in this language game of being troubled and doubting and believing philosophers in search of the real. That's what true philosophy is, isn't it? I guess some philosophers may be more interesting what makes us happy. Anyways....

BMK: For sure. I'll have to watch that movie again, as you are bringing out some really interesting things to look for. Btw, the immortal chant of the *Upanishads* - *'asatoma sadgamaya'* - was played to a mesmerising chorus in the third film of the trilogy *via* "The Matrix Revolutions." Particularly, the last line of the verse, *'mrityorma amrutamgamaya'* is relevant to our philosophical work; it means, 'lead me from the fear of death to the knowledge of immortality.'

RMF: Nice. It's easy to miss this deep philosophical inquiry in the entire trilogy because it was put into a genre of noir film about the future of humans and machines and it is sort of a horror action film at the same time as a film about 'waking up.' Can we actually come out of our everyday stupor, as Plato's Cave story brings forth for humanity to consider. It is a clever and universal story this film. But let's get back to your noticing that our Parts in the book are labeled with the same form. You are right of course, but you are also wrong, in part.

I think you'll notice it, if you hadn't, that when I was designing the names for the Parts, and this idea spontaneously arrived to use "as/is" in between

Fearlessness and the theme for that whole part—there, was a moment when I realized I had made errors in typing this out in the Outline I gave you and in the actual typing out of the Parts. What I'm saying is, there was 'shift' that took place. Notice that Chapter Five which starts off Part IV has a 'glitch' in it. The term glitch was used by the way in the sci-fi Matrix films to explain when something went wrong—or was amiss—in the Program, as they called it. I'll not try to explain the complexity of its meaning, but let's just call it an error for our purposes and go from there in reading carefully that any such error in the repetition, is well, like a 'slip of the tongue'—as Sigmund Freud would say. So, Chapter Five is a 'reversal' phenomenon because the title reads "Fearlessness is/as Philosophy"—note, no longer am I typing "as/is" but the reverse appeared. I was not conscious of it until now in Chapter Eight, and the glitch thing that happened in the 15 lines above.

A *'new' voice* entered the conversation. I ended up typing it later in italics and gave it a wider margin in the formatting as well, compared to the narrower margin of our voicing in the dialogue itself. So, in effect, that was a formative move, an aesthetic-literary device to show that some 'shift,' was happening and that it was more concrete and conscious. It indicates an 'edge' appearance on the stage from out-of-the-box so to speak; from the abnormal, from beyond-the-margins of the 'normal' repetitive conforming text.

The 'new' arrived. It is a double talking text at that point revealed. Which doesn't mean that double talking has not been going on elsewhere in our book and the dialogue and all the writing we're doing. It just became undeniably obvious suddenly. That's sort of a symptom showing itself—asking for attention(?)

BMK: What do you mean by symptom?

RMF: Without sounding so clinical and therapist-like, I'm saying a clue showed up for the mystery 'crime' that you and I have been talking about with our fearism and forensic lens on the whole dynamic of the Fear and Fearlessness....

BMK: Game? You mean we have been in a game, Michael. As Wittgenstein, the great postmodern philosopher argued, more or less, that everything going on in communications, in text, in culture, is fundamentally a word or language game. We are using words, but what the bright Wittgenstein tells us is that at the same time, like a double duty performance, there is the intricate and invisible phenomenon of *words which are using us*. Thus, there is no one and only absolute 'free agent' that rationally uses words to make meaning. But the meaning of the words in language, and in linguistic structures, are actually making us—into its pons.[427] It's a big game.

RMF: Wittgenstein, Foucault, Derrida and others of the so-called *linguistic turn* in philosophy really turned traditional modern philosophy up-side-down. Here these philosophers were telling us that philosophy is not what it seems, it is only operating AS IF it is telling the truth and the whole truth—but it is by fact of being caught in a particular or set of language games, or paradigms, that philosophy is only in some sense repeating the form and half-baked truths of the language game and/or paradigm. That's why paradigm has been used a lot in this book and in my work. I am trying to help people see that they are in a Paradigm of Fear and then while studying my work they are in a Paradigm of Fearlessness. At least, that's what I argue is going on. I believe I have at least some leverage to make that claim that that is what is going on. But of course, it is near impossible to 'prove' to those who want empirical evidence that this is what is going on. Most just get confused quickly, if you think back the pattern of discourse of the response to my book by Bruce.

BMK: Let me see if I understand what you are saying. A clue appeared in this Chapter Eight, when you realized a new voice had to enter. I mean you were the one who entered it in the text and made it into italics and then you are the one really who made up the dialogue of those 15 lines of text above. So, "you" are the creator of the matrix here and the way this whole discussion about glitches, clues, slips-of-the-tongue etc. are happening. Same with the creation of the 'shift' as you call it in the way you labeled the Parts and when "as/is" became "is/as" for the latter Parts of the text. You did it!

RMF: Ah, single-causal explanation. Remember, that's not the mutual-causal 21st-century paradigm of Maruyama that was delineated in Chapter Seven. Your discourse sounds more like...well, it sounds an awe-full lot like a police officer who has caught the culprit in the act of the fooling around, or worse, the crime scene. "You did it!" Now, admit you did it? I'm smiling while I write. This dialogue is getting so interesting to me in its self-reflexive properties of writing and at the same time writing about writing, and thinking about the thinking of our actual thinking in the moment while writing. That's self-reflexive working through the text and the problematics and the potentials for awakening to our text. Isn't it?

BMK: I'm aware this language gaming, is intriguing philosophically alright. It makes me think more carefully about what's going on between us as dialogue partners. It makes me think more about my own voice, and my own thinking about thinking. That's the level scientists and philosophers now are calling *meta-thinking* or meta-cognition. It's what you Michael often call "meta-theory" as core to your work on Fearlessness, that is, from a holistic-integral-meta-perspective. You ask of us as readers of your work to theorize and philosophize with you in a co-construct-ion, right? You are not saying that you have all the best answers about fear/ fearlessness and you are going to enlighten us.

RMF: Exactly. No, that would be the old paradigm of linear-causal pedagogy and knowledge construction. That's been highly refuted now in the field of communications and postmodern philosophy. So, we are up-grading our "program" here about the very nature of philosophy itself. And, I argue my case for this up-grade rather uniquely amongst philosophers, at least that I know of in the world. And that's because what I present is the complete, virtually opposite, language game for Philosophy itself. I do the same for Psychology—for Education, etc. I offer a Fearlessness Philosophy or paradigm in juxtaposition with and/or *in parallel* with a Fear Philosophy or paradigm.

I do more than that however. It is *not* merely an alternative difference and parallel of truth-telling and reality-making I am asking of my peers, students, readers and listeners. I am saying, the difference I propose to you is a difference that *really* makes a difference—and, if you aren't careful and are merely naive in adopting this Fearlessness, you'll get your ass kicked. I mean, you may transform yourself in the process. You will also being transforming your world, of course. It is dialectic: self/world is in movement and is 'working through' as the psychoanalysts call it—working on itself to correct itself.

Remember all our talk about Fearlessness at the Id level and how it is a basic system of flow whereby when *fear* or distress appears so then does that begin to change the moment it arrives. What is it changing into? It's opposite. It's reversing itself. *Thanatos* is becoming *Agape*, as Ken Wilber would argue.[428] Fear is becoming Fearlessness—again, this is metaphysical and biological at the same time; or so this is what integral and transformative theory would suggest. And remember the reversal is also back the other way, always already primed to 'shift' back-n-forth, back-n-forth.[429] It's wild.

BMK: Wow. Stop. I need to decelerate a bit. That's a lot to take in but I basically agree with it. I think(?). You have steeped yourself in this making this new philosophy for so long, like over three decades. Most people can't keep up, I suppose. That's why they become resistant not just to fearlessness but to you Michael. But, if your work is a prophetic teaching, as are all the world's fearlessness teachings before you, then history has already proven empirically that "prophets" are not typically understood, liked or...well, mostly, by the vast majority they are hated.

RMF: And, prophets are loved by some too. There's that tension of Love/hate....

BMK: Okay, I guess I agree now with your challenge that I was using a police tactic, or a detective tactic, to see if you'd bite. I was telling you that *You did it!* It's tactic of how to get people to tell the truth, when they are already in a situation that to tell the truth would put them in jail or worse. It would harm them. It would harm their self-esteem. Right? As a forensic analysis in the field, one has to operate by 'tricking' the person a bit. You have to play with the language game of their motivational schema. I simply mean, if you ask them straight questions over and over about the potential that they caused the crime, maybe you'll get some where, most likely not. Well, that always gives them and the deception strategy of defence, that is, if they are really guilty I mean, a clever way to double talk their way around your doubt. They are, if like all seasoned criminal-types of personalities, highly trained to "lie" and look like they are telling the "truth." Nothing quite seems as it appears in this game of 'hide-n'-seek.' Or they even learn to 'lie' so they'll get caught on that lie; only because it was likely their least worst of the lies and of their crimes committed. No one under pressured surveillance wants to disclose their unpublished 'record' of all crimes and lies. And so, they may sacrifice the least lie because it will potentially distract the detectives, lawyers and judges away from the real crime that was much worse than the one they got caught on and are currently admitting they were involved in.

RMF: Analogously, when a client comes into my therapy room for "help" and presents their case as a "symptom" they wish to disclose as "the problem"— typically that is not the real problem that needs therapy. The therapist and client may do a complicated dance, for some time, before they can agree on *what problem* *is really the most important problem.* Often, this is never achieved and only the lesser worst problem 'steals' all the therapeutic time and attention—and, no deep cure or transformation is possible for the client.

BMK: Okay, without going into all that, I merely want to say that *you* Michael made some clues or glitches in this text, that you admitted to, more or less. You are not in denial of that. But your more subtle critical point is that the clues above, like the 15 lines above, are there because they *co-emerged* from the dialogue with me. So, they are co-mutual and emergent realities. It's odd how they look sort of like fiction and games of fiction discourse. They are kind of *unreal*, relative to the straight-up presentation we were happily carrying on in this chapter and all other chapters of the book prior to this chapter.

RMF: I like how you are describing all this dynamic of double talking, double-tale telling. Deeper *unconscious* connections, or "strings" as Ettinger describes,[430] are informing us all the time—and, across time/space dimensions. Meta-motivations, even as archaic and archetypal as *Thanatos'* Death drive is part of our conversation. The arrival of *words* on a page are part of a language and mythic structure, says the archetypal depth psychotherapist James Hillman, in his many critical books on therapy and why analytical or behavioral therapies[431] are such 'games' of 'lies' and 'deceptions'; basically because they start on the psychological premise that there is only *one-self* in the therapy room and they are over there, and they are telling the therapist what is wrong with them. The assumption of this reductionist rationalist model of therapy is that it works to help the situation. Hillman argues, I think convincingly, that we need to question exactly who is in the room? Who is dialoguing? He says, the person is real but they are *not the only one* in the room nor is the therapist the only second one in the room. There are, he claims, myths and their characters and archetypes also in the room with the analyst/analysand relationality. The client, in other words, is pre-personal and transpersonal at the same time as person.

Note that Hillman is not saying there is no self in the room. There is, but it just happens to be a multi-layered, if not protean-self in shape-shifting dynamics, that is, a 'self' that by definition is no longer a stable, fixed ego-self; but it is a complex involving the Id and the Super Ego and the coalition of the Id and the Super Ego of the therapist are also are in the room. And, the whole "telling" going on both ways between the therapist-client or analyst/analysand is a 'unit' of systems of communications of past-present-future. Because I have been a practicing therapist for many years, I have found this and many other theories and meta-theories about "therapy" very informative to the process-based systems way I think.

King Fear vs. King Fearlessness: A Telling of the Truth

So, when I present *Fearlessness talking* into the world now,[432] for example, or in the past since 1989, as I'm building this new philosophy, I have seen that at the same time I am having to fight-off all defenses of the 'Fear' Matrix that wants to keep the Fear Paradigm and its philosophy in its dominating place. No 'king' likes to be dethroned, to put it bluntly. No dictator likes to lose. No empire likes to become second place, not once they have tasted the 'bitter-sweet' victory of Domination and rule. Fear will not let Fearlessness usurp it. I know, that's not a big insight. Anyone reading my work will have read about this relationship of Fear and Fearlessness, of which you and I often prefer to write as fear/fearlessness dialectics at the base of the Fearlessness Paradigm and philosophy we are creating here. Yet, it is a big deal. It is in fact, a very troubling deal. There is a "dealing" or negotiating going on between the two potential Rulers. The one rule, is *King Fear*, who has led for many millennia as the top-dogs of the hierarchy, that is, of Fear's Empire. They are purportedly having a conversation with the new kid on the block. The latter, who wants an *equal* say—that is, the King Fearlessness. Guess what? It's not an even-even table for negotiation. Why? Because King Fear has all the cards and language game down fixed, and static—as it is represented by the table or paradigm to use more technical language—and, they even have full control of the conversation as it takes shape. They have the power-over and all their soldiers with arms around the edges of the table, just to make sure the King's wishes are maintained. King Fear thus has set the rules of the conversation before it is even started with King Fearlessness.

It isn't an ethical "pure" negotiation table, even if the King Fear and their cronies are willing to be nice now and then and give a voice to the Fearlessness boys, like me. I became super-aware of this problem not only in the therapy room with clients and how the whole Psychological Establishment based on King Fear sets up the 'table' of 'therapy' and what should happen and what shouldn't happen, and that if the psychologists for example wants to keep their licence and get paid from the State, as if often the case, then that "psychologist" or "therapist" has to follow the King Fear rules from the start. What I learned working with adolescents, many with 'crimes' on their record, who don't follow King Fear or King Fearlessness rules very well, they are going into therapy because they are coerced to. The State sets the entire agenda. And, we have to ask what is at-stake and motivating the State to have control over these adolescents and/or criminals. By the way, the same is the case in form with the Education State-run systems.

BMK: That must be the similar power-imbalance dynamic that happens when an oppressor group appears to try to listen to the oppressed group at some point. I'm thinking of what I have read about Indigenous peoples trying to talk to White Dominant people who are the State, the latter whom are the 'colonizers' and hold most of the elite positions. They have the capital power.

RMF: Indeed, that is similar for sure. My colleague Four Arrows has taught me a good deal about this problematic meeting ground problem of oppressors and the oppressed, as has Willie Ermine, an Indigenous Canadian scholar of law.[433] In my phone conversation with Ermine many years ago, he told me as I'm paraphrasing now from memory, that *'We are not colonized.'* I listened. He was talking about something deeper in the Indigenous soul. He said, that only the colonizer wants us all to believe this is the case. Of course, the colonizer tried to hide their crime of genocide for eons. Yet, once they got caught, then they finally reluctantly admitted their crime, but it was not the real crime in depth that they are admitting. All they will admit—tell the 'truth' about—is that they weren't fair and made some bad mistakes. They are sorry.

He really meant, that too often that language of conquest, keeps depicting Indigenous peoples as "colonized" is but another tricky language game of the oppressors; even when White people admit they are colonizers, try to be nice to Indigenous people, and want to apologize and make reparations, like the Canadian government does now and then. No, there is a toxic underbelly to the niceness and admission of a crime. Deception and double talk in such initiatives is still the problem—still hiding as a "lie."

Ermine sees through it all and writes about this deception in the talk of "negotiations" and "laws" and is not willing to participate in it because it is already cast in victimizing the victims. But Ermine goes beyond that problem, he offers a philosophical argument that shows that to have an ethical negotiation 'at the table' truly *in/with* such opposing worldviews as Indigenous vs. Dominant, then the very language game of the set-up of the two worldviews needs to be a structural and values-based part of the negotiations. In other words, he is saying to the colonizers not to just bring your money and apologies to the table and make it look like you are understanding us. No, rather you must come to the table under our preferred language game of rules—that is, the sacred Indigenous ways.

Four Arrows and his Indigenous scholar colleagues have written a great book on the problem of "Unlearning the Language of Conquest."[434] For my analogy here in this teaching, I have my own translation and agenda for the Fearlessness Movement and fearlessnessizing, which is like Four Arrows' teaching Indigenizing—whereby everyone needs to de-colonize their minds and their ways and their very formations of trying to now 'help' the Indigenous peoples. How do you begin this "unlearning" of language that always reproduces its own language game of "conquest"? It's not easy. King Fear will not want to change its language game conquest either. Be prepared. Four Arrows says that there is an ideological "anti-Indianism" that infiltrates everything in, at least, North American society and history. We are all, more or less indoctrinated into that conquest language game of anti-Indianism. I suggest reading his edited book on this. But to note, the book he edited under his Lakota name *Wahinkpe Topa*, begins on the title page of the book with a small font text in italics. It is not a typical sub-title, because he already has one there in larger bold font *"Scholars Expose Anti-Indianism in America."* Something subversive, like another voice, a glitch, a clue, a symptomatology is being revealed like a dripping blood spot on the page, perhaps(?). I wonder. I had not seen this before[435] until now as I am looking at the book and typing, it says:

(Deceptions that influence war and peace, civil liberties, public education, religion and spirituality, democratic ideals, the environment, law, literature, film, and happiness)

What just happened? What is that subversive text? It's *Wahinkpe Topa* telling the truth in 20 chosen words which he wrote in italics but that are not easy to put anywhere for the reader, not the title, not the sub-title—what is going on?[436] This is an invocation of sorts for those who read it, who are paying attention, that says something like this, in my words: *Only read this book if you are sincere about what you are to discover in these pages and between the words of these pages. Only read this book if you are willing to engage actually the 'ethical space' a la Ermine of an Indigenous perspective and worldview on what has gone on historically and what is going on historically—between the oppressor and the oppressed. Note: this is a text from the oppressed position talking to you but we are not 'the oppressed' that you may want to imagine we are—especially, if you are an oppressor and White person who is trying to understand us. Be prepared. Read this at your own risk. Read it now in this little small font, because there in this message in parentheses is the indictment and is the judgement already passed by the awakened Indigenous intelligences that 'know what is really going on.' Read this book only if you are willing to face the "Deceptions" that are like the viruses that flow in the lies of the systems of language of the Dominators—and, like in you, dear reader.*

Maria, that is amazing in terms of the analogy of my own take on trying to write a book on Fearlessness teachings in 2010 and having it read by people who don't or won't see through what I am actually writing about and what the many peoples in the world's fearlessness teachings and traditions are talking about—that is, that there is a big lie that has gone on and is still going on and it is conceived and controlled by King Fear and their Fear Empire, by the 'Fear' Project(ion)—the 'Fear' Matrix. So, I wished I had the where-with-all then when writing that first major tome to write something like *Wahinkpe Topa* had, and sure even if I could have written it in a sub-versive small font italics text like an insert from 'another world' reality.

It's a double talking that is appearing, like a ghost or doppelganger effect. It attempts to invoke and wake you up from trance, shake you, and making you aware that you are *co-involved in the crime* of which you are about to read about. It's a phenomen-ological "stop." Now, really look at what you are reading about. This is not just some abstract text or philosophy on the page. This is about a bloody crime and the blood is on your hands too. You dear reader, will be best served by this book by serving this book's voice—that is the voice of trauma, tragedy, horror, nightmare, crime, and yes, 'evil.' But again, all those are descriptive words and won't do justice to the phenomenon of oppression 'speaking' through in these pages.

If you now go back up to the 15 lines out-on-the-edge of our 'normal' dialogue, way above now somewhere in the *past* but still ringing *a presence* in their absence in virtually everything I have been saying/writing here for pages and pages—in after thought, and in echoes, and in systematic following-through. Please go back!

Yes, there is in that 15 line interchange an unconscious slip-of-the-tongue indicating as a clue to a presence of motivational impulse and desire or so it seems—that is, to have a "purpose" to make you and I *stop*—and check-up on our normal talk, and enter a *talk of a different kind via* a 'shift.' And with a new sensitivity. We may have to listen more deeply. It may change everything we write from here on in—or not. Just as the shift in the words in our Parts from "as/is" to "is/as" may actually mean something much more profound than what is on the surface of its presentation—as a language/game/trick—or is it even some latent deceit appearing?

I'm not sure at this point what all is going on, I'm merely probing-as-process thinking—and, as part of our honest and self-reflexive detective work—that you and I have agreed to partake in for this book project. I'm wonder what you are thinking and feeling around all this? At some point, soon, we're going to have to end this chapter—and, our next Part V is "Fearlessness is/as "Uncanny"—where we'll dip into Freud and psychoanalysis and who knows what else. I will say, I'm pretty sure that we won't really be able now, perhaps ever, to *fully explain* rationally in analytic text what is happening. I'm actually sensing, and my journaling some hours ago revealed this, that we are going to have to turn to literature and literary devices to pursue this investigation of fear/fearlessness, narrative, story-telling, truth-telling, and especially if we want to 'work through' deeper with what has 'plopped out' on the above few page in this somewhat unpredictable Chapter Eight. Over to you.

BMK: I agree Michael! King Fear is like the Ptolemaic geocentric perspective of the universe. As long as its reign continued up to the 16th century, people lived under the spell of lies and darkness. The collective motivation was to reproduce and sustain the geocentric and deny and/or eliminate competing views. Now the heliocentric model has revolutionised science but beneath that shift is still basically the same old King Fear. It is internal and more invisible in its operations. This still dominates the psyche of not only commoners but also rulers and intellectuals.

As you have been advocating for decades, this is the time that the world should switch to operate from fearlessness lens. King Fearlessness will show amazing ways of experiencing a beautiful life. There will be a positive twist in every effort we put in. Philosophy, psychology, biology, sociology, economics and most notably politics have been under the dictates of King Fear. Because of this latter pessimistic approach, fear has been spreading its tentacles more and more deeply into human lives. Human relations, ranging from interpersonal to international, need to be refurbished with the aid of King Fearlessness.

Four Arrows and Ermine have rightly pointed out that the dominators' language of conquest and colonisation are nothing but fear tactics. Hence, King Fear has still been dividing and ruling most of humanity. The world looks forward to seeing a united humanity now. It is only the fearlessness paradigm that is compatible with brotherhood of humanity. Let us be optimistic about our efforts.

RMF: I wish to end the chapter with the invoking of literary devices, or simply arts/literature/film capabilities that are potentially great allies to the Fearlessness Project. I'm also well aware such literary means may simply operate in the Fear Paradigm and reinforce that Paradigm. Most do. There are however, now and then literary works that provoke enlightened discourse and move us a little along the way to better understanding resistances to Fearlessness, example *The Matrix* trilogy.

I thought of the rough outline for a play script while I was writing about the above clue to the crime that true Fearlessness is always going to expose. To better try to demonstrate, even explain, what the 15 lines were about and all the dialogue that followed, it's a simple story that's on my imagination. Think of the protagonist, Dan, of this play who moves to a new village on the outskirts, in the country side. They want to build this new house on a small piece of land there that he purchased. Dan knows no one and they don't know him. But he is quickly the 'talk' of the village people as the stranger. Days of shopping for supplies in the village, talking a little with people haphazardly about his house project, and everyone is so nice. He's starting to love people there. We watch scene after scene of Dan working alone to clear the land and start his wood and cement foundation. An enormous amount of work, but he is loving the labor of it. By the end of the day of his work he heads back to the village to stay in a motel. Then, early each morning he is off again to work, and the repetitive cycle repeats.

On one day we see that Dan has nearly completed the foundation, and has put up his framing of the first wall of the house. He goes home. He has a bad dream about a wind that blows his wall down and ruins some of the foundation. In the morning, like always he goes back to his land and is shocked to see the wall is smashed up and fallen along with much of his foundation. He is devastated. Looking carefully at the mess, he notices a beer can in the grass nearby. He looks for more clues. No tracks, nothing. Dan immediately knows that someone who is not supposed to be there on his property was there that night and he begins to suspect there's something not quite right. His worst thoughts move towards fear and thinking a crime has occurred, called vandalism.

He has worse nightmares that night, and not knowing what to do. He can't stand thinking the thought of reporting a crime and doesn't want to create a problem as he is quite a shy fellow. He keeps his mouth shut. He wants to trust. Skip several scenes now. The story unfolds that every day he fixes the house and vandalism but it is there again. He tries putting up hidden cameras at night and hides in the bushes near by, but he sees nothing and ends up falling asleep. More vandalism happens, to his car. And on it goes. He's getting enraged with the situation and his house is not getting built. He goes to a neighbor and asks if they have seen any unusual signs around of strangers, potential vandals and he finally tells them that he's experienced this vandalism on his house. The neighbors appear to be listening but do not register a thing he said about the vandalism. They talk in ways that make Dan feel like he is hallucinating. He's deeply troubled by troubling them and then becomes to question his own insanity. Turns out he cannot talk to them about "vandals" or "vandalism" because everyone he tries to mention it to in the village doesn't understand the term, apparently. They always give what Dan says to them around the crime events on his land, a completely different meaning. At some points, Dan is shaking his repeatedly shaking his head in talking to them, not to be seen as rude in regard to their responses, it was merely that he was trying to shake things around in his head to find an order for making sense that was effective with them. It never happened.

In writing in his motel room, journaling in the midst of this and a storm outside, he wrote by candle light: *"The term seems to have disappeared from their vocabulary."* Then he paused, and wrote, *"Today, the village psychiatrist approached me, and said, 'You should get your head injury looked at.' And she smiled, and walked away. It took me a few minutes to figure out that she was talking about my constantly shaking my head in disbelief about the people here. In my growing paranoia, I knew she had the power to put me in a mental institute for having a disturbed,* 'injured' head. It's called mental disorder. This is really freaking me out."

After coming to terms with struggling thoughts in his mind for days as to whether he should just get the hell out of this place and sell his land, or he should fight back, the decision came to dig in with both heels. He starts doing research on any clues as to how this ignoreance happened in this whole village town. What could be so universal that it has brought about this strange behavior pattern? Another late night, when he couldn't sleep and drank too much wine, he falls out of his bed accidentally and starts shaking uncontrollably for several minutes. Eventually, calming himself down a bit, he grabs his journal and wrote: *"What are they all so afraid of?"*

The story gets complex...far beyond the scope of my short telling the tale here; but the point is, that he now has a different problem on his hands than what has been happening to his house night after night. He is now tracking a much more serious problem re: the erasure of "vandalism" from the village. It's this problem that obsesses him. But his efforts and diversions from people he tries to interview, finally pays off. He ends up walking into the village historical library in an old rundown part of the village and, to make a long story short, he finds early village incorporation documents from 85 years ago. He reads through, and at a magical moment something catches his attention. The first mayor of the village and his wife were named "George and Myrtle Vandle." He stares at the word. His vision goes double he was staring so long and Vandle blurred and in parallel on the page like a mirage was the word Vandal. That's it! Vandal and vandalism. Vandal and vandals. That was the clue, he was sure to what happened in this village 85 years ago...

But no matter where he searched in the old library, he could find nothing more than the usual bureaucratic documents where the mayor Mr. Vandle signed, or made a motion to pass a policy in some meeting. Frustrated again, he asks people about the original Mayor and his wife, and residents of the village smiled and said odd things like "My aunt was the first to open a seamstress shop in our village. She was a great lady and did so much for the community" or another example, "Fine furniture he made, nothing built like that today. All the good craftsmanship is nearly gone." At one point, Dan answered the questions and tried to get them to go deeper but it only led to more nonsense, sometimes sounding like fast verbal 'word salad" combinations like when one is in a psychotic episode and delusional.

He gets so mad one night that he vandalizes the large outside wall of a bank with spray paint, and writes in huge letters "This is Vandalism." He manages to fool some of the villagers with a lie that he has cooked a barbecue down the street and they follow him upon his invite to share it with them. They were the handful of people who seemed to trust him a little bit more than the average. Then he shows them this wall. He points at the wall which he painted all kinds of images, like moons and starts and in the center of them all the actual word vandalism. He desperately says, while pointing: "That's vandalism."

Once again, they are dumbfounded by his getting all upset about this painted walled. And they make conversation about all kinds of things about the bank and the friendly tellers and where they are investing their money and all were very optimistic about the future. They twisted everything he said that is negative about vandalism into something positive and they saw no issue with the paint on the wall. No problem exists for them.

This drives Dan really mad...long story. He cannot communicate in their language game. He can't understand what would motivate it either. He loses all control of his shy and calm personality. You can fill in the rest of the film, and even imagine an ending for it. I have not got one but I do sense at some point in the play, Dan finds out information secretly hidden about the Vandles and some horrific incident that is of unimaginable 'evil' like they were involved in a child molestation ring, etc.

I've simplified this literary outline of a play. It has little details left out. You get the general sense of Dan's frustration, however. It is related to what happened above in the text in Chapter Eight. BMK's frustration in the short 15 line dialogue is related to Dan's experience, that is, indirectly. Why? Because of a double talking going on. What double talking is going on in the fictional play *per se* is less obvious but there is this wonderful image worth contemplating—of Dan trying so hard to teach the villagers to 'wake up' about the vandalism on his land, that he does it by painting graffiti: "This is vandalism." Arational painting, with some beautiful aesthetics for its modality is one language—combined with the letters of a word and his body posture as another modality—'body talk.' None of it, apparently, 'worked.' Certainly Dan got no sympathy or empathy for his crime problem. It all cost him a lot more than lumber and cement. It cost him his health and sanity in the end. It became totally paranoid. Every time the village psychiatrist walked by him, she stared and had a bigger and bigger smile. It gave him the shivers.

Dan had to figure out the best way to communicate with a system in denial—and, traumatized, in fear so long, they didn't know they were in fear—and, none of them apparently know, or need to know that their way of coping with the situation of what happened with the Vandles in their village is inadequate or inaccurate. Such criteria do not matter when people are living in terror of the 'unspeakable.' Research on Holocaust survivors shows how pain and horror in memory can virtually disappear. Only many decades later, if at all, could some things, some stories, be 'told.' A lot of double speak went on to refer to horrible things, but at the same time does not speak directly about the horror and rather double duties in fact to deny and help forget what is there in the unconscious. I simply don't have space here to go into this and yet, maybe some of the consequences of double talking fearlessness will show through in the next Part V.

Oh, I don't want to forget, if you haven't seen the fiction thriller film *The* Village (2004),[437] I highly recommend it for 'explaining' how the dynamic of a close community and their leaders set-up a language game of avoidance of the truth—yes, I mean deception and even coated the whole performance of daily life in spiritual terms. Fear is at the roots of such a village. And, the near poetic details and method of the mind-manipulation and social collusion dynamics, like the Super Ego layer, is really astounding to watch and hear in a drama on film. Totally sensory experience is something else way beyond reading text. The *unsaid* in that particular film sticks with me, more than the said. It was ghostly all the way through but one can't actually tell what, where, who... is the real ghost. That's an oxymoron, I realize. Double take. Therein are some great quotes, as well. I call this dynamic a "culture of fear." It could be also a "family" or "organizational" defense pattern. But to learn about it through narrative-based arts performances is way more subtle than through reading political science and sociology texts describing what a culture of fear is. That same literary devices is what I experimented with in my dissertation and what I analyzed in *The Matrix* trilogy.

This philosophical-literary combo of devices for analysis and resolving trauma are totally relevant to *why* people 'don't really' want to be free from fear, that is free from King Fear and the kingdom of oppression. Mostly, they won't tell the true story of their *village*—as metaphor for their *paradigm* of where they live inside. Like Dan, many of the people that responded to my philosophical book on the world's fearlessness teachings, wrote things that sort of seemed relevant to communicate with me but I had always to take a double-look at their speech acts. Through one eye, so to speak, I would listen and appreciate they at least responded to my book advertisement; but through the other eye I had my doubts and worse, I had my forensic lens on the whole exchange. For example, a world famous scholar and political activist of the Left, wrote back upon receiving my email on my book:

Noam: "Looks most intriguing. Glad to hear that it is out." (Dec. 10, 2009)

In the back of my mind, I reply to myself and the world: "Do you really mean it?"

BMK: Thanks for that explication. I keep sensing that there's some *absurdity* always lingering in human thought and especially human communications. The great existential philosopher, Albert Camus, viewed human life as full of absurd situations and reasoned that the solution to being human is within the human's search for meaning, which ultimately lies in accepting the truth of absurdity itself as the foundation to human existence. Such acceptance, he argued, would lead to a vulnerable but sturdy sense of self-dignity, esteem, and why? Because at least, they are free of deceit, of deceiving themselves that the world situation and human situation are not absurd. Seemingly paradoxically, however, Camus went further to clarify that *rebellion*, not really different than the *resistance* we are foregrounding in this book, has a key role to play in meaning making and how we tell meaning stories about what is reality and who we are and what is the purpose of life.

Have you thought of resistance that way, Michael? Why you care about resistance so much in your Fearlessness philosophizing. Contentment and freedom were still near enough for Camus and worthy to attain, but we have to go through the existential crisis of a kind of dismemberment of our 'untruths.' Anyways, Though every philosophy has got its own perspective, be it secular or theistic, one commonality is that all schools of thought agree about the perpetuity of one unsolved riddle—that is: "the problem of human misery and how to fix it?"

Coincidences between belief and intended outcome give credence to each school of philosophy and the concerned followers strengthen their confidence in such schools and also come to terms whenever there are anomalies, acquiescing that their own actions might have had shortcomings but not the school of philosophy *per se*. Most of the world's philosophies rely on the premise that an individual is the fulcrum around whom all the affairs of world move. It is a logical assertion and the individual's pivotal importance has been recognised since time immemorial like what has been stated in an olden dictum, *Homo Mensura*.

But the fact is that a human is as strong as her own weakness. She is as weak as her strength. That means, a human is strong when her neighbour or opponent is weak. Once the opponent turns stronger, she remains weak. And the affairs of the society revolve around the stronger person. As long as philosophy views things from a single person's perspective, the sole purpose of philosophy of life does not seem to be in order.

Jean-Paul Sartre's idea of human freedom fixes responsibility for decisions and the individual is accountable not only for herself but also for all other human beings. If Sartre's freedom is oriented towards choosing choices for making destiny, Camus's freedom, aims at rebellion to handle the problem of absurdity. If Marx's freedom is understood as redemption of the working class and oppressed people from the capitalist exploitation, Kierkegaard's freedom seeks to fetch meaning to human life through the "leap of faith." Here, one crucial element of antithesis is that freedom does not happen *suo moto*. Freedom means *lack of fear*.

Unless the Fear Problem is solved, the idea of freedom cannot be explained in full terms.

Choices require different definitions tinged with fearlessness. Absurdity is *best* to be analysed from a fearlessness lens or paradigm. Whether the goal of human life is considered as happiness, heaven or achievement etc., depending upon the respective of the school of thought concerned, the ultimate and pivotal ingredient of such a goal is invariably *freedom*.[438] Because...simply, one cannot be happy without freedom. And/or one cannot believe to attain salvation unless she is given freedom to worship God to the best of her own satisfaction. One will not be able to achieve things in life in restricted socioeconomic political environments that disregard the high value of freedom. But the fact, which needs to be remembered always, is that freedom itself depends upon the fundamental duo i.e., *fear and fearlessness*. Hence philosophy of freedom requires a fearlessness model.

As co-authors we are sharing a dialogue with our readers that is *both* real *and* fictional. We live at opposite ends of the world and cannot easily communicate other than by emails. We both write to each other, as well as to ourselves, and from that combination comes the book you are reading, rallied from chaos-into-order but not along a smooth road, a linear-causal and fine finished elite production. Rather, there is a gritty creative manipulation within these book covers—a manipulation of time, space, emails, and revisions bursting at times *to create* what looks like a seamless piece of work built on rational foundations but resting on shifting sand dunes. Welcome to Fearlessnessland. Welcome: come and survey this landscape/mindscape.

Because we both are comfortable with a trandisciplinary approach, compatible with a philosophy of fearism and fearlessness, we read, think, and write in-and-out of fiction/non-fiction matrixial borderspaces—like diving from a cliff, in and swimming out of the depths and waves of a great sea. And we do so as explorers and investigators of the pre-rational, magical, mythic, rational and post-rational (integral) worlds of reality. Fearlessness is that all-encompassing of a holistic and originary conception and creative phenomenon. *The moment a reader travels with fearlessness in their one pocket and fear in the other pocket, and forgets they are creative—is the moment one forgets who they really are.*

Many of the Figures in this book depict visually dynamic architectures for ways of under-standing fear/fearlessness and all the developmental and evolutionary dynamics around that dialectic. The Figures are like lenses of perception, to 'shift' our normal uncreative gaze. And, so we as co-authors swim--changing lenses as frequently as needed or as happens. It's unpredict-able when the next lens is on and the other off. No one lens put on for too long satisfies. We are *"in search of fearlessness"* and trying to build a house, a boat, a philosophy, in order to fulfill adequately that forensic search. But as soon as we are a bit over-confident that we have 'got it' and are proud to have built the foundations of that house/boat/philosophy—we return the next day and find it *vandalized* by some unknown entity, force, reversal—or merely what was real at some point dissolved, and we expect it did because of time/space three dimensionality, illusory and yet persistent, that keeps closing in on the more expanded integral dimensionality we have touched, that is timeless.

Ultimately, we are both interested in dialogue, of course, the question is, "What kind of dialogue is it that really matters today, in this kind of world we live in?" This work together through dialogue, at least, has to be imbued *via* the nature of creativity itself—in what Jean Gebser called "an originary phenomenon."[439] That curiosity is why we opened this chapter with a quote from a Gebserian integral perspective. However, to be honest, we only added that quote after this chapter was finished. What led this chapter seemingly was the double, perhaps twin—of deception, an impeccable character of 'tricks'—a trickster—to confuse and clarity what we sought. A deception perhaps of not merely a negative connotation. For like fear it too cannot be so contained alone. Fearism has taught us that lesson. But a more positive connotation, from a fearlessness perspective, perhaps, therein and imbued with the nature of creativity. Twins nonetheless always have this creativity/destructivity—enabling a 'blowing up of the ark'[440] as the great 19th century playwright Henrik Ibsen is most well-known for.

> **RMF:** I hear an echo from a ghostly past. I imagine our book coming out in a few months. Then an email from a reviewer of our book brochure comes in one morning and I open it. "Looks most intriguing. Glad to hear that it is out." Another one, and another one. I'm delighted. Then, another one, which hits me like none of the others' responses: "You seem to rely on dialectic for your so-called Fearlessness Philosophy. At the risk of sounding, and being accused of being, "resistant to fearlessness," I must say, your own very investigation has not near done justice, from an arational integral perspective, or a deep psychoanalytical perspective, or from the hackery of double talking fearlessness itself—you have not unveiled the inherent weaknesses of the dialectic form and methodology itself.[441] Surely, you could have caught that before you published this book. The sharp reader of philosophy expects that kind of rigor. I'm disappointed and have my doubts."

Dialogue, Morphing, Mutation and Unplugging

> Unguarded by the fear of losing its orientation, the [will for] freedom *for* [good] action [Arendt] is susceptible of surreptitiously morphing into a freedom [*aka* fear] *from* action....re: Sartre is quite aware that the ego makes most of this 'monstrous freedom' [*aka faux* fearlessness] invisible to itself.
>
> -Alin Cristian[442]

The focus in Part IV on Fearlessness is/as Philosophy is one that has a much larger story than the one we've told in these two Chapters Seven and Eight. Time will tell if others will support this aspect of investigation. Yet, there is some lament afoot. We (as co-authors) wish there was more time...we wish 'fear' and 'freedom' would stop morphing. But then we know, change cannot be stopped.

"You believe the year is 1999 when in fact it is much closer to 2199."[443] We are drawn to abruptly close with a brief excerpt from Scene 35 from the first film of the sci-fi trilogy *The Matrix*, where the protagonist Neo ('new man') is being restored, *via* a serious make-over, by the crew, led by captain Morpheus. Neo has just been through a dramatic first-step of a paradigm 'shift' from his life-inside-the-matrix to now a life-inside-the-hovercraft ('of the real'):

Neo: "What are doing?"

Morpheus: Your muscles have atrophied. We're rebuilding them.

Neo: Why do my eyes hurt?

Morpheus: You've never used them before....Rest, Neo. The answers are coming.[444]

****

PART V

FEARLESSNESS IS/ AS "UNCANNY"

CHAPTER NINE

Fearlessness is/as "Uncanny"

She is seemingly crazy—but is she?....[and] so the chord that links compassion to its shadow is coiled.
                                    -Bracha L. Ettinger[445]

Sigmund Freud's *uncanny* arises when something seems both frighteningly alien and strangely familiar, when we are reminded of a repressed and forgotten aspect of ourselves.
                                    –Joseph Dodds[446]

When fear appears, so does fearlessness to resist....Of course, there is still risk of extinction, and always will be.
                                    -R. Michael Fisher[447]

In this last chapter of our co-inquiry, other than Part VI chapter on Recommendations, it became an imperative to both share our personal experiences of the "uncanny" and to elaborate and modify Freud's notion. The chapter has two parts, distinct but interrelated. We begin with Kumar's experiences and his addition of a new type of uncanny that swerves from traditional ways of conceptualization. Secondly, we enter into a philosophical co-inquiry into Fearlessness that seems to lie in the latent uncanny territory of being human. Fisher introduces his potent experience of coming across a quote from Albert Camus during his research. The dialogue to follow that discover 'shifts'—along lines of a creative improvisation of theorizing, sure to stimulate the brain neurons and imaginaries of the future.

> **BMK:** Uncanny phenomena may be categorised into three types depending upon perception: that is, whether *fear-rooted* or *neutral* or *fearlessness-based*. The first type: is the Freudian account of uncanny sights and insights largely revolves around traumatic childhood and/or a saddened early life. In the second category, where life moves in more 'normal' circumstances, without being perturbed by fearful past events or memories, uncanny experiences may occur in a different way. They are different in the sense that they are not frightening *per se*. Too many fearful memories increase the frequency of painful uncanny occurrences. Too many curiosities in normal situations also increase the frequency of solution-oriented uncanny experience.
>
> As a student, I had personally experienced such uncanny instances, I would like to categorise as the second type. For example, I'd usually come across an academic problem which I was curious to know and understand or resolve but could not get it immediately. Later, when I found the solution without any obvious intended effort, it produced, invariably, a strange feeling. For example, say you are going to have an examination in the university and you want a book. Suppose you don't have the book at the moment. You will naturally go to a book shop because you know that the book stall sells the books and you can get it there. After you have bought the book, the problem of searching for the book is solved.
>
> Now, consider another case. Say, tomorrow you are going to face an examination. But you don't have the

book which enables you to prepare for the examination. There is no book stall in the village where you are residing. There is no other way to get the book. You are in a disappointed mood. Somewhat disturbed, you stroll along the road. But to your great surprise, you find the same book beside the road. You have a vast mixture of feelings—of the uncanny sort.

The former case is different from the latter in the sense that it is about physical search for solution and is within the sphere of your knowledge. You know where you to find the book in all likelihood. It is not a matter of huge surprise. But in the second case, you don't search for it physically as to where the book would be because there is no book stall as such to go for. But your unconscious mind directs you where you will get the book. This is one explanation. Similarly, another reasoning is about the unconscious mental ability that directs the individual from the problem event to the solution event within a span of time. The third interpretation is that the world around us is so small both in terms of physical requirements—here in this example about book but not about intergalactic ship—and thinking of an academic examination but not of alien life, that coincidences are most likely to happen, provided we are ready to take cognisance of them.

Some experts argue that there is no causal connection in the coincidence. But evidence shows that fear-based perception tends to end up in nightmare and a more fearless perception confronts the irrational imaginary for positive perspectives and results. Normal perception entails a normal situation albeit sometimes towards interesting coincidence. But whatever is the type of coincidence, it looks uncanny.

Here are some uncanny situations of the second type that I had experienced myself when I was pursuing my studies in the university during 1980-82. Those days, I coined this kind of phenomenon as Nestorism. I had named it after one of the oldest and wisest warriors in Homer's *The Iliad*, called Nestōr, who was known to be ever ready with advice and solution when solicited.

Cleopatra case: In the first week of January 1982, while I was reading a children's book entitled "The How and Why Wonder Book of Kings and Queens" in the library, I read the sentence, "it has been said that if the nose of Cleopatra had been shorter, the whole face of the earth would have been changed." At first I did not understand the epigrammatic meaning behind the sentence, hence it left a blank space in my mind. In the evening on the same day, when I opened my younger brother's English text book, I spotted the very same quotation in the lesson under the title "The Human Nose." The proverbial explanation was given by Pascal metaphorically with special reference to Cleopatra, and it clarified my pending doubt.

Duke case: In the morning of January 10, 1982, I went to the library and read something about Duke University. Then I actually felt curious to find where the university is situated. But I could not find it in the book. I didn't go for referring to either encyclopaedias or universities' directory. In the afternoon after having had my grub at home, I went to see a matinee at a local theatre. Due to failure of power there was no show and I again turned to the library. When I took the *Indian Express* newspaper, I happen to read that the Duke University is in North Carolina, U.S.A.

Joshua case: In the afternoon of January 15, 1982, I was reading a book under the title *The Wisdom of India*. The book deals with the vedic literature of ancient India. It also mentioned about the *Bhagavadgita* and *Upanishads* apart from the great Indian epics *viz.,* Mahabharata and the Ramayana. In the introductory pages of the *Upanishads*, the author quoted the reference from the Bible, which read as "it is said that Joshua prayed to God to stay the sun in order to allow his time to annihilate the enemies." Here I was anxious to know if it was really Joshua for whose sake God made the sun stand still. I also thought whether I could find it for clarification in the Bible, which is so vast that I could not afford to locate the verse timely in the Old Testament. And hence I gave up the idea of exploration. Later, I approached another shelf for books of general interest. There I found a book called *The Changing Concept of the Universe*, which was of astronomical interest. While I was reading Lucretius' concept and the Ptolemic geocentric model of the universe, to my unforgettable wonder, I caught the very same sentence about Joshua which read as "Sun! thou stand still' -this is what was said about Joshua and the Sun stood still."

Astronomy case: On Saturday the 16th January 1982, I sat in the study room of the library, reading the newspaper *Indian Express*. I read that there would be a configuration of planets on March 10, resulting in the gathering of all planets in a line except the Earth on one side. As usual, I was inquisitive to know how the planets could be grouped. Later, I entered the maintenance section of the library and took casually the book titled *Our Wonderful World*, Vol. 9. While I was turning the last pages in the book, to my utmost surprise, I found a beautiful illustration on the planets' configuration with clear astronomical explanation under the title "Planets and Ratio." I felt it strange to have approached the solution without my intended efforts.

6 x 6 case: As far back as 1980, I had experienced another incident of strange feeling. I was fond of framing magic squares. I developed nine numbered, sixteen numbered and twenty five numbered magic squares in my own method, different from the existing mathematical approach. I also formulated forty nine numbered and eighty one numbered magic squares. But the thirty six numbered, 6 x 6, was still elusive. I didn't consult the teachers. Hence I almost gave up the idea of doing it. Later, I went to library. One of my friends had previously asked me about books on tantra. But to my strange observation, I found the book under the title, *Secret Lore of Magic*, written by Idris Shah. It was written entirely on tantras, necromancy etc. Not only that, when I was browsing through pages in the second half of the book, I found the 6 x 6 magic square which was given with a view to explaining tantras. This magic square enabled me to carry on my research work on magic squares successfully.

Turning now to the third category, which is fearlessness-based, has the ability to turn the painful memories into hopeful moments. I will explain this phenomenon with the help of a movie. Kieslowski's masterpiece, *Three Colours: Red* is a mind-stirring uncanny picturization of a more uncanny theme. One who watches this film for the first time will feel like seeing it again because the weaving of the story is such that there remain some crucial gaps in understanding the underlying philosophical essence.

A young woman named Valentine is a student at the University of Geneva, who works as a model on part time basis. Kern is a retired judge, living alone in an apartment nearby. Valentine has a possessive boyfriend, a sceptical person based in London. Auguste. He lives in Valentine's neighbourhood and is a law student preparing to become a judge. He has a girlfriend who cheats on him and he feels dejected. One day Valentine hits a dog accidentally while driving her car and happens to meet the dog's owner Kern. Their association soon grows familiar to know each other over a couple of occasions. Kern confesses to her that he was betrayed by his girlfriend 37 years ago. Valentine takes a ferry across the English Channel to meet her boyfriend but her ferry sinks due to a sudden storm. But there are seven survivors and among them are Auguste and Valentine. The viewer of the film gets a hint that both Kern and Auguste are one and the same, existing 37 years apart but in the same spatial dimension. The most uncanny part of the movie is that they both are also living in the present and are within the same neighbourhood where Valentine lives.

For Auguste, the future is already rolling in front of him. Past is very much alive in the present as regards to Kern's perception. Valentine exists in the past, present and future simultaneously. Director of the film, Kieslowski handled the uncanny scenes in such a brilliant manner that both the past and the future would merge seamlessly into the present. Particularly, the ferry survivor scene shows how fear gives in to fearlessness. Auguste represents the feared past of Kern. As long as Kern feels alienated from the world and makes himself a recluse in his apartment, he has been in the grip of fear. His first encounter with Valentine sews the seeds of not only love but also fearlessness. He then starts looking at things from the lens of beauty and hope.

Actually, the film's plot has been woven from Kern's perspective. When Valentine invites him for her fashion show, he is there well attired. His face and body movements become more and more lively since the time his friendship with her grows step by step on a positive and optimistic track. We can say that there has been a radical metamorphosis in his psyche from gloomy and fearful state to active and fearless mode. Kern also dreams that Valentine is 50 years old, an age socially suitable to his. Among the survivors of the storm, Auguste and Valentine are seen on a TV news channel, who appear talking to each other. While watching the TV, Kern feels so relieved that he is full of confidence for a new life. He understands that Valentine sees Kern in Auguste. But the viewer of the film knows that Auguste does not exist separately from Kern for they are one. Valentine sees youthful Auguste in Kern and oldish Kern in Auguste. Body and mind are in continuum like space and time or matter and energy.

Questions Seeking: Answers Appearing

If there is any overt teaching fairly easy to grasp from these fascinating experiences and stories told by Kumar, it is that,

Metamorphosis
It's curiosity that leads, and
curiosity that will succeed;
fold not for a moment...
so dare...
to brave and endure
each and every deed.

> It's curiosity we
> plead, to fill holes
> and redeem
> every deadening curriculum
> totally gone beserk.

1. *Where is* Fearism located?
2. *Where is* Fear located?
3. *Where is* Fearlessness located?

RMF: In a paradigm. In a worldview...in consciousness... in D-ness [see Part II].

BMK: Yes Michael! Your A/D-ness survey is a very handy and useful tool to help interpret the world around us and it enables us to formulate views and ideas about how the world has been evolving. You have judged that D-ness is the best, most alive, most creative and most healthy among other quality attributes. Though you have conceived the instrument, some of your friends, colleagues and subjects of the survey would not have agreed with your opinions. But most might have done. That's an uncanny likeness of your viewpoint to that of most of those who coincidentally tick-marked the same choices in the questionnaire [see Part II].

The 'uncanny' is as natural as life is. The more experiences that life collects, the greater is the possibility for the uncanny to happen. If fear, through repression, dominates the process between the past and the present or between the unconscious and the conscious, the uncanny feelings will likely be dreadful. If fearlessness excels, the uncanny will be promising.

RMF: Promising and made good use of by the experiencer because the repression barrier against the unconscious processes and D-ness are not so on-guard and not so resistant to the unknown, weird, and strange. Rather, such experiences are embraced in/with creativity *via* fearlessness. Thus, the uncanny will be expected, even though such experiences can't be willed or predicted. Indeed, that makes a big difference, because we all are susceptible to fearing and avoiding 'the unknown' as a major component of the *aka* the uncanny. There's a lot of controlaholism going on....

BMK: Besides the everyday implications, with rigid defences against the uncanny, it has significant importance in philosophical terms as well. Fear does not let the individual live freely. The frightening experiences of fearful nature will impact life unfavourably, to the point where critical and open-minded thinking is developmentally delayed, if not 'frozen' in time. People don't easily mature as thinkers. It restricts the cognitive abilities to think curiously in the liminal in between and negative spaces, and even within pessimistic modes and the 'dark.' Unless there is cognitive modification as interventions, frightening uncanny experiences will continue to recur like dejections or bad dreams. The more they are repressed, as Nietzsche philosophized long ago *via* "eternal recurrence," the more passionately they return—with a vengeance, carrying more fear-loading behind them. Paranoia results[448] as part of this syndrome.

Coincidence of similar or parallel event-encounters occurs depending upon the frequency of the same type of thoughts and actions. If an individual suffered trauma due to a swimming accident, the coincidence depends upon the frequency of his or her approach to movements around water bodies. If fear controls the nostalgia every time, the uncanny coincidence will continue to reprise more painfully. It also depends upon the individual's attention and perception when he or she is moving around water bodies. Despite passing by the side of a lake in a car, if they are distracted by talking to a friend on mobile phone and unaware of the presence of a lake near by their side, they are unlikely to experience anxiety, restlessness, and more direct painful uncanny feelings.

Since fear tends to restrict thoughts and imaginations within certain limits, the possible uncanny experience will not be able to showcase the alternative and even better picture of life. Jose Saramago said that, "chaos is order yet undeciphered"; thus, we can also infer that 'fear is merely fearlessness waiting to be deciphered.' Because chaos is disorder, more or less, ridden with fear *via* randomness. Fearlessness or order is its opposite facet. Fear has a limited human perspective. It exists in encrypted mysterious form which needs to be deciphered and unravelled.

RMF: Nice. Encrypted, needing deciphering and unravelling...sounds like forensic work. Welcome to fearwork, fearanalysis and, to any good critical fearism work also.

BMK: That's what Freud's investigative brilliance shines forth upon, and is famous for.

RMF: It's easy to critique Freud, in many ways like personality and cultural role, he's a 19th century European white man. Rebellious as he was, he's largely caught deeply in the unconscious dynamics and commitments of Cartesian anxiety and the denial that such anxiety is there in methodologies and thinking of the "Sciences." These are the 21 cognitive pathologies as Maslow has argued.[449] But I think you and I are aware that the best of Freudian investigative strategies unveiling the nature and role of fear, the Id, Ego, Super Ego motivational investments, etc. will only be truly recognized when people can get beyond their Freudophobia. Which is not to say we ought not be critical of Freud and his work as well.

BMK: Right. At the practical side of things. Sometimes, we feel agitated out of severe anxiety. Yet, if when we sit calmly without concentrating on painful thoughts, we may feel a 'shift' and that our mind is clear and able to decide things peacefully and even cheerfully. It means that pessimism and optimism, the opposites of the same coin, can flip so fast that bad mood turns good in no time. Same is the case with uncanny feelings which, depending upon the time taken for cognitive modification, may become either pleasant or unpleasant.

RMF: Fine. Let me turn to our beginning questions. *Where?* Not *what is?* Notice that opening confrontation in thinking about these topics fearism, fear, fearlessness. Location is emphasized first. You know it is near impossible to get people to think outside of their hegemonic imaginaries and compulsion for definitions and the concomitant form of verbalizing that preference manifests. The hidden paradigm formation and regime of the 'best' way to think seems, amongst modern people at least, to privilege: "What is fear?" or "What is fearism?" or "What is fearlessness?" In many interviews that Desh Subba and I have had independently, the interviewer/host typically starts with that question. It controls the discourse and thinking. I do not like it. In an alternative critical paradigm, which we've spoken of in this book repeatedly, the orientation basically comes down to what investigative questioning is going to dominate the discussion. I no longer care much about "what is fear" but I really care about "How do we think about fear(lessness)?" Okay, enough.

The three questions above are framed for philosophical analysis and understanding. It is interesting and problematic that the general tendency of the modern mind, at least, in its quest for knowledge will invariably run its programmed 'Search' for understanding by going for the order of *positive description*.[450] By positive description, in contrast to *negative description*, the positive way searches immediately for a definition under the aegis of the flag of truth and reality that assumes there is a definition—or, there should be.

So, in a search for the definition, the positive philosophical orientation asks particular kinds of positive questions: most frequently, (a) *What is...* (?). Therefore, for the vast majority, when they hear the term *fearism*, as Desh Subba has introduced it in his classic text *Philosophy of Fearism*, the learner will ask quite predictably a set of self-reinforcing positive questions of matter and form, in the classic Aristotelean[451] way of pursuit of understanding: (i) What is fearism? How do you define it?

I'm sure Subba has been asked this a thousand times in his many interviews, conference presentations and discussions with people he encounters and shares his vision for this new philosophy for the 21st century. I can almost guarantee that no one, of those thousands, has asked Subba, "*Where is* fearism?"

BMK: I don't want to interrupt the flow...but it strikes me that getting a definition in this positivist tradition you speak of is a way to contain it—Fear—and, the experience of fear of fear. The anxiety is immediately quelled. But is that fully what we ought to be doing?

RMF: Good point. It's a concern. *What is fearism, what is fear, what is* fearlessness—it doesn't matter which, clearly the god of DEFINITION has trumped so much of modern thinking; whereas if one was to approach a magical and mythic-based pre-industrialized tribal peoples or an individual pre-modern nomadic sheep herder far from modern urban city life, in all likelihood they would encounter Subba very differently. Subba would perhaps say, "I bring fearism to you...", as he is attempting to bring the 'gift' of this teaching of his new philosophy. The tribal person would likely look puzzled and say, "*Where is* this fearism?"

They would gesture with their hands pointing, eyes gazing all over in many directions, and whole body moving, indicating they are verbally and somatically asking for an embodied answer, and they are expecting the answer to fit into their landscape of places, things, and actions that make a significant difference to their lives. The places could be visible or invisible it matters not, but the answer Subba gives will have to be coordinate with the significant places they live—because for basic primal peoples their quality of life and survival is dependent not on definitions for understanding but *locations* for understanding. Everything is located spatially and dimensionally, even if in the invisible world which they also cherish. In other words, Subba's answer just won't be real if this location is not immediately revealed in Subba's reply. Now we can ponder: So, under this condition of their particular naturalistic-magical worldview operating in the exchange, what would Subba reply to such peoples?

"Fear is a universe," "Fear is a black hole of space." These are two out of 21 definitions which Subba offers that form the basis of his philosophy of fearism. To the premodern Greek mind, and the modern, scientific, and postmodern mind, such definitions are absurd. Perhaps they are literary. If you read Subba's text you see that he is dead serious with these fantastic definitions. Of them all, the two above use the "Fear is..." definitional form of Aristotelian semantic structuration and not the way the primal peoples would be able to find interesting or significant to their life and thus their way of thinking practically and embodied. Now, if Subba was innovative in the moment, standing in front of these primal peoples waiting for an answer to their question to him, "*Where is* this fearism?," his re-phrasing of the two spatial definitions above could easily be converted to fit his audience. He might answer simply, "Fearism makes fear go everywhere." While saying this, through the translator, Subba would likely do best in his communication and to do justice to his concept, to make a full-bodied gesture with a big smile on his face, eyes wide open, then eyes shut, while he is slowly spinning 360 degrees and holding his arms outstretched—more looking like a dance of connection with all things, places, events—at the same time.

He could elaborate this expression, and then sing the word *fearism, fearism, fearism* in soft, medium and loud voice, low notes, medium and then high notes and back—creating a scale of sounds, rhythms, movements. He could then gesture and nod to the listeners to dance and sound with him as they mimic at first Subba's perform-ance. If all goes well and is convincing of the audience to do so, the various co-participants would turn this into a ritual ecstatic event of "Fearism." They would improvise in the singing, harmonizing, dancing their own variations. All brought as 'gift' from Subba to them, and they in turn could give this 'gift' back to Subba by their understanding his fearism—*via* their way.

In such a speculative description it is clear that the god of DEFINITION is not what is important or that brings about the understanding of one-person-to-another, as collective understanding and meaning. The fictional scene is meant to show a performance of fearism, could be fear, could be fearlessness. It is not too weird perhaps to think today in our Chapter Nine about this meaning-making coherence of word to lived experience, of concept to theory and to cosmology.

Surely, not Subba nor I have pursued the study of fear(ism) or fearlessness because we wanted to define fear(ism) or fearlessness. No, that god of positive description from the Aristotelian legacy would become only flattened and hard like steel. It would lay on the table of knowledge of the modern world, and it would be ugly, if not dead, if not a sign of the end of the pursuit of fearology—and, end of the fearologist.[452] Perhaps, at that point, if we had let it go that way, our pursuit re: a philosophy of fearism would end up in some arbitrary AI machine-computing performance done for the purpose of cranking out new definitions of fear and fearlessness in endless reams for eternity—without a soul—without a human presence—without an existential importance.

Maria, you and I, also have avoided the Aristotelian definitional entrapment in this book on fearlessness. We have not asked anywhere in the text, nor asked our readers, to pursue defining *fearlessness* as positive description. There is no point where we promote or care to declare absolutely: *Fearlessness is....*

BMK: True. We attempted from the start to co-inquire with child-like, beginner's mind, even primal sacred mind, taking into account the peripheries, the blurred and the outskirts of understanding that surround and flow in and through Fearlessness. We embrace the uncanny and unknown of our engagement with fearlessness. At most, we did attempt to define a Fearlessness Paradigm. Michael, you've well delineated the outline, albeit in a fictional narrative on one of your videos, of how this paradigm would work to solve real wicked problems.[453] And, I suppose that does point out that we located Fearlessness, as you say, in a paradigm, worldview, a cosmology itself. Rather than focus on just the word and concept AS IF it should have only one clear definition so everyone knows what we are talking about when we use that word.

Such, is the kind of pragmatic approach many would desire. We want to concretize fearlessness in behaviors, for example, as if it means brave or fearless—without fear. Yet, I am learning from working with you in this book that there are other conceptual alternatives to that harsh modernist approach. Maybe, you want us all to 'dance' without you Michael as you explain *this is where fearlessness exists*. And, maybe you are deciphering codes that we get hung up on—and, maybe you are asking us to think about how we think about fearlessness, as more important than anything else. For you, it's ethical. But fearlessness was also that for the Eastern traditions, and Gandhi's political and cultural revolution to free itself from Britain's empire—an, Empire of Fear....

RMF: Yeah, dancing, singing, all of that too. And, yet you can see I am also a very systematic thinker about definitions, meanings, classifications, taxonomies, etc. So is Subba. Him and I began a formal Glossary of defined terms in our East-West dialogue book which sound an awe full lot like Aristotle's way of thinking, or any social scientist would prefer. But the question is, what do you prefer, Maria. What does Subba prefer? What do the fearism philosophers prefer in how they all like their "fearism" and "fearlessness" laid out and bare? Graspable. Contained? My point is, I do think it is a conceptual revolution at stake here in the way we come to the study of fear(ism) and fear(lessness)? In our book here we chose to name the Parts of the book with the form "Fearlessness as/is..." do you recall?

BMK: Right. The as/is form is important. It signifies no one definition is presented or expected, neither expected of ourselves as authors nor from the readership.

RMF: It strikes me now as "uncanny," to use Sigmund Freud's term, to describe the sense going on inside me and between us in the liminal of our communication and between the words flying across the page here. All so clear, this text as print but also so unclear at the same time. It's weird to me that when I named those Parts with "as/is" and then they shifted to "is/as"—that meant something. Oh, I just was typing and actually typed "as/if" but deleted and corrected it right away. That's a Freudian slip, perhaps(?). "As/if" makes for an even more interesting disruption of the god of DEFINITION. It turns everything into a story-like fictional, performative, literary, metaphorical modality. And, with that a lot more affect, feelings, emotions. Hey, isn't that what the topic Fear is all about?

Not that I have said we should have one and only one definition of fear either. I'm a big critic of "fear is an emotion" type definitions. But we have to use words, and we have to define them generally because of the demands of this so-called rationalist and scientific world. We cannot easily show *dancing* with fear(ism) on the page, nor with fear(lessness). Subba and I have a preference for open-ended thinking. This can be all quite worrisome I would imagine for readers of our work, trained in analytical thinking, who might suggest that we are a bunch of 'air head' philosophers. Fearism is too 'fluffy' to be taken seriously. No academy anywhere in the world would put up with a "fearism" philosopher on faculty. Hey, I have heard these things from people who encounter this work overall and/or encounter Subba's work; but typically, they don't criticize outright. They just don't invite Subba or myself back for another 'lecture,' interview, etc. They get their single taste, and that's about all they want.

And, then, in a moment, there are other uncanny experiences happening at the edges of our discourse here. For example, I open Subba's classic text and read the first "Review" endorsement by a professor from Nehru University in the *Khashi* Language Department, who read Subba's philosophy of fearism book and wrote,

> *'Fearism is a new concept; it is utilized to keep the cultural dominance and the matrix of superiority intact...for the purpose of wielding abusive power and justifying such acts using other's fear. Identification of the practice of fearism would take us to deeper layers of psychological impact that the victims suffer from....'*[454]

Because we (Fisher & Kumar) have dedicated the subtitle of our new book to the philosophy of fearism perspective, it is uncanny somewhat to have to defend it—and ourselves—and, to feel that we are being undermined in our defense because it's so unclear, and problematic, re: what "fearism" means. Why would the first Reviewer (an endorsement) of Subba's book be offering a definition of *fearism* ("a new concept"), in their own words, and giving one that is quite contrary to Subba's own definitions/meanings?

The reviewer above is giving more a definition that fits the phenomenon of fearmongering typically used by many authors and disciplines. They are also using the definition originally coined by Fisher in 1990,[455] nearly a decade before Subba's inventing the term with a very different definition than Fisher's. What is going on? It's uncanny. Why would Subba include this first reviewer in his new book which tries to articulate his new meaning of this new term? It is disruptive, at least for me. It's uncanny, because it is so easy to read through reviews as endorsements and think that they are all in agreement with the finding of Subba, when they all are except the first one that is a re-defining of Subba's own definition. This is problematic in that it then comes down to us as co-authors in our new book having to decide what it is that we are referring to as "philosophy of fearism perspective"(?).

Of course, most readers would completely miss this anomaly we are pointing out in Subba's text. Maybe it does not matter. But that's the very kind of rationalizing that comes about when one encounters the uncanny. It's easy to miss, ignore, and move on from. We are now in the territory of psychoanalysis in the Freudian tradition. We are now entering a 'shift' in the zone from positive description to negative description. The latter, is what we give attention to in terms of a means of description/methodology/understanding. Knowledge itself 'shifts' when one leaves the near addiction to positive description (and positivism) to negativist explanation. *Fearlessness is/as Negative.*

> **BMK:** I looked up "Freud" in Subba's classic text and see "Fear in Error Theory of Freud," as one amongst several E. and W. theorist-philosopher types that have written about fear; Subba then *locates* "fear" "in error theory" (*a la* Freud), "in false concept" (*a la* Francis Bacon), "in illusion" (*a la* Shankaracharya) etc.[456] He's not seeking a typical definitional positive description here *per se*. He's playing with correspondences between the thinker's views, metaphors, stories and conceptualizations. Yet, with Freud, poignantly, we are drawn to what Subba is asking us to consider re: the location of fear-in-action phenomenologically *via* the unconscious-conscious juxtapositioning. Subba wants us to see "small errors," as Freud noticed and theorized, and that they occur many times in daily life: "Mistake in recognition," "Forgetting names," "slip of pen," "slip of tongue,"... "mislaying of objects" etc.
>
> If fear is *in* the error(s) of judgements and actions, as Freud suggested, it is still impossible to recognize that fear, because it is encrypted so to speak in the error(s) which get the overt attention. They get social attention too. That's what errors do. We typically notice them, albeit, we may quickly try to pretend we didn't make them and/or we just correct them immediately and carry on as if it is not meaningful. Yet, to notice the errors is to communicate with the errors, especially in the psychoanalytic techniques of free association and elaboration, etc. Having the errors witnessed unconditionally as well is fruitful to self-revelation. Without going into detailed psychoanalysis reading of

this all we can switch to fearanalysis, and re-member what Subba is asking us to investigate. He points us to see fear in the positive behavioral concrete act going on but *fear is absent* in the overt act going on—these error(s) so-called, which tend to hide their own source of motivation.

With that, if we move from Subba's actual positive description approach here with his lists of positive recorded phenomenon, in contradistinction negative description is where deeper things may be illuminated in terms of motivation based on Id and/or fear and need-based latencies. "Fear occurs when man knows that he has made an error....fear is the final point for all of them [the 8 listed errors]...,"[457] writes Subba.

RMF: That is a by-pass by Subba, I think. He is focusing now in that claim that fear is arising from the inappropriate behavior, as error, in the social sphere. Perhaps, the individual can be alone and still feel loss of self-esteem with making an error, but usually the worst affective potency is experienced with an error in public, even if people around don't seem to point it out. The by-pass is in categorical philosophizing. Subba skirts around the deeper fear-based manifestation of the symptom 'error' and only remarks on the "fear" as felt by the person making it. I see that as the surface of the fear phenomenon and is incomplete description. The way to a more determinate, even if speculative, negative description of say any Freudian error like those mentioned above, is to avoid the by-passing and rather probe into what is in "omission" or "absence" in the entire event of an error manifesting?

For example, I would negatively describe a 'slip of the tongue' as an uncanny arising not yet deciphered, something Kumar has pointed to earlier. Perhaps, fearlessness is the abject and omitted in all the describing by Freud and Subba. Perhaps, fearlessness is denied access by the very person making the 'error.' And, maybe the error is made because fearlessness was already there and arising at the site of fear, but the person wasn't registering a need for fearlessness—because, they weren't acknowledging they were in fear in that moment. The error looks like an accident. But that is a foil. What if these errors are fearlessness being deciphered—albeit, inadequately, because? Because the person hasn't the critical nuanced awareness and/or the theory of Fearlessness in place and useable for them to recognize and interpret their experience. So, in other words, without the Fearlessness Paradigm and practices developed, they can only 'miss' fearlessness and turn it into something it isn't. The easy ways is to call it an error. That double-duty of misplaced categorization is avoiding (a) fear and, (b) fearlessness arising when fear is present. Recall my dictum.

No wonder, we get so confused when an error arises. We may not feel that confusion *per se*. We do try to just ignore it though. We quickly correct it—but not with fearlessness. We correct, as Subba is right to say, *with fear* –as fear is the beginning and "final point," says Subba. In this scenario there is really a massive patterning of repetition to create more errors, and more fear of making errors, but also to not even feel the feeling of fear anymore that is there causing the errors and impacting our affective and cognitive processes. Yet, as I am suggesting, hypothetically, what may actually be manifesting in/as the 'error' is fearlessness undeciphered. Such a finding, if true, would lead to a conceptual revolution overall in our understanding of human behavior/thinking but it would revolutionize Freudian thought. It may very well also revolutionize our understanding of the Freudian uncanny itself. That would be really uncanny, wouldn't it?

We pause...to let the reader absorb, and digest somewhat that last claim....

Fourth Conceptual Revolution: Fearlessness

All along from the start of writing Chapter Nine, in the back of our minds was the thought *'that, really, there's no point in articulating the Fearlessness Paradigm, unless the reader is aware of being aware that this book is all about a conceptual (r)evolution.'* Despite that being in the back of our minds, it wasn't there as a formal thought to put on paper *per se*. That's why it is not written down in the Introduction 1 of this book. It was 'floating,' you could say, in the in between spaces of our dialogues—of our consciousness—and co-consciousness infused and not always communicated overtly, ideas for this book. Fearlessness located itself from the start of this book in an idea—and/or ideas flowed from us and were continually locating themselves in Fearlessness—or what we imagined as a Fearlessness Paradigm—Fearlessness Philosophy—Fearlessness Psychology and, yes, Fearlessness Movement/Tradition in-action to become a Fearlessness (R)Evolution for our times. Why? Because the latter is so needed today. King Fear is near completely ruling everything and everyone. An alternative comes in like a law of Nature abhorring a vacuum—and, the vacuum is Fear ('Fear') (?). Fearlessness—> blows as/is wind.

In Bois's summary of Alfred Korzybski's[458] general semantics philosophizing, we are told that there have been four major historical "conceptual revolutions" since the beginning of our species. They are: (1) Greek Conceptual Revolution –parted from magical-mythic consciousness of "primitive man"; (2) Classical Science Conceptual Revolution –when systematic doubt and questioning challenged "maxims of common sense" and put forward "induction" as "lead over deduction"—leading to the "scientific method"; (3) Relativity Conceptual Revolution- the new physics exploded ideas about reality and ways of thinking about reality at the same time—a huge 'shift' of systems in dynamic flows and how our very identity as an 'observer' is implicated in that which we 'observe.' This revolution brought the "subjective" element directly into the "objective" and science(s) would never be the same.

Although Albert Einstein is a major part of this third revolution it ought not to be forgotten that "Freud was upsetting the young sciences of psychiatry and psychology"[459]—bringing forth his new 'science' (some call more an art) of *psychoanalysis*—and his methodology of communicating with and interpreting the unconscious mind. Freud's psychoanalysis has a good deal of room for and patience with, anything we might call "double talk" (see Chapter Eight), whereas in all the other conceptual revolutions there would be no interest and/or likely awareness of double talk and 'slips of the tongue' or the uncanny. This is a vast generalization, but it is an arguable case, beyond the scope of this chapter. Yet, what is poignant in raising this distinction is that by the third conceptual revolution the modern mind is being forced into a new way of perceiving and thinking of the self/system/world.

And, that's exciting for us as co-authors, because we are situating the very dialectical study of fear/fearlessness in the last blurred edges of the third conceptual revolution and into the fourth conceptual revolution— which Bois never labeled in the mid-1960s understandably, but which we can now label *"Fearism Conceptual Revolution."*

Surely, that may sound preposterous at first. It is absurd. It seems irrational even, to place and locate an entire global conceptual revolution to be laid in the arms of one emotion—fear? That's what it looks and sounds like, in the concrete and practical interpretation of what we are writing here. But remember, we are writing this from two lenses: (a) perspective of the philosophy of fearism, and (b) from a Fearlessness Paradigm. While doing that, we realize such lenses/ perspectives are still in the process of being formed, recognized, and located in themselves. Their worthiness is not even fully tested. YET, we are at a moment of uncanny recognition being perhaps in a 'tsunami' MAJOR wave hitting a 'Crystal Castle' built on sand.

Everything is quite unstable. True enough. The fourth conceptual revolution is of this nature. At least, that's our take on it. It is nascent. It is postmodern and post-postmodern in the quick slide of changing paradigms, worldviews, and post-truth—with all that, and rapid change everywhere—collapsing systems—and existential terror and dread. Welcome to the fourth conceptual revolution—welcome to Fearism is/as Conceptual Revolution. Fearlessness lives there—lives here.

Deciphering History, Deciphering 'The Crime'

Is there a sign-post when you arrive at the Fearlessness 'edge' of one universe of conceptual thought and enter another? Can one make such a reference point? We are not sure, but we do have a rather uncanny discovery that came to mean something important to us while in the investigation of the 'crime' that is not easily seen to be a crime because there is not yet the awareness of the awareness that such would even be a crime. Would it be a crime...(?) we ask Albert Camus, the great 20th century existential philosopher-poet-fiction writer, AS IF he is alive and communicating with us in the pages of this book unfolding:

Dear Albert Camus,

> Something shifted on this planet. Turn to S. America in the mid-1980s with the new controversial interdisciplinary studies of dictatorships in the Southern Cone, so-called of Latin America—and, then in the early '90s, when Fisher was researching on the subject/object of *fear* and *fearlessness*, and found your 1992 edited book *Fear At The Edge*. It intrigued him from the title because of the location of which "fear" was placed,

rather than defined, the latter, as would be typical in a psychology of fear discourse or a social science regime of categorization of emotions. What could it mean? Why, fear-at-the-edge—what is this? An abyss?

So, Mr. Camus, even after you had long-departed from this earthly plane in 1960, you may not have realize yet that your words as poetic indictment of W. modern civilization, was positively invoked at one point in this book *via* an epigram to chapter fourteen by the political/cultural critic and research Juan E. Corradi.[460] In your original French, *Le XVIIe siécle a été le siécle des mathématiques, le XIIIe*....Fisher felt this uncanny reconnection to this text of yours even though he did not speak much French nor read it but he did know from his research on fear since 1989 that *la peur* meant "fear." Weeks later, this quote from you kept coming back and back at him through his moments of reverie and journaling, and he got up the nerve to do something he had never done before as a first speaker in English—he asked a graduate student colleague he knew who was bi-lingual to translate the epigram. He photocopied it and sent it in a letter request. In less than 24 hrs, his colleague wrote back, Camus was writing: "The 17th century was the century of mathematics, the 18th century was of physical sciences, and the 19th century biology. Our 20th century is the century of fear."[461] [the letter to be continued...]

"Our 20th Century is the Century of Fear"

RMF: Oh, Camus! "Century of fear" double-tasks here as a longitude of 'progress of fear'—over, an equal-long 'progress of knowledge'; but even more chilling—it imputes a thick emotional and ethical layer of indictment. Camus names the name of which I was conceived to know. Fear. He named the human condition as (arguably) the cause-and-effect of 'the failure of love' through developmental, intellectual and moral history—and, perhaps of evolution and consciousness itself, the address of which Camus would some six years later, in 1952, the year of my birth on this planet, in the brief years after the collective world trauma of Nazism in Germany, declare: "In the clamour in which we live, love is impossible and justice does not suffice." It's a courageous, if not fearless, voicing of 'my blood' soul and lament—emanating on my mother's side from her coursing veins wrought with the terror she lived on the streets in Belgium for some three years under the occupation of the Third Reich. In the womb... my mother...in the after-womb my nemesis, we meet, I can't scream. "Let me out of your fear, mother."[462] Those are the words from the opening epigram quote that began my doctoral dissertation on "Fearless Leadership In and Out of the 'Fear' Matrix."

I still get hair stand-up on the back of my neck now, even after 29 years from when discovering that quote by Camus. Well, if I don't actually have that physical reaction in the moment, I have this internal subtle *memory-glow*[463] of it happening just like it originally did when I received the English translation. Kind of like finding my first love and touching....It's uncanny that I remember now to remember to cite Camus's indictment, and that's exactly what it is/was. It's astounding poetry to my ears and Camus wrote it that way in c.1946; I am sure—even though it was originally penned as a section of a larger political text in his own underground war magazine in France called *Combat*. I get 'zinged' sometimes when I connect with certain historical ideas, consciousness and imagination—still alive and flowing through words and imagery just like in this epigram as I go back to it for our book. I cannot think of a more powerful quote involving fear. It has to be here, Maria. Have you seen this before, from Camus? Have you read any Camus? How has it influenced you—in the past—and/or now?

BMK: Yes Michael! As I was a fan of Greek mythology since my school days, Camusian Sisyphus always interested me, since I first came across his book, 'Myth of Sisyphus' during the early 1980's. How Camus interpreted the fate of Sisyphus in modern human context was something that all of us could compare and identify with in our respective lives.

People in general are ambitious to achieve what they desire for but only a few would succeed. But most of the people however don't quit despite their repeated failures in life. They are like Sisyphus. They might lose in elections but wouldn't leave the political arena. *Enjoying the struggle* is what gives happiness according to Camus. Apart from Sisyphus, there are other characters in Greek mythology like Prometheus, Tantalus, Arachne and Atlas, all who also suffered eternal punishments for offending the gods. We can imply that the gods denote unavoidable situations created for the humans by the absurd world.

Some of the 'offences' perpetrated by Prometheus and others were actually benevolent in nature. Prometheus stole fire from the heavens and brought it to humans who were living in a lightless world. Tantalus pilfered the divine ambrosia from gods in order to keep his friends happy. Arachne excelled in weaving and took pride in her talent. Atlas had to carry the load of heavens on his shoulders eternally because he fought against the gods to help his brother and co-titans. Despite their unending suffering, they never thought of committing suicide. Like Sisyphus, they seemed to enjoy life in the way they were able to carry on in spite of the pain, fear, and limitations.

All these five characters, Sisyphus, Prometheus, Tantalus, Arachne and Atlas, had an uncanny bravado in the commonality of not only facing the endless penalty but also living through the same with optimism. Similar uncanny resemblance to the Greek quintet is seen in the great Indian epic, 'Mahabharata' in which five warriors namely Bheema, Duryodhana, Keechaka, Jarasandha and Bakasura are known as 'Panchakam—a quintet. Four of them are destined to die in the hands of the fifth warrior. As the oracle said, Bheema would be the eventual survivor. Bheema was an uncanny hero.

Such strange instances might look fictitious when we read about them in literature but Freud would say that myths and legends actually mirror the real life of human motivational and behavioural tendencies and hence they were documented by the authors in the form of stories.

The postmodern existential Camusian interpretation of Sisyphus myth appears stranger not because it is fiction but because it is truth. A note on Kafka's character 'Josef K.' was appended to the essay of Sisyphus by Camus. Why he did it that way is easily understandable from the fact that the fictional Josef K. has got an uncanny resemblance to the mythical Sisyphus. Josef K. like Sisyphus lives through struggling events forced upon him by the weird society without any sane reason or sensible logic but at the same time he would not avoid eating nicely, enjoying female companionship or pursuing the hobby of newspaper reading.

The Camusian absurd world is full of uncanny events, which emerge in the same way as the orderly things look conspicuously separate in the background of disorderly chaos. Being free of distractions, maintaining acute attentiveness and most importantly fearlessness, and compassion, all facilitate the actor/observer to witness uncanny phenomena in favourable settings.

RMF: True. The post-Lacanian, Ettingerian view, is that there is inherently a psychodynamic balance of "uncanny awe" on the way to compassion as much as there is the Freudian "uncanny anxiety."[464] We can think of this as the Life-drive and Death-drive complexes, respectively. It is just that our phallocentric world driven by *Thanatos*[465], especially in the West, has so extracted itself from uncanny awe and fearlessness as the foundation of restorative practices and ethics, that the latter uncanny anxiety—that is, a fear-based paranoid orientation of mistrust has led away from the former. Ettinger argues the latter is the result of repressing desire and the M/Other overall and taking the civilizational trajectory of the Father archetype and Oedipal complex—even though, that is *not* the only way to go. This latter path ends up with the dominating "*fear of other*" patterning everywhere—as cultural critics today call *Othering*. The trust and cooperation dives low and sociality is fragmented into constant divisiveness and toxic conflict. And from thereon in, violence of some form is the result of this basic pathological *xenophobia* embedded in our relationality to the strange and stranger. The "culture of fear" is another way to explain this. We see this crisis really exacerbated today in the whole nightmare of global migration problems, refugees etc. "Fearism" is being used as a concept in a lot of research to explain this phenomenon of rejecting the stranger, aliens, migrants, asylum seekers, whatever we call them.[466] Fear and its role in all this is surely being magnified as the world goes deeper into this crisis of migrants 'trying to find home' and basic care, hospitality and ultimately compassion.

And then there's Camus' *The Plague*, so ripe for our critical self-reflection today, starting in 2020 with COVID-19. There's Camus' "absurd lifestyle" in his philosophical work *The Myth of Sisyphus*, as you've mentioned was important in your early philosophical studies and development. One interpreter noted that one chief characteristic of the Camusian absurd lifestyle (*a la* Sisyphus book) is "simultaneously awareness and rejection of death"[467]—meaning, in terror management theory (TMT) terms, that any awareness gain is a gain in awareness that life is folded into the larger reality of inevitability that is death. This is hard on the psyche, said Freud and Camus and many others. But more interesting to me is that it is profound in its social implications re: social philosophy. Fearism is a social philosophy and that's important. TMT is a social psychology theory with key lessons for all of humanity.[468] The absurd in the sense above for Camus, as well as his historical indictment of knowledge itself—both, are realizations of 'waking up' to a point where one reflects on the past, on life, and assesses it clearly without much fear—and, then simultaneously realizes that fear is the major driver and outcome of the whole 'game' of this absurd life. And for the 20th century, fear has grown and located itself at the heart of the outcome of history, progress, the Enlightenment, ending up as the signified form of "century of fear" for Camus. That means *aka* 'century of death'—and, as I have written elsewhere, the 21st century is then, following this trajectory, logically and experientially—via post-9/11 era, nothing other than what can accurately be called the "century of terror."[469] COVID-19 plague has validated this indictment—and its uncanny problematic.[470]

The latest TMT book has the subtitle "On the Role of Death in Life." It seems to me uncanny in its connection with Desh Subba's *Fearism* subtitle "Life is Conducted, Directed and Controlled by the Fear." TMT is all about *fear* but they just chose to call it *terror*. Subba's subtitle could be read the same except to Fear one could add /Death. Death prompts and Fear prompts—as various forms and means of reminding one of Death and/or Fear—are arguably, in negative description, *the most powerful* forces shaping human personality and sociality—that is, history itself. And, are the vectors shaping the "absurd lifestyle" we live. The above mentioned cultural and conceptual revolutions, in other words, like the knowledge and disciplinary pursuits of the centuries, *a la* Camus' indictment 'poem,' and 'civilization process' overall, are displacements and sublimation *a la* Freud.[471] They are cultural/conceptual defenses *via* "towards abstractions [opposed and counter] than feelings"—thus, a general move away from uncanny feelings, a point we see dramatized in Camus' novel and philosophical works above, according to Bisht.[472]

I feel out of my league discussing all this but it is a growing fascinating awareness I have of late for the psychoanalytical and fearanalytical perspective on making sense of the *resistances* to Fearlessness *via* a circulating pattern of paranoid reactivity, abjection and other defenses, including sublimation. Maybe humans are just so habitually used to the sublimated 'second choice'[473] or what Hall calls "second best"[474] means of sublimation of psychic energy. I have called this the "coping paradigm" earlier in this book—that is, Fear-like is then the more Human-like outcome of this compensation and accommodation. Fearlessness is the foreign, uncanny itself, by the predisposed inevitability that it is, supposedly, 'opposite' to Fear— or so this appears the case within the coded familiarity of the hegemonic Fear Paradigm. But this is certainly not the case within the marginalized and discredited Fearlessness Paradigm, the far lesser known. So, at the same time, with the two Paradigms in juxtaposition all the time, the double lens upon which I look at the world, there is the familiar/ unfamiliar anxiety played out all the time, even below the level of conscious awareness. I'm aware of what happens when people in the Fear Paradigm encounter something outside their paradigmatic comfort zone—that is, their familiarity of what appears as 'human' and what is a facsimile of 'human.'

I submit that an "Uncanny Valley" phenomenon, and potential explanation, is at play here. Let me explain a fascinating empirical research study, by MacDorman, connecting android objects with human responses to the objects—and the emergence at times of the uncanny, as well as TMT, and nearly 500 test subjects. Research and theorizing on androids as human-like machines has shown that when humans view a typical industrial android that works in a factory to build something, like say automobiles, the recordings of the observer's stress and anxiety levels is very low and in fact it registers as a 'positive' evaluation and affinity to be around such devices. As the same observers are then given images of more humanoid looking androids there is still a good deal of fascination, if not awe, and relatively little amount of uncanny feelings hardly registering *via* measured stress and anxiety levels. The 'positive' evaluation still remains but only up to a threshold point. That's when a very sudden and unexpected 'valley' drop in the data began showing up because the observers were shown more and more androids that looked real, very human, and even parts thereof like prostheses made to mimic the real hand, say of a human.

People generally all showed they were physiologically feeling anxiety and were frightened. This was labeled uncanny responses by the researchers. Often the android experimental observers were not aware of this internal state that was measured by physiological parameters and later made evident in self-reports and/or interviews. The participants may have talked about the androids in these latter facsimile forms as interesting and awesome etc., but the actual internal 'shift' had already occurred onto the 'negative' scale of affinity. It was statistically significant. One would not predict this outcome necessarily, because of an assumption that humans are comfortable with their own species and human shape, they are narcissistic, etc. But of course, even the most real human-looking androids are 'unreal.' They are machines, they are dead. Researchers have theorized that living-dead hybrids, like for example, zombies from movies or ghosts have long been greatly feared. They've been linked to traumatic experiences of all kinds. The great terror of burying humans alive, when they merely looked dead is well known in anthropology as well. Yet, there are still likely other reasons for the 'uncanny valley' phenomenon. The original hypothesis of Masahiro Mori on this problem of the uncanny valley re: robots/humans came to the probable conclusion that "robot designers [ought] not to make...total human likeness" in their machines because it would turn-off the affinity and empathy reflexes; and people wouldn't want to have such humanoids around them or work with them in cooperative ventures. Bottomline, they wouldn't sell well as a product on the market.

Several research studies have confirmed empirically that Mori's hypothesis was accurate. It was simply first called the "unnerving effect" of being in the presence of something so humanly real but unreal at the same time. It generally freaks people out—even if they are unaware of being freaked out. It is this unawareness of such, that intrigues me to continue to tell this story of the uncanny valley and its implications for uncovering resistances to Fearlessness. Let me continue.

The paradoxical 'double affective' of real *and* unreal, living *and* dead, is challenging to human perception and psychology overall. I wish to pull this out further because of our interest in Part V especially re: "double talking" and Fearlessness. We argued that Fear and Fearlessness are in a historical, philosophical, psychological, and sociological competing set of discourse patterns. Philosophically, and dialectically, we argued that one ought not try to talk about or understand one without the other. One the one hand that sounds nice, logical and abstract, on the other hand it may in actuality be psychologically problematic. In the energetic, affective and emotional register such a dialectical integration is typically being highly defended off by the psyche—probably at the Ego and Super Ego dimensions of the personality.

Simply, we stated that double talking was going on regularly but not noticed—often completely below consciousness. The near total predominance of the Fear Paradigm and its shaping of near everything about us as modern humans, including our very social identities, is having big effects. Concomitantly, there is always already a defense posturing to deny the Fearlessness Paradigm any access, reality and/or valuation. Fearlessness is being sublimated,[475] and Fear takes over the operational aspects of existence and is allowed its free reign to do so. The exclusion in this dynamic is profound, at least theoretically. People may mouthed their valuation of "fearless" and so on but it is double talk for the most part. We then suggested, and more so now in Part VI, that there is an uncanny anxiety elicited that troubles people in hearing about a Fearlessness Paradigm or Project—and thus, it has to be avoided and likewise even the impulse of fearlessness experiencing as a 'corrective' to excess fear and 'fear.' So, if it is true that the word *fear* elicits fear *a la* Sardello,[476] then what we are saying here is that fearlessness, ironically, elicits even more fear, if not dread. Fearlessness predictably elicits the degree of uncanny anxiety that easily stifles any positive engagement with the uncanny object—be that of the real human-looking android or fearlessness itself and what it is symbolic of. The analogy here could be a fruitful inquiry in the future. Of course, Kumar in the above examples of the three types of the uncanny, offers a slightly modified understanding with his third type.[477]

Let me now bring in the really poignant research finding when the uncanny valley is hooked to what researchers call "mortality salience" from TMT. Remember, all of this, including TMT, is just another form of *fear management* going on and theorizing about universals of fear management *via* systems and strategies. The Fearlessness Paradigm itself is totally interested in understanding 'how we think about fear' and its management. Okay, back to the study by MacDorman.

So the story here of the uncanny valley phenomenon starts to expand when we examine further the paradoxical *real/unreal* and *living/dead* juxtapositions. Dodd called such juxtapositions to be the core of "the *primary uncanny* of our culture."[478] It generally freaks people out—even if they are unaware of being freaked out. The *unaware* aspect is what I am concerned with here; and likewise TMT is concerned with in the social psychology processes of Othering and its destructive, if not violent, effects. I won't go into all the details of TMT as that would take up too much space here, but I highly recommend people study this research and theory of human behavior. It's deep stuff re: fear/terror management strategies and the unconscious mechanisms of self-esteem and cultural worldview protection mechanisms. TMT says,

"Our cultures also offer hope of symbolic immortality, the sense that we are part of something greater than ourselves that will continue long after we die. This is why we strive to be part of meaningful groups.... The desire for self-esteem drives us all, and drives us hard. [By both culture and self-generated means via narcissism] Self-esteem shields us against the rumblings of dread [due to death anticipation]...."[479]

MacDorman initiated TMT findings and theory as an added dimension of testing the Mori hypothesis and explaining further the dynamics of the uncanny valley. MacDorman was intrigued that the "living dead"[480] experience of the android observers encountering the very humanly real robots might be connected to what TMT research has found about "morality salience" and empathy research. The latter universal finding of TMT is that basically when people in the lab under controlled conditions, are given a stimuli that triggers mortality ideation, even if subliminal, the person invariably responds to anything that is 'different' than them, including beliefs, values, worldview, that person triggered will exaggerate their reaction against the 'difference' to the point of implied and/or real aggression toward the other. In other words, they lose their flexibility of having empathy for any difference. Without the mortality prompting by the researchers, the subjects may acknowledge the difference but they don't elaborate it nor show overt signs of aggression against the difference. Only with a death reminder does the phenomenon unfold. The more intense the death prompt stimuli, generally the more intense the hatred toward the other—the difference that is different from them. The threat from the other is positively correlated with thinking about one's own mortality—that is, fear of death and/or dying. This individual reactivity is primal. It equally shows in TMT research to be applied to when one's culture and its symbols, like a national flag, is involved in the experiments. The triggered individual will attack other nation's flags and peoples who are foreigners. All that is required is a stimuli that brings about fear—that is, mortality reminders.

Indeed, MacDorman's research on androids show a positive correlation as well in that subjects studied had the same TMT othering reactivity of aggression, disgust, hatred, and fear with a death prompt as they did with exposure to androids that were at the high end of 'real' human looking. The complexity of explanation has not fully been researched in these findings. Basically it seems the most human looking of machines brings about strong uncanny anxiety aligned with strong reminders of one's death and mortality. One reason I think this may be is because the android is going to likely 'live' beyond the human—as machines are less vulnerable because they are Mechanical not Organic— if you recall the A-ness vs. D-ness test of Part II, you may see the connections.[481] And The Wachowski Bros. film *The Matrix* also shows this battle of Machine World vs. Human World and a good deal of uncanny anxiety in between for the movie characters and perhaps for viewers of the movie. It's actually quite dark and terrifying in many scenes where we see Machines and Digital Facsimile have enslaved the humans, who remain unconscious of their enslavement in the Cyberworld. They are living in an illusion.

I wonder if the analogy I'm offering is valid. A Fearlessness human is going to be seen as unreal/real. The Fear Paradigm has constructed a world where Fear is accepted as the motivational main operating 'fuel and engine.' *Fear is what makes us human.* I have seen that slogan many times in our modern society and perhaps even back to premodern. Fearlessness Paradigm challenges that notion of being human— and, thus, it will be coded as a threat to the belief of the Fear Paradigm. Make sense? A human operating from fearlessness will be received as a threat to being human—that human will be make an 'it' and 'different' to the point of being a death reminder. A death reminder to the old paradigm and way of seeing ourselves as human. Fearlessness is uncanny.

TMT has offered several principle patterns of behaviors of the "System" of protection that the Dominant worldview, fear-based worldview, operates to ensure all excess 'difference' is more or less ignored, neutralized and/or destroyed at any cost.[482] Being triggered in TMT experiences in the lab is of course correlated with and explains real behaviors in the real world too. Violence is typically enacted when the perpetrator, individual or collective, is reminded of their own mortality. The 9/11 incident in the U.S.A. is arguably, according to TMT, classic as to show how the theory works on mass scale in cultural-political-geographic dimensions.[483] The mass waves of refugees, asylum seekers and migrants all over the planet now with ecological and economic collapsing systems underway, the encounters of people 'at home' are now having to manage constant death reminders from the migrants appearance on their shores and borders—and, we all know what is happening for the most part. The situation is not pretty and will only get worse. A Fearlessness Paradigm is urgent now to begin to counter the Fear Paradigm and the uncanny anxiety invoked by witnessing the arrival of the living/near-dead into your 'house'—of which so many people who are horribly suffering remind the privileged people of their own coming dying and death. Now, the whole ecosphere is dying. Expect more outbreaks of violence than ever under this regime of the Fear Paradigm because it simply cannot cope any longer with the accumulating fear and 'fear' and death reminders—it will resort to reactive desperation and elimination strategies—called violence—which is, itself a fear management strategy or "anxiety-buffering"[484] as TMT says. Welcome to the insanity of 'the real.' Just as Camus welcomed us in his poetic indictment of history in 1946 to the same.

Camus' Path to a Century of Terror

How can one not be 'struck' by the brilliant synopsis, albeit poetics, of Camus' indictment of human history? Well, no doubt many would write off this "century of fear" as typical of Camus and his dark view of history. The positivists would not give his poetic conclusion a moment's extra thought and they would move on to their 'normal' everyday, if not they would replace Camusian diagnostics of pessimism with their own brand of optimism about the progress of humankind and success of the W. mind, etc. It is not that we totally disagree with the optimistic view of human progress as pointed out by Stephen Pinker[485] as one recent example. We merely think it is insufficient for a full spectrum 'reading' of human progress. Wilber posits a "dialectic of progress" view, based in critical philosophy, but one that is both optimistic and pessimistic (*aka* realistic). This Wilberian integral perspective is part-n-parcel of our own view as co-authors. Humans have a great creative possibility, while heading into the tornado of their own making, largely based on fear ('fear') = ignore-ance and arrogance[486]—with it's unbelievable global destructivity.

Camus, extremist at times as he may be, 'corrects' the over-optimistic, and sets them onto their heels—even if for only a moment. With Fisher's discovery and uncanny experience with Camus' "century of fear" conclusion, we simply cannot ignore what is to be learned from it. Others have called it (the 20th) a tragic, if not apocalyptic "post-traumatic century."[487] A Fearlessness Paradigm, by any other name, is a curious one that will not shy away from tragedy, the uncanny and/or such a truthing diagnosis from a great philosopher-artist in our midst, living or dead. A year after his poetic indictment writing Camus produces *The Plague* "in the wake of Nazism" which "inaugurates the

Age of Testimony as the age of the imperative of bearing witness to the trauma and the implications of survival."[488] (i.e., to be a 'survivor' of The Death and Destruction). Indeed, this is a turn in art and philosophy, ethics and psychology—there is a whole re-orientation required, argues Felman, in order to re-find our very 'humanity' and sense of discernment about what is 'progress' and what is not? The future, of course, is highly dependent on this deep and painful inquiry and process of witnessing. Camus, and *The Plague*—are not going to let us forget. To witness is to offer the magic elixir, what Freud called "free-floating attention" capable of deep listening and compassion. Anything less, is not the path of fearlessness.

Thus, with Camus, the road map for a modern to postmodern transition is presented and persistent to keep us on the double duty of healing and remembering—call it grief work, call it conflict work, call it fear work. There is no escape from it—that is, not as long as Camus stays in our face! Fisher must have discovered a universal fossil-like conscience of the ages—found marked and scared as: 'this Face' of History—of Trauma—like a Ghost staring at him the moment he deciphered the French penned epigram. Everything changed and Fisher's marginal and struggling work to promote fear studies was then reinforced by Camus's calling out and rebellion against forgetting— that the nature and role of fear (and 'fear') ought to be *central* to the entire Human Knowledge Project—that is, fear needs to be central in the critical analysis of Progress, however one wants to define it. As of 1946, arguably, Fear was not going to be so easily forgotten as it had in human history, thanks to Camus and this new postmodern age of Testimony and Witnessing.

Albert Camus' work is a signature exposé that we (as co-authors) would expect from a fearlessness genre of inquiry (testimony, witnessing)—and yes, from any high quality existential philosophy worth its salt. And, yes, it too is incomplete in and of itself. Thus, we continue the search for a holistic-integral approach that includes existentialism, fearism in their best aspects but also transcends them. We cannot claim such a philosophy has fully appeared as yet. Though, we sense it and write about it in this book as a nascent form, and perhaps, more a gestation than anything else.

What we are intrigued by is the postmodern Camusian 'shift' as real and as metaphorical, if not as a new *meta-mythical* foundation for our times—that is, the 20th-21st century, where by all accounts, that without a major transformation of humanity's common ways of carrying out their 'business', there will be no 22nd century to experience for our species (and, unfortunately, many other species). The world is quickly spiralling into eco-collapse. But such emergency-time was not on top of the public discourse of Camus' times. Rather, there was a brief respite of germination of possibilities and yet tragedies to process—coming off from the horrific World Wars that tore the fabric of modern Europe (at least) apart.

In this climate of fear/terror and destruction, Camus took a breath, and in 1946 penned his wonderful poetics of indictment of a crime going on in all of W. history. He challenged and still challenges humanity to seriously look at the outcome of the 'great' knowledge production—called "Education" and "Science." What happened? How could "fear" be the final outcome—at least, in this Camusian declaration? The literary device, in the hand of artistic-philosophical genius, was Camus' *The Fall* about a 'story of suicide' and the culpability of *witnessing it*. Though we cannot go into the depths of that novel, Camus's narrator says, "It's too late now"—or equally, could has said, 'it's history.' Gone. But Felman pointed out that Camus was reframing for us all, including the narrator and himself as author, "not just to listen to, but to articulate the very inarticulateness of the narrative, to *be* the story and to repeat its unrepeatability"[489] (echoes of the Holocaust and its near-impossibility to be articulated from any 'normal' perspective).

What we take from this, in this moment, is that we (as co-authors) are asking also "not just to listen to" what is on these pages of *Resistances to Fearlessness*. We are asking to be open to the uncanny of encountering Fearlessness. We asking "to articulate the very inarticulateness" of Fearlessness, not as abstract philosophy and ideas alone, but as Witness—or better yet, what Ettinger calls "wit(h)nessing"—that is, to truly be willing to "perform" the act of co-encountering and co-creating in the spaces in between 'normal' history and the absurd—that is, inside and outside of the 20th century—to 21st century—of fear/terror—to be with Fearlessness in its juxtaposition with Fear, yes, dialectically—but also on a much subtler plane of experiencing—yes, perhaps only fully can be touched by the uncanny that Fearlessness seems to lie. Felman's revisionist historian is a post-traumatic historian, and we think that a perfect analogy for the revisionist fearologist, fearanalyst and historian of fear/fearlessness. Felman concluded that the canon of work of Camus,

> ...succeeds in giving to the very silence of a generation—and to very voicelessness of history—the power of a *call*: the possibility, the chance, of our [ethical] *response-ability*.[490]

RMF: Re: Camus' poetic indictment of history—it is not *only a quote* involving *fear*—for that is the obvious *pharmakon* character and maneuver that arrives finally at the end of his 'poem.' Maybe it is not even his at all. Maybe it is his generation's poem—universal and transpersonal. Anyways, one gets lured at the beginning into thinking he is talking about *anything but fear*—he's rather talking about knowledge and progress and the great W. Enlightenment project we can be so proud of as humanity. But then suddenly, he like 'blows up the ark'—and drops in the 20th century—the one he and his readers were living in at the time he penned this. So now what? Where does all that pride and progress go? What is left behind? Are we left now to study fear itself? It would seem that is the unsaid left-over, which even Camus was not capable of articulating. For example, he could have then added the line: "Now, knowing what you know, what we know, Fear Studies is the next knowledge that makes sense to pursue." But he didn't say it. And, humanity didn't say it, either. Consciousness apparently wasn't ready to say it.

Clearly and concretely in the word expressed on paper, "fear" is there for us to read and thus it is in that sense a "positive" description approach. To claim and name it, as he does, because it is an outcome, a product, that can be described in the positive—yet, you realize it only appeared as the latent "negative" shadow hidden beneath the surfaces of pride/progress/greatness, all as dialectical really, in the double talk of tongue-in-cheek Camusian 'progress' through the 300 years of mathematics and sciences. What else would an existentialist true to the cause, do but so reveal that which is our collective anxiety, denied, yet felt, yet ... [etc....]

BMK: Michael, this is so pertinent. Sorry to interrupt, but you said it, and Subba said it.

RMF: What?

BMK: You said, 'let there be Fear Studies' c. 2000. Even if it was 70+ years after Camus' call. You said it! Philosophy of Fearism also says it! I think this is great and worth celebrating, despite all the resistances you both have had from others towards your projects.

Fearlessness is already here...and it was there in Camus—and his generation—but as you've said, it was a problem of inadequacy of vocabulary and lack of theory of Fearlessness in the W. world especially, that prevented it from blooming then. Voicelessness was prevalent, while the 'voice' of Fearlessness was awaiting its time. Things are developmental and logical in a sense; things emerge for good reason when the conditions are right. Like a seed germinating needs the right conditions to break free of dormancy. Ideas are similar in they need right conditions to break out of the 'Fear' Matrix, as you call it. A developed Fearlessness would have been so useful then, of course. Their response-ability was restricted. They were unconsciously trapped in their own collective *resistance* to Fearlessness.

Retrospective thought is easy now for us, for we did not live in those challenging times of Camus. No one yet had offered the full negative description of history and the omission of Fearlessness, especially in the West. And, not enough of the Eastern thought had yet come to penetrate European thought, even though the great philosopher Arthur Schopenhauer, followed by Nietzsche, had been slowly exposing the E. philosophies in hybridization potentials with W. philosophies.[491] The integration wasn't there and would not really show up until the E-W explosion of the boomer's generation and cultural and spiritual rebellion in the 1960s-70s in North America and much of the W. in general. Michael, you had the benefit of that explosion, and I suspect from that, you would be channeling the Fearlessness 'voice' to come out of silence by the time of late 1989 and your uncanny mystical experience that birthed In Search of Fearlessness Project. Everything changed.

And this change should continue to explore and achieve better prospects. The fearlessness voice and type three uncanny has a positive connotation. It makes one to think and act with an open mind. On the contrary, negative connotations restrict ideas so as to focus only on particular issues. Positive connotations like fearlessness approach will empower. Negative connotations of fear can alert people to be cautious of dangers in a certain line of actions. Both have got their own areas of operations and are relevant in the sense that they are required for balancing human life. But as Camus already prophesied, 'fear' voice has been alarmingly cacophonous since especially the last 20th century. Fear needs to be moderated, to say it euphemistically. As you Michael have emphasised on the new Fearlessness conceptual revolution for 21st century, it is time now to embrace change towards a fearlessness perspective regarding our worldview, and thus. for moderation in national life as well as in world politics. It will be more likely to pave the way for immense possibilities and vast opportunities towards peace, friendship, and progress among world nations. Yes, it is plausible through a fearlessness voice and even the uncanny.

CHAPTER TEN

Recommendations

The Fearology Institute is something about fearology. And, what is fearology, and who's to say what fearology is, becomes a very interesting issue. [Fearology- is the study of the interrelationship of fear and life]....this very intimate relationship has been something that's been going on since the beginning of Life really, we're looking at four billion years or so, that fearology is something that could be important today. And it's been important to all of history, except we haven't talked about fear directly or fearology directly throughout history. We've only probably, recently particularly, and I'm thinking in the last 100+ years, really started to think about as a species our relationship with fear in a systematic way, not just in a way that we knew fear was always important to human existence and to all organisms really, but we've really started to now come to see that we have to understand fear in a new way, in a different way, a more systematic way, so here we are in 2018, it's taken us a long time as a species to gather the intelligence, to gather the awareness, to come out of our own denial, to come out of our own fear enough to actually say, 'Hey, we really need to talk more about fear...wherever it might be... [like] we want to study fear actually by putting a fearist lens or a fearological lens on the topic of fear itself; ahhh, now there becomes the shift in consciousness.... 	-R. Michael Fisher[492]

Motivation, especially at its deepest roots, intrigues me. I see myself as an educational architect....To focus on fearlessness and its many forms, however, is not wise if such focus denies or takes flight from the fear-based historical, economic, sociopolitical and cultural context in which most of humanity is living today. Though my in depth critical writings on fear are found elsewhere, the introduction material of *The World's Fearlessness Teachings* gives fear its due credence. Clearly, fear and fearlessness are dialectical conceptions and phenomena, neither of which can be understood well without knowing the other.
	-R. Michael Fisher[493]

This book *Resistances to Fearlessness* begins this overt restoration of Fearlessness. 	-RMF

I (Fisher) am committed to add to the world's vocabulary a new study called "fearology." It struck me after writing this book with Kumar that there is an invisible double talking going on in the above quote, which is taken from my first teaching video for my new Youtube channel. With all attempts to do justice to the fear/fearlessness dialectic in my own philosophy of liberation, the reality is that I have typically privileged and given over most of my overt writing to the study of "fear" (and 'fear') and what I have called fear management/education. Yet, paradoxically, and as part of the double speaking herein, "fearlessness" is the lesser, at times invisible, cousin in most of the conversations and in my writing and teaching. Although such emphasis has a good purpose, it is somewhat a tragedy that this has ended up being the case, because the very original inspiration for my life shift and transformation in 1989 to become a 'teacher' was coined under the umbrella In Search of Fearlessness

Project, as a counter-education to the growing and prevailing insidious strength of the 'Fear' Project and Fear Problem.

From Project to Problem emphasis, eventually I named the Fearlessness Movement as a consciousness and political movement that any of us could tap into and carry forth the mission. Yet, upon the shoulders of the many great historical figures and groups who have been part of the Fearlessness Movement historically, I again seemed destined to focus most of the development of scholarship and pedagogy upon the concept and phenomenon of fear. The philosophy of fearism itself, both East (e.g., Desh Subba) and West (e.g., myself) has also favored the discussion of the nature and role of fear and explicated new ways to talk about fear(ism). This penchant of heart-felt desire to push a conscious fear-agenda into philosophy and the world-at-large has had great consequences, at least theoretically—and, it's ended up supporting my call for a new field of 'Fear' Studies, as a transdisciplinary endeavor and eventually a new *International Journal of Fear Studies* (2018). The slippage from emphasis on original focus on fearlessness to then on fear is a pattern I am just noticing in writing this Recommendation section, and it is replicated in my founding of not-for-profit Institutes to carry out this work. The original, and long-lasting In Search of Fearlessness Research Institute eventually was usurped in 2018 with promotion of the newly coined Fearology Institute. Although, these are social experiments and great victories at some level, they are also a double talking of which there is a down-side not acknowledged in their positive description—and, it is only by negative description and honest and sincere critical reflection does one encounter the shadow-side of such progress around fear management/education.[494] My conclusion, Fear ought not ever be held as the greater cousin of the dialectical pair.

Let's look at the recent accumulated vocabulary expansion of the term *fear* within the discourses of the fearism philosophers, which I include myself as part of that movement. In a recent article I created a Glossary of 70+ terms[495] that were currently in use, more or less, within the group of thinkers and writers following mostly Desh Subba's[496] lead. From the whole list which all center on expansion of prefixes and suffixes added to the "fear" word (e.g., feardom, fearagentic, etc.) only four such terms have "fearlessness" in them.[497] In other words, there's been virtually no expansive building on the lesser cousin of the dialectical pair. And sadly, from my view, no one, not even myself, notice this bias was happening. That warns me of the power of dissociation within the language structures that are dominating today, and it seems eastern and western thinkers and writers who have contributed to fearism work have equally been caught in this 'trap' and 'double talk' unconsciously. So, now I am making this conscious so we can learn from it. Much of what is in this book *Resistances to Fearlessness* is a reclamation of the lesser cousin and there are many clues to the 'crime'[498] that has been perpetrated for so long. I recommend readers, who are most keen, to take this approach to reading this book. It is time for serious self-reflection on what we have all taken for granted by focusing mostly on only one half of the dialectical pair. I'm delighted to recently have edited a volume of scholarly work on ecofear as the theme, mostly with Eastern-based writers from India especially, and I noticed a new term coined that I have never seen, "ecofearlessness."[499] Wow. That's a movement in the right direction.

"My theory of fearlessness creates more room for customizing fear management/education in a postmodern sensitive, developmental and evolutionary framework....I contend we need to develop a *critical literacy of* fearlessness that has rarely if ever been taught to us...".[500] I always thought I taught and wrote mindfully of that dialectical equality of value of both halves of the pair fear/fearlessness, and maybe it is true. Yet, it is undeniable that the former greater cousin has sort of 'stole the show.' There are many reasons for that, not that they are the focus here for Chapter Ten, but more so I mention all this because of my long criticism of why humanity has constructed several scholarly works on the *history of fear* but not on the *history of fearlessness*. This is again mentioned in *Resistances to Fearlessness* overtly at points, yet one ought not forget that the double talking is so thick everywhere around the term "fear" and "fearlessness" that so much is occluded continually—and, typically the principle of the dialectic of fear/fearlessness, which is core to Fearlessness philosophy and paradigm and fearism, is not given its due. We have to take responsibility for this, and thus I forefront this omission, if not a 'crime,' here in Chapter Ten but from this point will not mention it again below. The implication is, of course, to do the upgraded and appropriate holistic-integral research, writing and teaching, to bring the dialectic into balance as an overall aim. To ignore this, will truly continue to compromise the quality of any fear management/education we offer. This book *Resistances to Fearlessness* begins this overt restoration of Fearlessness.

Questions/Exercises to Practice True Fearlessness

I could literally fill another book with questions, exercises, or what is called "praxis" reflectivity in regard to fear/fearlessness advancement. There is yet so much to be thought about and done. Fearlessness in particular is so far behind in its knowledge-base, especially in the modern West, that I'll focus all of this section to it, and what for colloquial purposes we can call the aim of "true fearlessness." However, such a concept is radical, and far beyond what most people can even imagine that such a term and distinction might mean. But let me get practical and give you as readers the benefit of the doubt so you may do your own searching on what I offer below as a start.

1. What makes the distinction between "true fearlessness" and what is referred to as "*faux* fearlessness" a few times in this book? Utilize your already pre-given knowledge, your readings and study from this book and elsewhere, and begin your own philosophizing, and writing, about this distinction. Then follow that reflection up with discussion with peers. Then follow that up with more writing and reflection and take note of any of the *resistances you noticed* during these above activities—especially, if you were able to find some peers to discuss this with. And, finally take a look at the concept (movement) put forward by Arianna Huffington, she dubbed as the need for an "epidemic of fearlessness." Research this, write about it, and critique

it—especially, in light of your own burgeoning philosophy of the distinction between true fearlessness and not.

2. Construct a found-poem, as long as you like, and in whatever style you like, from any chapter or many chapters from this book. This does not require you to be a 'poet' *per se*. Rather, this technique is well-known in certain circles of research and amongst writers and poets, whereby you take someone else's text (i.e., prose) and you convert it for your own learning purposes. Contemplative practitioners like to do this, as a means of picking and choosing a 'cut down' version of the larger original text, and making it simpler, giving it more space, and allowing another part of your brain (right-side) to take-over a little more than the analytic (left-side) functions. See what happens. Share it with others. And, continue to utilize this contemplative approach to research and deepening understanding of fearlessness (and, whatever else).

3. Do some research on the three primary pillars that are threaded throughout this book, mainly as Fisher brings them forward in terms of leading-edge routes to expanding the understanding of fearlessness (and fear). The three pillars can be boiled down to "Fisherian," "Indigenous" and "Matrixial." Search this book on these terms and the discussion, make notes, and then pursue reading about the others whom Fisher mentions as pivotal leading-edge thinkers on fearlessness (i.e., Indigenous – Four Arrows; Matrixial – Bracha L. Ettinger). In doing this, you may find your research takes you into other directions and perhaps uncovering other 'pillars' that are not covered by the three pillars. Consider developing an essay on this research and submitting it to the *International Journal of Fear Studies* (RMF is Senior Editor).

4. Research from this book, as a starting point, on the issue of aesthetics (e.g., Part II) and the application of the arational domain of methodology and way of perceiving, thinking and acting in the world to promote fearlessness. Arational is distinct from irrational and rational. What is Fisher's agenda, do you

think, in bringing forth the arational as much as he does in this book, and what is Kumar's notion of this domain and how do the two co-authors differ and how are they similar in their thinking around this? Where do you stand in this regard?

5. Explore the way "resistance" is talked about in this book. List and describe all the different connotations you can find, like definitions, meanings, and framings for understanding resistance. What do you think are the strengths and weaknesses of resistance in the world generally and in your particular life? What experiences have you had, where resistance was actually therapeutic? Does a Fearlessness Paradigm re-invent in some way, the very meaning of resistance? Explain in detail, and contrast that with a Fear Paradigm view of resistance.

6. How do you think COVID-19 pandemic has impacted the world in terms of humanity's lessons being learned? Giving examples, specifically study this book and pull out what it has to say about this pandemic. Then, make your critique of this book's approach to the pandemic topic and add your own contribution of how you could improve this book's approach and write your complementary "Addendum" to this book in this regard.

7. Based on Fisher's critique that there is simply no equivalency of attention given to the history of fear compared to the history of fearlessness, where would you want to start your research and writing a history of fearlessness? Start with your own autobiographical history in your development as a human, person, and citizen, etc. Then, start on the entire history (and herstory) of the world—where would you begin that story? Follow-up, do more research, and begin to write a history of fearlessness from your own slant. Fisher would be glad to see what you have come up with; maybe you could co-author and publish a paper with him and/or Kumar for starters.

8. How would you engage a child under 7 years of age, on the topic of fearlessness? Pretend you are a school teacher or parent, if you aren't actually one, and advance your curriculum or even

one class lesson on this topic. For some clues to this potential and its details go to the video FearTalk 7 as Fisher and Debbie (a kindergarten teacher)[501] discuss this topic.

9. How do you think public school administrators generally, would react, respond etc. to this book? What 'bridge' is needed, describe in details, in re: to communicating some of the ideas in this book to others, like public school stakeholders, or governments, etc. The emphasis of your research and creative thoughts on this question have to do with the problem of communicating effectively about fearlessness. Add your own ideas and share them with the co-authors and others, as appropriate.

10. Because the dialectical principle of the Fearlessness Paradigm, and all of this book, is based on Fisher's dictum: *When fear appears, so then does fearlessness,* what is your understanding of what this means? Do you think it is accurate? Why or why not? How do you think it could be improved upon as a dictum and philosophical principle?

11. Based on your investment into the above questions, how would you further like to "plan" to become involved, or more involved, in making the Fearlessness Movement more robust and influential in the months and years ahead. Map out your plan and set dates for this action on your part. Share it with others and build the necessary coalitions required.

12. Based on what is written in this book, and beyond, what do you currently believe are the strengths and weaknesses of the philosophy of fearism and its approach?

13. The growth of fascism around the world in the last decade and especially the last couple years is very controversial and very important in how our societies are going to be governed. Because much of what is in this book could be labeled "progressive" and Leftist, take time to examine what are the main signatures of such liberal/progressive/Left thinking in the book and what are some of the things written/said by the co-authors that are not so easily aligned with the progressivism? Look also at an article by Fisher recently on the radical Leftist, Dr. Cornel West,[502] written

as a critique, and how "moral courage" is a more comfortable term it seems with Leftist generally and traditionally. How could fearlessness *re-vision* the very notion of progressivism (and/or revolution) and up-date it for the 21st century? How could a Fearlessness Paradigm also embrace the best of conservativism and attract their attention—even, attract fascist's and other extremists to engage in a more fruitful conversation with the Left? Is that even possible? Is that dangerous? Note: Fisher calls himself an "integralist" and is non-partisan in his approach to improving and evolving the political sphere as a whole.

14. Quoting from Fisher's first major book: "On the more conservative side (using that word in its widest sense) there is a large contingent in fact, who believe notions or actions of 'fearlessness' are the very problem with humanity not the solution. They prescribe *more fear* to keep us and things in order. They may prescribe governments should be afraid of the people. I will argue against these types of fear-based prescriptions and instead pursue a model and theory which suggests we are progressing and very rapidly indeed and less fear not more is the way to go. Our means of fear management are, unfortunately, well behind the rate of change...".[503] Write your views of these issues raised here, and then provide rationale to back-them-up using your own thinking, the thinking in this co-authored book by Fisher & Kumar, etc.

15. What do you make of the quotes, not well-known, by two great (Eastern) world leaders (philosophers) of the contemporary era: (1) the late Mahatma Gandhi- "God is fearlessness" and, (2) XIVth Dalai Lama- "Don't fear fearlessness."

REFERENCES

Adhikari, B. S. (2020). *Exotic fearology.* Xlibris.

Adhikari, B. S., Kalu, O. A. & Subba, D. (2020). *Eco-fearism: Prospects and burning issues.* Xlibris.

Ainsworth-Land, G. T. (1973/97). *Grow or die: The unifying principle of transformation.* John Wiley & Sons.

Alex, R. K., & P. S., Sachindev (2021). Editorial: Naturecultures, ecofears, cultural texts. *International Journal of Fear Studies, 3*(1), 7-10.

Alexander, C. (1977). *A pattern language: Towns, buildings, construction.* Oxford University Press.

Anonymous (2020). 'Fear spreads like a virus': How coronavirus panic is taking a toll on N. J.'s mental health. Retrieved from https://www.nj.com/coronavirus/2020/03/fear-spreads-just-like-a-virus-coronavirus-panic-is-taking-a-toll-on-njs-mental-health.html

Anonymous (2008). II: Gift of fear of the Lord. In R. Karris & Z. Hayes (Eds.), *Collations on the seven gifts of the Holy Spirit.* Franciscan Institute Publications.

Anonymous (2004). Editorial. *Planning Theory & Practice, 5*(2), 141-4.

Azarian, B. (in press). *The romance of reality: How emergence creates life, consciousness, and increasing cosmic complexity.*

Bader-Saye, S. (2007). *Following Jesus in a culture of fear: Christian practice of everyday life.* Brazos Press.

Barber, B. (2003). *Fear's empire: War, terrorism, and democracy.* W. W. Norton.

Barr, L., & Barr, N. (1989). *The leadership equation: Leadership, management, and the Myers-Briggs.* Eakin Press.

Barrett, W. (1979). *The illusion of technique.* Anchor.

Bateson, G. (1979). *Mind and nature: A necessary unity.* E. P. Dutton.

Bateson, G. (1972). *Steps to an ecology of mind.* Ballantine Books.

Beck, D., & Cowan, C. (1996). *Spiral Dynamics: Mastering values, leadership and change.* Blackwell.

Becker, E. (1973/97). *The denial of death.* Simon & Schuster.

Bickel, B. (2020). *Art, ritual, and trance inquiry: Arational learning in an irrational world.* Palgrave Macmillan.

Bickel, B., & Fisher, R. M. (1993). *Opening doors: A guide to spontaneous creation-making.* In Search of Fearlessness Research Institute.

Bisht, K. (2020). Mental sublimation: The anchor of survival in Albert Camus *The Plague*. *International Journal of Creative Research Thoughts, 8*(5), 3039-43.

Bois, J. S. (1973). *The art of awareness: A textbook on general semantics and epistemics.* Wm. C. Brown Co. [original published in 1966]

Boje, D. M., Fedor, D. B. & Rowland, K. M. (1982). Myth making: A qualitative step in OD interventions. *The Journal of Applied Behavioral Science, 18*(1), 17-28.

Boschman, C. (2007). Researching the fear factor:' Fearologist' has mapped out different fear management systems. *The Lethbridge Herald,* July 5, A1-A2.

Brown, J. S., Laundré, J. W. & Gurung, M. (1999). The ecology of fear: Optimal foraging, game theory, and trophic interactions. *Journal of Mammology, 80*(2), 385-99.

Campbell, J. (with Moyers, B.) (1988). *The power of myth.* Ed. S. Flowers. Doubleday.

Chödrön, P. (2001). *The places that scare you: A guide to fearlessness in difficult times.* Shambhala.

Cohl, H. A. (1997). *Are we scaring ourselves to death?: How pessimism, paranoia, and a misguided media are leading us toward disaster.* St. Martin's Griffin.

Connor, K. R. (2017). Mystery and bad manners: Flannery O'Connor and Mary Karr's resemblance across generations. *Flannery O'Connor Review, 15*, 70-9.

Corradi, J. E. (1992). Toward societies without fear. In J. E. Corradi, P. W. Fagen & M. A. Garretón (Eds.), *Fear at the edge: State terror and resistance in Latin America* (pp. 267-92). University of California Press.

Corradi, J. E., Fagen, P. W. & Garretón, M. A. (1992). Introduction, Fear: A cultural and political construct. In J. E. Corradi, P. W. Fagen & M. A. Garretón (Eds.), *Fear at the edge: State terror and resistance in Latin America* (pp. 1-10). University of California Press.

Creed, B. (2005). *Phallic panic: Film, horror and the primal uncanny.* Melbourne UP.

Cristian, A. (2012). Daring to fear: Optimizing the encounter of danger through education. *Meta: Research in Hermeneutics, Phenomenology, and Practical Philosophy, 4*(1), 9-36.

Davis, M. (1999). *Ecology of fear: Los Angeles and the imagination of disaster.* Vintage/Random House. de Becker, G. (1997). *The gift of fear: Survival signals that protect us from violence.* A Dell Book.

Devereux, G. (1967). *From anxiety to method in the behavioral sciences.* Mouton & Co.

Dodds, J. (2020, April). Elemental catastrophe: Ecopsychoanalysis and the viral uncanny of COVID-19. *Stillpoint, 4*, 1-12.

Dotson, K. (2011, Spring). Tracking epistemic violence, tracking practices of silencing. *Hypatia, 26*(2), 237-57.

Dubos, R. (1970). *Reason awake: Science for man.* Columbia University Press.

Eisler, R. (1987). *The chalice and the blade: Our history, our future.* Harper & Row.

Eneyo, M. (2019). *Philosophy of fear: A move to overcoming negative fear.* Xlibris, Lightening Source.

English, A., & Stengel, B. (2010). Exploring fear: Rousseau, Dewey, and Freire on fear and learning. *Educational Theory, 60*, 521-42.

Ermine, W. (2007). The ethical space of engagement. *Indigenous Law Journal, 6*(1), 194-203.

Ettinger, B. L. (2011). Uncanny awe, uncanny compassion and matrixial transjectivity beyond uncanny anxiety. *FLS (Psychoanalysis) 38*, 1-35.

Evernden, N. (1993). *The natural alien.* 2nd Ed. University of Toronto [original published in 1985].

Fazekas, P., & Kampis, G. (n.d.). Turning negative causation back to positive. Unpublished paper.

Felman, S. (1992). Education and crisis, or the vicissitudes of teaching. In S. Felman & D. Laub (Eds.), *Testimony: Crises of witnessing in literature, psychoanalysis, and history* (pp. 1-56). Routledge.

Felman, S. (1992a). The betrayal of the witness: Camus' *The Fall*. In S. Felman & D. Laub (Eds.), *Testimony: Crises of witnessing in literature, psychoanalysis, and history* (pp. 165-). Routledge.

Ferguson, M. (2005). *Aquarius now: Radical common sense and reclaiming our personal sovereignty.* Weiser Books.

Fisher, R. M. (in prep.). *The Fear Problematique: Role of philosophy of education in speaking truths to powers.* Information Age Publishing.

Fisher, R. M. (2021). Fear is social. Technical Paper No. 122. In Search of Fearlessness Research Institute.

Fisher, R. M. (2021a). Solving global wicked problems: Fearlessness. Retrieved from https://www.youtube.com/watch?v=-yF36_-NV7I&t=1079s

Fisher, R. M. (2021b). Status update on fear education: Jiddu Krishnamurti teachings. Technical Paper No. 123. In Search of Fearlessness Research Institute.

Fisher, R. M. (2021c). *The Marianne Williamson presidential phenomenon: Cultural (r)evolution in a dangerous time.* Peter Lang.

Fisher, R. M. (2021d). Hot button twin archetypes clash: Williamson vs. Trump. Retrieved from https://www.youtube.com/watch?v=G4sYleZOf5g

Fisher, R. M. (2021e). Fearism philosopher on beauty: B. Maria Kumar. Retrieved from https://fearlessnessmovement.ning.com/blog/fearism-philosopher-on-beauty-b-maria-kumar

Fisher, R. M. (2021f). Do 40,000 people believe fear is the answer in politics? Retrieved from https://fearlessnessmovement.ning.com/blog/do-40-000-people-believe-fear-is-the-answer-in-politics

Fisher, R. M. (2021g). Fearanalysis in action. Retrieved from https://www.youtube.com/watch?v=iH4PQYsO1OI

Fisher, R. M. (2021h). Elders have to speak the truth: David Suzuki. Retrieved from https://fearlessnessmovement.ning.com/blog/elders-have-to-speak-the-truth-david-suzuki

Fisher, R. M. (2020). Fearism: With R. Michael Fisher. Retrieved from https://www.youtube.com/watch?v=EPB9oVZnI4A

Fisher, R. M. (2020a). Resisting fearlessness: Resisting Life. Retrieved from https://www.youtube.com/watch?v=IyiaNVmPRO8

Fisher, R. M. (2020b). History of fearlessness: Interpreting the world through conspiracy theory. Technical Paper No. 103. In Search of Fearlessness Research Institute.

Fisher, R. M. (2020c). Samuel N. Gillian's Beckerian educational philosophy of terror. Technical Paper No. 102. In Search of Fearlessness Research Institute.

Fisher, R. M. (2020d). Review of "Immortality Project" Concept: Misinterpretation in terror management theory. Technical Paper 108. In Search of Fearlessness Research Institute.

Fisher, R. M. (2020e). Psychotic 1: Loss of baselines for sanity. Retrieved from https://prism.ucalgary.ca/handle/1880/110810

Fisher, R. M. (2020f). The League *for* Fearlessness—birthed in 1931. Retrieved from https://fearlessnessmovement.ning.com/blog/the-league-for-fearlessness-birthed-in-1931

Fisher, R. M. (2020g). The Love & Fear problem: A response to Michael Bassey Eneyo. *International Journal of Fear Studies, 1*(2), 75-112.

Fisher, R. M. (2020h). Fear management and education: Status of a failing relationship. Technical Paper No. 97. In Search of Fearlessness Research Institute.

Fisher, R. M. (2020i). Book review: *An education in 'evil': Implications for curriculum, pedagogy, and beyond,* by Catherine van Kessel, 2019. *International Journal of Fear Studies, 2*(2), 85-94.

Fisher, R. M. (2019). "Fearism" coined in 1990: New discovery. Retrieved from https://fearlessnessmovement.ning.com/main/search/search?q=fearism+new+coining

Fisher, R. M. (2019a). Fearless standpoint theory: Origins of FMS-9 in Arthur Schopenhauer's work. Technical Paper No. 86. In Search of Fearlessness Research Institute.

Fisher, R. M. (2019b). Fearlessness psychology: An introduction. Retrieved from https://prism.ucalgary.ca/handle/1880/110441

Fisher, R. M. (2019c). Fearlessnessizing. Retrieved from https://fearlessnessmovement.ning.com/blog/fearlessnessizing

Fisher, R. M. (2019d). Notes and drawings to myself: A fearlessness future. Technical Paper No. 82. In Search of Fearlessness Research Institute.

Fisher, R. M. (2019e). In Search of Fearlessness Project: Archival memory 1989-91 (30th anniversary). Technical Paper No. 80. In Search of Fearlessness Research Institute.

Fisher, R. M. (2019f). New fear vocabulary. *International Journal of Fear Studies, 1*(2), 10-14.

Fisher, R. M. (2019g). L.E.T. 1: Shifting from a coping culture to a healing culture. Retrieved from https://www.youtube.com/watch?v=iYX1x3sZoac

Fisher, R. M. (2019i). "Fearism" coined in 1990: New discovery. Retrieved from https://fearlessnessmovement.ning.com/blog/fearism-coined-in-1990-new-discovery

Fisher, R. M. (2019j). Schopenhauer on fear. Technical Paper No. 84. In Search of Fearlessness Research Institute.

Fisher, R. M. (2019k). How the "culture of positivity" debilitates Fear Studies. Technical Paper No. 81. In Search of Fearlessness Research Institute.

Fisher, R. M. (2019l). FearTalk 7: Debbie L. Kasman and R. Michael Fisher. Retrieved from https://www.youtube.com/watch?v=rlkclDeRKpA

Fisher, R. M. (2019m). Cornel West, and the Left, on fearlessness. Retrieved from https://fearlessnessmovement.ning.com/blog/cornel-west-on-fearlessness

Fisher, R. M. (2018). *Fearless engagement of Four Arrows: The true story of an Indigenous-based social transformer.* Peter Lang.

Fisher, R. M. (2018a). The Fearlessness Movement: Meta-context exposed! Technical Paper No. 72. In Search of Fearlessness Research Institute.

Fisher, R. M. (2018b). Delineating "The Movement": Regarding study of fear. Retrieved from https://fearlessnessmovement.ning.com/blog/delineating-the-movement-regarding-study-of-fear

Fisher, R. M. (2018c). FearTalk 1: Four Arrows and R. Michael Fisher. Retrieved from https://www.youtube.com/watch?v=GKKNWEfl_nY

Fisher, R. M. (2018d). "Fear has no place...": The youth movement for fearlessness in need of critique. Technical Paper No. 76. In Search of Fearlessness Research Institute.

Fisher, R. M. (2018e). Liberation Peer Counseling outside of distress. Retrieved from https://www.youtube.com/watch?v=5bE7-z0-0iE

Fisher, R. M. (2018d). Ethical practice of fearology. Retrieved from https://www.youtube.com/watch?v=13agg3VYg5U&t=78s

Fisher, R. M. (2017). Radical love—is it radical enough? *International Journal of Critical Pedagogy, 8*(1), 261-81.

Fisher, R. M. (2017a). De-hypnotizing technology of CAT-FAWN. Retrieved from https://fearlessnessmovement.ning.com/blog/de-hypnotizing-technology-of-cat-fawn-by-four-arrows

Fisher, R. M. (2017b). "Fearism": A critical analysis of uses and discourses in global migration studies. Technical Paper No. 64. In Search of Fearlessness Research Institute.

Fisher, R. M. (2016). Feariatry: A first conceptual mapping. Retrieved from https://fearlessnessmovement.ning.com/blog/feariatry-a-first-conceptual-mapping

Fisher, R. M. (2016a). Ideological underpinnings of colonial domination in understanding fear itself. Technical Paper No. 60. In Search of Fearlessness Research Institute.

Fisher, R. M. (2016b). Problem of branding "fearlessness" in education and leadership. Technical Paper No. 59. In Search of Fearlessness Research Institute.

Fisher, R. M. (2016c). New 7th 'fear' vaccine added. Retrieved from https://fearlessnessmovement.ning.com/blog/new-7th-fear-vaccine-added

Fisher, R. M. (2014). Towards a theory of fearism. Technical Paper No. 51. In Search of Fearlessness Research Institute.

Fisher, R. M. (2015). What is the West's problem with fearlessness? Technical Paper No. 53. In Search of Fearlessness Research Institute.

Fisher, R. M. (2013). The problem of defining the concept of "fear-based." Technical Paper No. 48. In Search of Fearlessness Research Institute.

Fisher, R. M. (2012). Love and fear. A CSIIE Yellow Paper, DIFS-6. Center for Spiritual Inquiry & Integral Education.

Fisher, R. M. (2012a). Do we really want a fearless society? Technical Paper No. 40. In Search of Fearlessness Research Institute.

Fisher, R. M. (2012b). Erich Fromm and universal humane experience: Application in the aesthetic domain for art educators. Technical Paper No. 39. In Search of Fearlessness Research Institute.

Fisher, R. M. (2012c). *Fearanalysis: A first guidebook.* In Search of Fearlessness Research Institute.

Fisher, R. M. (2012d). Do we really want a fearless society? Technical Paper No. 40. In Search of Fearlessness Research Institute.

Fisher, R. M. (2011). A critique of critical thinking: Towards a critical integral pedagogy of fearlessness. *NUML: Journal of Critical Inquiry, 9*(2), 92-164.

Fisher, R. M. (2011a). A 'Fear' Studies perspective and critique: Analyzing English and Stengel's progressive study of fear and learning in *Educational Theory*. Technical Paper No. 37. In Search of Fearlessness Research Institute.

Fisher, R. M. (2010). *The world's fearlessness teachings: A critical integral approach to fear management/education for the 21st century.* University Press of America/Rowman & Littlefield.

Fisher, R. M. (2009). "Unplugging" as real and metaphoric: Emancipatory dimensions to *The Matrix* trilogy. Technical Paper No. 33. In Search of Fearlessness Research Institute.

Fisher, R. M. (2006). Invoking 'Fear' Studies. *Journal of Curriculum Theorizing, 22*(4), 39-71.

Fisher, R. M. (2006a). Integral fearlessness paradigm. Technical Paper 20. In Search of Fearlessness Research Institute.

Fisher, R. M. (2003). Fearless leadership in and out of the 'Fear' Matrix. Unpublished dissertation. The University of British Columbia.

Fisher, R. M. (2003a). Report on the status of Fear Education. Technical Paper No. 15. In Search of Fearlessness Research Institute.

Fisher, R. M. (2000). Toward a 'conflict' pedagogy: A critical discourse analysis of 'conflict' in conflict management education. Unpublished masters thesis. The University of British Columbia.

Fisher, R. M. (1998/2012). Culture of 'fear': Toxification of landscape-mindscape as meta-context for education in the 21st century. Technical Paper No. 7. In Search of Fearlessness Research Institute.

Fisher, R. M. (1997). A guide to Wilberland: Some common misunderstandings of the critics of Ken Wilber and his work on transpersonal theory prior to 1995. *Journal of Humanistic Psychology, 37*(4), 30-73.

Fisher, R. M. (1997a). Defining the 'enemy' of fearlessness. Technical Paper No. 6. In Search of Fearlessness Research Institute.

Fisher, R. M. (1997b). *Thanatos* and *Phobos*: 'Fear' and its role in Ken Wilber's transpersonal theory. Technical Paper No. 4. In Search of Fearlessness Research Institute.

Fisher, R.M. (1995). An introduction to defining 'fear': A spectrum approach. Technical Paper No. 1. In Search of Fearlessness Research Institute.

Fisher, R. M. (1995a). An epistemology of 'fear': A fearlessness paradigm. Technical Paper No. 2. In Search of Fearlessness Research Institute.

Fisher, R. M. (1986). Education and beauty: Skin-deep or life-deep? *Elements: A Journal for Elementary Education, 8*(1), 13-16.

Fisher, R. M., & Bickel, B. (in prep.). *Creative practices for community care: Education, healing and transformation*. Routledge.

Fisher, R. M., & Four Arrows (aka Jacobs, D. T.) (2020). Indigenizing conscientization and critical pedagogy: Nature, Spirit and Fearlessness as foundational concepts. In S. Steinberg & B. Down Eds.), *Sage Handbook of Critical Pedagogies (Vol.2)* (pp. 551-60). SAGE.

Fisher, R. M., Quaye, S. J. & Pope, B. (2008). "Fearless leadership": R. Michael Fisher's story. In Four Arrows (aka D. T. Jacobs) (Ed.), *The authentic dissertation: Alternative ways of knowing, research, and representation* (pp. 143-8). Routledge.

Fisher, R. M., & Subba, D. (2016). *Philosophy of fearism: A first East-West dialogue.* Xlibris.

Fisher, R. M. & Subba, D. (2016a). Terrorism: A guide to fearful times based on a philosophy of fearism. Technical Paper No. 57. In Search of Fearlessness Research Institute.

Fisher, R. M., Subba, D. & Kumar, B. M. (2018). *Fear, law and criminology: Critical issues in applying the philosophy of fearism.* Xlibris.

Fixmer-Oraiz, N. (2019). *Homeland maternity: U.S. security culture and the new reproductive regime.* University of Illinois Press.

Forman, M. D. (2010). *A guide to integral psychotherapy: Complexity, integration, and spirituality in practice.* State University of New York Press.

Fromm, E. (1941/69). *Escape from freedom.* Avon.

Four Arrows (*aka Wahinkpe Topa*, Jacobs, D. T.) (2021). *Sitting Bull's words: For a world in crisis.* DiO.

Four Arrows (*aka* Jacobs, D. T.) (2018). From a deeper place: Indigenous worlding as the next step in holistic education. In J. P. Miller, K. Nigh, & M. J. Binder (Eds.), *International Handbook of Holistic Education* (Chapter Four). Routledge.

Four Arrows (*aka* Jacobs, D. T.) (2016). *Point of departure: Returning to a more authentic worldview for education and survival.* Information Age Publishing.

Fowler, J. W., & Keen, S. (1985). *Life maps: Conversations on the journey of faith.* World Books.

Fox, M. (1986). *Original blessing: A primer in creation spirituality presented in four paths, twenty-six themes, and two questions.* Bear & Co.

Freire, P. (1973). *Education for critical consciousness.* Continuum.

Freire, P. (1970). *Pedagogy of the oppressed.* [Trans. M. B. Ramos]. A Continuum Book/The Seabury Press.

Furedi, F. (2006). *Culture of fear revisited: Risk-taking and the morality of low expectation.* Continuum.

Gebser, J. (1949/84). *The ever-present origin.* [Trans. N. Barstad with A. Mickunas]. Ohio University Press.

Geist, V. (1978). *Life strategies, human evolution, environmental design: Toward a biological theory of health.* Springer-Verlag.

Gibb, J. (1991). *Trust: A new vision of human relationships for business, education, family, and personal living.* Newcastle Publishing.

Gillian, S. N. (2002). *The beauty of fear: How to positively enjoy being afraid.* Phemore Press.

Giroux, H. A. (2014). *Neoliberalism's war on higher education.* Haymarket Books.

Glassner, B. (1999). *The culture of fear: Why Americans are afraid of the wrong things.* Basic Books.

Goldman, M. (1999). *Ibsen: The dramaturgy of fear.* Columbia University Press.

Goleman, D. (1995). *Emotional intelligence: Why it can matter more than IQ.* Bantam.

Gur-Zé ev, I. (2010). *Diasporic philosophy and counter-education.* Sense.

Guy, D. (1995, July/Aug.). The world according to Wilber. *New Age Journal,* 77-9, 93-6.

Hall, C. S. (1960). *A primer of Freudian psychology.* New American Library.

Hallward, P. (2005). The politics of representation. *The South Atlantic Quarterly, 104* (4), 769-78.

Heim, M. (2004). *Theories of the gift in south Asia: Hindu, Buddhist, and Jain reflections on dāna.* Routledge.

Herbert, F. (1965). *Dune.* Chilton.

Hibbets, M. (1999). Saving them from yourself: An inquiry into the south Asian gift of fearlessness. *Journal of Religious Ethics, 27,* 437-62.

Hillman, J. (1972). *The myth of analysis: Three essays in archetypal psychology.* Harper & Row.

Hillman, J., and Ventura, M. (1993). *We've had a hundred years of psychotherapy—and the world's getting worse.* HarperSanFrancisco.

hooks, b. (2000). *All about love.* William Morrow.

Horsley, J. (2003). *Matrix Warrior: Being the One*: The unofficial handbook of Jake Horsley. Gollancz.

Jackins, H. (1972). *The uses of beauty and order.* Rational Island Publishers.

Jackins, H. (1965/85). *The human side of human beings.* Rational Island Publishers.

Jacobs, D. T. (1998). *Primal awareness: A true story of survival, transformation, and awakening with the Rarámuri shamans of Mexico.* Inner Traditions.

Jingpa, T. (2016). *A fearless heart: How the courage to be compassionate can transform our lives.* Penguin.

Kahane, A. (2010). *Power and love: A theory and practice of social change.* Berrett-Koehler.

Kalu, O. A. (2017). *The first stage of the fearologist.* Self-published.

Kalu, O. A. (2016). *Conquering the beast fear: Philosophical cum psychological approach.* Self-published.

Kapsch, S. G. (1997). A Lutheran reflection on the twelve steps of AA. *Journal of Ministry in Addiction & Recovery, 4*(2), 53-67.

Keen, S. (1983). *The passionate life: Stages of loving.* Harper & Row.

Keeney, B. P. (1985). *Aesthetics of change.* The Guilford Press.

Kizel, A. (2021). The facilitator as self-liberator and enabler: Ethical responsibility in communities of philosophical inquiry. *Childhood and Philosophy, 7,* 1-20.

Kizel, A. (2016). Pedagogy out of fear of philosophy as a way of pathologizing children. *Journal of Unschooling and Alternative Learning, 10*(20), 28-47.

Klein, N. (2008). *The shock doctrine: The rise of disaster capitalism.* Picador.

Koros, V. (2012). *Secret techniques for controlling sadness, anger, fear, anxiety, and other emotions.* Book Baby.

Korten, D. C. (2005). *The great turning: From empire to earth community.* Berrett-Koehler.

Krishnamurti, J. (1995). *On fear.* HarperCollins.

Krishnamurti, J. (1976). *The awakening of intelligence.* Discus Book/Avalon Books.

Krishnamurti, J. (1953/81). *Education and the significance of life.* Harper & Row.

Kuhn, T. (1962/96). *The structure of scientific revolutions.* [3rd ed.]. The University of Chicago Press.

Kumar, A. (2019). Music as meditative inquiry: Dialogical reflections on learning and composing Indian classical music. *Artizein: Arts and Teaching Journal, 4*(1), 98-121.

Kumar, B. M. (2021). Being fearless in the Republic. *The Hans India,* Jan. 25.

Kumar, B. M. (2020). Coexisting with corona, not fear. *Surya,* Teluga Newspaper, July 31.

Kumar, B. M. (2020a). Curing the corona fear. *The Hans India,* n.d.

Kumar, B. M. (2019). Chapter Three: Fear Factor. In *India, a nation of fear and prejudice: Race of the third kind* (pp. 7-9), by B. M. Kumar, R. M. Fisher & D. Subba. Xlibris.

Kumar, B. M. (2019a). Tax, they name is fear. *Telengana Today,* Aug. 28.

Kumar, B. M. (2019b). A tale of two Siddharthas. *Telengana Today,* Aug. 7.

Kumar, B. M., Fisher, R. M. & Subba, D. (2019). *India, a nation of fear and prejudice: Race of the third kind.* Xlibris.

Kumar, B. M., & Sushmita, B. S. (2018). *The youth don't cry: A critical commentary on the youth about their fears and hopes amidst adversities and opportunities.* Indra Publishing House.

Laing, R. D. (1960/73). *The divided self: An existential study in sanity and madness.* Penguin Books.

Lawler, J. (2002). We are (the) One!: Kant explains how to manipulate the Matrix. In J. Lawler (Ed.), *The Matrix and philosophy: Welcome to the desert of the real* (pp. 138-52). Open Court.

LeBeau, M. (1971). *Beyond doubt: A record of a psychic experience.* Harper & Row.

Leggo, C. (2011). Living love: Confessions of a fearful teacher. *Journal of the Canadian Association for Curriculum Studies, 9*(1), 115-44.

Lerner, H. D., & Lerner, P. M. (1988). *Primitive mental states and the Rorschach.* International Universities Press.

Levine, P. (2021). Immobility and fear. Retrieved from https://www.youtube.com/watch?v=LkqC2JEEe2o

Little, G. C. (1973). The gift of fear. *Good Housekeeping, 176*(3), 26, 28, 32, 34.

MacDorman, K. F. (2005). Mortality salience and the uncanny valley. *Proceedings of the 5th IEEE-RAS International Conference on Humanoid Robots,* pp. 399-405.

Mackie, F. (1985). *The status of everyday life: A sociological excavation of the prevailing framework of perception.* Routlege.

MacKeracher, D. (2007). *Making sense of adult learning.* [2nd ed.]. University of Toronto Press.

Martin, R. (2010). Integral situational ethical pluralism: An overview of a second-tier ethic for the twenty-first century. In S. Esbjörn-Hargens (Ed.), *Integral theory in action: Applied, theoretical, and constructive perspectives on the AQAL model* (pp. 253-72). State University of New York Press.

Maslow, A. H. (1966). *The psychology of science: A reconnaissance.* Gateway Editions.

Massumi, B. 2014). *What animals teach us about politics.* Duke University Press.

Massumi, B. (1993). Preface. In B. Massumi (Ed.), *The politics of everyday fear* (pp. vii-x). University of Minnesota Press.

Mathew, D. (2015). *Fragile learning: The influence of anxiety.* Karnac.

May, R. (1977). *The meaning of anxiety* (rev. ed.). Norton. [original published in 1950].

McHarg, I. (1971). *Design with nature.* Doubleday/Natural History Press.

McManaman, D. (2007). The gift of fear (teaching religion and fear of God to criminals). *Catholic Insight, 15*(1). n.p.

Mindell, A. (1993). *The leader as martial artist: An introduction to deep democracy.* HarperSanFrancisco.

Mobbs, D., et al. (2019). On the nature of fear. *Nature,* Oct. 10. Retrieved from https://www.scientificamerican.com/article/on-the-nature-of-fear/

Moreno, F. J. (1977). *Between faith and reason: Basic fear and the human condition*. Harper & Row.

Moreva, L. (2003). Reflections on paradigms of philosophizing. *Diogenes, 50*(1), 83-96.

Morin, M-T. (1998). Paradigm shifts. In S. M. Scott, B. Spencer, A. M. Thomas (Eds.), *Learning for life: Canadian readings in adult education* (pp. 59-70). Thompson Educational Publishing.

Murdock, M. (1990). *The heroine's journey*. Shambhala.

Narvaez, D. (2014). *Neurobiology and the development of human morality: Evolution, culture, and wisdom*. W. W. Norton.

Nelson, R. (1981). *A person-centered understanding of work and its implications*. A paper commissioned by the Labour Market Development Task Force, Government of Canada. Labour Market Development Task Force Technical Studies Series

Neufeld, H. D. (1979). *Cancerophobia: We are scaring ourselves to death*. Vantage Press.

Norcross, J. C. (1987). A rational and empirical analysis of existential psychotherapy. *Journal of Humanistic Psychology, 27*(1), 41-68.

O'Donohue, J. (with Tippett, K.) (2017). John O'Donohue: The inner landscape of beauty. Retrieved from https://onbeing.org/programs/john-odonohue-the-inner-landscape-of-beauty-aug2017/

Overstreet, B. W. (1951/71). *Understanding fear in ourselves and others*. Harper & Row.

Peale, N. V. (1963). *The power of positive thinking*. Fawcett.

Peck, M. S. (1988). *The different drum: Community making and peace*. Simon & Schuster.

Peters, T. J., & Waterman, R. H. (Jr.) (1982). *In search of excellence: Lessons from America's best-run companies*. Harper & Row.

Pinker, S. (2011). *The better angels of our nature: Why violence has declined*. Brilliance Audio.

Pirsig, R. (1984). *Zen and the art of motorcycle maintenance: An inquiry into values*. Bantam New Age Book.

Pirsig, R. (1976). *Zen and the art of motorcycle maintenance: An inquiry into values*. Bantam Books.

Portnoy, J. et al. (2014). Heart rate and antisocial behavior: The mediating role of impulsive sensation seeking. *Criminology, 52*(2), 292-311.

Pulcini, E. (2013). *Care of the world: Fear, responsibility, and justice in the global age.* [Trans. K. Whittle]. Springer.

Pyszczynski, T., Greenberg, J. & Arndt, J. (2011). Freedom vs. fear revisited: An integrative analysis of the dynamics of the defense and growth of self. In M. Leary & J. Tangney (Eds.), *Handbook of self and idenity* (pp. 378-404). (2nd ed.). Guilford.

Pyszczynski, T., Solomon, S. & Greenberg, J. (2002). *In the wake of 9/11: The psychology of terror.* American Psychological Association.

Reeves, A. N. (2012). *The next IQ: The next level of intelligence for 21st century leaders.* The American Bar Association.

Rella, F. (1994). The myth of the other: Lacan, Deleuze, Foucault, Bataille. *Postmodern Positions,* Vol. 7 [Trans. Nelson Moe]. Maisonneuve Press.

Reynolds, B. (2006). *Where's Wilber at?: Ken Wilber's Integral vision in the new millenium.* Paragon House.

Reynolds, B. (2004). *Embracing reality, the integral vision of Ken Wilber: A historical survey and chapter-by-chapter guide to Wilber's major works.* Jeremy P. Tarcher/Penguin.

Riley, S. (2004). U. S. culture of fear is expertly tilled to keep one from thinking. *Edmonton Journal,* July 18, A14.

Robin, C. (2004). *Fear: The political history of an idea.* Oxford University Press.

Rothenberg, Albert. 1971. "The Process of Janusian Thinking in Creativity." *Archives of General Psychiatry 24* (3) (March 1): 195-205.

Sandoval, C. (2000). *Methodology of the oppressed.* University of Minnesota Press.

Sardello, R. (1999). *Freeing the soul from fear.* Putnam Penguin.

Schaef, A. W. (1989). *Escape from intimacy: The pseudo-relationship addictions: Untangling the "love" addictions: Sex, romance, relationships.* Harper & Row.

Schaef, A. W. (1987). *When society becomes an addict.* HarperCollins.

Schumacher, E. F. (1977). *A guide for the perplexed.* Fitzhenry & Whiteside.

Seaton, E. (2001). The commodification of fear. *Topia: Canadian Journal of Cultural Studies, 5,* 1-18.

Simpkinson, C. H. (1995, May/June). Kosmological therapist. *Common Boundary, 7.*

Solomon, S., Greenberg, J. & Pyszczynski, T. (2015). *The worm at the core: On the role of death in life.* Random House.

Stiopu, A. L. (2020). Review [of book, *Exotic Fearology* by B. S. Adhikari] (pp. xiii-xxviii). Xlibris.

Subba, D. (2015). *The tribesman's journey to fearless: A novel based on fearism.* Xlibris.

Subba, D. (2014). *Philosophy of fearism: Life is conducted, directed and controlled by the fear.* Xlibris.

Svendsen, L. (2008). *A philosophy of fear.* Reaktion Books.

Tinnin, L. (1990). Obligatory resistance to insight. *The American Journal of Art Therapy, 28,* 68-70.

Toffler, A. (1981). *The Third Wave.* Bantam Books.

Trungpa, C. (2007). *Shambhala: The sacred path of the warrior.* C. R. Gimian (Ed.). Shambhala. [original published in 1984]

Turner, L. (2016). The gift of fear: Anxiety has been my constant companion. It has also kept me tethered to God. *Christianity Today, 60*(6), 76-81.

van Kessel, C., & Burke, K. (2018). Teaching as an immortality project: Positing weakness in response to terror. *Journal of Philosophy of Education, 52*(2), 216-29.

Varela, F. J., Thompson, E. & Rosch, E. (1992). *The embodied mind: Cognitive science and human experience.* The MIT Press.

Verdecchia, R. (n.d.) [with Suzuki, D.]. Be Afraid: The Science of Fear. Retrieved from https://www.cbc.ca/natureofthings/episodes/be-afraid-the-science-of-fear

Wachowski, L., & Wachowski, A. (2000). The Matrix. In S. Lamm (Ed.), *The art of The Matrix* (pp. 271-394). Newmarket Press.

Wahinkpe Topa (*Four Arrows*) (*aka* Jacobs, D. T.) (Ed.) (2006). *Unlearning the language of conquest: Scholars expose anti-Indianism in America.* University of Texas Press.

Walker, F. N. (1985). Avoiding a technological eclipse of education. *Elements: A Journal for Elementary Education, 27*(1), 7-10.

Walsh, R., & Vaughan, F. (Eds.) (1993). *Paths beyond ego: The transpersonal vision.* Tarcher/Perigree.

Watkins, A., & Wilber, K. (2015). *Wicked and wise: How to solve the world's toughest problems.* Urbane Publications.

Watts, A. (1972). *The book: On the taboo against knowing who you are.* Vintage Books.

Wheatley, M. J. (interviewed by A. Kleiner) (2007). Fearlessness: The last organizational change strategy. Retrieved from http://www.strategy-business.com/li/leadingideas/li00044?pg=1

Wheatley, M. J. (1999). *Leadership and the new science: Discovering order in a chaotic world.* Berrett-Koehler.

Whitfield, C. L. (1987). *Healing the child within: Discovery and recovery for adult children of dysfunctional families.* Health Communications, Inc.

Wilber, K. (2000). *Integral psychology: Consciousness, spirit, psychology, therapy.* Shambhala.

Wilber, K. (1995). *Sex, ecology and spirituality: The spirit in evolution* [Vol. 1]. Shambhala.

Wilber, K. (1982). *The Atman Project: A transpersonal view of human development.* The Theosophical Publishing House. [original published in 1980]

Wilber, K. (1981). *Up from Eden: A transpersonal view of human evolution.* Anchor Press/Doubleday.

Wilber, K. (1977/82). *Spectrum of consciousness.* The Theosophical Publishing House.

Williamson, M. (2021). Spirituality and psychedelics with Rick Doblin. Retrieved from https://podcasts.apple.com/us/podcast/spirituality-psychedelics-with-rick-doblin/id1536043190?i=1000512523635

Williamson, M. (1992). *A return to love: Reflections on the principles of A Course in Miracles.* HarperCollins.

ENDNOTES

1. Throughout the book we use *fear* (small letter) and *Fear* (capitalized), same with *fearlessness* and *Fearlessness*. It is a complicated reasoning, far beyond the scope of this book, to go into all of the theorizing for such distinctions. Suffice it to say, that when a capital is added to those terms, something grander, and more politically radical, is being represented than mere individual, emotional and behavioral psychological fear or fearlessness, the latter which is the common dictionary framing of their meaning.
2. "Fear's Empire" is a term borrowed from the sociologist Barber (2003).
3. E.g., Fisher (2018a).
4. Fisher (2010).
5. E.g., Furedi (2006), Glassner (1999).
6. Fisher (2019k).
7. E.g., Fisher (2021c).
8. Fisher & Subba (2016), see Introduction: Why Focus on Fear, Not Love? (pp. xxxi- xlii).
9. "Fear, even fearlessness, is still negative sounding," (Fisher, 2018, p. 167) referring to a dialogue between Indigenous-holistic educator Four Arrows and holistic educator Jack Miller, the latter who promotes love pedagogy. See also Fisher (2018), pp. 225-7 on energetics debate and New Age interpretations.
10. The scholarly and political history of "negative philosophy" over "positive philosophy" is complicated and not with only one set of interpretations, as it depends on the author describing these. Suffice it to say, generally, a "negative philosophy" is interested to focus on what is absent in the presentation of the "positive" thrust of a philosophy; or in other words, what is 'not being said, nor recognized as the deeper driver' of what is assumed most visible in the positive descriptions of a positive philosophical approach. E.g., a Love philosophy is a positive philosophy and a Fearism philosophy (*a la* Subba) is a negative philosophy because the "fear" (and/or fearlessness) aspects are excluded for the most part by the Love philosophy and its positivity (i.e., hopefulness). The negative philosophies typically are not classic progressive and liberal hope-mongering philosophies, a point that will come forth later in this book.

Guy Lardreau suggested that the new post-revolutionary condition after the 1970s in the Western world, at least, required a shift away from impossible old visions of "absolute revolt" (*a la* Marx, etc.) paradigms and politics of hope/promises of freedom/emancipation overall—and thereby, suggested: "Negative [political] philosophy is ineluctably worth more than any affirmation for, affirming nothing, it has no interest in [more] betrayal, and it never lies" (cited in Hallward, 2005, p. 770). In many ways, nondual philosophy, that arises at times in this book (e.g., the "fearless standpoint theory" of Fisher; *a la* Ken Wilber) is a negative philosophy.

11 Levine (2021).
12 Ibid.
13 Fisher (2012d).
14 Gebser (1949/84), p. 4.
15 Kumar & Sushmita (2018), Preface.
16 E.g., "culture of fear" has a vast literature but Furedi (2006) and Glassner (1999) are basic good references.
17 *Fear education* is discussed, for e.g., in Fisher (2003a, 2021b).
18 Of several publications on the *fearlessness paradigm*, e.g., see Fisher (2006a).
19 Robin (2004) called it a "politics of fear."
20 E.g. Fisher (2010, 2012).
21 Ibid., p. 165.
22 We do not romantically idolize youth today. We know they too are quickly conditioned by a culture of fear and thus will often lose-touch (i.e., repress) some of the best instincts and knowing that is in their unconscious and youthful memory systems. We have to be discerning and rigorous in any attachment of and valuation of wisdom to youth, but that also applies for all people.
23 Ibid., Preface.
24 Ibid., Desh Subba wrote, "The ocean is always youthful....It never feels tired, desperate, anxious and depressive. It has [an] enthusiastic, progressive and helpful mind. Our youth must make the ocean as their [ideal] role model" [for being fearless] (p. 18). Subba shows, like us, a reasonable reluctance to making adults role models for youth, especially, when it comes to the search and claiming of the best of true fearlessness. Re: "fearless," Fisher (2018) and Subba (2015) have pursued this interest of (alternative) radical ideal role models for good ways of living, through adopting an Indigenous worldview (perspective).
25 Fisher (2021).
26 Fisher (2000).
27 The two brothers, Cain and Abel, in the Biblical story is another example.
28 E.g., see Rothenberg (1971).
29 Azarian (in press).
30 See also "Why Focus on Fear, Not Love?" (Fisher & Subba, 2016, p. xxxi).

31 This premodern St. Augustinian theological idea may have some partial truth; but it is overly binary and static—and, thus, will not likely serve us well today in a 21st century complex world. Unfortunately, I (Michael) have seen this ontological claim revive itself in the new age movement around the teachings of *A Course in Miracles* (and the spiritual politics of Marianne Williamson).

32 Fisher (2012).

33 Fisher (2017).

34 In fact, Subba (2014) has 21 definitions of fear, and Fisher (2010) has 15+ definitions (and meanings) of fearlessness.

35 The use of a postmodern, critical, holistic-integral approach (*a la* Ken Wilber), philosophically and methodologically, is core to my work. And I have argued how it would challenge any kind of non-holistic definitions of fear *via* their inevitable skewing (reducing) reality and ways of knowing fear itself (e.g., see Fisher, 1995, 2006).

36 Kumar (2021).

37 Kumar, Fisher & Subba (2019).

38 Fisher (2003).

39 E.g., see Wilber (1977, 1995).

40 Williamson on her Twitter, Nov. 5, 2019. Retrieved from https://twitter.com/marwilliamson/status/ 1191844144240644096

41 Reason and rationality (rationalism) are the modernist's king pins to the W. unities, order/domination, advances, successes, and high status of knowledge/power (especially, *via* empiricism and science). But also, and much lesser known, are the disasters that have come from the W. Enlightenment in philosophy and values. Within relatively recent decades of postmodern thinking (e.g., Lacan, Deleuze, Foucault, Bataille to name a few, and with roots of dissent to ruling rationalism going back to Schopenhauer and Nietzsche in the 19th century) "A whole constellation of rationalities and discourses have arisen in opposition to this model of classical reason, which are the products of divergent, emergent social groups and classes, the products of the expansion of the 'sphere of conscious protagonists of social existence'....The crisis [philosophically and otherwise] consists not only of disorder and ill: is an imbalance but also a tense towards new orders. The contradictions cannot be [so easily] 'resolved,' but rather transformed. The terrain of this is undoubtedly political; it is the struggle, the fight..." (Rella, 1994, pp. 14-5). These new postmodern philosophies make up a *resistance* that has appealed to Fisher, in part, because of the disruption of the order of thought (rationality) that presumes it has the definition, meaning, and location of "fear" already figured out—and, thus, it likewise has (more implicitly) done so with "fearlessness." Fisher resists rationalism on this grounds, as well as on philosophical-asthetic-ontological-epistemological grounds (see Part II on A-ness and D-ness as models in his theory which reflect this conflict

between Rationalism and Arationalism, respectively).

42 See Subba (2014), Chapter 3.
43 Cited in Fisher (2010), p. 211.
44 Cited in Fisher (2010), p. 221.
45 Fisher (2021), p. 4.
46 From Jacobs (1998), p. 167.
47 "Learning is a dialectical process" (p. 8), wrote MacKeracher (2007), of which she classifies three major dimensions: interactive, constructive and transformative. Such learning is "a dialogical process" (p. 8)—and for us as co-authors, we are most particularly interested in our book on all these learning ways, therefore we often dialogue in the text, but ultimately our hearts are aimed toward the "transformative dimension": "Learning is *transformative* because it has the potential to lead to change. Personal meanings and one's personal model of reality can be changed during the constructive and interactive dimensions...One may retreat [i.e., resist] from possible changes and return to what is already know [comfortable, convenient]. But learning normally results in new or modified meanings that are then used to reconstruct previously existing meanings.... Transformations occur through differentiation (separating, distinguishing) and integration (connecting, combining), resulting in increasing complexity and inclusiveness" (p. 10). Throughout this co-authored book you will notice the emphasis on understanding "resistances" as part of transformative learning and that we continually encourage a learning that moves readers to experience and hold (i.e., integrate) more complex forms of knowledge, knowing and understanding re: fear/fearlessness than is typically taught to us in our fear management/education training in societies.
48 Fisher (2018), p. 2; see also Furedi (2006), Glassner (1999).
49 See further definition of "integral" in relation to "holistic" in terms of the "fearlessness paradigm" (e.g., Fisher, 2006a).
50 Four Arrows (2021) invokes 17 complementary opposites and two worldviews (Dominant and Indigenous) in which to organize them, of which #4 is "Anthropocentric ---> Non-Anthropocentric." The arrow indicates that ultimately the more heathy, sane and sustainable way of the polarity is an Indigenous worldview, that had operated well for 99% of human evolutionary history before the Dominant worldview onset around 10-12, 000 years ago (see also Four Arrows, 2016). His #2 of the pairs is "Fear-Based ---> Fearlessness-Based" and this is the crux of the motivational directionality (*telos*) that we as co-authors are most interested in for our book.
51 E.g., Fisher (1995, 1995a). "What exactly constitutes a 'definition' of 'fear'? I don't know and I am not sure anyone does. Imagine attempting to come up with a precise definition of 'Love'? Perhaps, with such large concepts/phenomenon as 'fear' and 'Love' we would better let poets assist us to understand. I do know

'fear' can be explored as an artist-scientist-philosopher in a type of 'renaissance approach.' With a new initiative and effort, 'fear' will be defined *better than* in the past" (Fisher, 1995, p. 6).

52   Fear and *consciousness* (i.e., waking up and/or going back asleep) are dialectical *via* Subba (2014), p. 24. More forthright, Subba (2014) claimed, "Fear can be considered consciousness, as knowledge and as disease. Liberation from fear needs medicine made for fear" (p. 25).

53   Kalu (2016).

54   LeBeau (1971), p. 177.

55   All fearism writers drift into this simple binary but it is also very common amongst most all writers on the subject and is part of the clinical psychological (and medical) paradigm. Fearist (Christian) philosopher-theologian, Eneyo (2019) relies heavily on this binary.

56   See Four Arrows (2016). By "Indigenous" for this book, we utilize the meaning as applying to primal peoples, Indians, Natives, First Nations, etc.—meaning those that have close natural ancestral connections to archaic cultures of people who lived off the land by the 'old ways' in "pre-contact" and/or "pre-colonized," and/or "pre-civilized" (so-called) ways. Arguably, these peoples were in much greater harmony with the laws of Nature than later evolved agriculturalized, urbanized and industrialized (now digitalized) societies. Four Arrows (2016) offers a great generic summary of their Indigenous worldview, contra the Dominant worldview of non-Indigenous cultures/societies.

57   Campbell & Moyers (1988), pp. 50-1.

58   Says Campbell, (Ibid., p. 51).

59   Adhikari (2020).

60   Stiopu (2020), p. xxiii.

61   A complex topic, beyond the scope of this book; yet, the great philosopher Alfred North Whitehead has been inspiring to Fisher over the years, off and on, in developing the basis of process philosophy.

62   This is hard to pin down but it means something to us. *Consciousness* is centralized as part of the philosophy we ascribe to—some other examples of philosophers of consciousness are Hegel, Wilber, etc. Desh Subba (2014) has also given consciousness great emphasis in his philosophy of fearism. Note, mind-based does not exclude body-based, it is merely a particular emphasis of orientation. Consciousness is part of everything (matter and spirit) in the (holistic-integral) consciousness philosophy approach.

63   "Fear can be considered consciousness....[historically] Fear was powerful, yet it remained invisible in knowledge" (Subba, 2014, p. 25). This invisibility issue is core to the fearist perspective of both Subba and Fisher—a type of "hidden" themata (i.e., a tricky epistemological problem in studying fear and fearlessness) that will come back at various moments in this book (see also Fisher & Subba,

2016, Chapter Three).

64 Excerpt from an interview with Fisher (2020).
65 Kumar (2019), p. 9.
66 Ibid., p. 8.
67 I'm (Fisher) struck by the similarity that Desh Subba also took an MBA in a W. university, as did A. K. Osinakachi in some form of business education degree—all of you some of the most astute supporters of the philosophy of fearism and my fearwork. I am the farthest away from ever being interested in a business education. That's part of a 'gap' I perceived long ago in encountering the fearist writings and attitudes, where the MBA-types are more conformist (if not conservative) societally and politically, than I am.
68 E.g., Fisher (2010), pp. 231, 265.
69 "In its established usage, a paradigm is an accepted [group-determined, and de-limited] model or pattern" for carrying out experimentation, data analysis, forming questions to research, and determining how to represent and share the data and results (e.g., in publications) (Kuhn, 1962, p 23).
70 Merton also wrote: "At the root of all war is fear." He hardly gave fear a lot of credit as benevolent, from what I have read of his mystical texts. See all quotes here from Merton, as cited in Fisher (2010), p. xi.
71 Excerpt from Fisher (2020).
72 de Becker (1997), p. 339.
73 Regardless what people may think about their *panic* experiences (and that can be subtle and diverse), de Becker (1997) makes a very confident mono-judgment/claim about it: "Panic, the great enemy of survival..." (p. 341). For him (pragmatically), terror is not the worst thing that can happen to someone, especially under high duress; rather, it is what one does with that terror (i.e., how they manage fear and panic) that concerns him most in terms of protecting them and them protecting themselves from harm—or even death.
74 Meg is following her fear instincts (so-called), while de Becker is giving her his expertise: "Ideally, when there is fear, we look around, follow the fear, ask [ourselves intuitively] what we are perceiving. If we are looking for some [pre-given] specific, expected danger, we are less likely to see the unexpected danger. I urge that she pay relaxed attention to her environment rather than paying rapt attention [i.e., worry] to her imagination [of possibilities, and specific worst scenarios that terrify her most]" (de Becker, 1997, p. 340). She's caught into a cycle of fear-positivity that in the short-run seems like it is useful, but in the long-run it is 'scaring her to death.' This latter paranoid phenomenon is incredibly insidious and contagious in a "culture of fear" (e.g., Glassner, 1999; Cohl, 1997).
75 Little (1973), p. 34.
76 Turner (2016), p. 77.

77 E.g., Anon (2008), McMahaman (2007).
78 These Christian stories all fall within the exoteric forms of the institutional mainstream of Christianity and not the mystical (esoteric) forms of the religion. The latter, are much more based on fearlessness-based, I would argue.
79 Fisher (2018), p. 241.
80 Ibid., (Chapter 7), p. 241.
81 See Fisher (2018).
82 Nathalie Moelhausen, 27 years old at the time—placed 5th in the 2016 Olympics.
83 Excerpt from Fisher (2018), p. 215.
84 This last quote is specifically from the scholar Raymond Aron (Robin, 2004, p. 27).
85 Although Robin himself was critical of this position they took (generally), he respected their views—see p. 30.
86 Ibid., p. 38.
87 I wrote, "people get addicted to "hope" (/fear),"—for a more nuanced conversation see e.n. 234 (in Fisher, 2010, p. 206); see also Fisher & Subba (2016), pp. xxxi, xxxiv.
88 It is my own conception, which I developed when I was in my early thirties. I made then some rough jottings now and then in my journal/diary.
89 We have as co-authors in some way been on a mission to promote a Gospel of Fearlessness in contradistinction (not in total opposition) to the Gospel of Fear (cf. "Gospel of Fearlessness" from a Gandhian philosophy website as cited in Fisher, 2010, p. 142-3). We also have not taken up all the streams of contributions to the fear-positivism directive, and at least we want to mention a powerful channel in the last few decades, especially recently is the conceptualization by biologists, ecologists, and evolutionists, that there is an "ecology of fear" that is a major vector of influence in ecological systems *via* predatory-prey balancing (i.e., biological regulation; e.g., see Brown, Laundré & Gurung, 1999). These scientists are contributing to make fear positive and essential to healthy systems. Again, their definition of "fear" is reductionistic and dubious. Not yet examined, is the contrasting cultural critic's conceptualization of an "ecology of fear" in urban studies (e.g., Davis, 1999), which posits a much less benign view of fear and its role in nature-culture juxtapositions.
90 E.g., the *abhaya dāna* (gift of fearlessness) tradition in S. Asian cultures, religions and philosophies has been studied by the scholar Hibbets (1999) and Heim (2004)—which, is the same person, who just changed their surname over time. We will return to this notion in much greater detail at various points throughout our book.
91 Cited from Ferguson (2005), p. 154.
92 From the fictional account of the life of Jesus, as interpreted by the film Director, Martin Scorese, ©1988 Universal Pictures.

93 Fisher (2021a).
94 Excerpt from book endorsement in Fisher & Subba (2016), front matter.
95 Subba (2014), pp. 19, 21, 13.
96 Ibid., p. ix.
97 Ibid., p. ix.
98 Fisher (2020).
99 E.g., Subba (2014).
100 Krishnamurit (1953/81), p. 34.
101 E.g., Fisher (2010), p. 231.
102 Dr. Daniel Goleman (1995) and many others have advanced this field of studies. Emotional Intelligence (EI) theory, is conceptually weak in our view because it only treats "fear," as one of the many emotions, through a neurobiological and psychological lens. This reductionism is hardly sufficient for a holistic-integral "fear education." The latter, treats fear as entirely unique (as a phenomenon) compared to all the other emotions (in EI).
103 "Fear is like Proteus—assuming a thousand different forms," (Assagioli, 1991, p. 169); for several other astute authors also making this association of *fear* with guises, shadows, etc. (see e.n. 7 in Fisher, 1995, p. 9; and see a great discussion by Overstreet, 1951/71, pp. 11-13).
104 "Our task is to look at the world and see it whole," (Schumacher, 1977, p. 15). The vision for working with a continuity spectrum of "Levels of Being" (and/or Consciousness, says Wilber, 1995), says Schumacher, points us in the direction of an ethical and epistemic search for multiple ways of seeing, knowing, understanding etc. that are adequate to the task of two basic processes: (a) cleaning-up the current dominating ways of knowing that have made us fearful, confused, delusion, depressed, unhealthy and violent etc., and (b) offering the bigger 'map' and directions for a true transformation and emancipation from that slavery that (a) represents, that is a path of Liberation from Oppression— which, Fisher calls "path of fearlessness" (e.g., Fisher, 2010). The four great levels of being, according to Schumacher, have each their distinct, but interrelated, concomitant demands of *"adaequatio"* (*aka* "adequateness") (p. 39).
105 Krishnamurti (1951/83), p. 35.
106 The great motivational psychologist noted a distinction between "growth-oriented" and "deficit-oriented" methodologies and knowledges—which, he ultimately called the latter "cognitive pathologies." Fisher calls these fear-based. These cognitive pathologies (he lists 21 of them) are so powerful in shaping the entire scientific way of knowing because of a chronic insecurity (i.e., "afraid of not knowing")—that they lead to a compulsive syndrome and situation whereby "reality itself doesn't matter," says Maslow, as long as a secure 'story' (of 'facts') can be concocted around it, and defended by so-called 'science.' In other words, he wrote, "knowledge-seeking behavior is primarily defensive" in

the deficit-oriented motivational paradigm (Maslow, 1966, p. 26).
107 Massumi (1993), pp. viii-ix.
108 Krishnamurti (1976), pp. 470-74.
109 Ibid., p. viii.
110 Krishnamurti (1976), pp. 470-74.
111 Ibid., [excerpted front matter Quotations].
112 Subba in Fisher, Kumar & Subba (2018), p. 113.
113 Kumar in Ibid., p. 112.
114 Ibid., p. 113.
115 Fisher & Subba (2016a); re-quoted in Ibid., p. 102.
116 Ibid., p. 100.
117 Ibid., p. 102.
118 Fisher coined this c. 2015-16 to distinguish it from Subba's fearism.
119 Barber (2003).
120 E.g., also called "War of Fear" (rather than "War on Terror"), Fisher (2010), p. xvii. Fisher, originally coined the term "Fear Wars" c.1998 during his graduate work; see also in Fisher (2003a), p. 17.
121 This is discussed in more detail under "Fearless" (FMS-9) in Fisher (2010), pp. 76-7.
122 See Fisher (2010); note, Subba (2014) also saw this trajectory, independently of Fisher; see Subba's (2014) "Fear Ages" which end in a "Fearless Age" theoretically (pp. 44-6).
123 This causal relationality of fear/fearlessness is discussed in the dialectical thinking of Introduction 1; it is also generally a demonstration of Fisher's notion, based in genetics and instinct (i.e., Defense Intelligence), that all living systems regulate themselves *via* this kind of dynamic 'correction.'
124 Fearism includes but also transcends existentialism, according to Fisher & Subba (2016), pp. xxv, 2, 97, 157.
125 Subba (2014), p. 307.
126 Ibid., p. 312.
127 Ibid., p 301.
128 Ibid., p. 296.
129 Ibid., p. 299.
130 Ibid., p. 273.
131 Ibid., p. 164.
132 Ibid., p. 152.
133 Subba (2015), p. 85.
134 Ibid., p. 72.
135 Adhikari (2020), p. 159.
136 Ibid., p. 156.
137 Kalu (2017), p. 56.

138 Ibid., p. 51.
139 Kumar (2021).
140 Kumar (2020).
141 Kumar (2020a).
142 Kumar (2019).
143 His exact term is "quantum of fear", see pp. 76-81 in Fisher, Kumar & Subba (2018).
144 Kumar (2019b).
145 Adhikari, Kalu & Subba (2020), p. 160.
146 Ibid., p. 167.
147 Quoted from Hindu spiritual guru Sai Baba Gita (cited in Fisher, 2010, pp. 180-1).
148 See Fisher (2019).
149 E.g., see Furedi (2006), Glassner (1999).
150 Subba (2014), p. 11.
151 Go to https://fearismstudies.blogspot.com/
152 Quotes from Ibid., pp. 11-12.
153 "Second attention" is taken, in part, from the concept as developed in shamanistic traditions of Indigenous peoples—in part, as explicated by the mystical anthropologist Carlos Castaneda (e.g., https://www.carlos-castaneda.com/category/the-second-attention/).
154 For more info. on The Sedona Method, see https://www.youtube.com/watch?v=CADTkM1aoP8
155 For a fearism perspective on law, criminology and policing, see discussion by Fisher, Subba & Kumar (2018).
156 E.g., see Fisher & Subba (2016), p. 40. The reason a "cultural therapy" (*via* transdisciplinarity) is suggested by Fisher's work is because of the meta-context of the "culture of fear." The basic logic is: if you now live not just in a culture and have a fear problem, and evidence shows, you live in a culture of fear now, then you have a Fear Problem on a scale far greater than the first instance of carrying on one's existence as a sociocultural being. In the latter instance, therefore, one needs not just a psychological therapy but a cultural therapy; and, ideally, one needs both to be highly integrated. That is the point of all the mentioning of the term "holistic-integral" throughout our book.
157 See Whitfield (1987).
158 All Whitfield quotes from pp. 10-11.
159 Laing (1960).
160 E.g., see the 1972 documentary film *Asylum* (https://www.youtube.com/watch?v=_8-Z4clSrRM).
161 There is a vast growing, transdisciplinary study, of "schizo" and "schizoidal" and "schizoanalysis" which we have not studied sufficiently here. We recommend

it, however, as very important in understanding the nature of the 'crime' (i.e., *escape*) that this Chapter One addresses in the first part. Laing (1960), wrote, "The term schizoid refers to an individual the totality of whose experience is split in two main ways: in the first place, there is a rent in his [sic] relation with his world and, in the second, there is a disruption of his relation with himself. Such a person is not able to experience himself 'together with' others or 'at home in' the world, but, on the contrary, he experiences himself in despairing aloneness and isolation...not...as a complete person but rather as 'split' in various ways, perhaps as a mind more or less tenuously linked to a body, as two or more selves, and so on" (p. 17) [note: link with Marx's philosophy/theory of alienation or Freud's philosophy/theory of dissociation]

162 E.g., see Fisher (2016).
163 Four Arrows (2016).
164 E.g., Schaef (1989).
165 Schaef (1987).
166 Ibid., p. 150.
167 Schaef (1989), p. 101.
168 E.g., Fromm (1941).
169 For a good review of the literature, see Pyszczynski, Greenberg & Arndt (2011).
170 Fromm (1941), p. 160.
171 Trungpa (1984), pp. 33, 75.
172 Fisher (2008), pp. 143-4.
173 Leggo (2011). The late Dr. Carl Leggo was my former research co-supervisor.
174 Fisher (2008), p. 145.
175 Fisher, Quaye & Pope (2008).
176 Dr. Blaine Pope [at the time] was a Columbia University Professor of Environmental Science and Policy.
177 The actual voice/writing here is by Four Arrows for the fictional character Dr. Samson (DS).
178 Pope in Fisher, Quaye & Pope (2008), p. 148.
179 Reeves (2012).
180 Peters & Waterman (1982).
181 Fisher's exploration here led him back to the early 1980s and the breakthrough work and theory of "total quality management" (TQM) *via* the great (American) leader of his movement, W. Edwards Deming; Fisher (2010) wrote, "Some other important names...that stand out as leaders of fearlessness [i.e., Fearlessness Movement, see Part III] in a revolutionary sense are the late W. Edwards Deming and his "without fear" principle in organizational manage-ment and leadership (TQM)" (p. 21).
182 Pirsig (1976).
183 Wheatley & Kleiner, (2007).

184 Quoted in Kumar & Sushmita (2018), p. 86.

185 Ibid., p. 87.

186 Other than a natural attraction to 'Indians' and their warriors in child stories I heard or watched on TV, my commitment to what great teachings come from warrior traditions then led to study the E. martial arts philosophies and finally I began a School of Sacred Warriorship (1993-97), later evolved to Neo-Rebel School, for teens and adults in Calgary, AB, an essential component of the 'fear' vaccines, as part of my work in the In Search of Fearlessness Community.

187 Trungpa (1984), p. 37.

188 Mindell (1993), p. 40.

189 Kahane (2010) has refined this paradigmatic practice of social change into "Power" and "Love"—and, argues they can be working against each other, or for each other. Fisher's reading of this dual motivational theory by Kahane is very interconnected to the grand archetypal meta-motivations of "Fear" and "Love" respectively. Unfortunately, Kahane has no theory of fearlessness in between Fear and Love.

190 Dr. Randall Auxier (book endorsement review) in front matter of Fisher (2021c).

191 Williamson (1992), pp. 190-1.

192 Fisher (2021d).

193 See Fisher's (2021c) rationale for his position particularly on Williamson's political and cultural leadership in these times.

194 This echoes the dictum of H. G. Wells in the early 20th century: "Civilization is in a race between education and catastrophe."

195 See the "Mechanical" [19th century] Paradigm is contrasted in Part III with the "Organic" [20th-21st century] Paradigm in terms of aesthetic-metaphoric models (designed by Fisher for teaching purposes).

196 Fisher (2010), pp. 50-1.

197 Desh Subba, equally is very cognitively-oriented in his philosophy of fearism book (2014).

198 E.g., "Existential psychotherapy [or sociology] facilitates the client's exploration of what he or she really longs for, not only in the instinctual [Id] unconscious but also in spiritual aspirations. Existentialism is not an ego psychology if the ego is a reflection of the outer world, a compromiser, and a relatively weak portion of the personality. In contrast, being is the total experiencing person—prior to the subject-object dichotomy. A new mode of feeling and living emerges when a person begins to understand that existence [itself—and, reflecting in being itself] is tremendously important to him or her, and that the fact *that* he or she is quite different from the fact that she or he is a person. Being implies nonbeing or nothingness. If people are to grasp what it means to exist, they must confront the fact that at any given moment they may cease to exist. People may become alienated from the source of their being because of their [and society's] anxiety

about the inevitability of death....Anxiety [fear] is an ontological characteristic of every person....Anxiety is not something we have, but something we are (May, 1977)" (Norcross, 1987, p. 46). Thus fearlessness, as Fisher would argue from a transdisciplinary and transpersonal perspective, is the path of the existential-plus onward to the ultimate potential of existence, with its unique characteristics that are 'human' and beyond merely animal-laden consciousness that knows of death on its way. Such an existential to fearlessness existence does not try to erase fear/anxiety per se, but focuses on higher developmental processes and consciousness and self-identity structures that eventually can become more nondual in their structuring of what it means to be a self-in-the-world of Creation. Yes, spiritual is the dimension being referred to as one touches into the existential, and thus, as co-authors we invoke all good leaders and leadership for the 21st century to be well-knowledgeable if not steeped in spirituality dimensions. It is absolutely necessary to transform the toxic anxiety, fear, dread, terror and panic that will continue to rise—that is, until there is a paradigm shift from a Fear Paradigm (culture) to a Fearlessness Paradigm (culture).

199 Wilber (1977), p. 151.
200 Krishnamurti (1995).
201 Philosophically (arguably), our predominant consciousness is based in egoistic dualism; it takes nondualism (at least theoretically) as a trans-egoic standpoint and consciousness in operation to see beyond dualism (e.g., see the new psychological field of transpersonal or trans-egoic studies—e.g., Walsh & Vaughan (1993). Fisher has studied this tradition and as well has studied the new postmodern cultural approaches to getting outside of these egoistic-dualistic structurations *via* what he calls *fearlessness as a path*; and a good example, is the way of becoming a "Matrix Warrior" (Horsley, 2003; Fisher, 2003).
202 E.g., Watkins & Wilber (2015). "At this stage in our evolution, as a species there are simply not enough people who are sufficiently mature or evolved in their thinking [perspectives] to really appreciate this [complexity] dynamic. Wicked problems are therefore fundamentally developmental problems, and if we really want to find a constructive way forward we need to adapt and take a quantum leap in our level of thinking [i.e., to integral and FMS-7/8] so we can address the issues instead of just pretending that they don't exist or that they don't concern us because the nasty unpleasant symptoms are occurring on a different continent to a different 'tribe.' And this means very specifically...that part of the solution to wicked problems will involve the actual growth and development of the consciousness of the change agents themselves" (p. 41). The Fear Problem, in Fisher's view, is a wicked problem. And, Fearlessness is, more or less, its ultimate solution.
203 Subba (2014), pp. 14-18.
204 For Fisher, the very meaning of *fear-based* (Fisher, 2013) and the imbued

oppressive colonializing of the very commonest definitions and meanings of *fear* (Fisher, 2016a) have to be carefully tweezed out, something Subba's philosophy of fearism has ignored, creating the epistemological weakness Fisher points to. Fisher (2019b, 2019c) brings a radical "fearlessnessizing" as a new form of fearlessness psychology itself to correct this.

205 Fisher's *fearless standpoint theory* (also FMS-9) is important to understanding the transpersonal, kosmological, nature of my critical integral framework of fear management systems (FMSs) and consciousness itself (i.e., nondual standpoint). See Fisher (2010) and for e.g., Fisher (2019a). "Fearless" is thus categorically unique from "Fearlessness," of which I am vigilant to distinguish, and most everyone else is not.

206 E.g., Fisher (2019b).

207 However, the *return* is never into the same river. Something prior to the return has been experienced, learned, and some growth achieved. Perspective changes, perhaps with each of these leavings and returnings—in a grand *spiral of development* inherent in the design of evolution of consciousness itself—and, the nature of the self-identity with that.

208 See "Fishbowls: Integral Dialectics of Love and Fear" (Fisher & Subba, 2016, pp. 34-5).

209 Fisher distinction of toxic fearism (e.g., Fisher, 2006, p. 51), which is directly linked to oppression systems/discourses and "political fear" and the "culture of fear" and 'Fear' Matrix. This is also connected to the culturally modified 'fear' that Fisher often uses in his work. *Fearism-t* was coined by Fisher to distinguish it from Subba's *Fearism* notion (see definitions in Fisher & Subba, 2016, p. 157).

210 Most people would not think "vulnerability" is a core quality of *fearlessness*, especially in how the W. tends to construct this term—believing that fearless(ness) ought to be about invulnerability—like a 'bullet proof' psychology—etc. That needs to be balanced and corrected by a much more ancient E. wisdom/tradition re: fearlessness (as gift; e.g., see Heim, 2004), of which Trungpa (2007) addresses and as recognized well within Buddhism and the "fearless heart" dharma teachings; for example: "We are born at the mercy [gift] of someone else's care. We grew up and survived into adulthood because we received care from others. Even at the height of our autonomy as adults, the presence or absence of others' affection [attention] powerfully defines our happiness or misery. *This is human nature—we're vulnerable...*" (quote from Thupten Jinpa (2016), n.p., in a book review). Chödrön (2001), a pupil of Trungpa, summarized the "Disciplines of Mind Training" in the practice of fearlessness and gives several commandments, two of which are intriguing in terms of poignant practices to bring up one's sense of vulnerability—especially, in the context of the rugged individualist, competitive, goal-seeking daily living 'norm' of a typical modern culture/society. They are: "Always maintain only a joyful mind....Abandon any hope of fruition"

(i.e., of one's aims and ideologies) (p. 127). Ultimately, Chödrön (2001) advises, "go to the places that scare you."
211 Gibb (1991).
212 E.g., https://www.verywellmind.com/trust-versus-mistrust-2795741
213 Eisler (1987).
214 E.g., Fisher (2012, 2017).
215 Watts (1972).
216 Two versions are out there: (1) *autophobia* -Fear of self: An irrational fear of oneself, an intense self-fear that is groundless. Fear of oneself is termed *autophobia,* which comes from two Greek words: "autos" (self) and "phobos" (fear) = literally, self-fear, fear of oneself and (2) the one Subba (2014) uses: "fear of being alone or by oneself" (p. 337). Our discussion is more directly about the pathology of the first version but the versions overlap. *Anthrophobia-* fear of people or society (Subba, 2014, p. 336)—is also, directly related to autophobia. The deeper issue beyond phobias, is what is happening that makes one fear themselves, their species, their society? (or as Cohl, 1997 put it, *Why are we scaring ourselves to death?*). At what point, are our many-named and listed phobias actually an oppressive structural form of even further scaring ourselves to death? A legitimate, liberational, philosophy of fearism and fearlessness have to ask (at least) this question. Psychiatrists and psychologists who rely on the phobias list, for example, are not likely ever going to be a solution to the Fear Problem—they may, easily become part of it.
217 Whitfield (1987), Laing (1960).
218 E.g., Keen (1985), Murdock (1990).
219 Fisher (2010), p. 48-52.
220 Fisher's suggests this map (defense design) may also apply, to some degree, to all living creatures/systems.
221 See Beck & Cowan (1996) on Spiral Dynamics and Leadership.
222 It would take a long explanation to explain these different conceptions Fisher has re: human nature, condition, potential; but he has defined them briefly in Fisher (1997), p. 47. Basically (generalizing grossly), FMS-0 is closest to our "human nature" and FMS-1 to 6 is closest to our "human condition" (especially, the 'Fear' Matrix in Figure 3); and FMS-7 to 9 is our "human potential." Fearlessness *is* our human potential—it *leads* us to our human potential.
223 We are referring to a very expanded conception of the "magician" than what most people associate in the everyday world. Today, in organizational development and management literature, studies have shown that some people learn skills of the sort that are outstanding in how to work with creativity, vision, conflict, problems, people and systems. They think not just 'magically' (as in say, irrational), but they are highly intuitive, see in the invisible and energetic realms of reality—and, are several steps around the corner in vision/consciousness

development compared to most; that is, where others cannot see what is going on beyond the obvious and what is right in front of their face (i.e., the visible aspects of a system). For e.g., Borje, Fedor & Rowland, 1982) spoke about the role here of magician as intertwined with "myth-making" in modern organizations and leadership in order to bring about change and transformation (p. 19).

224 "Truly, the [authentic, fearless, wise] leader is more fearless...for fears have already been confronted....They are old familiar foes of the [sacred] warrior" (Barr & Barr, 1989, p. 173); see also Fisher (2003), Horsley (2003), Trungpa (2007).

225 We are not the only ones to suggest this. It starts and ends with the cycle of oppression, which in more basic terms is the cycle of hurting—where, hurting people hurt others and pass it on (see e.g., Jackins, 1965)—when there is no feasible alternative—like healing and self-regulation of distress and unhealed painful memories.

226 See the analogy with *Indigenizing* that is being introduced by many Indigenous-based scholars and educators—of which, I have taken this to *fearlessnessizing* (e.g., Fisher & Four Arrows, 2020; Fisher, 2019c).

227 Trungpa (2007).

228 There's a larger debate about whether the Fearlessness Paradigm has within it a "competition" drive or not. Fisher says 'not.' It is the Fear Paradigm that has such an egoic-death-drive and it is the 'enemy' thus of Fearlessness; but not the other way around, according to Fisher and his "fearless standpoint theory" perspective on this reality of wars over ideas and paradigms, etc.

229 Kuhn (1962).

230 E.g., Wilber (1995).

231 Fisher (2000).

232 Cited In Fisher (2010), p. 266.

233 Cited in Ibid., p. 267.

234 Narvaez (2014), n.p.

235 E.g., Fisher (2016b).

236 E.g., Fisher (2019d).

237 E.g., Fisher (2012a).

238 Ferguson (2005), p. 154.

239 Hindu spiritual teacher Sai Baba Gita says "Of all the great virtues, fearlessness occupies the place of primary importance. It is the ideal virtue"; and according to *Brihadaranyaka Upanishad 1.4.2* "Fearlessness is the fruit of perfect Self Realization," a cardinal virtue (cited e.g., here in Fisher, 2010, pp. 180, 79).

240 Cited in Cristian (2012); in Sartre's own words: "Maybe its [the ego's] essential role is to conceal [*masquer*] from consciousness its own spontaneity [i.e., expressions of authentic freedom]" (p. 34).

241 Throughout this book we have referenced the importance in our theorizing

and philosophy of fearism that it ought to be *holistic-integral*. Desh Subba has agreed with this overall approach (Fisher & Subba, 2016). It is considered the better way to go to achieve a richer, diverse, healthier and 'whole' sense of what the Fear and Fearlessness phenomena actually are (and, thus, this has included the transdisciplinary approach). Wilber (1995) has offered extensive philosophizing around the classic 'Big Three' spheres of reality and knowing, and so, we are relying somewhat on that Wilberian integral context in this book. What Wilber has made very evident is that each of the three great spheres need to be in intimate communication with each other ongoing, to enable a greater integrity and health of the 'Whole.' With modernity, Wilber argues, there's been a tendency of over-differentiation, and even pathological dissociation, in the three spheres—which has had disastrous results. For example, *the True* (Sciences and the "It" perspective) has really dominated the other two spheres since the 17th century and W. Enlightenment. See Wilber for more analysis. *The Beauty* (Arts and Humanities and "I" perspective) have, with *the Good* (Religion and Morality and "We" perspective), been forced into subordinate (if not distorted) roles in society and the production of knowledge/power. Any good 'new' holistic-integral education (and "Fear Education" and/or "Fear Studies") ought to take into account this need for a correction of balance in the three spheres. Our emphasis on Beauty (and the "I" perspective) in this chapter is thus an intervention for a more balanced reflectivity, methodology, and understanding of fear/fearlessness.

242 E.g., Alexander (1977).
243 E.g., Bickel (2020).
244 E.g., Jackins (1965).
245 Fisher has long argued, and it's not an original notion, that 'evil' is 'live' spelled and operating backwards—more technically, it is a movement/pattern/design in retro-regression and de-evolutionary spiralling.
246 E.g., Keeney (1985).
247 E.g., Bateson (1979).
248 Geist (1978), Chapter Five.
249 McHarg (1971).
250 See Jackins (1972).
251 See Kumar's 11 questions in Fisher (2021e).
252 One musician-academic-educator, Ashwani, wrote, "Rather than worrying about seeking approval from the authority figures or following the defined stages of learning music, I intuitively sensed my potential [and creativity], and I carried on learning and composing music....this is what I call *intrinsic intelligence* or an intuitive trust in life [the universe]....Slowly, I realized that what I was singing, playing, and composing was good *because it was coming from my heart.* After I realised that, I didn't care [fear] if anyone enjoyed and approved it or

not" (Kumar, 2019, p. 104).

253 In teaching A-D/ness theory, I (Fisher) often tell a story from the mid-to-late 1980s, when I was working as a family therapist at Quest Ranch. I got called to present at a professional development day for 12 psychologists and psychiatrists, who were working at an established and prestigious adolescent treatment center in Calgary. Before going far with my workshop and lecture, I handed out the 10+ original questions that go with A-D/ness model. I projected with a 35 mm slide the image on a screen so everyone (btw: all white males) in the room could see them clearly. I gave the minimum description of my Creator's originary question to the survey and then gave them a sheet of the questions to answer about the diagrams. The short of the story is, at one point in going over their collective data results, we arrived at the question "Which is the most healthy?" and I asked them to show their hands regarding who chose 'A' – zero; who chose 'B'—all hands arose, except one. I then said, "I would choose 'D' as the healthiest." Oh, wow. The room went completely silent and still and their faces were obviously bewildered and some very angry. One young man shouted out, "That's wrong!" Meaning, my answer was 'wrong' in his view. I told them I had done years of research on the background bases, rationale and philosophy for why I gave my answers on the questions the way I did, for after all I was the 'test-maker' designer and I better (ought to) know the 'right' answers (to many of the questions, not all). Well, that surely wasn't going over well at all. The young man was so agitated that I did not back down from my view of D-ness as healthiest. I asked him: "What is the problem you have with D-ness, then?" He immediately shouted with absolute certainty in his body and voice, although, I could see he was trembling with obvious anger, and more subtly with fear, if not terror in his voice: "D is schizophrenic!" I stayed calm, almost predicting this would be a typical judgement from a typically-trained psychiatrist or psychologist these days. I said, "Why would you diagnose D that way?" And, he replied, "Because it has no boundaries?" By which, he implied it was pathological—a representation of a psychological disorder. I replied: "Sir, do you see a rectangular shape in the model 'D'?" He reluctantly looked at the projection on the screen and pondered momentarily, of which of course, all the people in the room were also doing the same; and, with some resistance he admitted, "yes." I replied: "Exactly. Then it is a model of drawing/coloring and making that is with boundaries, otherwise you would not see a rectangular shape." My point, and critique of his assessment was made. There was no argument from that point. I concluded: "D-ness just represents a very different way of getting to a rectangle, that's all—it is still a rectangle." I went on further to explain the Organic Paradigm (based on C-ness and D-ness)—and gave a little fuller articulation of my model of human nature and what happens in "culture" to trim down D-ness to move and reshape itself as a way of organizing reality and a sense of self—to eventually, with enough

traumatization, it becomes A-ness. Wow. What a teaching moment that was for us all. Btw, the one dissenter in the room? It was their senior supervisor of the entire clinical staff. Later, I looked at his data sheet, which he had put his name on, and he was near totally in agreement with all my answers to the questions in the test. He was definitely D-ness positive—that is, he saw the Organic paradigm of organizing reality as the "healthiest" and a good deal more, he showed results on the test quite different in most cases from his staff members. I knew that was going to be a deep problem for that organization in the years to come unless they could talk about their worldview differences, if not conflicts, and the impacts it has on everything going on in that institution. I still cringe to this day when I think about all those B-ness psychiatrists and psychologists making judgements upon young adolescents' lives and behaviors, values and ideas, because they as "adults" and as "experts" supposedly 'know best' what is healthy and what is not. I dare say, these psychiatrists and psychologists as a collective are 'schizoid' (of which, I could provide many other labels).

254 Kalu (2016).
255 E.g., Fisher (1986, 2012b).
256 E.g., Fisher (2020a).
257 A more nuanced reading, would suggest A-ness is the most fragile—and, explosive, aimed at self/system-destruction most of the time. It is in crisis, but doesn't recognize it is. That's the worst form of ignore-ance (pathology—cum evil) on the planet.
258 Jackins (1965).
259 Anonymous (2020).
260 The A-ness method is used by artists at times, like the famous Mondrian—albeit, they use it consciously in exploration rather than as unconscious habit.
261 Pirsig (1984), p. 263.
262 For any critics, who want to immediately think that I am creating an absolute philosophy/ideology of *objectivism* that therefore cannot be challenged, you can forget it; because I have no such intention to promote it or state anything, and then claim it is absolutely objective—meaning *only* objective. Fundamentalists of all stripes do that. That would be a ridiculously untenable, and deluded, as a posture to take by myself or anyone really. Critics will have to recall my holistic-integral approach, always critical, and doubtful, is a fearlessness perspective, far from such a stance that is so *fear-based* and *A-ness-based* that it is utterly ugly, violent, and abominable, if not evil.
263 Since late-1989, I (Fisher) have labeled it *'fear' pattern virus* (FPV+). This is not the same, by quantum measure, as "fear" by which humans typically define it. Most everyone, ignores this part of my *fear theory* when they discuss my work. Thus, I get a lot of (mis-)interpretations and citing of my work, which is only partially accurate, and mostly distortive in many cases.

264 Some of this loss of Quality, comes from Martin Heidegger's critique of "technological thinking" and Barrett's (1979) critique of "technique" over-infatuation (e.g., see Walker, 1985, p. 7). There's a tremendous Quantification over Quality that is happening in this techno-digital revolution and eclipse and it is still going on. A-ness is the perfect symbol/template of *quantification*—that is, you can measure A-model and reproduce it exactly quite easily, like on an assembly line of widgets all the same; whereas, D-ness is impossible to do so. D-ness resists that homogenization. Alfred North Whitehead said, "as we think, we live," meaning as we pattern our thinking on certain preferred templates/designs/architectures then the pattern of our lives follows that (Walker, p. 7). For example, wanting all schools to have computers and their template programs at every students desk, and in their homes, is a sign of this near-total eclipse that's so dangerous to our holistic aesthetic development, critical thinking, and our ability to live healthy lives. Further on the theme of Whitehead, the epistemologist Gregory Bateson (1972) wrote, "Beliefs [mostly unconscious] about what sort of world it is will determine how [one] sees it and acts within it, and [one's] ways of perceiving and acting will determine [one's] beliefs about its nature. The living is thus bound within a net of epistemological and ontological premises which—regardless of ultimate truth or falsity—become partially self-validating..." (p. 314).
265 Fisher (2021).
266 Gillian (2002) book title; he also wrote within that book: "Courage is positive fear" (p. 22). Gillian is one of the exceedingly rare few of African-Americans, who is non-Christianized, to specialize in the topic *fear*—and, specifically, fear and education (see Fisher, 2020c).
267 Toffler (1981), p. 9.
268 Wilber (1996), p. 198.
269 Martin (2010), p. 253.
270 Four Arrows (2018).
271 Fisher (2020d).
272 I (Fisher) have a long and sophisticated integral philosophical meaning frame by which "deep" is made meaning and defined. You can read some of that in Ken Wilber's *philosophia* work (Reynolds, 2004, p. xx), for e.g., re: 'deep sciences" and "deep structures" in consciousness and evolution or "Deeper Order" and "deeper psychic" phenomenon, etc. (e.g., see Reynolds, 2004, pp. 167, 190, 222, 229, 290, 345). Wilber (2000) wrote in his deep poetic nondual Zen Buddhistic way: "A person's deepest drive—the major drive of which all others are derivative—is the drive to actualize the entire Great Nest [of Being] through the vehicle of one's own being, so that one becomes, in full realization, a vehicle of Spirit shining radiantly into the world, as the entire world. We are all the sons and daughters of a Godhead that is the Goal and Ground of every

gesture in the Kosmos, and we will not rest until our own Original Face greets us with each dawn" (quoted from *Integral Psychology* (2000) by Ken Wilber, in Reynolds, 2004, front matter).

273 Many postmodern, existential and spiritual-based progressive theorists have talked of this ontological "fragility" and/or or "fragile learning" (e.g., Mathew, 2015) within the context of ontological insecurity (anxiety, angst), and precarity, etc. The old Rationalism and Modernism (R & M) discourses have repudiate this reality and attempted to defend it off; one can see this resistance of such stable (R & M) discourses reflected in the Mechanical (solid) vs. the Organic (liquid) paradigms in the A to D models, respectively. Whatever the form of defense (and/or ideology) present and working, and trying to dominate the reality-scene, one could assess this all through the fearism lens and concluded such 'devices' (i.e., defenses) are themselves "anxiety containers" attempting to manage anxiety itself. Now, just substitute the word "fear" for "anxiety" as fearists do, and you start to see the underlying methodology of analysis in this book and others we have co-authored together prior. Basically, A, B, C, D as diagrams are literally and symbolically anxiety-containers. Many techniques for relaxation and mindfulness and emotional management, including Fear Management Systems (Fisher, 2010) are "anxiety containers" (e.g., Koros, 2012). The question is, that the fearist and fearanalyst must ask: Are anxiety containers the only or *best* way to manage anxiety? What are their limitations, in terms of a larger liberation potential along the path of fearlessness? Fisher talks of this problem a good deal in his work on the limitations of fear management/education discourses of the first-tier (e.g., FMS-1 to 6).

274 This intentional holarchical ordering of importance of these platforms or dimensions, is based on Fisher's reading of the artist-psychoanalyst-theorist-activist Bracha L. Ettinger, founder of "matrixial theory," and is also found in other's writings like the philosopher John Dewey and Fisher & Bickel (in preparation).

275 From a holistic-integral perspective, "Kosmos" is favored, in resisting materialist reductionism, because conceptually it has more depth over "Cosmos," as explained by Ken Wilber (see Reynolds, 2004, e.g., pp. 8, 68, 227, 284, 342).

276 Evernden (1993), p. xi.

277 The essence of this 'Fear' Matrix is well demonstrated in the deep artful reflection that comes from *The Matrix* sci-fi trilogy of films (1999-2003) by The Wachowski's (see Fisher, 2003). According to critical analysis of the films, the philosopher James Lawler (2002) wrote, "The world of the Matrix is a world of fear" (i.e., run by the *illusion* of *separation* or dualism; when there is liberation *via* non-dualism available in the Oneness of the existence and principles of the Universe as the really Real) (p. 147).

278 Although there are several other social critics who have mentioned "flatland"

and "one-dimensional" thinking and humans, etc., the critique of integral philosopher Ken Wilber (1996, pp. 336-9) is by far the most outstanding and relevant to what is going on ontologically in contemporary (and postmodern) discourse power/knowledge regimes to undermine anything with depth, holistic-integral dimensionality. For e.g., Wilber wrote, "Only by rejecting flatland can the Good and the True and the Beautiful be integrated" (pp. 336-7).

279 Lerner & Lerner (1988), p. 420.
280 Kizel (2021), p. 5.
281 He cites here Kizel (2016), p. 28.
282 See Four Arrows' CAT-FAW/N model (e.g., Four Arrows, 2016), where 'A' in FAW stands for *Authority*, by which we need to be conscious of the hypnotic impacts authority-figures have, especially when we are in a state of *Fear* (the 'F' in FAW). This is core to his arational-centric TBL (Trance-based Learning) theory of education (and pedagogy).
283 Kizel (2021), p. 5.
284 Fisher (2020e).
285 E.g., Gur-Zé ev (2010).
286 E.g., Fisher (2011).
287 See Kizel (2016). In my own work, I have linked *fearism-t* with *adultism*—as core to the deepest ideological fear-based forms of all oppressions (e.g., Fisher, 2003). If adults fear children (*a la* Kizel, *a la* Alice Miller, etc.) then indeed, that will manifest as adultism—which is the basic oppression that adults purvey onto children and youth, who are classified as "non-adults."
288 In 32 years of researching and teaching, I (Fisher) have found North Americans to be by far the most resistant of all peoples to Fearlessness.
289 Fisher (2020b).
290 This is not my term but was coined by the sociologist Benjamin Barber (2003).
291 I (Fisher) make a big deal about this distinction in terms of competing discourses along the spectrum from *conservative* to *radical* to *transformational* in discussions within fearism; see Fisher, Subba & Kumar (2018, p. 14).
292 We use Ken Wilber's *kosmology* over cosmology, because the latter typically excludes the interior depths of existence and focuses on the materiality and exteriors only. The ancient Greek Pythagorians also used *kosmos*.
293 I (Fisher) am aware this may sound overly like dualism, binaries, and such, as poststructuralists are quick to discard. I won't make the longer case for why I make this distinction, as it is complex metaphysics and experiential etc. Yet, I am very aware that at some level, all of what is Cultural is also Natural and/or they are intimately interrelated. I refuse the strict radical constructivism and relativism of everything is Natural and/or everything is Cultural (i.e., human perceived and constructed in terms of meaning and existence). My take is more integralist than that but in the end any disagreements with my thought here

would depend on how one defines these terms and spheres of reality.

294 E.g., Fisher (2016b); and, the "No Fear!" slogan-wear marketing was one of the first waves of this tendency, and a few years later the popular *Cosmopolitan* magazine trended their "Fun, Fearless, Female" marketing campaign. By the post-9/11 era, I (Fisher) was finding many mainstream (often liberal) colleges and universities using "fearless" in their slogans for (mostly American) higher education at their institution; and thus as their goal for their student's. Of course, it was the branding agencies/corporations of the mainstream that promoted this to those educational institutions and charged them a lot of dollars for their brand-image advice. It's all image—superficial—without much substance, and certainly without any theory of fear/fearlessness. It's one big distraction. The trend also disappeared some years later, more or less, and new slogans have come on board for colleges and universities—of which I find even more superficial, airy, unthoughtful, if not totally meaningless. My using the term "fearlessness" in my pre-graduate school days was hard enough to swing, academic culture even resisted it more. I have a copy of a 1996 Sept. 9, email I sent to Laura, who was a business consultant on a spirituality in leadership email-group. I wrote her with the subject line: "Re: *Fearlessness and not watering things down.*" And she replied "Thank you so much for your recent post [to the group site]. I admire and applaud your work, you're doing, and how you're standing up to the 'business minded' [as you called them] folks who say the name is too scary." I had to learn to receive a lot of social rejection where ever I posted my "fearlessness" campaign.

295 BMK wrote to Fisher in response to the survey: "The 16th century English philosopher Thomas More's fictional work *Utopia* may be taken as an example of A-ness. Utopia is an imaginary island where people live happily without fear or worries."

296 Earlier in this chapter I argued D-ness most represents Kizel's "pedagogy of searching" as progressive teaching/paradigm in contrast with a pedagogy of fear. It is now worthy to ask: Is D-ness the most valued and operationalized, that is, and representational of those many educators who say they promote a *"pedagogy of love"*? Anyways, with that question in mind, I did have the opportunity to talk to a very advanced-thinking progressive educator and theologian-in-training once, after I gave them the A-D/ness survey. And luckily I made notes (Feb. 15, c. 2000): Emi and I had a long talk. She saw D-ness as having the most 'fear' in it. It didn't matter how we conversed about it, and even though she saw it as most like the qualities of Nel Noddings [i.e., pedagogy of caring] etc., we didn't disagree [totally]. But her view was that there was a terror of letting go of the "old" rigid dualities [inherent in D-ness]—and, that which she hates at the same time and yet is so terrified [of doing]. She is now saying her very theology is being challenged [by this 'test' result], where she thought she believed in 'God'—is now, that she sees she believes in 'fear'—and yet, she wanted to conclude the

new place of communication [with me where] she would rather call [D-ness] love than fearlessness. Wow! She said "loveness" [is best for D-ness] and that is her tradition of a place of breaking bread and communion. We disagreed and agreed. She is not so sure about the [Sacred] Warrior positioning I put forward, and yet, she is considering it and interested, though she thinks in many ways we are already overly constructed [as people in the West] in 'warrior' mode [and, it offers little positive in her eyes]...". For a very similar (i.e., Christian) twisting of "fearlessness" into what they prefer as "love" (or loveness) can be found in the extensive article by my former doctoral research co-supervisor (Leggo, 2011).

297 E.g., Fixmer-Oriaz (2019).
298 Tinnin (1990).
299 I (Fisher) keep wondering when humans are going to get their Fear Education 101 down... to where they are no longer needing to spend all their attention and writing/speaking/preaching on the vices and virtues of fear interplay—drama—victory? Let's move on to Fear Education 201... please. The latest version (Yan & Slattery), a defense of Levinasian ethics and its role for education and society-at-large, is another defense of fear-positivism and a rejection of a nuanced "fearlessness" as the highest aim for the liberated citizen for an Enlightened Age (e.g., Fearless Age of Subba's). This argument, classically Abrahamic in ground, carriers another version of the *reverential fear* argumentations of the eco-fear thinkers/theorists and of the Christian fearists in general (but not only). My (Fisher) take on this is problematic. It presents an idealized image of "fearless" to burn like a straw-man and then reasserts, as if one wouldn't notice, an idealized fear(fulness) as the new 'be brave, be humble' dictum of the van Kessel & Burke Hypothesis (see Fisher's critique)...
300 See a summary in Fisher & Subba (2016), pp. 47, 95.
301 E.g., Gillian (2002).
302 Bader-Saye (2007).
303 Yan & Slattery (2021), p. 84.
304 E.g., Cristian (2012), Pulcini (2013).
305 Fisher (1997a).
306 Fisher (2021c).
307 Giroux (2014).
308 Dubos (1968), p. xi.
309 Fisher (2010), p. xxx-xxxi.
310 I highly recommend, for e.g., respectively, Seaton (2001), Massumi (1993), and Klein (2008).
311 Fisher (2010), p. xxv.
312 Ibid., p. xxv.
313 Front matter in Kumar, Fisher & Subba (2019).
314 Although intuited as something akin to the one arm of the Trinity (say, like in

Christian theology), this spirit is easily adopted as "holy spirit" by Fisher, who coined this term *spirit of fearlessness* specifically in the early 1990s and gave it a qualified form for action-in-the-world *via* In Search of Fearlessness Project (e.g., Fisher, 2019e). In an analogous form, Fisher (2010) makes a case for a "spiral of fearlessness" in evolution of consciousness (p. 28).

315 Fisher (2010), p. xxviii; equally, "...the pathway to growth, development, and evolution itself can be seen as one from *fear to fearlessness* individually and from a *culture of fear* to a *culture of fearlessness* on a macro-scale (p. 47); see also Chapter Two in Four Arrows (2021), "Fear —> Fearlessness."

316 E.g., "The social consequences of increased knowledge and technological innovations [of 19-20th centuries] caused as much uneasiness and alarm [fear] among Western Europeans 400 years ago as they do among us today. In 1575 the French scholar and jurist Louis Le Roy...as the French Plato" published *Vicissitude* as a detailed articulation of the social impacts (e.g., social order disturbances) of such potent changes, especially that Science had brought and was going to bring in the future (Dubos, 1970, pp. 3-4). Even in the mid-16th century "It seemed to him [Le Roy] that an era of darkness and perhaps self-destruction might be at hand" (p. 6).

317 E.g., see Fisher (2010), Chapter One.

318 Ibid., pp. 3, 4, 10, 11, 134, 152, 165, 167-72, 229, 234, 245-6, 249, 251.

319 Ibid., 48, 97; or "path of maturity" p. 246, and "path of liberation" p. 21. etc.

320 E.g., Fisher (2021b).

321 "There appears to be a general blind-spot to seeing fearlessness flowing and crafting history equally as has fear," (Fisher, 2010, p. xxx).

322 Fisher conceives *fearlessness* as a 'gift' of Nature (p. 24) and its Intelligence, that is, of the evolutionary intelligence from the beginning of Life and perhaps before. Billions of years in the making, this Defense Intelligence (Fisher, 2010, pp. 34, 109, 152, 164, 166) is part of a Fear/Fearlessness System of self/system regulation processes made to ensure survivability and thrivability, including sustainability.

323 Defense is susceptible to become (violent) offense—that is, "neurosis" (Fisher, 2010, pp. 195, 85) as its pathological form of chronic protectionism (e.g., recall A-ness in Chapter Three).

324 See Fisher (1997b) for such a metaphysical model of the dynamic dialectic and interplay of Love (Life) Instinct and Fear (Death) Instinct, through a Wilberian integral perspective.

325 See discussions of 'fear' patterns (e.g., Fisher, 1995, 1995a) and *culturally commodified 'fear'* as in the contemporary postmodern problems at the core of 'Fear' Studies as proposed by Fisher (2003, 2006)—all as operating now in a "culture of fear" meta-context (e.g., Fisher, 1998, 2018a).

326 A term offered by Dubos (1970), p. 8. "All knowledge is good, but not all

advances in knowledge are equally good or urgent" (p. 8).
327 Fisher (2018b).
328 Fisher (2021f).
329 Fisher (2014).
330 Front matter of Fisher & Subba (2016).
331 See definition distinctions in Fisher & Subba (2016), p. 157.
332 Ibid., p. 37.
333 Subba (2014), pp. 46, 300-2, 304-5, 351.
334 Although beyond the scope of this book, Fisher has for several decades been developing a "rebel theory" based on evolutionary principles, that far transcend merely an anthropocentric view of "rebellion" and the nature of human nature within such a limited lens. There remains lots to theorize yet about the Rebel archetype in not only evolution, human history, development itself in psychological and social terms, but as to its core role in revitalization, restoration and healing in systems—*via* the Id, Ego and Super Ego, etc. He first learned of this by his experiences living a 60-70s life as a hippie-type musician/artist and then eco-activist in rebellion against the status quo of virtually everything. Intellectually he was encouraged by Dubos (1968) who wrote of the rebel in biological self/system regulatory terms: "Rebellion...should reach beyond conventional political and social issues. Even if perfect social justice and complete freedom from want [from fear] were to prevail in a world at peace, rebels would still be needed wherever the world is out of joint [balance], which now means everywhere. Rebellion permeates all aspects of human life. It originates from the subconscious....This [current modern] society has more comfort, safety, and power than any before it, but the quality of life is cheapened by the physical and emotional junk heap we have created" but the true rebel know this is not the way to go and they must rebel to such loss of quality (pp. 6-7).
335 E.g., Fisher (2010), pp. 29-32.
336 Ibid., p. 33.
337 Kuhn (1962/96), pp. 109.
338 Wright (1994), pp. 12-13.
339 The infamous Dr. David Suzuki, Canadian environmentalist, on his 85th birthday on The National (CBC TV March 23, 2021) was asked what is the most important thing you would say to the younger generations; he replied, "You are an animal." In search of an "integrally animal politics," Canadian philosopher Brian Massumi turns particularly to mammals and their play and what it has to teach us humans. He wrote, "understanding the flourishing of play at the level [of animality] necessitates theorizing wellsprings of sympathy and creativity, the qualitative and even the subjective, everywhere on the continuum of animal life. The very nature of instinct—and thus of animality itself—must be rethought as a consequence. This [philosophical] project requires replacing

the human on the animal continuum. This must be done in a way that does not erase what is different about the human, but respects that difference while bringing it to a new expression on the continuum: immanent to animality.... [which has important] political implications, as do all questions of belonging.... to investigate what lessons might be learned by playing animality in this way about our usual, all-too-human ways of working the political. The hope is that in the course of the investigation we might move beyond our anthropomorphism *as regards ourselves*: our image of ourselves as humanly standing apart from other animals; our inveterate vanity regarding our assumed species [superiority] identity... [etc.]" (Massumi, 2014, pp. 2-3). In retrospect, I (Fisher) was greatly influenced by Dubos (1968) when I was in my early 20s as he interwove the scientific perspective, with cultural and ecological issues and asked humans to see themselves first and foremost as understandable as animals living with nature rather than always obsessively trying to conquer it. He wrote, that true sustainable alternatives ways to live will emerge with development which "demands an intellectual and emotional revolution. We cannot transform the world until we eliminate from our collective mind the concept that man's goals are the conquest of nature and the subjection of the human mind. Such a change in attitude will not be easy....[we need] a new social ethic—almost a new social religion" (p. 7).

340 Becker (1973/97), p. 79.
341 Within W. Psychology and its worldview, both "fearlessness" (and/or within behavioral "fearlessness theory" so-called, Portnoy et al., 2014) are clinically predisposed to defining fearlessness as if it was only literal, physiological-behavioral, individual, and a psychiatric and criminological tendency and/or pathology (e.g., Fisher, 2010, pp. xxix, 133, 157, 232; Fisher & Subba, 2016, p. 82).
342 E.g., Fisher (2020f).
343 Ferguson (2005), p. 154.
344 E.g., see Wilber (1977, 1995).
345 Arguably, some religious believers who suggest that God, or some other divine variant, has more significance potency than humans.
346 CBC TV The National, an interview with host Andrew Chang, March 24, 2021.
347 Suzuki critiqued CBC's The Nature of Things program philosophy and David Suzuki Foundation in this interview (see Fisher, 2021).
348 I am actually more interested in comparing Near Death Experience (NDE) with Near Psychotic Experience (NPE). What is their potential for transformation?
349 Suzuki narrates this program on "Be Afraid: The Science of Fear" but it was actually written by Roberto Verdecchia, who wrote in the script: "[this fear episode] is a fun, freaky and fact-filled tour through the strange and

exciting places..." (Verdecchia, n.d.). Clearly, another case of fear-positivism, psychologism/scientism, where ultimately this is so popular as to become entertainment or info-tainment, and *not* very good "Fear Education," compared to what could be if FME (fear management/education) was done within the critical lens of fearism or fearlessness. I (Fisher) find this approach more harmful actually than good. It skirts really deep issues. And, always these approaches start with the unquestioned premise: "this most primal of emotions" (meaning, "fear"). I both agree that Fear is operating intensely in the Id dimension, but to say that it is "primal" alone and that's the way to understand fear in the world reality and history of things, is a great reductionistic distortion, of which Robin (2004) has made one of the best arguments on in regard to "fear" as an "idea" and its nature and role in political history in the last 400 years or so. Fear is not that primal or mysterious. The fear-positivism, with its "primal" emotionalist discourse hegemony is a great 'enemy' (resistance and distraction) to the becoming of Fearlessness; see also part of this argumentation in Introduction 2.

350 Sardello (1999), p. xvi.

351 In the early 1990s I developed "Rebel Theory," of which is too complex to go into here, but to suffice it to say I was greatly influenced by Sam Keen's (1983) model of development and from my own cutting-my-teeth boot-camp training in an adolescent therapeutic treatment facility (and healing community), specializing in the "behaviorally-disordered" (so-called). I helped build the program and worked there for 10 years in the 1980s-90s. Talk about "rebels." What I eventually theorized is a tri-partite model of rebellion essential to healthy development for all humans, which developmentally begins in the 18-24 mo. period and manifests in full in the two-year olds and the next year, when "No!" is one of their favorite words and *resistance*, that is rebellion, is core to their means of defining who they are as distinct but related autonomous beings in the social sphere. There are healthy and wounded dimensions to the tripartite categories: (a) Essential Rebel, (b) Normal Rebel, (c) Twisted Rebel. For sure, this Rebel archetype is linked directly to the Sacred Warrior/Magician archetype which I talk about mostly in this book. But an adequate presentation on the Sacred Warrior's nature and role in society (like the "hero" archetype) requires a much more in depth presentation than what I can offer here. It has been mentioned many times in my work on Fearlessness that the Eastern philosophies have generally been much more favorable to the acceptance and utilization of the path of fearlessness—however, I think Keen (1983) is right when he says "The rebel impulse is not encouraged within Eastern philosophy and culture" overall. This makes the Eastern philosophies and culture a co-participant in *resistance* to Fearlessness, unfortunately. Thus, a more integrated East-West model is required to advance the spirit of fearlessness; I think The Wachowski's sci-fi trilogy of films (1999-2003) is a near-perfect blend of such an East-West

archetypal dramatization of this Rebel and "Resistance" Movement (*aka* an implicit Fearlessness Movement).

352 Re-cited in Fisher & Subba (2016), p. 100.
353 For e.g., look at the philosophy of fear books by fearism philosophers (e.g., Michael Eneyo) or others like Svendsen (2008)—there is no such cautionary; and arguably, there is thus no possibility of true Fearlessness. They are actually, in their own way an ideological and implicit *resistance* to the Fearlessness Movement. I could go even farther to say, by their omission, and collusion with the Fear Paradigm, they are sliding into an epistemic violence within the field of fearism and/or FME and Fear Studies (e.g., see Fisher, 2020g).
354 hooks (2000), p. 93.
355 van Kessel & Burke (2018), p. 216.
356 Ibid., p. 226.
357 Ibid., p. 226.
358 Ibid., p. 226.
359 Fisher (2020h).
360 Trungpa (1984), p. 37.
361 We are referring to a very expanded conception of the "magician" than what most people associate in the everyday world. Today, in organizational development and management literature, studies have shown that some people learn skills of the sort that are outstanding in how to work with creativity, vision, conflict, problems, people and systems. They think not just 'magically' (as in say, irrational), but they are highly intuitive, see in the invisible and energetic realms of reality—and, are several steps around the corner in vision/consciousness development compared to most; that is, where others cannot see what is going on beyond the obvious and what is right in front of their face (i.e., the visible aspects of a system). For e.g., Borje, Fedor & Rowland, 1982) spoke about the role here of magician as intertwined with "myth-making" in modern organizations and leadership in order to bring about change and transformation (p. 19).
362 "Truly, the [authentic, fearless, wise] leader is more fearless...for fears have already been confronted....They are old familiar foes of the [sacred] warrior" (Barr & Barr, 1989, p. 173); see also Fisher (2003), Horsley (2003), Trungpa (2007).
363 Leggo (2011), p. 115.
364 Personal communication, Nov. 30, 2009.
365 Varela, Thompson & Rosch (1992), p. 130.
366 See Subba (2014). He defines "fearist" on p. 11. "Fearism," "fearist" and "fearist perspective" are defined in Fisher & Subba (2016), p. 157.
367 Officially he articulated this in Fisher (2006), and in 2019 he founded the *International Journal of Fear Studies.*
368 Fisher (2018d).

369 Fisher (2006), p. 57.
370 We are aware at times of switching from Fear Studies to 'Fear' Studies. Fisher has always played with this switching—this double-tasking, as he calls it. Adding (') marks to any terms in the fear lexicon has a long history and philosophizing that one ought not ignore (e.g., its roots are articulated in Fisher, 1995, 1995a). For convenience in the short-run, readers may simply code this as a problematic ongoing tension, if not conflict, whereby some rare few authors conform to Fisher's call for advancing the (') marks regularly in discourses about fear/fearlessness and fearism. However, virtually no one else but Fisher attends to this systematically. The simplest advice: when you see no (') on the word fear, you know you are in a conversation, that is a discourse regime (*a la* Foucault), where you can count more or less on there being a rather widespread agreement amongst the public and even professionals and academics as to what definition is commonly assigned to fear, as that within the dictionary, for example. Otherwise, when the (') marks are invoked, one is asked by Fisher and by good philosophy itself, to attend to something of a quantum difference that makes a difference in re: the entire conceptualization, methodology and philosophy of the topic—that is, fear (and 'fear'). Such strategies of adding (') marks in this technical way are known to be used in postmodern deconstructionist approaches—and, although Fisher is following in some way that precedent, he is also not confined to it and prefers to use the signification of (') marks in a critical integral post-postmodern sense—and, even beyond that he has invoked matrixial theory and Indigenous-based postcolonial philosophical critiques into language (and its games) all through his work. See Chapter Eight, where Fisher especially goes *wild* at creative junctures in the text to articulate this problematic of double talking fearlessness (and fear) (and 'fear').
371 Fisher's claim here is similar to the one he made in Fisher (2010): "The theory of fearlessness I put forth is optimistic and unique among the fear management literature humanity has produced [p. xvii]....[however] Something is wrong in the field of fear management" (p. xxvii). Turns out it is horribly under-theorized and under-philosophized—and, it lacks a Fearlessness Perspective/Paradigm and a "fearless standpoint theory" (e.g., Fisher, 2019a) for starters—which, is all part of what a good quality 'Fear' Studies field would embrace rather than shun.
372 Subba (2014), pp. 44-5.
373 As well as being legitimate academic and cognitive scientists, they also have adopted, more or less, a Buddhist-friendly philosophy underneath their analysis and conclusions.
374 See Fisher (2010), pp. 151-78.
375 Varela et al. (1992), p. 140. Of course, Descartes and his acolytes since have thought their way of knowing reality was incredibly brave and self-assertive and a sign of human greatness etc. Arguably, from a nascent 21st century Fearlessness

Paradigm and our philosophical critique in this book, there is a hidden shadow and curriculum of the Cartesian Dominant worldview/paradigm/philosophy. It is a twisted bravado on the surface and fear-based structure underneath—yes, it arguably is a pursuit of knowledge based on a deep ontological anxiety/terror of existence itself. This is a very important but too complex topic for us to cover adequately here (e.g., see Varela et al., and Maslow, 1966).

376 See Maslow (1966) who contrasted a bipolar paradigm model: "deficit-motivated" vs. "growth-motivated" science/knowledges (cf. to Fisher, 2010, respectively: Fear vs. Love meta-motivational paradigm and Pyszcyznski, Greenberg & Arndt, 2011, respectively "fear" vs. "freedom" motivational psychologies). Psychological motivation cannot be extracted from the so-called observer or *objective* scientist. No. According to the 'new paradigm' of 20-21st century thought, the scientist like everyone else, is more or less, also *subjective* and psychologically motivated with their own and/or their discipline's and/or their funder's needs. This latter heavily influences research and influences accuracy and distortion of knowledge(s). Deficit-motivated science, which Maslow argues is by far most common, and also dominates other ways, in the Sciences, is *fear-based*.

377 Morin (1998), p. 60.

378 Fisher (2006), p. 43. Albert Camus' postmodern philosophical-ethical indictment, based on his observation, is that our W. knowledge pursuits (mathematics, physical sciences, biology) of the last 300 years are in doubt, once we realize that they have led to the predomination of (in Camus' words in c. 1946) "Our 20th century is the century of fear" (see Fisher, 2006, p. 43). Arguably, the 21st century is turning out to be the "century of terror." Camus' calling out here is fundamental to any taking *responsibility for philosophy* and its relationship to reality and the world (i.e., human nature, human condition, human potential). Any philosophy that shirks that responsibility, and worldliness, to us is an unethical philosophy at core—even if, it may be a philosophy that produces interesting results.

379 Both faith and reason, argues, Moreno (1977), are the sources of fear and are the distorting elements in thinking itself—that is, so-called "rational" thinking and philosophizing. Michael A. Weinstein wrote on the back cover [from the Introduction] of Moreno's classic work that *"Moreno's description of how reason generates fear through an internal dialectic markes a decisive, original, and far-reaching step beyond previous contextual critiques of rationalism....His contribution is an important achievement, not only to political, social and psychological theory, but to the attainment of civilized values."* Moreno's thesis is backed-up by recent social psychology experimental research, including the work of Ernest Becker (see Terror Management Theory)—"consciousness and self-awareness also necessarily engender dread: fear, trepidation, anxiety, alarm, fright, horror,

and, in due course, unmitigated terror. First, knowing that one is alive and being able to anticipate the future inevitably produces the unsettling awareness of one's inexorable death" (Pyszczynski, Solomon & Greenberg, 2002, p. 15).

380 Moreva (2003), p. 83.
381 Maslow (1966).
382 Cited from Morin (1998), p. 61.
383 Subba (2014), Fisher (2010).
384 There is a growing body of researchers and thinkers who are recommending *transdisciplinarity* in contrast to multi- or inter- disciplinarity and who are critical of 'old paradigm' singular disciplinarity. This progressive movement is largely due to the problems of a complex world, complexity theory itself, and how humans are going to have to become much more complex thinkers in analyzing and solving the world's worst (wicked) problems (e.g., see "integral" (and holistic) approach as transdisciplinary, in its working with global "wicked problems" (Watkins & Wilber, 2015). In this context, Fisher has long claimed that the Fear Problem is a global wicked problem.
385 An extensive new vocabulary for Fear Studies is already being compiled, e.g., see Fisher et al. (2019f).
386 Retrieved from http://www.thegreatcourses.com/tgc/courses/course_detail.aspx?cid=449
387 By Barbara Scott, 2011, retrieved from http://www.amazon.com/Becoming-Fearless-Love-Work-Life/dp/B001Q3M79C
388 Cited in Nelson (1981), A-6/7.
389 Fisher has long been influenced by Alfred N. Whitehead's "process philosophy," albeit, he acknowledges he only scantily knows its depths but it 'fits' his own evolutionary/organic (D-ness) sensibilities.
390 *"Praxis"* is a deeply meaningful term from the critical traditions of philosophy and political movements, in which both theory/practice give 'feedback' to each other in the unfolding of the operations of whatever people and their organizations are involved in.
391 In the 1980s-90s, Fisher has been involved in two other intense conscious communities prior to founding In Search of Fearlessness. One was an organic hippie-like community in a rural setting called Common Ground and the other a therapeutic community for adolescent boys and their families in a rural setting. These were invaluable training grounds to prepare him for starting his own conscious community and the 'fear' vaccines as the praxis tools for it.
392 The notion of the intervention of a 'fear' vaccine (vaccination process) concomitantly implies a notion of a "virus of fear" (e.g., Peale, 1963, n.p.), of which both notions have some historical roots in the human imaginary—but the 'fear' vaccine *per se* is original to Fisher's work, within the context of an overall evolutionary view of fear management/theory/education.

393 The potent psychological defense mechanism, typically called by psychologists, "*projection*," is at the base of the thinking that Fisher went through, as well as his ontological and epistemological philosophizing around this conception/dynamic as foundational to consciousness itself. The larger history of this notion is available in much of Fisher's writings but it is beyond the scope of this chapter to discuss further. For keen philosophical readers, you may also see the parallel of this project(ion) phenomenon in Wilber's work, e.g., his "Dualism-Repression-Projection" conception (e.g., Wilber, 1977/82) and "The Atman Project" (e.g., Wilber, 1982).

394 One ought not only equate the 'Fear' Project(ion) with the Fear Problem. The latter, is Fisher's preferred term for most public discourse he engages. It is also a larger umbrella term, typically disregarded by those who read and write about his work (see Fisher's (2021g) critique of this dismissal of his capitalized version of the Fear Problem).

395 For problems with wounded and fearful people becoming addicted enlightenment and/or "to the (spiritual) light" (of faith and religion) see Kapsch (1997) and Connor (2017), for critique examples. A fully articulated Fearlessness Philosophy remains to be explicated adequately. Fisher is well aware of the problems of his endarkenment path—e.g., getting 'stuck' in the dark-side, in the Shadow projections themselves while trying to understand them and free oneself from them. The psychotic potential of such explorations is always there, as many an artist, mystic and shaman in human history have fallen prey. Yet, Fisher gives great credence, theoretically and experientially, to Jung's warning in his analysis of the "enantiodromia syndrome"—wherein, as Jung's research showed, 'the pursuit of virtues typically ends up the expression of vices'—or in other words, do-gooders easily and predictably often end up doing the opposite of what they intended. Although it is arguably correct to say that "fearlessness" is a virtue (e.g., as we see in Eastern philosophies especially), it is a virtue, as Fisher argues, by its virtue of *resisting* the seductive pursuit of Love, Light, Peace, Harmony—and, takes another route to Enlightenment, so to speak (e.g., see Fisher & Subba's (2016) critique of "Love" as the professed best way; pp. xxxi-xlii). This is a large topic beyond the scope of this chapter (see Part VI).

396 This *via negativa* mystical path (e.g., see Fox, 1986) and/or negative philosophy/methodology tradition, including "negative description" in the therapeutic intervention paradigm, is a topic Fisher loves to engage. But it would require a long explication beyond the scope of this chapter and book *per se*. Albeit, in the final Part VI, he does talk about the "negativist" traditions as really important to understand and utilize in understanding resistances to fearlessness and Fearlessness Philosophy and Paradigm.

397 Originally this practice was adapted from Jackins (1965) Re-evaluation Co-counseling; Fisher & Bickel turned their version into LPC (Liberation Peer

Counseling) (see Fisher, 2018e). Fisher (2019g) recently re-adapted this as the Life Enhancement Training Program (L.E.T.).
398 "Second-tier" is part of the developmentalist values-classification of Spiral Dynamics integral discourse (see the Internet).
399 E.g., Freire (1970, 1973).
400 E.g., Fisher (2012c).
401 Bickel & Fisher (1993); and, Fisher & Bickel, *Creative Practices for Caring Community* (in prep., Routledge, 2022).
402 E.g., Peck (1988).
403 See "Credo of Fearlessness" in Fisher (2010), e.g., pp. 39, 126, 205.
404 E.g., Fisher (2015).
405 E.g., Fisher (2016) and Fisher (2017a).
406 E.g., see Four Arrows (2016) and Fisher (2018).
407 The helpful side of "negative philosophy" and its problematics are taken up in Chapter Eight. Fear(lessness) articulates the valuation of a "*less*" or *minus-ing* trend and imperative and this is one signal to show is it a negative philosophy not a positive philosophy *per se.*
408 This is #7 from out of 10 fear management systems he has catalogued and placed in an evolutionary spectrum of developmental logic/theory, using Ken Wilber's integral philosophy (see Fisher, 2010).
409 All quotes taken from Fisher (2010), pp. 168-71.
410 Chödrön (2001), p. 123.
411 The late Dr. Carl Leggo, from The University of British Columbia, was research co-supervisor for my dissertation (2000-03). He is a great mentor in my memory and many other students during his decades long career as professor in English and Literacy. He's deeply regarded and will be greatly missed. Yet, his positive legacy lives on, I (Fisher) think it is great because he was so unusually transparent and 'vulnerable' within an institution that coerces people not to be. In that stream of practice then, he is in my view well along the path of fearlessness, even though, in the end of our exchanges and his 2011 article etc., I never thought he ever really understood fully what my work was about, meaning, that he resisted (as a Christian) Fearlessness could be so important—he preferred Love.
412 Leggo (2011).
413 Wilber's integral reconstruction of the "spectrum of consciousness" and "Great Chain of Being" philosophies is very nuanced and does not easily fall into the critics' simplified attacks on such holarchical models. See Wilber (1995).
414 Korten (2005), p. 34.
415 Ibid., pp. 46-7.
416 *deliberately evasive-* speech using nonsense syllables along with words in a rapid patter...[i.e.,] ambiguous language: When you try to get a straight answer, he gives you *double-talk* (excerpt from http://dictionary.com).

417 "Every statement about creativity is open to doubt. Since creativity is a potency or energy it cannot be grasped systematically and can at best be perceived systatically....In any event, creativity is more than a creative, imaginary, intuitive, productive, or reproductive element" (p. 313). At the four-dimensional *integral perspective*, which Gebser is a master teach of, there is recognition of a new kind of "integration" which "can be completed through synairesis" and "unsystematic systasis"—whereby, according to Gebser (1949) we are in a world of meaning making and creativity which "takes leave of the three-dimensional world of polar [dualism] movement or providing a possible escape into the unitary-relatedness of magic. Systasis is in no way irrational or prerational but rather arational....a new form of statement...a form of expression and realization that renders perceptible the content and principal motif of the new mutation which at the same time consciously fulfilling its impartation of truth" (p. 312). Chapter Eight is a beginning take-off from the rest of our book along the 'flight-lines' of potency of orign/creativity in the Gebserian arational sense. This is why there is a decided literary and artistic 'field' that is engaged and a very rewarding result; although, for many readers within a time/space three-dimensional rational thinking framework only, they will find this chapter likely most disconcerting, if not chaotic, fear-invoking, if not fearsome. Theorizing and imagining Fearlessness Paradigm and Philosophy within a fourth-dimension is a goal of this text *Resistances to Fearlessness*.

418 Personal communication, Nov. 30, 2009.

419 See end note 5 in Chapter Seven, which explicates Fisher's distinction and rationale for (') mark significations within the language game of his ventures in Fear Studies ('Fear' Studies). Double talking fear ('fear') in other words, was the first sign that there was real trouble, epistemically and ethically, in Fisher's pursuit of the In Search of Fearlessness Project (1989-). Chapter Eight is a more complicated double talking fearlessness discourse of which is nascent in comparison to his earlier work (e.g., Fisher, 1995, 1995a). Note: I (Fisher) have added (') to *fearlessness* at times, e.g., in Fisher (2010). This latter strategy has not held to systematization, for some reason but after writing Chapter Eight, maybe I ought to reconsider this.

420 Referencing here is to many critical philosophical arguments, from queer theory, critical shamanism and anthropology, sociology, and from Black Studies and/or critical Indigenous Studies, etc., where there is the problem of (critical) consciousness (and identity and language) of the (so-called) "oppressed"—operating within the circulating economy of signifiers near totally controlled by the oppressors (controlled by a fear-based worldview). It is a topic too expansive to enter for our purposes but is potent in describing the issues Fisher raises with *resistances to Fearlessness* within a 'Fear' Matrix regime. Specifically, in Black Studies, "double consciousness" philosophizing; of which psychological

implications can be found in the work of W. E. B. Du Bois. At times "the double" is either stated or implied in our writing in this book, especially in Chapter Eight, with a tone of the emergence of the ghostly, the haunting—see also, Derrida's notion of hauntology. In one of the better articulations of this double talking (consciousness/identity) issue one has to analyze all situations in societies "within the dominant cultural matrix" (*a la* Fanon; cited in Sandoval, 2000, p. 127). "Fanon exhorts every enslaved consciousness (those who have become [the] dominant image) to 'burst apart' all they have become—an eruption that will fragment the self, he warns. But these fragments can be put together again when another kind of transformative self arises....This new self can liberate citizen-subjects from any 'archetype' [i.e., regime of historical discourse of intractable oppositions, like the civilized vs. the barbaric or enslaved] (Sandoval, 2000, p. 128). And, one cannot ignore the critique that many Indigenous peoples and scholars have had of the 'European' colonizer and their Dominant worldview and its insanity-making properties, which Four Arrows' wrote "deception was [still is] at the root of Western culture's loss of balance and illogical, contradictory lives" –and "lies" (quoted in Fisher, 2018, pp. 124-5). It is well-known, pre-industrial Indigenous natives in North America characterized the European settlers and leaders as 'speaking with forked-tongues'—which is a poetic code for double-speak in its pathological connotation and form. What Fisher's point in Chapter Eight is exploring is that Fearlessness is really by necessity within the 'Fear' Matrix always already pre-written so to speak in a 'forked tongue' as well—but, he implies, perhaps it is not always a pathological form but actually a double speaking of liberation. In other words, Fearlessness philosophy is a negation of the negation of the Fear Paradigmatic of making sense.

421 Referring to the great ethical theorist and humanitarian, Immanuel Levinas.

422 E.g., see the cases made by Eneyo (2019), English & Stengel (2010), Cristian (2012), and Yan & Slattery (2021). One of the great problems these kinds of rationalist, even if spiritual, thinkers make is that they so poorly make any distinction of quantum 'leap' difference between ordinary (psychological) fear and 'fear' (as in the morphing-kind, the mutational and/or the culturally-constructed). To make ethical arguments about a fixed fear that is (supposedly located) inside the individual as a rational agent and can thus be managed as such by virtues ethics and moralism is, in my view, faulty of unethical practice itself; because of its reductionism of the nature and meaning of fear itself—that is, within ideological psychologism. See Fisher (2011a) for one example of my critical fearanalysis of this situation/trend. I will pursue this problematic in great detail in my upcoming book in preparation (Fisher, in prep.).

423 I say this from experience teaching this in the larger community, and especially in a continuing education night class (titled "Basics to the Path of Fearlessness") for three years at the University of Calgary (1992-5), but also an intense group

experience with several students during my tenure at the School of Sacred Warriorship (1993-97), which I founded and taught at.

424 All quotes here from Anon. (2004), p. 141.

425 Barrett argues *fear-and-evolution* go hand-in-hand all the way. "Probably most controversial about Barrett's theory is that it proposes that fear, like other emotion categories, does not have a hard-wired neuroanatomical profile but is part of a dynamic system in which prediction signals are understood as ad hoc, abstract categories or concepts that are generatively assembled from past experiences that are similar to present conditions. In this view, the brain is a categorization machine, continually creating contextually relevant concepts that are appropriate to an animal's niche" (Mobbs, 2019). Fisher would interpret her findings and speculation as a good staging for an advanced "ecology of fear" notion that is more holistic than the typical bio-neurological "psychology of fear" reductionistic understandings. This could influence an as yet to be explicitly articulated *ecology of fearlessness* idea.

426 Several literary/film critics and philosophers have seen this meta-mythic universal thematization focus in this movie, of which I developed my own view of as emancipatory 21st curriculum (Fisher, 2009).

427 Michel Foucault said the same thing, more or less, about discourses that an "agent" may utter but potentially at the same time the (capital 'D') Discourse (historically) is using the agent to transmit it into time/space and even 'immortality.' To view words/language/linguistic at this subtle critical level is an achieved skill of awareness and consciousness, according to integral theory—few people reach this developmental capability in their life-time; e.g., within the overall 11 spectrum stages of "identity development" with 6 stages of "cognition" known by developmentalists, being 'construct-aware' of how one is being forged by the very structures that they are using (like language games) is also called "postformal" and/or "Ego-aware-paradoxical" at cognition level 5/6 (Forman, 2010, p. 81).

428 See Fisher (1997b); e.g., Wilber (1995).

429 Indeed, based on transformation theory (e.g., Ainsworth-Land, 1973), the repetition herein, is not merely linear-causal and fixed back-n-forth, but in living systems they are moving more on a "spiral" of dynamics (*a la* Wilber), meaning the system is never quite the same when it goes 'back' for it knows a little more—as learning is always part of the change/transformation processes of development. This is where *transformation philosophy* (e.g., *a la* "integral," "holistic," "matrixial," and/or "Indigenous") are fundamental to the way I think of philosophy overall.

430 E.g., "matrixial strings" as proposed in the post-Lacanian matrixial psychoanalysis of Bracha L. Ettinger (see in Part V).

431 E.g., see *archetypal psychology* in contradistinction to *analytical psychology*

(Hillman, 1972, p. 3); and, Hillman & Ventura (1993).

432 Typically, I use the more easy to digest term re-translated for public consumption—as you can watch on my video series called "FearTalks" (e.g., see Fisher, 2018c

433 See Ermine (2007).

434 *Wahinkpe Topa* (Four Arrows) (2006).

435 It appears to be a 'literary device' of some kind, which I have not seen in any book before.

436 One gets a fuller sense of the subversiveness by contrasting this Indigenous voicing within the context of the book being published by University of Texas Press. The Indigenous voicing is 'working through' then within the totally White Dominator's publishing house and its control. But clearly, *Wahinkpe Topa* found a leak in the White armor and shared the 'real' messaging truth that needed to be told on the opening page.

437 *The Village* film was written and directed by M. Night Shyamalan.

438 In Fisher's four-layered meta-motivational model there is *Freedom* at the 'top' of the developmental schema of that which is most of significance, but less foundational—all, as located in the Fearlessness paradigm/philosophy (see Figure 5 in Chapter Six).

439 E.g., see Chapter Three, Part Two in Gebser (1949). If we had more space, I (Fisher) would want to pursue the comparison of Othering/(M)Othering in matrixial theory (*a la* Ettinger) as analogous with Fearing/Fearlessness. Perhaps, in a later work, someday. Unplugging from the 'Fear' Matrix is as hard as unplugging from the phallocentric Patriarchy that has (arguably) dominated W. civilization for 5000+ years (Eisler, 1987). We've called it *Fear's Empire* (*a la* Barber, 2003) in this text at times, ruled by King Fear and its Fear Philosophy.

440 Paraphrased from Goldman (1999). Note: end note 5 in relation to blowing-up and "burst apart" (a la Fanon's call for the oppressed and their "double consciousness" (*a la* Du Bois) and the necessity of transformative re-subjectification 'in and out' of the dominant cultural matrix (*a la* Fisher's 'Fear' Matrix).

441 This reflects my (Fisher) haunting in writing this ending. At one point during the 15 'glitch' (mutational) lines of interruption, intervention, if not 'chaos' in the main text of this chapter, while still in a kind of light-trance of consciousness—and, a beautiful state of fearlessness, I must say—there was a cleared opening for such a critique of dialecticism. With alacrity, I saw through the weakness of the fear/fearlessness justification in this entire discourse with Kumar. I thought it would make up a good deal of this Chapter Eight. But with various doctor's appointments and other interruptions in real-time of the banal worldly-world, such insight disappeared. Although, some traces still remain. Like a few days later, I now see there is a critique sitting in my work. I have theorized a "Bi-centric" paradigm/theorem over the years (e.g., Fisher, 2010, p. 167) and it

suggests that when confronting certain really important ethical polarities like Fear vs. Fearlessness or Fear vs. Love or "Addiction vs. Living Process" (*a la* Schaef) the premise is that one *canno*t be practicing one side of the polarity and the other at the same time—they are mutually exclusive. This kinda puts a cramp down on the over-simplicity of dialecticism as it is traditionally defined as co-evolving opposites (which Kumar and I tend to trade in within this text). Anyways, try as I may to reconnect with the original sense of the weakness in dialectic use, the time ran out. We had to finish this manuscript draft and move on. Someday, I'll get back to it, or maybe someone else will help articulate this welcomed critique.

442 Cristian (2012), p. 34.

443 This is such a pivotal line in The Wachowski's story, in *The Matrix* (1999) movie, as it leads all of us to question "What time is it, really?" and "What is time?" and "What is reality?" based on time—and, timelessness? Truly, these are Gebserian types of questions for us as co-authors and relevant to the problematics of a philosophy that we are playing with in this book—that somehow or other, will have to come to terms with "What has happened to people's sense of time?" be they *in* or *out* of the 'Fear' Matrix?" Note: I (Fisher) have slightly altered the years (as did the actual final film) from the original 1998 play script by The Wachowski's, which originally reads "1997" and "2197" (in Wachowski & Wachowski, 2000, p. 37).

444 The Wachowski's 1998 script, p. 37 (cited in Wachowski & Wachowski, 2000, p. 307).

445 Ettinger (2011), p. 1, 5.

446 Dodds (2020), p. 1.

447 Fisher (2010), p. xv.

448 And, arguably, paranoia is the cause as well. According to Ettinger's matrixial theory, the entire phallocentric sphere is already paranoic-based (i.e., anxiety-driven and fear-based) in orientation towards the world—part of what feminists have called the "pathological patriarchy." Mistrust vs. Trust, is Erik Erikson's first stage of affective development as well—so, one can put together several theoretical threads here to make a case of intersecting vectors that create the entire "culture of fear" phenomenon (and/or 'Fear' Project, 'Fear' Matrix, *a la* Fisher).

449 Maslow (1966). See also the same kind of unveiling of a fear-based structuration beneath "Science" and "Method" in Devereux (1967). Sadly, these two powerful studies/theories are virtually totally ignored in conversations about epistemology today.

450 Unfortunately, there are a lot of researchers who use these terms *positive description* and *negative description* in their research and common discourse as only simple 'flat' notions of positive-association and negative-association, as in

positive-values and negative-values. Although that is somewhat valid, it is overly-psychological in use. The philosophical (and some systems-communications therapy) traditions carry a much deeper epistemic and nuanced understanding of these terms, of which we are referring to in our discourse here. *Negative causation* orientation, for example, in philosophical analysis or otherwise, is about "absence" or "omission" as being (supposed as) the primary motivational background of importance for registering causality and actuality in things we can see and document in the sense of being a "positive" presence (cf. Fazekas & Kampis, n.d., p. 3).

451 "The [premodern but post-magical/mythic] Greek philosophers, beginning with Thales of Miletus and including such well-known thinkers as Pythagoras, Democritus, Heraclitus, Socrates, Plato, and Aristotle, gave up these [primal people's thinking and] beliefs about the gods and their compelling whims [for explanations of phenomenon]. They [rather] looked for permanency and regularity [i.e., patterns, principles, laws, theories] in nature, and theorized about a common element in everything that existed [and was explanatory of reality]: Heraclitus called it fire; Democritis spoke of the 'atom'; Pythagoras thought of numbers; and Aristotle devised his explanation in terms of matter and form. They did not agree in their theories, but all held the revolutionary idea that there was such a thing as *the nature of things*, and that whatever existed remained identical with its natural self: a man was a man, and he could not originate from a dragon's tooth, nor could he be transformed into a snake. On this principle of identity [as basis to a philosophy we could call "scientific" or "rational"], there was no disagreement [amongst these great Greek philosophers], and Aristotle used it as the basis of his system of logic [and definitional-based classification system of things, processes, and of everything]" (Bois, 1973, p. 6).

452 I (Fisher) do identify as a "fearologist" and have informally since 2000. The public news media has only briefly acknowledged my expertise as such: (a) "Critics, including University of British Columbia "fearologist" R. Michael Fisher, say it only makes people more fearful" (Riley, 2004), (b) a 25 min. live interview with Shelagh Rogers, *Sounds Like Canada*, CBC Radio One, June 10, 2004 and, (c) "'Fearologist' has mapped out different fear management systems" (Boschman, 2007). For reasons unknown to me, media have since then stayed away from talking with serious fearologists.

453 See Fisher (2021a).

454 Excerpt from "Reviews," on the top of front page, of the front matter of Subba (2014).

455 Fisher (2019i). Interestingly, "fearism" used like this reviewer, has been *the most* popularized of all of Fisher's hundreds of terms around his fear/fearlessness research and writing—unfortunately, virtually all of those diverse and numerous scholars who have used (cited) Fisher's "fearism" concept have distorted and

reduced it—of which Fisher has recently critiqued this 'sloppy' tendency (Fisher, 2017b).

456 Subba (2014), p. 197.

457 Ibid., p. 197.

458 Lesser-known today, Korzybski was well-known 50-90 years ago, and admired by many thinkers as a meta-thinker who made famous the notion of "the map is not the territory." Which means it is a logical categorical error (illusion) to mistake our concepts/words/images/diagrams/theories of explanation for the Real territory of experiential reality and/or the reality beyond what is humanly (culturally)-constructed (e.g., Nature-constructed). Bois (1973) suggested Korzybski's system as third-to-fourth order potential of "the new episteme-in-becoming, with the new general system of knowing-feeling-behaving that makes us view ourselves and our world in a perspective so far unforeseen" (p. xi). Bois believed Korzybski's system "if properly developed, could assume in the future the role of Aristotelian epistemology and logic [that have] played for centuries in the Western world" (p. xvi). In many ways, this is foundational systems-communication epistemic-philosophy that 'fits' well into the holistic-integral epistemic perspective of our (Fisher & Kumar) co-authored book.

459 All quotes above from Bois (1973), p. 8.

460 Excerpt from Corradi (1992), p. 267.

461 An excerpt from the 1946 essay in *Combat* newspaper, "Neither Victim Nor Executioner." Retrieved from http://www.ppu.org.uk/e_publications/camus1.html

462 Another uncanny quote (p. 190) that I found c. 2000, by the most bizarre research means—synchrony—or accident (?). Nevertheless, it is the potent line that stood out from all the doctoral work in Mackie's (1985) pivotal book on the nature of fear ('fear') embedded in everyday life and knowledge systems. Synchronously, by chance, or by any other means, it is fascinating that in that same year of Mackie's publication, independently, the scholars studying the Latin American S. Cone region of past dictatorships, uncovered the term "culture of fear" (Corradi, Fagen & Garretón, 1992, p. 3).

463 I (Fisher) have always resonated with this invoking of this uncanny-like term as defined and actualized in the incredible (sociological) phenomenological study of Mackie (1985). She introduced me during my graduate research to the "fear-barrier" concept, which became crucial in my growing imaginary of fear (and 'fear'). Her work needs to be studied by anyone who wants to better understand the *phenomenology of fear*, with and through a psycho-historical-sociopolitical lens.

464 Ettinger (2011).

465 I (Fisher) am simplifying this for this text but a more accurate integral perspective is one that would distinguish between *Phobos* and *Thanatos* drives—that is,

meta-motivational great ontological forces of what can be called 'Fear' forces (*a la* Wilber, 1995); see Fisher (1997b).

466 Fisher (2017b).

467 Bisht (2020), p. 3039.

468 Based on the research, philosophy and theorizing of the late Ernest Becker and his existentialist orientation, for nearly 40 years of empirical social psychology (experimental) research on human social behavior has been conducted using basic "death prompts" (i.e., morality salience factor) in various forms, to show there is conclusive evidence that (fearing) *othering* processes and violent thought/actions towards 'differences' will predictably follow such prompts—that is, follow such reminders (perceived as threats) re: our death and/or threats *via* death potential of our cultural symbols, even when they are subliminally primed below any conscious awareness (e.g., see Solomon, Greenberg & Pyszczynski, 2015). A good documentary film on this is *Flight From Death* (2005).

469 E.g., Fisher (2003, p. 4).

470 E.g., Dodds (2020).

471 I am following the explication of these Freudian concepts based on Hall (1960).

472 Bisht (2020), p. 3039.

473 The unsaid here is Fearlessness as "first choice" (i.e., as the instinctual Id choice) via the Fisherian dictum: *When fear appears, so then does fearlessness*. Once this is denied culturally and via sublimation effects, often forced by the "culture of fear" (coping)—and, not healing. Then, fearlessness is going to be turned into something not natural as it is, according to Fisher. Fearlessness then is located as 'the alien' experienced as 'uncanny anxiety'—or at least, it is latently predisposed to this location of human psychic experiencing—and sociality experiencing. Of course, this is all rather fresh hypothesis-making and theorizing based on an intuitive 'hunch' that I had when designing the book outline and coming to make a commitment to write and title Part V.

474 "Freud points out that a person never actually relinquishes his [sic] original object-cathexis [i.e., vehicle of latent life-bonding energy to "love" and "desire" and "heal" with the unconditional attending m/other—who is typically the mother or main caregiver and/or an introjected symbol thereof]. By this he [Freud] means that a person is always looking for his first love in the substitute object. Failing to find a completely satisfactory substitute, he either continues his search or reconciles himself to something that is second best. When a person accepts a substitute he is said to be *compensating* for the original goal object" (Hall, 1962, p. 83). There is of course, a psychological narcissistic wound-effect-affect going on in this "split" from the mother/matrix (*a la* Ettinger). A coping paradigm, based on fear (if not paranoia eventually) reproduces a neurosis-effect-affect patterning in relating to 'objects' and eventually (when healing is denied) one's self-sense becomes an object in the process; note, it is easier to

then self-wound oneself as an 'object' (e.g., self-cutting behaviors) because one is split and 'cut off' phenomenologically from a matrixial subjectivity based on love and carriance (*a la* Ettinger). A fascinating philosophical variant of this "search for the original goal object" on a macro-ontological scale re: the evolution of Consciousness itself (i.e., dynamics of development itself) can be found in the Wilberian kosmo-psychoanalytic theory put forth most explicitly in his earliest books (Wilber, 1977, 1981, 1982). Wilber basically argues, as have others that he cites in his summary transpersonal theory and integral philosophy, (using Hindu sacred terms) that Brahman (Absolute One) is sought as original Source (i.e., Oneness) by all consciousness formations (fragmentations *via* dualism) that are in the process of evolution/development/historical unfolding. This deep metaphysical (nondualistic) theory and worldview is core to understanding my own work and conceptualizing meta-motivational forces, like the 'Fear' Project(ion) and Fearlessness—as fundamentally a simultaneous *fear management* and *love management*—"in search" for Brahman through Atman (Relative Many). Atman substitutes for Brahman identity (ultimately fail and compensate as second-best and) create the process of "a search" driving the wheel of evolution of consciousness—and, this can 'failure', under certain conditions create troublesome neuroses (like with Freudian notions of object-cathexis processes that are ultimately unsatisfactory substitutes—and, desire moves to needs to addictions)—at worst, it creates *pathologies*, which are attempts to heal the original ontological split-wound-dualism of differentiation. These pathologies carry that double-duty core of trying to heal while trying to cope— and, depending on cultural and experiences in environmental conditions—this can be exacerbated to "cultural pathologies" (e.g., what has been referred to as "culture of fear" in this text and Fisher's variation of deep interpretation *via* fearanalysis). Note: it is this philosophical integral analysis by Wilber that is so compelling to understand what is going on in the world and is probably one of the best guides to repair of the pathologies in the most complete ways (see Wilber's AQAL model and integral vision—e.g., a good summary by Reynolds, 2006)— not surprisingly then, Wilber, "freelance philosopher...something of an enigma" (Guy, 1995, p. 77) was once labeled "kosmological therapist" (Simpkinson, 1995, p. 7)—and, equally the Wilberian philosophy has been resisted and attacked like "no other figure in the field of transpersonal psychology" (Fisher, 1997, p. 33). Fearlessness work is also striving to be a kosmological therapy or more accurately, what Wilber (1995) called a "*therapia*" (pp. 73, 201).

475 That Fearlessness is sublimated is a big topic, and we cannot go into here further other than to say, the link would be with Part III, whereby we argue that the primal healing instinct is suppressed in this modern world—coping culture.
476 Sardello (1999).
477 And, likewise Ettinger (2011) would offer the matrixial theory perspective

on uncanny as well, whereby having the uncanny experience brings about connectivity not anxiety and separation.
478 Dodd (2020, p. 7) is citing Barbara Creed's (2005) thesis in *Phallic Panic*.
479 Solomon, Greenberg & Pyszczynski (2015), pp. 8-9.
480 "Machines that appeared too lifelike would be unsettling or even frightening inasmuch as they resemble figures from nightmares or films about the living dead" (MacDorman, 2005, p. 399).
481 One hint: Why do 50% of the population surveyed pick "A" as most "fear" in it and 50% pick "D" for that same question? Which diagram of the A-ness/D-ness survey, in other words, is the most uncanny? And, is that a 'good' uncanny (as in "awful") or a 'bad' uncanny (as in anxiety-provoking)?
482 "Conversion," "Derogation," "Assimilation," "Accommodation," and "Annihilation" (Pyszczynski, Solomon & Greenberg, 2002, pp. 30-3).
483 Pyszczynski, Solomon & Greenberg (2002).
484 Ibid., p. 26.
485 E.g., Pinker (2011).
486 Wilber (1995) called these: ignore-ance (*Thanatos*) and arrogance (*Phobos*), more or less from Plotinus, and what Fisher (1997b) has adapted ontologically to call the 'Fear' Project (ion). These are the forces underneath the more simple label "Fear Problem."
487 E.g., Felman (1992), p. 1.
488 Felman (1992a), p. 165.
489 Ibid., p. 202.
490 Ibid., p. 203.
491 E.g., Fisher (2019
492 Fisher (2018d).
493 Fisher (2010), p. x.
494 Upon reflection now, I think big part of the struggle of whether to talk more about fear or fearlessness has come down to a troublesome 'marketing' problem. I had to figure out what was going to 'sell.' I don't mean literally in economic terms, but I also don't deny that played a part in my decisions. I have never been systematically funded to do any of this fearwork and I have virtually no expendable income to do so. It's a voluntary effort of lot of blood, sweat and tears. I wouldn't want to do anything else, of course, because of my recalcitrant "idealist" self that guides me to make many of these choices to be 'impractical' in the world of the capitalist economy. I rather support and live the 'gift economy' alternative, yet this latter has not been well supported in modern times. Many do not know it but when I started to write my 2010 book as the tome that summarized so much of my efforts since 1989, I made a clear decision, which I describe in the book (p. xxix) in the beginning sections, to not follow my first impulse to write a book summarizing all the "fear theories" and

philosophies and practices I could find around the world and turn that into a huge book—something along the lines of the "World's Fear Teachings." As I started to research and conceive that kind of book, the amount of material was overwhelming for me to do without research grants and assistants. So, I did some soul-searching and came up with a compromise solution and that was to focus on "The World's Fearlessness Teachings" (Fisher, 2010) because it seemed a more 'marketable' term in the positivity sense—better to give "fearlessness" offerings than just more talk about "fear." That marketing hypothesis, you might call it, was efficient and workable in size because there truly is less information about fearlessness to synthesize than about fear, yet I now see that which I didn't see back then in 2008, when I began working on that book, that "fearlessness" was really 'hated' at some level deep in the collective unconscious and culture (especially of the modern West).

495 Fisher (2019f).

496 Subba, a Nepalese philosopher, poet/writer is the recognized leader of the philosophy of fearism movement, with origins of his coining the term "fearism" in 1999. Fisher has used the same term, independently derived, as early as 1990 but with a more specific political and cultural meaning than Subba's more generic wide meaning. Both of these authors joined forces as colleagues in late 2014, with an E-W book on the topic (Fisher & Subba, 2016). Although Subba had talked of "fearlessness" a few times in his work, Fisher (a Canadian philosopher-educator-artist) brought this concept to a higher profile within the Subbaian fearism discourse.

497 The four (excluding one mention of "fearless") are: (1) 'fearlessness,' (2) fearlessness, (3) fearlessnessizing, (4) Fearlessnessland (Fisher, 2019f, pp. 12-13). All these terms are coined by myself (RMF)—albeit, (2) is not my own creation at all, it has a long and dignified history of use in Eastern cultures, religions, spiritualities and philosophies, especially.

498 Although Kumar and I have chosen this term 'crime' often in this book, there is another term one could use as a replacement or complement, that is, 'violence.' In particular, my own philosophy of fearwork from the start has been interested in "epistemic violence" and the politics of knowledge construction, distribution and what is deemed as the (somewhat 'neutral' domain of) "education" which trades in knowledge/power/fear dynamics.

499 Alex & P.S. (2021), p. 9.
500 Fisher (2010), p. xiv.
501 Fisher (2019l).
502 Fisher (2019m).
503 Fisher (2010), p. xvi.

INDEX

A

A-D/ness 74, 78, 79, 82-90, 92-4, 102, 111, 116, 124-8, 160, 221, 295, 296, 326, 365, 380-2, 385, 386, 394, 406; *see also* aesthetics

Abel, 364

abhaya (dāna), xxxi, 65, 183, 369 ; *see also* fearlessness

Abrahamic Tradition(s), xc, 386; *see also* Christianity

abstract(ion), xiii, xxxix, lxxxi, lxxxvii, 69, 98, 115, 159, 192, 269, 319, 322, 330, 399; *see also* artificial, dissociation, dualism, functionalism, logical, mechanical, objectification

absurd(ity), 136, 218, 279, 280, 281, 301, 311, 315, 318, 319, 331; *see also* Camusian, Fearlessness Paradigm, uncanny

addict(ive)(ion), liv, ci, cii, cv, cxiv, 9-10, 13-14, 15, 16, 32, 60, 96, 113, 117, 136, 193-4, 224, 225, 307, 356, 360, 369, 395, 401, 405; process, 229; righteousness (moralism), xvi; *see also* Alcoholics Anonymous, defense(s), dissociation, pathologies

Adhikari, B. S., cxxiii, cxxiv, cxxvii, 345, 367, 371, 372

adualism, 55; *see also* dualism, nondualism

aesthetics, 36, 43, 69, 73-74, 87, 93, 102, 225; inquiry, 70-2; *see also* A-D/ness, arationality, art(s), beauty

affect(ive)(s), xxiii, 179-86, 208; *see also* aesthetics, beauty, bonding, emotion(s), feelings, libidinal, *libido*, ugly

Agape, 229, 260; *see also* bonding, *Eros*, Love

agriculturalized, 367

agriculture, lxiv, 147; revolution, 187; *see also* cultural, Dominant worldview, Nature (vs.)

Ainsworth-Land, G. T., 345, 399

Alcoholics Anonymous, xci, 10, 226; *see also* addict(ive)(ion), F.E.A.R

Alex, R. K., 345, 407

Alexander, C., 73, 345, 379

Alexander the Great, xcix

aliens: *see* enemies

409

altered states: *see* arational, consciousness, dreams, mind, trance
Ambedkar, B. R., xl, lxvii, 77-8
Amundsen, 147
amygdala, lxxxi; *see also* body/brain
anger, xiv, xx, 186, 356, 380; *see also* betrayal, madness
angst, xiv, 383; *see also* dread
animal(ity), xviii, lxxiv, lxxvi, lxxxiv, xci, 110, 122, 135, 160, 163, 173, 175, 185, 186, 226, 230, 258, 375, 388-9, 399; *see also* Id, humans, mammals
anxiety, xviii, xxi, liii, lxxxix, xcii, xcvii-iii, c, cxix, 32, 51, 80, 112, 180, 214, 218, 297-8, 300, 321, 327, 332, 356, 358, 361, 383, 401, 406; awe and, 317, 348, buffering, 328; Cartesian, 218, 219; container, 110, 383; death, 374-5; disorder, xc; method and, 347; ontological, 393; Platonian, 219; uncanny, 317, 320, 323, 326, 348, 404; *see also* Cartesian anxiety, fear of death, existentialism, Platonic anxiety, reason, pathologies
apathy, xxi, xlix; *see also* culture of fear, helplessness
Aphrodite, xxxi
Arachne, 315, 316
arationality, 40, 74, 75, 76, 132, 238, 276, 283, 340-1, 346, 366, 384, 397; *see also* art(s), dreams, Gebserian, imagination, integral, irrationality
archetype(s), 56, 204, 263, 348, 390, 398; *see also* Father, hero, leadership (Royal), Magician, myth(s), Puer, Rebel, Sacred Warrior, Senex, Shadow, Twins
Arendt, H., xcvi, 283

Ares, xxxi
Aristotle, 304, 402
Aristotelean, 240, 301, 302-03, 402
Arndt, J., 393
Aron, R., 369
arrogance, 328, 406; *see also* ignore-ance, pathologies, *Phobos*
art(s): *see* A-D/ness, arationality, literary
artificial, xxxix, 110, 123, 192; *see also* abstract(ion), dualism, illusion(s), mechanical, walls
Artificial intelligence (AI problems), xxii-xxiii, 96, 114
Assagioli, R., 370
Atlas, lxvii, 315, 316
Atman, 405; *see also* Brahman, Hinduism
Atman Project, 395
attachment(s), xviii, lxxxvi, lxxxvii, 192; fear itself versus fears, xviii; *see also* bonding, coping, defense(s), Eros, love, object-cathexis, objectification
attention, l, xciv, cxxvii, 5, 22-4, 262; free-floating, 329; unconditional, 40
Auguste (character), 293-4
Auschwitz: *see* Nazism, Third Reich
authenticity, 6, 10, 14, 50, 97, 124, 205, 354, 378; *see also* truth(s)
authoritarian(ism), xlvii, xllvii, 32, 50, 113, 203; *see also* autocratic, dicatorships, ideology, oppression, right-wing
autocratic governments, xxvi, 63, 153; *see also* authoritarian(ism), Dominant worldview
Auxier, R., 28, 374
Azarian, B., 345, 364

B

Baby Boomers, lxix

Bacon, F., 307
Bader-Saye, S., 345, 385
Bailey, A., 182
Bailey, F. W., 182
Bailey's (The), xi
Bakasura, 316
Barber, B., 345, 363, 371, 384, 400
Barr, L., 346, 378, 391
Barr, N., 346, 378, 391
Barrett, L. F., 249, 346, 382, 399
barriers, xiii; Fear (2), 228; defensive, 235; 'fear,' 403; negative, xxx; repression, 296; see also boundaries (vs.), defense(s), resistance(s), walls
Bateson, G., 75, 346, 379, 382
Bataille, G., 360, 365
Beautiful (The), lv, cxvi, 75, 379
beauty, xxiii, 69, 72, 73, 85, 95, 124, 131, 270; fearlessness and, 58, 400; goodness and, 81; see also A-D/ness, aesthetics
Beck, D., 346, 377
Becker, E., 179, 389, 393, 404
Beckerian, lxxxv, 349; see also Terror Management theory
behavior(ism), xv, xix, cxviii, cxxvi, 122, 145, 327; addiction, 9, 13; cognitive, cxxii; disordered, 390; fearlessness as, 303; self-abusive, 77, 191, 405; social, 404; therapies, 262; see also cognitivism, functionalism, psychologism, psychology, reductionism
Belmi, P., lxxiii
betrayal, xx, xxviii, 50, 51, 348, 364; see also anger, lies, mistrust, woundedness
Bhagavad Gita, 65, 291; see also Hinduism, *Vedas*, *Upanishads*

Bhave, V., lii
bhaya, xxxi; see also *abhaya*, fear
Bheema, 316
Bible, xli, xlviii, xc, lxviii, cii, 264, 291; see also Christian(ity)
Bickel, B., xi, 48, 346, 379, 383, 396
binary, xxxiii, xxxvii, xl, xliii, lvii, 131, 132, 133, 159, 365, 367, 384; see also barriers, dualism, dialectical (vs.), opposites, wall(s)
Binder, M. J., 354
Biomedical worldview, 181; see also Science(s)
Bisht, K., 319, 346, 404
Black (people of color), 64, 197, 244, 397; see also racism
Black Panthers, 244
bodies/brain, xvii, lxxxix, xci, civ-cv, cxi, cxv, 64, 70, 167, 219; see also amygdala
Boethius, A. M. S., 39
Bois, J. S., 311, 346, 403
Boje, D. M., 346, 378, 391
bonding, lxxxvii, 13, 192, 404; fear-, xc, ci, cii, civ; love-, xc, ci; see also attachment(s), narcissistic
Boschman, C., 346, 402
boundaries, lviii, cxv, 72, 100, 125, 225; D-ness, 92; invaded, 14; without, 85, 380; see also barriers (vs.), walls (vs.)
Brahman, 405; see also Atman, Hinduism
branding (slogans), 385, fearlessness, 351; see also commodification
bravado: see bravery
brave(ry), xcviii, cxii, 25, 55, 61, 131, 181, 200, 204, 303; be humble, more, 202-03; bravado and, 142; virtues, 164; see also courage(ousness), Fear Management Systems
British Raj, lxvii

411

Broditsky, L., 220-1
Brown, J. S., 346, 369
Bruce, 242-6, 247, 249, 258
Buddha, xxxiv, cxvi, 57, 154, 198
Buddhism, 21, 25, 60, 115, 204, 230, 355, 376, 382, 392; *see also* Shambhala, nondualism, Zen
Burke, E., 77
Burke, K., 200-01, 205, 206, 361, 385, 391

C

Cain, 364
Campbell, J., lviii-ix, 55, 346, 367
Camus, A., 279-80, 287, 312-19, 328-32, 333, 346, 348, 393, 403
Camusian: absurd, 317, 318; declaration, 330; pessimism, 328; progress critiqued, 332; shift (meta-mythic), 330; Sisyphus, 315-6; *see also* existentialism, postmodernism
cancer(ophobia), lxxxviii, 135, 150, 162, 186, 189-90, 359; *see also* dis-ease, virus(es)
capitalism: disaster, 141, 356; predatory, xx, 123; *see also* economics, ideology
caring, xxi, 129, 206; pedagogy of, 385; theory (Fisher), xx, xxiii; *see also* compassion, Creation, ethics, helping, service
Cartesian anxiety, 218, 219, 298; *see also* cognitivism, modernism, rationalism
Cartesian dominant worldview, 393
Cassandra, xxx
Castaneda, C., 372

caste(s), xxii, xlvii, lxii-iii, lxvii, lxxii
casteism, lxvi, lxxvii, 41, 144, 151
CAT-FAWN, xci-xcii, 351, 384
cathexis: *see* attachment, bonding, healing
Catholic: *see* Roman Catholic
century of fear (Camus), 293, 393
century of terror (Fisher), 328, 331, 393
Chang, A., 389
change(s), xiv-xv, xxi, xlvi, 33, 133, 218; agent of, 375; *see also* apathy, conflict theory, development, functionalism, reform, (r)evolution, transformation
Charybdis, 27
Chödrön, P. 230, 346, 376-7, 396
Chopra, D., xxi
Christ: *see* Christianity, Jesus
Christian(ity), lxiii, lxix, lxxxviii, lxxxix, xc, 66, 173, 174, 240, 249, 367, 369, 385, 396; *see also* Abrahamic Tradition, *Bible*, Jesus, religion(s)
classism: *see* casteism, economics, poverty
Cleopatra, 290
climate change: *see* Global Warming
cognitive, xv, xviii, xcviii, cxxii, 16, 36, 44, 236; six stages, 399; pathologies, 298; *see also* behavior(ism), symbolic, thinking (thought)
Cohl, A., 188, 190, 346, 368, 377
colonization, 112, 118, 265, 266, 398; *see also* domination
commodification, xiv, xxi; *see also* branding, economics
communism, 157, 159; *see also* left-wing, socialism
compassion: *see* caring, matrixial theory
complexity theory, 394
conditional: *see* unconditional

conditioning, xliv, lxvi, lxxiv, cxx; fear-, liv; 'Fear' Matrix, 47; mind, cxvi; see also habits, human condition, illusion(s), norm(s)
conflict(s), xxxiv, xlix, 58; fear and, cxxiii; unhealthy, xxxiii; ontological, civ; political, xxxv; psychic, xxxviii; resolution, xxxvi; xxxvii; toxic, 317; see also defense(s), rebellion, resistance(s), politics, psychology, revolution(s), distress
conflict management/education (CME), xxxv, xl, xliii; see also DCFV theory
conflict theory, 59, 142; functionalism (vs.); see also critical theory, DCFV theory, left-wing, politics, structuralism
Connor, K. R., 347, 395
consciousness, xviii, lvii, 4, 30, 90, 224, 311, 314, 315, 367; double, 397; dualistic, lvii, lviii, lxi, 89, 131, 205, 375; evolution of (struggle), xvii; levels of, 59; spectrum of, xiv; structures, 82; see also altered state, false, fear, mythic, thinking
conservative, li, xcvi, xcvii, 159, 170; see also politics
conservativism, 19, 343; Christian, 173; see also right-wing
conspiracy theory, 117; see also critical theory
constructivist: see cognitive, functionalism, knowledge(s), poststructuralism
cooperation vs. competition, xvii, xviv, xx, xii
coping, 95, 197; see also defense(s), healing
Corradi, J. E., 313, 347, 403

corruption, cxvi, 136; compulsive security-seeking, cxiv; development, 66; fear and, lix; fear-based, 204; human condition, 175, 177; human nature, 174; leaders, 56; lower forces, 204; original sin, 174; psychology, 12; ugliness, 136; youth, 114; see also deception, distortion, false, fear, ideologies, neoliberalism, pathologies, State
cosmogenesis, xli; see also Bible
cosmos, xxxv, xlii, 109; see also kosmos
courage(ousness), xiv, xxiii, liv, xcvi, cxii, 61, 153, 181; moral, 343; see also brave(ry), Fear Management Systems
Course in Miracles (A), 143, 362, 365
Covey, S., 22
COVID-19, xvii, xviv, xxii, c, 32, 37, 128, 130, 318; lessons, xix, xx; responses (fearlessness), xx; responses (positive and negative), xx; responses (shut-down), xx; see also care, trauma
Cowan, C., 346, 377
Creation: see Mother (Nature), Nature
creativity: see arationality, art(s), Janus(ian), timelessness
Creed, B., 347, 406
crime, lxxi, cxiii, cxvi, 7-9, 11, 12, 13, 14, 24, 179, 181, 182, 218, 226, 239, 240, 250, 257, 258, 261, 265, 266, 268, 269, 271, 272, 273, 276, 312, 330, 338, 339, 373, 407; see also fearlessness
criminalisation, xxii
crises (global), xvii, xx, xxi-xx; see also COVID-19; ecological, economic, nuclear, political
Cristian, A., 283, 347, 378, 385, 398, 401

413

critical integral framework, 376
critical lens: fearism, 390
critical literacy, xiii, xviii; *see also* education
critical praxis, liv, 95, 195, 394; fearlessness and, 57
critical theory, cxx, 117, 142; *see also* conflict theory, conspiracy theory, liberation, political, praxis
critique of Positive Paradigm, xv; *see also* positivism
Cultural (sphere), 127, 161, 384
cultural approaches (analysis), 204; postmodern, 205; psycho-, xliv; revolution, 304; therapy, 8; *see also* culturalism, culturalist lens, postmodernism
cultural: bias, 161; contexts, 175; creature (human), 172; critique, 73, 313, 317; duties, 179; dynamics, 65; events (domination), lxvii; evolution, lxxi, xcvii; field-mind, 18; history, 188; leadership, 374; lens, xl; matrix (dominant), 398, 400; mediation, lxxv; norms, 166, 179; political factions, 100; revolution, 304, 319; techno-, 175, 185; therapy, 8, 372; views, 152; world, 75; *see also* agriculture, fear, political, Terror Management Theory, trance
cultural matrix, 306, 398; 400; *see also* culture of fear, Dominant worldview, 'Fear' Matrix
culturally hypertrophied, 126
culturally-modified 'fear': *see* 'fear'
Culture Wars: *see* Fear Wars
culture (radical): sub-, lxix
culture of fear, xiv, xxvii, xliv, cxv, 2, 18, 127, 278, 387; *see also* apathy, Culture, fear management/ education, ideology, morality, nine/ eleven, oppression, Other(ing), Terror Management Theory, terrorism, victim
culture of positivism, xiv-xv, xx; *see also* positivism
cura, lxxxiv; *see also therapia*
curriculum: *see* education, fear management/education, pedagogy

D

DCFV theory (Domination-Conflict-Fear-Violence), 59; *see also* conflict theory, critical theory
da Gama, V., 147
Daedalus, 27
Dalai Lama (His Holiness, XIV), cvii, 57, 65, 183, 343
Darius (King), xcix
Darwin, C., 102, 174
Darwinian, 172-3; *see also* evolutionary, survival
Davis, M., 347, 369
Dean, J., 33
Death-drive, 13, 94, 149, 161, 162, 191, 192, 206, 242, 262, 317, 378; *see also* death, ego, motivation(al), *Thanatos*
death, xxxviii, xli, lxxxiv, lxxxviii, c, civ-v, 13, 27, 48, 51, 97, 111, 149, 242, 318; imperative, 161; near (experience), 389; prompts, 319, 404; *see also destrudo*, existentialism, denial of death, fear (of death), future(s), Terror Management Theory, *Thanatos*

de Becker, G., lxxiv, lxxxv, xcii, 24, 368
de Beckerian, lxxxv
deception, 261, 262, 266-8, 277, 282, 398; *see also* defense(s), distortion, Dominant worldview, false, fiction, psychotic, untruth
Descartes, R., 218, 392
defense(s), xvi, 41, 106, 203, 223, 319, 395; fear-based, xvii; moralism of, xvi; *see also* artificial, attachment, barriers, conflict(s), denial of death, dissociation, dualism, emotion(s), fear, flight-fight, freeze (response), immunity, mechanical, needs, Other(ing), phobias, pathologies, projection, psychotic, regress, repressed, splitting, sublimation, trauma
Defense Intelligence (DI), xiv, xxiii, 3, 9, 20, 47, 53, 160, 169, 250; *see also* defense(s), fear management/education, Fearlessness IQ, Nature, regulating, risk(s), survival, threat (system)
Deleuze, G., 360, 365
Deming, W. E., xxiii, 373
democracy, xxv-vi, xxxii, 26, 152, 167; *see also* political
Democritus, 402
demonic, xxiv, xlviii, 63, 146; *see also* dictatorships, evil, spell
demonisation, 62; *see also* Other(ing), projection
demons, 81
denial, 196, 197, 277, 298, 335; amnesia, 128; of truth, 187; self-, 123; *see also* defense(s), dissociation, psychotic
denial of death, 346; see also fear (of death), Terror Management Theory

depth (psychology), xxxv, lxxxiv, 20, 45, 112; archetypal, 262; darker approach, 224; knowing, 248; *see also* existentialism, psychoanalysis, transpersonal
Derrida, J., 257
despair, xiv, xx, xxix, xlviii, 155, 373; *see also* dread, hope
desacralization, xxi
destrudo, xxxviii, civ, 48, 149; *see also* death, *Thanatos*
de Tocqueville, A., xcvi
developmental, xxiii, xxvi, xxxviii, xlv, 21, 234; Fearlessness, xxiii; post-adult, 234; *see also* education, evolution
Devereux, G., 347, 401
Dewey, J., 347, 383
dialectic(al), xiii, xxiii, xxvi, xxxvii, lvi, 64, 195, 223, 332; *see also* dualism, fear/fearlessness, holistic, nonbinary
discourses, xv, xxvii, lvii, lxxviii, 6, 37, 158, 203, 227, 240, 365, 384, 392, 399; agent of, 399; dominant, 231; existential, 161; positivizing, xiv; unity, xxii; *see also* deception, knowledge(s)
dis-ease, xxi, xxiii, xxix, 10, 11, 17, 98, 188, 191, 216; *see also* anxiety, fear, pathologies
dissociation, 116, 338, 373, 379; *see also* defense(s), denial, distortion, double talk, dualism, objectification, Other(ing), pathologies, psychotic, Shadow
dictatorships, 62-3, 64, 234, 263, 312, 403; *see also* authoritarianism, demonic, domination, fascism, Nazism

415

distortion, cxxii, 207 ; ideology and, 192; of real self, 10-11; knowledge-seeking (deficit), 393; needs and, cxiv, cxxii, 393; reductionism and, 390; security-seeking, cxiv; *see also* corruption, double talk, dualism, false, fear, psychotic

distress(ed): *see* conflict(s), hurt(ing), trauma, woundedness

Doblin, R., 32, 362

Dodds, J., 287, 324, 347, 404, 406

Dominant worldview, 13, 94, 107, 227, 266, 327, 366, 367, 393, 398; *see also* autocratic governments, colonization, corruption, ideology, Indigenous worldview, oppression, paradigm(s), psychotic, untruth, violence, worldview(s)

domination, xv, xviii, 62, 181, 351; fear-based ways, xxx; *see also* authoritarianism, colonization, conflict(s), DCFV theory, fear, pathologies, politics

Dotson, K., 347

double: *see* consciousness, meaning, Twin

double talk, 238-52, 255, 262, 277, 322, 336; *see also* dissociation, distortion, dualism, Error Theory (Freud), schizoidal, splitting

Down, B., 353

dread, xx, 312, 323, 324, 375; *see also* angst

dreams, xxvii, lxv, 98, 159, 194, 272, 294, 296; *see also* aesthetic, arational, vision(ary)

drive(s): *see* Life Drive, Death Drive, Esteem, motivation(al)

dualism, xviii, xxxiii, xlii, 55, 192, 397; critiques of, xvi, xviii; moralism, xvi; *see also* abstract(ion), artificial, consciousness, dialectic(al), distortion, double talk, epistemology, ideology, moralism, nondualism (vs.), splitting, violence

Dualism-Repression-Projection, 395; *see also* Atman Project, 'Fear' Project

Du Bois, W. E. B., 398, 400

Dubos, R., 136, 347, 385, 387, 388, 389

Dunning, D., 63

Duryodhana, 316

E

Eastern, lxvi, 2, 209; philosophy/culture, xxxiii, 390; rebel and, 390

ecological, xx, xxiii, 115, 160; companions (viruses), xix; crises, xvii; Earth Day, lxix; *see also* Gaia, Global Warming, Green

economic crises, xvii; *see also* capitalism, commodification, gift (the)

education, xxvi-xxvii, l, li, lii, lxvi, 1, 16, 18, 123; adult, xi; minimalist, 200; new era, xi; positive, xiv-xv; *see also* critical literacy, fear management/education, knowledge(s), learning, liberation, pedagogy, Positive Paradigm, propaganda, State, teachers, thinking (thought)

Ego, xxii, xxxiv, xxxviii, lxxvii, c, 51, 184; *see also* Freudian, Id, psychoanalysis, self, Super-Ego

ego, 10-11, 37, 40, 41, 152, 283; *see also* egoic, esteem, identity, self
egoic: death-drive, 378; fear weaponry, 56, 205; trans-, 375; *see also* bravado
Eisler, R., 49, 347, 377, 400
Einstein, A., 311
Emi, 385-6
empiricism, 365; *see also* positivism, Science(s)
emotion(s), xx, 197, 305, 311; lower vibrations (fear), xv; *see also*, affect(ive)(s), anger, angst, anxiety, despair, dread, fear, feelings, love, panic, terror, worry
Endarkenment, 224, 395; *see also* existentialism
Eneyo, M., 347, 367, 391
Enlightened Age, 386; *see also* Fearless Age, New Age
Enlightenment, xxvi, xxx, lxx, c, cxxi, 125, 155, 365, 395
enemies (aliens), xvii, xix, xcviii, 77, 378; worst (inside), xix; *see also* Other(ing)
English, A., 347, 352, 398
environment(s) xvii, lviii, 102; fearless, xxii; Environmental Movement, lxix; *see also* Green
epistemic: *adequatio*, cxii; doubt, 218; violence, 347, 391, 407; *see also* epistemology, ethics, functionalism, knowing, knowledge(s), philosophy, reductionism
epistemology, 43, 195, 209, 346, 397, 402, 403; multiple ways, 370; *see also* metaphysics, ontological
Erikson, E., 49, 66
Ermine, W., 265-6, 268, 271, 347, 400

Eros, 149, 229; *see also Agape*, bonding, Immortality, Life Drive, Love, Mother, motivation(al)
Esbjörn-Hargens, S., 358
Eskimo (Inuit), lxxx
esteem, xxix, cii, 51, 166, 169, 179, 308; It-, xlv; tripartite model, xliii-iv; *see also* needs, Terror Management Theory
ethical: *see* epistemic
ethics, xxi, 13, 64, 97, 105, 202, 317; *see also* caring, moralism, virtue(s)
Ettinger, B. L., 191-2, 262, 287, 317, 330, 340, 348, 383, 399, 400, 401, 403, 404-05, 406
Eurydice, lxvii
Eve, lix
Evernden, N., 109, 348, 383
Evil, xxxv, 75, 81, 153, 202, 228, 229, 246, 269, 276, 349, 379, 381; *see also* demonic, Good (The), Love vs. Fear, *Phobos, Thanatos*, ugly
evolution, xiii, xvii, xxxii, xxxviii, lxxiv, cxx, 57, 102; de-, 379; of caring ('gift'), xx; *see also* consciousness, Darwinian, developmental, Fear Management Systems, (r) evolution
existentialism, cxx, 51, 110, 329, 404; anxiety (crisis), xxi; *see also*, authentic, Camus, depth psychology, Endarkenment, fear of death, postmodernism, self (unauthentic), Terror Management Theory

F

Fagen, P. W., 347, 403

false, 97, 109, 307; concept, 307; fearlessness, 50; game, 168; myths, 118; security, 98; self, 10-11, 50; wall, 244; *see also* consciousness, culturalism, culture of fear, deception, denial, distortion, dualism, F. E. A. R., illusion, Immortality Project, untruth

Fanon, F., 398

fascism, 62, 64, 118, 342; *see also* ideology, Third Reich

Father, 317; *see also* psychoanalysis

Fazekas, P., 347, 402

F. E. A. R. (false evidence appearing real), xci; *see also* Alcoholics Anonymous, Fear

Fear, xi; behaviorally (reduced), xix; complexity, xvi; consciousness itself, xviii; critics of, xv-xvi; definitions (possible), xvi; education, cxiii; emotion (lower vibration), xv; F.E.A.R. (false evidence appearing real), xci; God of (*Phobos*), xcix; history of, xiv; individualization of, xix; location of, xvii, xviii; moralistic locating, xvi; paradigms/worldviews, xviii; *see also* culture of fear, Love vs. Fear, *Phobos*, *Thanatos*

Fear Management Systems (theory), cxix-cxx, 53, 142, 324, 376, 383, 396; *see also* evolution, regulating

Fear Paradigm, xl, xlii, xliv-v, li, 26, 120, 184, 271; versus Fearlessness Paradigm, xv

Fear Problem, xiii, xxiii, 66, 337; *see also* culture of fear, fear dilemma, disease, trauma

Fear Project, xvi, cxi, 114, 117; *see also* Atman Project, Culture, Dualism-Repression-Projection, Immortality Project

Fear Psychology, 45

Fear Studies, xiv, xviii, xxxi, 137; harm to (*via* positivism), xiv-xv; *International Journal of*, 340

Fear Wars, cxix, 371

'Fear' Matrix, xliv, 1, 14, 17-8, 47, 48, 56, 60, 62, 110, 254; Agents of, 18; *see also* cultural matrix, Culture, culturalism

'Fear' Project(ion), xliv, 94, 113, 203; *see also* Culture, Immortality Project, ontology, *Phobos*, *Thanatos*

'Fear' Studies, 137, 352

'fear,' defined, lxxxii; culturally-commodified, 387; culturally-constructed, 398; culturally-modified, xl, 376 ; *see also* 'Fear' Matrix, 'Fear' Project, *Phobos*, *Thanatos*

fear, xx; attracts fear, xv; century of, 293; conditioning, liv; constructing, xviii; definitions as absurd, 301; education, xxiii; everywhere, xviv; excessive (regressive), xxii; factor, lxiii, lxxii; fear itself, xviii, lxxv; Fisher's dictum, xix; localize/locate, xvii, xviii; motivator, xxi; object attachments, xviii; of death, xviii, xxvi-ii, xxxviii, xcix, civ-v, 150, 161, 221; individualization of, xix; phenomenon, xvii; positive versus negative (spectrum), xvi; positivizing, xiv; reductionistic (meanings), xvi; response (understanding), xix; responses (fearlessness), xix; responses (immobility), xvii;

responses (hope/love), xx; scared (levels), xxi; sceptre of, xxii; self-awareness and, xviii; sex education (analogy), xxiii; shut-down, xviv; threat and, xviii; understanding (know thyself), xviii; virus of, xxi; without, xxiii; *see also bhaya*, culture of fear, Defense Intelligence, dialectic(al), enemies, existentialism, fearlessness, flight-fight, freezing, insecurity/uncertainty, regulating, risk(s), threat (system), trauma

fear(s), xviii, xlvii, lxxi, lxxvi, xcix, cxxi, 63, 121, 152, 155, 179, 205; identity (social), xxii; locating (place for), xviii; versus fear itself, xviii ; youth, xxix, xxx, 357; *see also* defense(s), phobias

fear/fearlessness (dialectic), xiii, xiv, xviii, lv, lvii, 64, 72, 145, 222, 264, 371

fear-based, xxvii, xxviii, xxix, xli, lxvi, cxviii, 14, 36, 56, 113, 179, 237, 336, 381, 401; A-ness, 100; architectures, 185; defenses, xvii; dominant ways, xxx; drives, cxii; ideologism, cxviii; Matrix, 112; needs, cxiv; oppression, cxviii, 384; *see also* Dominant worldview, domination, ideology

fear dilemma, xvii; *see also* Fear Problem

fear management/education, xiv, xxi, xxvii, xxxv, liii, lvi, xcii, 122, 137, 194, 338, 366, 383; *see also* conflict theory, Defense Intelligence, education, Fearism, Fearlessness, liberation

Fear's Empire, xiii; *see also* colonization, culture of fear, Dominant worldview

Fear's Rule, li

fear-positivism, 128, 129, 369, 386, 390; *see also* gift of fear

fearanalysis, lxxxii, lxxxiii, lxxxvii, xciv, cxix, 18, 225, 226, 297, 308, 348, 352, 398, 405; *see also* psychoanalysis

feariatry, 12, 351; *see also* psychiatry

Fearism community, xi; *see also* Fearism (philosophy of)

Fearism (philosophy of), xi, xvi, xxiv, xxv, xxviii, xxx, xxxix, lx, lxxix, lxxxii, cix, cxviii, cxxviii, 2, 12, 15, 20, 35, 36, 39, 44, 51, 158, 195, 217, 250, 299, 332, 337, 342, 354, 363, 368, 379, 391, 407; location of, xvii, xviii; Positive Paradigm and, xv; resistances to, xiii ; Subbaian, cxx; versus love, xv; *see also* Defense Intelligence, Subba, Subbaian-Fisherian

fearism (toxic form): fearism-t (Fisherian), cxviii, 48, 376; *see also* Other(ing), terrorism

Fearless Age, 386; *see also* Enlightened Age, New Age

fearless, xxviii, xlviii, cxxv, cxxviii, 27, 35-6, 53, 60, 80, 85, 99, 121, 130, 131, 148, 407; attitude, 17; authentic, 378; become, cxiv, 81; bravado, 50; children, lii; D-ness, 126; dialogue, cxxiii; distinguished (from fearlessness), cxxi, 376; double talk and, 323; environments (governments), xxii; *faux*, xxi; environment, xxii; Fear Management System-9, 124, 371; future, xxix; heart, 356; journey to, 361; leader, cv, 25, 26, 30, 60, 204, 205, ; leadership, xxvii, xli, 46, 314, 354; meet fear

419

with, 28; mental state, cxxvii; mode, 294; path, cxxiii; Republic, xxxiii, 357; society, xxii, 65; socioeconomic, cxxv; Subba on, cxxiii; terror threshold, cxx; voicing, 314; women can't be, cv; *see also* nondualism, standpoint theories

Fearlessness: birth right, xiv; complexity, xvi, xxiii; consciousness itself, xviii; definitions (possible), xvi; developmental, xxiii; Fear Management Systems-7, 396; Fisherian theory, cxx; Great Tradition, 229; locating, xvii-xviii; negative, xvi; open-minded investigation, xvi; paradigms, xviii; positive, xvi; Positive Paradigm and, xv; positivizing and, xiv; rescue world (not), xxiii; resistances to, xiii; subtle, xxiii; uncanny, xvii; way of, xi, xx; worldview, xviii; *see also* Fearlessness Movement, Fearlessness Paradigm, Indigenous worldview, gift of

Fearlessness IQ: *see* Defense Intelligence

Fearlessness Movement, xiv, xlix, l, lxxxiv, cxxiv, 20, 57, 141, 143, 145-50, 152, 154, 156, 160, 165, 168, 178, 194, 195, 197, 203, 228, 266, 337, 342, 351, 373, 391; resisted by, 179; *see also* In Search of Fearlessness Project, League *for* Fearlessness, nonviolence, resistance(s)

Fearlessness Paradigm, xvi, xviii, xxi, xxiii, xxvii, xxxi, xxxvi, xl, xlii, xliv, xlv, cxxvi, 21, 45, 47, 58, 123, 171, 392; absurdity and, 281; architecture (new), 137; competition debate, 375; conservativism and, 343; conspiracy theory, 117; D-ness, 126; definition, xxiii; dialectical, 184, 342; fearology and, 61; fear of death and, 161; four dimension, 397; human nature and, 174; infested by Fear Paradigm, 185; freedom and, 400; integral, 353; lesser known, 320; miss 'fearlessness' (not), 309; Nature/Life and, 172; negative, xvi; other dimension, 60; resistances to, xiii, 31, 62, 391, 395; road less travelled, xvi; solve Fear Problem, xxiii; theoretical, 42; versus Fear Paradigm, xv, 156, 168, 185, 202, 320, 375; versus Love Paradigm, xvi; versus Positive Paradigm, xv; *see also* Fearlessness Philosophy

Fearlessness Philosophy, xxx, 170, 213, 227, 230, 240, 283, 310, 338, 395, 397, 398, 400 ; negative (too), xv; *see also* Fearlessness Paradigm, Fear Philosophy (vs.), negative, philosophy (of fearlessness)

Fearlessness Psychology, 45, 310

fearlessness, xv, xix, xx, xlviii, 407; *abhaya hastam*, 66; afraid of, 18; as resistance itself, 48; -based, 288, 292; beauty and, 81; commodification of, 142; consciousness and, lxi; courage (distinct from), 143; critical literacy for, 224; culture of, 223; defends body, cv; define, lv, 300, 303; developing (promoting), 142; dialectical, xxxi; dictum (Fisher), xix, 53; discipline, lxxxiv; education, xlix; Elephant in the Room, 4, 14,

31; epistemology, 50; escape, 7; excellence and, 21; exercising its muscles, cxvii; false, 50; fearism and, 16; four freedoms and, 154; fragility, 116; fraternity as, xxii; Freudian Id and, xix; from fear to, 232; Gandhi's, 198, 304; ignored, 124, 141, 230, 250; haters of, 197; healing and, 223; historical omission, 333; imaginaries (new), lii; immortality and, 111; in search of, 224; Indigenous and, xcii; knowing, 50; latent (hidden), xix; leadership and, 20, 48; learning from fear, 143; lens, 16, 281; living process (practice), 224; looks opposite to fear, xxxiv; matrix and, 18; mature, xlvii; motivator (political), xcvii; movement, 154, 156; nonviolence and, 198; not in Abrahamic tradition, xc; organization, 224; path of, 51, 53, 124, 224; pathology, xxxix; perspective, 102, 157; philosophy, 222; primal, 199; rebellious, lxviii, 159; resistances to, lxxix, 48; resource of, 141; response to fear, xix; self- (philosophy), 222; simplistic, li; spirit of, l, 51, 54, 55; teachings, 278; theory, cii; threatens (norms), 326; transformative learning as, 9; true, 17, 56; truth (without righteousness), xvi; unconscious (instinct), lxviii; United Nations, xxii; uncanny, 287, 303; victim (not), xxi; voice, 334; vulnerability and, 116; warrior and, 205, 208; *see also abhaya*, courageousness, crime, dialectic(al), fear, gift of, Spirit

fearlessnessizing, 107, 266
Fearlessnessland, 281
fearmongering, xxx, lxxvi, cxix, 2, 306; *see also* Fear Wars, weaponizing
fearsome, lxx, 81, 397
fearwork, cx, cxx, cxxi, 182, 208, 242, 297, 368, 406, 407
Fedor, D. B., 346, 378, 391
feelings, xxii, xc, cxiii, 12, 84, 208, 305; binary of, 132; fear without, 193; exhaustion (pandemic), xviv; uncertainty, xxii; *see also* affect(ive)(s), emotion(s), Id, uncanny
Felman, S., 330-1, 348, 406
Ferguson, M., 65, 348, 369, 378, 389
fiction, cvi, 19, 58, 254; *see also* deception, imaginary, literary, stories
Fisher, R. M., xi, xiv, xv, xvi, xviii, xix, xxiv, xxv-xxvi, xxix, liii, lvi, lxii, lxxiv, lxxx, xcii, cvi, cix-cxii, cxvii-iii, cxxiii-iv, 1, 3-5, 6-7, 8-9, 12, 14-16, 17-19, 21, 35, 47, 48, 49, 51, 52-6, 57, 65, 83, 102-04, 132-6, 137, 141-3, 145-6, 149-50, 152, 157-9, 161-9, 171-8, 180-1, 184, 200, 202, 203-05, 207-08, 212, 215-16, 220-31, 232-33, 238, 239, 250-1, 263, 283, 287, 295, 298-300, 305-06, 308-10, 313-15, 317-29, 331-2, 335-9, 340-1, 342-3, 348-54, 357, 363, 364, 365, 366, 367, 368, 369, 370, 371, 372, 373, 374-5, 376, 377, 378, 379, 380-1, 382, 383, 384-5, 386-7, 388, 389, 390-1, 392, 393, 394, 395-6, 397-9, 400-01, 402-3, 405, 406-07,
Fisherian, cxix, cxx, cxxiv, cxxvi, 216, 217, 340; dictum, 404
Fixmer-Oraiz, N., 354, 385

421

flight-fight, xviii, xix; see also fear, defense(s)
Forman, M. D., 354, 399
Four Arrows, liii-lv, lvi, xci-xcv, 13, 28, 107, 113, 118, 204, 227, 266-7, 271, 340, 353, 354, 362, 363, 366, 367, 373, 378, 382, 384, 387, 396, 398, 400; see also Jacobs, D. T., *Wahinkpe Topa*
Foucault, M., 257, 360, 365, 392, 399
Fowler, J., W., 354
Fox, M., 395
Frankenstein, 64
fraternity, xxii, xxvi, 78; see also unity
Freedoms (Four), 152, 154, 160
freedom, xlix, lii, cxii, 15, 124, 169, 364; free agent, 208, 287; no. 1 aim, xx; see also Camus, fear of, fearless (society), fearlessness, politics, rebellion, rights
freeze (response), xvii; shut-down, xviv; see also fear, flight-fight, panic
Freire, P., 224, 347, 354, 396
Freud, S., xliv, 5, 94, 106, 172, 174, 175, 184, 191, 287, 297, 304, 311, 318, 319, 329, 373, 404
Freudian, xix, 88, 185, 298, 306, 307, 310, 317, 355, 405; slip, 305; see also Id, Ego, Super-Ego
Freudophobia, 298
Fromm, E., 15, 16, 100, 124, 352, 354, 373
functionalism, 113; see also conflict theory (vs.)
functionalist, xxxv, lxxviii, 142, 203; see also Dominant worldview, materialism, minimalism, reductionism
Furedi, F., 355, 363, 364, 366, 372

future(s), xxi, xxv, xxviii, xxix, xxxvi-xxxvii, xlviii, lxxxix, cix, 21, 28, 75, 144, 253, 283; fearlessness, 65; shrinking (i.e., extinction), xxi ; youth (symbolic), l; see also death, New Age

G

Gaia, 186, 191; Hypothesis, 88; see also ecological
Garden of Eden, lviii
Gandhi, M., xli, 28, 57, 148, 197, 198, 221, 304, 343
Gandhian, 369; see also nonviolence, Satyagraha
Garretón, M. A., 347, 403
Gebser, J., xxiv, 238, 282, 355, 364, 397
Gebserian, 282
Geist, V., 75, 355, 379
Gibb, J., 49, 355, 377
gift (the), xiv, xx; sacred and, xx; spirit of the, cvi-cvii; see also Mother
gift of fear, lvii, lxi-cv, 137; see also Defense Intelligence, fear-positivists
gift of fearlessness, xiv; liii, lvii, 24, 355, 387; caring, xx; sacred, xx; see also Defense Intelligence
Gillian, S. N., 105, 137, 349, 355, 382, 385
Gimian, C. R., 361
Giroux, H. A., 355, 385
Glassner, B., 355, 363, 364, 366, 368, 372
Global Warming, xiii, xxi-xxii
God(s), xv, xxv, xxxvi, xli, lxiii, lxiv, 7, 53, 65, 153, 185, 226, 281, 402; fear of, 129; is fearlessness, 343; of Fear (*Phobos*), xcix; of violence (Ares), xxxi; see also myth(s), Satan

422

goddess, 7, 65, 81, 153; of Love (Aphrodite), xxxi; *see also* Gaia, myth(s), religion(s)

Goldman, M., 355, 400

Goleman, D., 355, 370

Good (The), xv, xvi, 379, 384; *see also* Evil, gift (the), Love vs. Fear

government(s), xxii, xxvi, xxxii, xlvii, 37, 49, 62, 146; ideals, xxii; responsibility (re: fear/insecurity), xxii; *see also* autocratic, dictatorships

Greek: *see* mind, mythology, philosophers, Pythagoreans, revolution

Green, 109; *see also* ecological, environment(s), Nature

Greenberg, J., 360, 361, 373, 393-4, 404, 406

Gurung, M., 346, 369

Gur-Zé ev, I., 113, 355

Guy, D., 355, 405

H

habit(s): *see* conditioning, norm(s)

Hall, C. S., 220, 355, 404

Hallward, P., 355, 364

Haze, Z., 345

healing, xci, 7, 13, 22, 76, 167, 388; paradigm, 202; *see also* cathexis, immunity, regulating (system)

health (wellness), xiv, xxviii, cxxiv, 10-11, 13, 16, 71, 85, 101, 380-1; deterioration of, xxii, 23; mental, 11-12; no. 1 aim, xx; *see also* liberation, peace, sanity, sustainable,

Hebrew, 66

Hegel, G. W. F., 233, 367

Hegelian, xxxiii-xxxiv

Heidegger, M., 129, 382

Heim, M., 355, 369, 376

helping: *see* caring

helplessness, xlix, 77; *see also* apathy, hopelessness, victim

hero, lix, xcvi, 51, 205; *see also* archetype(s), Rebel, Sacred Warrior

Herbert, F., 355

Heraclitus, 402

Hibbets, M., 355, 369

Hillman, J., 262-3, 355, 400

Hinduism, lxiii, 65, 355, 372; *see also* Atman, *Bhagavad Gita*, Brahman, Krishna

Hitler, A., lxviii, 246

Hobbes, T., lxxv, xcvi

holistic, xxxvii, xli, lii, liv, 36, 354, 366; curriculum, xlvi; fearlessness and, xlix; -integral, xxxvii, l; xxxi, xxxvi, lv, cxii, 161, 203, 229 *see also* health, integral, sustainable, unity

holism, xiv

Holocaust, 277, 330; *see also* Third Reich

Holy Spirit, 387; *see also* spiritual(ity)

Homer, 290

homeopathy, 223; *see also* immunity, vaccine

hooks, b., 197, 391

hope, xxi, 52, 81, 364; abandon, 376; addiction, 369; fear and, 60-1; love and, xx; -mongering, 142, 363; paradigm, 229; *see also* defense(s), despair, Pollyana-ish, trust

hopelessness: *see* despair, helplessness, victim

423

horde, xxi; *see also* materialism
Horsley, J., 356, 375, 378, 391
Huffington, A., 221, 339
Hugh, 249, 250, 253
Hugill, T., 238-9
human(s), 109; better-angel side, xxiii; *Homo mensura*, 280; unique animal, xviii; social species, xx; *see also* animal(ity)
human condition, xxxviii, 175, 177, 190; *see also* conditioning, norm(s)
human nature, xxvii-iii, xxxviii, 56, 95, 112, 149, 170-7, 393; *see also* animal(ity), Id, instinct(ual)
human potential, xxvii, xxix, xxxviii, 47, 48, 101, 146, 208, 333, 375; *see also* development, evolution, liberation
Human Potential Movement, xv; *see also* Fearlessness Movement, New Age
hurt(ing), 10-11, 74, 75, 95, 165, 167, 224; cycle of, 378; unhealed, 225; *see also* distress(ed), mistrust, trauma
hypnosis, liv, xciii, xciv, 113, 127, 194, 384; de-, xliv, 227; ideology, 141; *see also* altered state, CAT-FAWN, false, illusion(s), spell, trance, unconscious

I

Ibsen, H., 283
Id, xix, xxxviii, xlv, lxxvii, 160; *see also* animal(ity), Ego, Freudian, instinct(ual), primal, Super-Ego
idealism, 116, 117, 406; *see also* politics, spiritual(ity)
ideologism, 116; *see also* ideology

identity cii, 51, 145, 311, 389, 399, 402; -based fears (social), xxii; Brahman, 405; *see also* culture of fear, ego, esteem, politics
ideology, lxvii, 2, 97, 114, 381, 383; capitalism, xx; communist, 147; fear-based, 181; hypnotic, 141; moralism/dualism, xvi; positivism, xv; *see also* authoritarian(ism), dictatorships, distortion, culture of fear, false, ideologism, propaganda, reductionism, weaponization
ignore-ance, xx, 39, 274, 328, 381, 406; *see also* arrogance, denial, pathologies
illusion(s), xliv, 47, 136, 145, 326, 383, 403; *see also* altered state, conditioning, false, hypnosis, psychotic
imaginary, xcviii, 44, 47, 123, 133, 171, 177, 184, 200, 289, 403; *see also* fiction
imagination, lv, lvii, 65, 97, 151, 213, 231, 271, 297, 315, 347, 368; *see also* arationality, imaginary
immaturity, xxiii, xxviii, 30, 195, 236; *see also* regress
immobility: *see* freeze (response)
immortality, lviii, 98, 107, 111, 235, 255, 399; symbolic, 324; *see also Eros*, Life Drive, motivation(al), Terror Management Theory
Immortality Project, 192, 201, 202, 349, 361; *see also* 'Fear' Project
immunity, 23, 131, 162, 223; *see also* defense(s), Defense Intelligence, resilience, vaccine(s)

In Search of Fearlessness Project (ISOF), xi, xxiv, 222, 226, 228, 229; critics of, xvi ; *see also* Fearlessness Movement

In Search of Love Project, xvi

India, xxii, xxv, xxx, xxxi, xl, xli, xlvi, xlvii, lxii, lxiii, lxiv, lxvi, lxvii, lxviii, lxx, lxxi, lxxii, lxxiii, lxxvi, lxxvii, c, 27, 62, 78, 79, 120, 144, 147, 148, 183, 267, 290, 291, 316, 338, 357

Indians, 367, 374; anti-, 267, 362; *see also* Indigenous

Indigenous, liii, xvi, lxxx, xcii, 118, 265, 266, 267, 340, 347, 351, 354, 363, 372, 378, 392, 397, 398, 399, 400; primal, xix, lvii; worldview, xix, 13, 107, 226, 227, 268, 364, 366, 367; *see also* Eskimo, Four Arrows, Indians, Lakota

individual, 172; agent, 113; agent (change), 375; agent (free), 208; agent (of discourses), 399; agent (rational), xcvi, 398; private self, 10-11

injustice: *see* crime

insanity: *see* madness

insecurity/uncertainty, xxii, lxxiii, cxxvii, 26, 154, 370, 383 ; *see also* fear, irrationality, risk(s), threat(s)

instinct(ual), xxxviii, xlv, lxi, lxviii, lxxvi, lxxvii, civ, 1, 22, 48, 70, 88, 147, 173, 184, 387; *see also* animal, Id, primal, human nature, Indigenous, Nature, unconscious

integral, xxiv, xlv, 51, 105; level, 54; perspective, 328; second-tier, 175; theory, 52; *see also* holistic, philosophy, transpersonal

integralism, 108

intelligence, xxiii, lxxiv, xcii, cxiii, cxv, 9, 83, 355, 379; ethical, 71; Fear, 62; primal, 164; reduced, xvi, somatic, 70; *see also* Defense Intelligence, dialogue, education

investigation, xvi, xxxii, xlii, lx; criminal, 7; deeper, xvi; forensic, cxii; open-minded (creative), xvi

irrationality, xxi, xxviii, lxxxv, 36, 74, 151, 180, 238, 289, 391, 397; *see also* arationality, conditioning, dis-ease, fear, hurt(ing), illusion, insecurity/uncertainty, pathologies, rationality

Islamism, 66; *see* Mohammed

J

Jackins, H., 74-5, 95, 356, 378, 379, 381, 395

Jacobs, D. T., 353, 354, 356, 362, 366 ; *see also* Four Arrows, *Wahinkpe Topa*

Jainism, 355

James (Hermitix), lxi, lxxx, lxxxiii

Janus(ian) thinking, xxxvi-viii, xxxix, xli, 360, 362; *see also* creativity

Jarasandha, 316

Jesus, lxxxix, cvii, 128, 369; *see also* Christian(ity)

Jingpa, T., 356, 376

Josef K., 316

journey, cxvi, 46, 49, 223; fearlessness, cxxii; heroine's, 359; soul's, 47, 53, 205, tribesman's, 361; *see also* hero

joy, xxiii, lxxx, 166, 168, 376; contraction of, xxi
Jung, C. G., xxxv, xlvii, xlix, 224, 395

K

Kafka, F., 316
Kahane, A., 356, 374
Kalu, O. A., cxxiii-iv, cxxvii, 345, 356, 367, 368, 371, 381
Kampis, G., 348, 402
Kant, I., 357
Kapsch, S. G., 356, 395
Karris, R., 345
karma, lxiv
Karr, M., 347
Kasman, D. L., 342, 350
Keechaka, 316
Keen, S., 354, 356, 377, 390
Keeney, B., 75, 356, 379
Kern, 293-4
Kierkegaard, S., 179, 280
Kieslowski, K., 292
King (Fear), 263
King, M. L. (Jr.), 28
Kizel, A., 111, 112-13, 114, 356, 384, 385
Klein, N., 356, 385
Kleiner, A., 61, 356, 373
know thyself, xviii, 50; *see also* philosophy
knowledge(s), xxxvii, li, liii, lxii, lxxvii, cxiv, cxxii, 16, 27, 144, 218, 393, 407; commodification of, cxiii; constructed, xviii; deficit-oriented, 370; fear and, 367; fearlessness-based, cxvi; industry, 133; /power, 365, 379; superficial, cxii; *see also* conditioning, education, epistemic, epistemology
knowing, cx, 39, 248, 370; fear, xviii, 365, cxii; fear-based, 174, 218; fearlessness, 40, 50; feeling-, 69; holistic, 40; norm ways, xliv; ourselves, 50; paradigm of, lvi; resistance to, xxiii, 180; wisdom, cxvi; *see also* conditioning, epistemic, epistemology
Koros, V., 356, 383
Korten, D., 234-5, 236, 356, 396
Korzybski, A., 310, 403
kosmos, 383, 384; *see also* cosmos
Krishna, cxvi; *see also* Hinduism
Krishnamurti, J., cxii-iv, cxv-vi, cxxi, 40-1, 348, 356-7, 370, 371, 375
Kruger, J., 63
Kuhn, T., 59, 220, 357, 368, 378, 388
Kumar, A., 379-80
Kumar, B. M., iii, xxv, xxix-xxxi, lv, lxi-ii, lxxxiv, xcvii, xcvii, cvi, cxiii, cxvii, cxxiv-vii, cxxv-vii, 1, 5, 7, 9, 17, 21, 35, 57, 72, 80, 106, 142, 144, 146, 155, 157, 159-60, 169, 178, 182, 197, 204-05, 212-13, 215, 222, 240, 250-1, 271, 276, 287-94, 295, 300, 307-08, 309, 315-17, 323, 336, 343, 348, 357, 364, 372 365, 368, 371, 374, 379, 384, 385, 400-01, 402, 403, 407

L

LGBTQ, 154; *see also* phobias, queer theory,
Lacan, J., 5, 360, 365
Lacanian: post-, 317, 399
Laing, R. D., 11-12, 14, 15, 357, 372-3, 377
Lakota, liii
Lamm, S., 361
Lao Tse, 98

Lardreau, G., 364
Laub, D., 348
Laundré, J. W., 346, 369
Lawler, J., 357, 383
Le Roy, L., 387
League *for* Fearlessness (The), xi, 182-3, 349
leadership, xi, 1, 31, 37-8, 42, 57, 185, 373, 374, 375, 377, 391; Democratic, xxxii; fearless, xxvii, xli, 17, 46; Fearlessness, 55; paradigm of, 52; Royal, 56; true, 30
Leary, M., 360
learning, xv, 71, 366, 399; re-(unlearning), xviii, 362; TBL (Trance-based), liv, 384; *see also* CAT-FAWN, education, hypnosis, pedagogy, trance, transformation, trauma
LeBeau, M., 357, 367
left-wing, 100, 159; *see also* fascism, ideology, liberal, right-wing, politics, socialism
legends, lxviii, ciii, 65, 81, 316; *see* myth(s), mythology
Leggo, C., xi, 213, 231-3, 235, 237, 357, 373, 385, 391, 396
Lerner, H. D., 110, 357, 384
Lerner, P. M., 110, 357, 384
Levinas, I., 129-30, 398
Levinasian, 240, 385
Levine, P., xvii, xviii, xx, 358
libidinal, 208; *see also* affect(ive)(s), libido
libido, xxxviii, civ, cv, 48, 149, 162; *see also Eros*, psychoanalysis
liberal: *see* neoliberalism
liberation, xi, xli, cxvi, cxx, cxxii, 7, 48, 75, 203, 223, 224, 241; free agent, 208; leaders, 226; path of, 337; philosophy, 227, 336; *see also* domination (vs.), freedom, healing, health, human potential, left-wing, liberty, nonviolence, oppression (vs.), peace, praxis, Reversal, theory
liberty, xxvi, xiii, xcvii, cxxvii, 152, 173; *see also* democracy, freedom, progressive
lie: *see* false, untruth
Life Drive, 94, 149, 160, 162; *see also Eros*, Immortality, Immortality Project, motivation(al), Nature
Life System, 185
Lincoln, A., 77
Lindberg, S., 62
Lisa, 246-8, 249
literary, lxviii, cxviii, 2, 157, 256, 270, 271, 276, 278, 301, 305, 330 397, 399, 400; *see also* art(s)
Little, G. C., 358, 368
localizing: *see* locating
locating, xvii, xviii: *see also* Fear, fear, Fearlessness, fearlessness
logic(al): *see* abstract(ion), rational
love, xx, xvi, xx, xxix, xxxviii, xxxix, lxxxviii, xc, civ, 57, 77, 241, 355, 356, 357, 385-6, 404, 405; addictions, 360; -based, 234, 235; fearlessness (inherently), 241; hate, 260; is the answer, xv; letting go of fear, 143; Paradigm, xvi; politics of, xv; radical, 351; return to, 362; romantic, 225; *see also* attachment(s), hope, In Search of Love Project
Love vs. Fear, xv, 15, 29, 49, 71, 191, 229, 349, 352, 363, 374, 393; dialectics of, 375; *see also* paradigm(s)
Lovelock, J., 89
Lucretius, 291
Lührmann, A., 62

427

M

MacDorman, K. F., 320, 324-6, 358, 406
machine, 33, 92, 93, 94, 97, 103, 186, 255, 302, 326, 406; *see also* artificial, mechanical
MacKeracher, D., 358, 366
Mackie, F., 358, 403
madness, 11, 18, 107, 189, 357; insanity, 17, 20, 50, 273, 328, 398; *see also* anger, Dominant worldview, existentialism, health (mental), methodologies, pathologies, psychiatry, psychoanalysis
magical, liii, 226, 274, 282, 377, 402; *see also* reality, shamanism
Magician archetype, 56, 204, 205, 377, 378, 390, 391; *see also* Rebel, Sacred Warrior
Mahabarata, lxvii, 290
Malthusian theory, cxxi
mammals, 122, 160, 388; *see also* animal(ity), human(s)
management, lxxvii, lxxxiv, 1, 27, 151, 346, 377, 391; conflict, xxxv, 353; emotional, 383; Quality, xxiii; without fear, xxiii; *see also* fear management/education, Terror Management Theory
Martin, R., 105-6, 358, 382
Maruyama, M., 221-2, 258
Marx, K., lxx, 109, 154, 280, 373
Marxian, 102, 157
Marxist, lxx; *see also* communism, conflict theory, politics, socialism, structuralism
Maslow, A., lxx, cxiv, 120, 154, 174, 220, 298, 358, 370-1, 393, 394, 401

Massumi, B., cxv, 358, 371, 385, 388-9,
materialism, lxxviii, 114, 136, 161, 383; *see also* functionalism, horde
Matthew, D., 358, 383
Matrix (The), 17, 253, 254, 255, 256, 271, 278, 284
matrixial theory, 191, 281, 340, 348, 383, 392, 399, 400; *see also* caring, (M)Other, Other(ing)
May, R., 358, 375
McHarg, I., 75, 358, 379
McManaman, D., 358, 369
meaning, xvi, xxix, xli, lvii, lxxvii, cv, 43, 44, 112, 179, 223, 236, 366, 397; double, xvii, 252; epigrammatic, 190; -less, 385; narratives of, 130; *see also* existentialism
mechanical, 74, 88, 115, 134; model, 92, 93, 95, 124; paradigm, 374; *see also* artificial, defense(s), dualism, machine
Mechanical vs. Organic, 74, 89, 94, 326, 383
meditation, xcviii, 225; *see also* mindfulness, regulating
Merton, T., lxxv, 368
metaphysics, lviii, ciii, 21, 150, 197, 260, 384, 387, 405; *see also* nondualism, philosophy
methodologies: challenges, 209; voluntary performative schizoidal praxis, 18, *see also* Cartesian anxiety, cognitive, madness, Platonic anxiety
Mill, J. S., 173-4
Miller, A., 384
Miller, J. P., 354, 363
mind, xxvi, lxxxv, c, civ, 12, 191: body/, cxii; change of, cxviii, 36; conditioned, cxi, cxiv; consciousness, lxi; cultural-field,

18; disturbed, 188; fear and, 36; fear-conditioned, cxv; games, xcix; Greek (premodern), 301, open-, cxxi; -power, 185; primal, lvi; without fear, cxxiv, 36; *see also* cognitive, conditioning, intelligence

mindfulness, lii, 26, 39, 223; *see also* meditation, peace

mindset, xxix, li, 33; *see also* mind

Mindell, A., 25-6, 358, 374

minimalism, 200, 203; minus-ing (less), 396; *see also* functionalist, narcissism, poststructuralism

mistrust, lxxii, 35, 49, 137, 317; fear and, 49, 401; *see also* betrayal, lies, trust

Mobbs, D., 358, 399

Mohammed, cxvi; *see also* Islamism

Mondrian, P., 381

monism, xlii; *see also* dualism (vs.), nondualism

Montesquieu, xcvi

morals, 114; *see also* virtue(s)

moralism, xvi, 58, 206, 398; commandments, xxi; defenses, xvi; meaning of fear, xvi; trap, xvi; *see also* addictive, dualism, ethics, morality, positivism, reductionism, virtues

morality, 379: conservative vs. liberal, 176; neurobiology of, 64, 359; of low expectations, 355; *see also*, culture of fear, minimalism, moralism, self, social

More, T., xxxiii

Moreno, F. J., 218, 359, 393

Moreva, L., 218-19, 359, 394

Mori, M., 322

Morin, M-T., 359, 393, 394

Morpheus, 284; *see also Matrix (The)*

mortality, 326, 327; ideation, 325; prompting, 325; salience, 324, 358; *see also* denial of death, existentialism, fear of death, Immortality Project, Terror Management Theory

Mother, xx; *see also* feminism, matrixial theory, post-Lacanian, psychoanalysis

Mother (Earth, Nature), xiv, xx, lvi

mother substitute (*via* fear), ci, cii, civ, 93, 192, 314; *see also* bonding, deception, fear (projection), illusion

mother/matrix, 404

motherhood and apple pie, xv

motivation(al), xiv, xxi, xxvii, lxxvii, 59, 65, 130, 161, 336; arche-, xxxix; bi-, 15; fear-based, xxviii; 'fear'-based, 216; investments, 298; map of, 207; meta- xliii, 71, 405; principle, xxv; psychology, 220; schema, 261; template, xxxiii, xlv, 219; *see also* Fear vs. Love, fear, fear of death. fear/fearlessness

Movement(s): negative, xvi; *see also* environment(s), Fearlessness Movement, Human Potential Movement, New Age, Positive Psychology, Positivists, Rebel, Resistance(s), revolution(s)

Moyers, B., lviii-ix, 346, 367

Murdock, M., 359, 377

mystery: *see* crime

mystic(al), xxiv, lxxv, 27, 69, 333, 368, 369, 372, 395; *see also* shamanism, spiritual(ity), transpersonal, vision(ary)

myth(s), xxxi, xxxvi, xxxviii, xli, xlix, li, lviii, lix, cv, 7, 29, 56, 81, 185, 262, 263, 316, 318, 346, 355,

360; casteism and, lxvi; Eastern, lxvi; false, 118; -making, 378, 391; meta- 253, 330, 399; post-, 402; *see also* mythology, religion(s), Royal Leadership, Sisyphus,
mytheme, xxxvii, xli; *see also* Bible
mythic consciousness, 310-11
mythic(-based) reality, 282, 300
mytho-psychological xxv
mythology, 51, 202; Greek, lxv, lxvii-iii, 15, 316; Indian, lxviii; Roman, xxxvi, lxv-vi; Twins, xxxvi; *see also* Janus(ian), myth(s), Sisyphus, symbolic

N

Naive, 56; *see also* Pollyana-ish
Napoleon, lxxiii
narcissism, 206, 324; *see also* self
narcissistic, 123, 192, 321; syndrome (twisted), 193; wounding, 404; *see also* attachment
Narvaez, D., 64, 359, 378
Natural, xlv, xcii, 73
natural, ci, cxiv, 64, 95, 103, 123; ancestors, 367; caring ('gift'), xx; fears, lxxxi, cxxi, 36; free-state, 241; organic, 89; philosophy, xx; progression (fear to fearlessness), 30; resistance, 48; resilience, 148; self, 402; super-, lxiv, xcix; *see also* Defense Intelligence System
Nature, xiv, xxx, xxxi, 147, 160, 192, 353; conquer (need), 136; design in, 75; laws of, xx, 107; *see also* animal(s), ecological, gift, human nature, Indigenous worldview, Mother Nature, Natural, natural, Organic paradigm

Nazism, lxviii, 314, 328; *see also* Evil, Third Reich
needs, 332; desire and, 405; ego's, xxxviii; esteem, 208; fearless, 60; me, cxv; personal, 28; security, cxiv; social animal, lxxxvi; unhealthy, 123; womb (mother), 55; wounds and, 225; youth, l; *see also* defense(s), esteem, Nest (evolutionary), survival
negative, xiii-xiv, xv, xvi, xx, xcvi, 169; barriers, xxx; D-ness, 126; fear, cxxv; feelings, xc; lower vibrations (emotion), xv; negation of negation, 398; resistance and, xiii; shadow, 332; spaces, 296; towards fear, 159; *see also* Fearlessness, In Search of Fearlessness Project, philosophy, rebellion, resistance(s), Shadow, unconscious
negativism, 307; *see also* negative, positivism (vs.)
Nelson, R., 359, 394
Neo, 284; *see also* Matrix (*The*)
neoliberalism, 134, 136, 355; *see also* capitalism, conservativism, ideology, politics
Nest (evolutionary) liv, 359; *see also* bonding, health, morality, needs, neurobiology
Nestor(ism), 290
Neufeld, H., 188-9, 190, 359
neurobiology: of fear, lxxviii; of morality, 64, 359
neurotic, xlix, 15, 16, 149, 190, 219; *see also* madness, pathologies
Neupane, T. P., 157-8
New Age, xv, 363, 365; *see also* Enlightened Age, Fearless Age, Human Potential Movement

Newtonian, xxxvii, 33
Nietzsche, F., 296, 333, 365
Nigh, K., 354
nine/eleven (9/11, 2001), xxii; *see also* culture of fear
No Fear! (slogandia, branding), 361, 385; *see also* fearless
Noam, 278
Nobunaga, xcviii-xcix, 204
nondualism, xlii, 6, 47, 71, 115, 168, 364, 375, 382; standpoint, 376; theory (metaphysics), 405; *see also* adualism, fearless, holistic, integralism, monism
nonviolence, 148, 198, 225; *see also* Gandhian, peace, *Satyagraha*
Norcross, J. C., 359, 375
norm(s), xlvii, cxxii, 166, 236; *see also* conditioning, cultural matrix
nuclear proliferation (crises), xxii

O

object-cathexis, 404, 405; *see also* attachment
object: gaze, 39; -relations, 404-05; -self, lviii; -uncanny, 323
object/subject, 5, 7, 374
objectification, lx; *see also* artificial, attachment(s), defense(s), dissociation, mechanical, Other(ing)
objectivism, 381
objectivist, xli, 98; science, 311, 393
objectivity (*faux*), 40
objects (attachment theory), xviii; *see also* coping, defense(s)
O'Connor, F., 347
O'Donohue, J., 69, 359
Odysseus, 27

Oedipal complex, 317; *see also* psychoanalysis
ontological, xxxix, cvi, 98, 219, 384, 404, 405; conflict, civ; insecurity, 383
ontology: flatland, 234; *see also* epistemology, metaphysics, reality, structuralism
opposites, xxxii-iii, xxxiv, xxxviii, xxxix, lviii, cvi, 89, 191, 298, 366, 401; *see also* binary, dualism, Other(ing), nondualism (vs.)
oppression, xxi, xxvi, xxix, xlix, cxviii, 49, 51, 62, 77, 118, 127, 145, 146, 156, 203, 269, 278, 370, 376, 378, 384; *see also* authoritarianism, culture of fear, Dominant worldview, politics, repression
Organic paradigm: *see* Mechanical vs. Organic
Orpheus, lxvii
Other(ing), xvii, xx, xxix, 73, 317, 324, 326, 400, 404; 'fear'-based, 78; *see also* defense(s), demonisation, dissociation, dualism, enemies, fearism-t, mechanical, (M) Othering, opposites, Shadow
Overstreet, B. W., 359, 370

P

pandemic: *see* COVID-19
panic, xxi, lxxxv, lxxxvii, 34, 190, 345, 368, 375, ; phallic, 347, 406; *see also* anxiety, fear, terror
paradigm(s) xiii, xv, xviii, lvi, lxxv, cxxiii, 81, 132, 250, 299, 367; holistic, xxxvii; shift, xxviii, 13, 43, 63, 145; split, 11; thinking (old), xxxiii, 259, 327; transformational, 9; *see also* Fearlessness Paradigm, Love

431

Paradigm, Positive Paradigm, worldview(s)

paranoia, 273, 296, 346, 401, 405; *see also* coping, fear, pathologies, phobias,

paranoid, 151, 277, 317, 320, 368; schizoidal-, 189

Pascal, 69, 290

pathologies, xxxix, 98, 113, 192, 206, 218, 377, 381, 389; *see also* arrogance, cognitive, defense(s), disease, dissociation, distortion, Dominant worldview, false, ignore-ance, madness, neurotic, phobias, psychology, psychotic, reality (distortions), schizoidal

Paudyal, M., cix

peace ; *see also* nonviolence

Peale, N. V., 359, 394

Peck, S., 225, 359, 396

pedagogy, liv, 111; conflict, 216; critical, 216 ; emancipatory, 200; integral, 352; love, 363; of fear, 113, 114, 385; of Fearlessness, 165; of oppressed, 354; of searching, 112, 385; trance-based, 384; *see also* education

perfection, 11, 96, 111; *see also* fear (no), spirit(uality)

Peters, T., 20-1, 359, 373

philosopher(s) xxiv, xxv, lii, lxxv, lxxx, lxxxi, cxii, cxxii, 8, 216, 220, 226, 399; classical, 76; Eastern, xxxi, cxv; eco-, xcii; existential, xviii, 38, 51; Greek, 79, 402; integral, xlv; mystic, 27; phenomenological, 12; poetic, 69;

political, xcv; Western, xxxix; *see also* Camus, fearism

Philosophia, 39, 128

philosophy, 42, 255, 260, 401, 402, 404; constructivism (postmodern), xviii; Eastern, 390; epistemic-, 403; fearlessness, 213, 400; Gandhian, 369; integral, 405; Marx's, 373; negative, xv, xvi; of fearlessness, cxxiv, 1, 110, 227, 237; phenomenological, 12; positive, 363; pragmatism, xiv; process, lxxviii, 394; transformation, 399; *see also* conflict theory, dialectic(al), dualism, epistemology, Fearism, Fearlessness Philosophy, functionalism, paradigm(s), knowledge(s), knowing, metaphysics, ontology

phobias, xviii, 149, 151, 190, 377; agoraphobia, lxxxvii; anthrophobia, 377; autophobia, 377; cancerophobia, 188, 189, 190; corona-, cxxvi; four hundred and fifty, lxxxi, lxxxiv, 50, 377; Freudophobia, 298; homophobia, 225; theriaphobia, 245; *see also* fear(s), paranoia, pathologies, taboos, xenophobia

Phobos, xcix, 229, 353, 377, 403, 406; *see also* arrogance, Fear, 'fear,' *Thanatos*

Pinker, S., 328, 359, 406

Pirsig, R., 21, 97-8, 99, 359, 373, 381

Plato, xxxix, 38, 82, 219, 402; *see also* idealism, Socrates

Plato (Fr. version), 387

Plato's cave, 255

Plotinus, 94, 406 ; *see also* integral

political, xvii, xxi, xxxii, xxxv, xlvii, li, lxxvi, ci, 100, 146, 160, 173, 236, 304, 315, 364, 374, 395, 403, 407; crises, xvii; *see also* cultural, leadership, politics, self (private vs. public)

politics, xxvii, xxx, 64, 127, 152, 153, 200, 334; agent (rational), xcvi; agents of State, xxvii; animal, 388; of fear, 157; fear-based, xxix; fearism, 157; fearlessness, 157; game of, xxvi; ; of hope, 364; of knowledge, 244, 407; of love, xv; phobo- xxix; polarities, xxxii; power-, 220; power sharing, xxxv; spiritual, 365; *see also* conflict theory, corruption, democracy, functionalism, government(s), idealism, ideology, leadership, neoliberalism, oppression, reform(ation), revolution(s), transformation

Pollyana-ish, lxxxviii ; *see also* hope, Naive

Pope, B., 19-20, 354, 373

Pope John XXIII, lxxv

Portnoy, J., 360, 389

Positive Paradigm (PP), xv, xvi ; resistance to Fearlessness, xiv-xv; *see also* Human Potential Movement, Love Paradigm, New Age, positivism, Positivists

Positive Psychology (movement), xvi; moralism (defenses), xvi

positive, xiii-xiv, xv, xvi, liii, lxxiv, xcviii, 130, 142, 161, 289; description, 299; educationists, xiv; fear as, xxxix, lxxxvi, xci, 105, 129; psychologists, xiv; righteousness, xlix; versus negative, xvi; *see also* hope, philosophy, positivism

Positivists, xv

positivism, xiv-xv, 117, 307; culture of, xiv-xv ; fear- 129, 369; discourses, 128; ideology, xv; resistance to Fearlessness, xiv-xv; *see also* culture of positivism, empiricism, functionalism, moralism, Positive Paradigm, righteousness, Science(s)

positivizing, xiv

postmodernism, xl, 73, 106, 131, 176, 205, 233, 329, 387; constructivism, xviii; Fearlessness, cxxii; *see also* Camusian, existentialism

poststructuralism, 195, 233, 384; *see also* constructivism, postmodernism

poverty (inequality), xxii, 154; *see also* classism

power: *see* politics, thinking (thought)

pragmatism, xiv

praxis: *see* critical praxis, critical theory, liberation

primal, xix, xxv, lvi, lvii, xcv, 70, 73, 160, 192, 242, 390; healing, 405; sacred mind, 303; *see also* emotion(s), Id, Indigenous (worldview)

progress (dialectic of), xxiii, 146, 328

progress vs. regress, xvii

progressive, xxvii, 21, 77, 246, 342, 385, 394; *see also* freedom, liberty

projection, 34, 94, 107, 205, 380, 395; see also defense(s), demonisation, Other(ing)

Prometheus, 315, 316

propaganda, xx

prophet(ess), xxv, 219, 226, 228, 231, 250, 260; *see also* vision(ary)

Proteus, cxii

433

psyche, xx, xxi, xxxvi, xlix, li, civ, 31, 63, 190, 294, 323; *see also* psychology, soul

psychiatry, lxxxiv, 12, 190, 311, 360; *see also* feariatry

psychoanalysis, 208, 224, 226, 270, 306, 307, 311, 347, 348, 399; theory, 5; *see also* defense(s), depth psychology, Father, fearanalysis, Freudian, Lacanian, Mother, Oedipal complex, psychology, repression, uncanny

psychologism, 119, 181, 248, 390, 398

psychology, xxv, xxvii, l, lxxxii, lxxxiv, 20, 181, 243, 259, 311; clinical, 181, 242; ego, 374; evolutionary, 173; Fearlessness, 45, 170, 222, 350; integral, 383; motivational, 220; of fear, 399; paradigm of, 218; paranoic-based, 188; positive, xiv, xvi; social, 120, 404; transpersonal, 246, 405; Western, 112; *see also* depth psychology, existentialism, fearlessnessizing, fearology, psyche, psychiatry, psychoanalysis, psychologism

psychotic, 275, 349, 395; near (experience), 113, 190-1, 389; *see also* dissociation, distortion, illusion, pathologies

Puer (archetype), xlix; *see also* youth

Pulcini, E., 360

Puranas, xxxi

Pythagoras, 402

Pythagorean(s), 384, 402; theorem, 131

Pyszczynski, T., 360, 361, 373, 393-4, 404, 406

Q

Quality, xxiii, 20, 21

quality, ciii, 23; rebel for, 388

Quaye, S. J., 354, 373

queer theory, 397; *see also* LGBTQ

R

racism, xxii, 41, 225; white (White), 64 ; *see also* Black, colonialism

radical(s), 118; *see also* rebel(s)

radicalization, 118

Ramayana, lxvii, 290

rational(ity), xxi, li, xcvi, 12, 365; *see also* abstract(ion), arationality, defense(s), irrationality, objectification, mind, reality, reason, thinking, truth(s)

reality, xxvi, lxxxviii, ci, cv, 10-11, 14, 46, 50; affective, xxiii; -awareness, 31; big picture, xvi; distortion, xix; integral, 282; magical, 282, mythic, 282, new self-awareness and, xviii; post-rational, 282; pre-rational, 282, rational, 282; self (Real), 10-11; *see also* defense(s), irrationality, logic(al), pathologies, True (The)

reason, 155; anti-, 193; *see also* abstraction, anxiety, fear, rational(ity), thinking

Rebel (archetype) 195, 388, 390-1; *see also* Sacred Warrior

Rebel (Neo-) School, 374

rebel(s), cvii; archetype, 390; essential, 390; immature, 195; impulse, 390; normal, 390; pathological,

434

118; regulatory (biological role), 388; revolutionaries, 118; twisted, 390; spirit, xxi; theory (Fisher's), 390; true, 388; *see also* radical(s), Spirit of fearlessness

rebellion, lx, 18, 184, 388; Camusian, 279, 280, 329; definition, 388; health and, 390; origins of, lix; spiritual, 333; tripartite model, 390; *see also* Camus, freedom, negative, resistance(s), revolutions

rebellionism, 225

rebellious, xxviii, lix, lx, lxviii, 152, 159, 297; *see also* fearlessness, resilience, youth

reductionism, xvi, xix, xxxv, li, cxxiv, 40, 203, 370, 398; *see also* distortion, dualism, epistemic, functionalism, ideology, knowledge(s), moralism

Reeves, A. N., 360, 373

reform(ation), xxxiv, li, 157; *see also* transformation

regress, xvii, xxii, 47, 145, 155, 224; *see also* defense(s), immaturity

regression, xxiii, 224; retro-, 379; *see also* de-evolutionary

regulating (systems), xliii, 53, 64, 164, 230, 241, 378, 387; *see also* change, defense(s), fear management/ education, government(s), healing, resilience, restoration, trauma

Rella, F., 360

religion(s), xxxiii, lxix, lxxii, 51, 154, 226; myths and, lxvi; *see also* Bible, Buddhism, Christianity, Hinduism, Islamism, Jainism, myth(s), *Upanishads*, Vedas

Renault, M., xcix

repressed, xxviii, 10-11, 287, 296, 317; *see also* defense(s), psychoanalysis, sublimation, unconscious

repression, xxi, 295; retro-, 379; barrier, 296; of self, 10-11; *see also* domination, oppression

resilience, xxii, 25, 204, 223; deterioration, xxii; *see also* Defense System Intelligence, healing, immunity, regulating (system)

Resistance Movement 391; *see also* Fearlessness Movement

resistance(s), xiii, cxxii, 3, 18, 62, 110, 184, 203, 244, 248, 320, 332, 395; against alternatives, xv; against critiques, xv; against ecological laws, xx; against "shut-down" (lock-down), xx; negative, xiii; self and, 50; to injustice, xxi; to knowing, xiii; to terror, cxix; *see also* conflict(s), defense(s), Fearlessness, rebellious, revolution(s)

restoration, xliv, 65, 208, 284, 336, 339, 388; *see* healing, regulating (system)

Reversal 227, 228, 229, 256, 260, 282; *see also* liberation, transformation

revolution(s), xiii, xliii, cxxii, 123, 157, 304, 310; Greek (conceptual), 304, 310-11; *see also* ideology, resistance(s)

Reynolds, B., 360, 382-3, 405

right-wing, 32, 100; *see also* authoritarian(ism), fascism, ideology, left-wing, politics

righteousness, xvi, xlix; *see also* ideology, moralism, positivism

rights (human), cxxiv, cxxv, 62, 63, 160; Civil, 153; Declaration

435

of Independence and Human Rights, 16; four freedoms, 152, 154, 160; Universal Declaration of Human Rights, 152
Riley, S., 360
risk(s), lxxxv, lxxxvii, 8, 26, 164, 206, 287, 355; at-, 225; discouraged, 112; predation, 13, 163; threat/fear phenomenon, xvii; *see also* fear, threat (system)
Robin, C., xcv-xcvii, 360, 364, 369
Robinian, xcvi
Roman, xxxvi, lxv, lxvi; Catholic, lxiv; *see also* Greek, mythology, religion(s)
Roosevelt, F. D., 152, 183
Rorschach, 84, 86, 110, 357
Rosch, E., 212, 361, 391
Rothenberg, A., 360
Rousseau, J. J., 175, 347
Rowland, K. M., 346, 378, 391
Ruck, D., 62
Russell, B., lii

S

Sachindev, P. S., 345, 407
sacred: see desacralization, spiritual
Sacred Warrior, 25, 56, 194, 198, 200, 208, 241, 242, 390; *see also* archetype(s), hero, Magician, Nobunaga, Rebel
safety: *see* needs
Sai Baba Gita, 372, 378
St. Anthony, lxx
St. Augustine, 365
Samson (Dr.) (character), 373
Sandoval, C., 360
sanity: *see* health, madness, sustainable
Sannuto, C., xi
Saramago, J., 85, 93, 297

Sardello, R., 194, 196, 323, 360, 390, 405
Sardelloian, 196
Sartre, J-P., 51, 69, 120, 280, 283
Satan, xxxv, 81
Satyagraha, 148; *see also* Movement(s), nonviolence
Schaef, A. W., 13-14, 360, 373, 401
schizoidal, 12, 14 ; *see also* double talk, distortion, false, paranoid, pathologies, psychotic, splitting
schizophrenics, 12
Schopenhauer, A., 333, 350, 365
Schumacher, E. F., 361, 370
Science(s), lv, cxiv, 8, 218; dominant, lx; new, xxxvii; power of, 155; *see also* Biomedical worldview, empiricism, positivism
Scott, B., 394
Scott, S. M., 359
Scorese, M., 369
Seaton, E., 361, 385
security: *see* needs
Segal, J., 35, 58
Self (true), lix, 11; -Fear-Other, lx
self, xviii, 34, 95, 100, 218, 232; /system regulation, 53; -abuse, 187; -centered, xxviii; -devouring, xxix; -dignity, 279; -esteem, 247; -fulfilling prophecy, 190; -made (youth), lxv; -need, xx; -reflective, cxii; -reflexive, 258; -sense, 404; -structure-system, lxxvii; -wounding, 405; change agent, 375; co-dependent, 10-11; divided, 50; Ego, xxii; false, 10-11, 50; fearful, 50; fixed, 217; free agent, 208, 257; new (awareness), xviii; object-, lviii; public, 10-11; private, 10-11; real, 10; sick, 10-11; true, 11, 50;

unauthentic, 10-11; *see also* ego, esteem, individual, narcissism, needs
Senex (archetype), xlix
service: *see* caring
Shadow, xxxv, cxi, 133, 185, 187, 287, 370; *see also* negative, unconscious
Shah, I., 292
Shakespeare, W., lxvii
shaman(ism), 25, 356, 372, 395, 397; *see also* arationality, magical, mystic(al), transpersonal
Shambhala, 25, 58, 204, 361; *see also* archetypes, Buddhism, Sacred Warrior, Magician
Shankaracharya, 307
shut-down: *see* COVID-19
Shyamalan, M. N., 400
sick(ness): *see* dis-ease, pathologies
Simpkinson, C. H., 361, 405
Sisyphus, 315-18
Slattery, P., 130, 385, 398
slip-of-the-tongue: Error Theory (Freud), 307; *see also* double talk, unconscious
social, xlvi, lxxxvii, 136, 175, 195, 236, 308, 383; approval, cxiv; experiments, xi, 337, 404; fearless society, xxii; life, xxviii; media, 133; movements, 146; philosophy, 228; prophecy, 249; public self, 10; reality, 249; rejection, 385; species, xx, 225; trust, lxxii; *see also* culture of fear, communism, esteem, government(s), psychology
socialism, 157; *see also* communism, left-wing, Marxist, politics
sociality, 128, 317, 319, 404
socialization: *see* conditioning, social
Socrates, 41, 50, 402; *see also* Plato

Socratic questioning, 254
Solomon, S., 360, 361, 373, 393-4, 404, 406
soul, xxi, cxi, 18, 47, 53, 56, 107, 219; -searching, 407; without, 303; *see also* psyche
spell, xxiv, 270; *see also* hypnosis, illusion(s), shamanism, trance
Spencer, B., 359
Spirit, v, 103, 116, 353, 382 ; fear of, iii; *see also* Holy Spirit, religion(s), spirit(uality)
Spirit of fearlessness, iii, xiii, xxi, l, lvii, cxx, cxxiv, 53, 54, 55, 60, 64, 145, 146-7, 169, 176, 387, 390; *see also* rebel
spirit, cxi, cxxix, 25, 32, 160; leadership, 3; rebel, xxi; *see also* fearlessness, rebel
spirit (fearless), 27
spirit of the gift, cvi-cvii
spiritual(ity), ci, 17, 71, 96, 116, 267, 354, 375; but not religious, lxxi; desacralization, xxi; deterioration, 14; sacred, xx; *see also* mystic(al), perfection, resonance
spirits, lii, lxxii, xcviii, xcix, 186
splitting, xxxvii, 14; *see also* defense(s), dissociation, double talk, dualism, schizoidal, walls
Sri, S., 72
standpoint theories: existentialist, 51; fearless, 44, 47, 350, 364, 376; Indigenous (primal awareness), xcii; nondual, 47, 376; trans-egoic, 375; *see also* praxis, theory
State, xcvi, 37, 127, 264, 265; *see also* politics
Steinberg, S., 353
Stengel, B., 347, 352, 398
Stiftung, K. A., xlvii

437

Stiopu, A. L., lx, 361, 367
stories, lxxxvii-ix, lxxxix-xci; Astronomy, 291-2; Cleopatra, 290; Dan, 271-8; Duke, 290; Inspirer, xcviii-ix; Intimidator, xcix; Joshua, 291; Meg's lxxxv-vii, 368, Nathalie, xci-xcv, 369; Robin, xcv-xcvii; Six-by-Six, 292-3; Suicide, xcix-ci; Survivor, xcvii-iii; *see also* fiction, myth(s)
structuralism: *see* conflict theory, development, evolution, Marxist, ontology, poststructuralism (vs.)
Subba, D., xi, xv, xvi, xxv-xxvi, xxx, xxxix, xl, xli, li, lxi, lxvi, lxxix, lxxxi, lxxxiii-iv, cvi, cix-x, cxvii-viii, cxx-iii, cxxv, cxxvii, 2-3, 12, 44-5, 47, 48, 50, 52, 59, 144, 150, 157-9, 195, 216-17, 220, 222, 298, 300-02, 304, 305-08, 309-10, 319, 337, 345, 361, 363, 365, 366, 367, 369, 370, 371, 372, 374-5, 376, 377, 379, 384, 385, 388, 391, 392, 393, 395, 402, 403, 407
Subba-Fisher-Kumar, 215
Subbaian, cxx, cxxiii, cxxiv, cxxvi, 220, 407
Subbaian-Fisherian, cxix
sublimation, 319, 320, 323, 346, 404; fearlessness and, 405; *see also* defense(s), repressed
Super-Ego, xxxiv, xxxviii, c, 10, 160, 184, 199, 208, 263, 277, 298, 323, 388; *see also* Freudian, Ego, Id,
superstitions, lvii, lxiii, lxiv, lxx, ci; *see also* taboos
survival, xxvii, xxix, lxxiii, 22, 23, 46, 89, 368; of the fittest, xcvi; *see also* Darwinian, death, deception, defense(s), fear, needs
Survivor, 56

Sushmita, B. S., xxv, 357, 364, 374
sustainable, xxviii, xxix, civ, 13, 21, 115; *see also* environment, health
Suzuki, D., 186-7, 191, 192, 199, 349, 361, 388, 389
Svendsen, L., 361, 391
Sylla, 27
symbolic, xviii, xlviii, 1, 29, 45, 111, 323, 324, 383; un-, xx; *see also* cognitive, immortality, mythology, thinking

T

taboos, 50, 51; against knowing yourself, 49, 362; *see also* phobias, superstitions
Tagore, R., cxxiv
Tangney, J., 360
Tantalus, 315, 316
Tao, 168
Tarnas, R., 220
teachers, xlii, l, lvi, 2, 112, 114, 200, 201; *see also* Sacred Warrior
Terror Management Theory (TMT), 318, 319, 320, 324-8; *see also* anxiety, Beckerian, culture of fear, fear of death, mortality, oppression, repression, pathologies
terror, xxii, lix, lxxxv, cxix, 12, 195, 198, 199, 368, 375, 394; century of, 328, 331, 393, existential, xxii, 201, 312; of future, 202; unspeakable, 277; War on, 371; *see also* death, insecurity/uncertainty, panic
terrorism, 22, cxvii-cxix, cxx, 1, 345, 354; *see also* authoritarianism, culture of fear, fearism-t
Thacker, E., 201

438

Thales of Miletus, 402
Thanatos, 94, 149, 161, 192, 206, 208, 229, 260, 262, 317, 353, 403, 406; *see also* death, *destrudo*, Fear, 'fear,' ignore-ance, *Phobos*
theology, xc, xci, cvi, 129, 201, 220, 235, 248, 249, 385, 387; *see also* Christian(ity)
theory, xxxi, xxxiv, xxxv, lv, lxi, xcvi; addiction's, 13; bi-motivational, 15; big story, 15; chaos/complexity, xxxviii; conspiracy (no), xcv; de-hypnosis, 227; developmental, 91; Error (Freud), 307; evolutionary, cxxi; fear bonding, cii; fearism, cxxi, 3; Fisherian (fearlessness), cxx; Freudian tripartite, xxxviii; holistic-integral, 161; liberation, 75; matrixial, 191; meta-, 56; motivation, 161; spectrum, 248; transformation learning, liv, 15; quantum, 20; Whitfield's, 12; *see also* CAT-FAWN, Fear Management Systems, Malthusian, praxis, psychoanalysis, standpoint theories, theoriaphobia
theoriaphobia, 245
therapia, lxxxiv, 7, 8, 226, 405; *see also cura*, healing, philosophy, therapy
therapy, 6, 8, 31, 95, 226, 261, 262, 263, 264, 355, 372, 402; existential, 374; kosmological, 405; *see also* cultural therapy, psychoanalysis, *therapia*
Theseus, lxvii
thinking (thought), xx, xxxvi, liii, 217; absolutist, cxxi; advanced, 385; analytical, 305; Aristotelian, 304; critical, 352, 382; dialectical, xxxvi, xxxvii, li, 371; distortions of, 393; dualistic, lxi, 205, 375; egoistic, 205, 375; fear-based, xli; flatland, 110; integral (leap), 375; liberal/left, 342; modern, 300; one-dimensional, 384; open-ended, 305; open-minded, 296; positive, xcviii, 359; postmodern, 365; power (cognitive), xviii; primal people's, 402; process, 5; rationalistic, 20, 393, 397; scientific, 21; structures and languages of, xviii; symbolic, xviii; systems, xlvi; technological, 98, 382; Thanatos-driven, 161; topographies, 82; unclear (pandemic effects), xviv; unhealthy, xiv; wise, 30; *see also* Janusian, knowledge(s), rationality
Third Reich, 183, 246, 314; *see also* fascism, Holocaust, Nazism
time/space, 262, 282, 397, 399
timelessness, cvi, 238, 282, 401; *see also* integral, nondual
Thomas, A. M., 359
Thompson, E., 212, 361, 391
threat (system), xiii, xvii-xviv, xx, xxii, xxix, lxxii, 3, 29, 37, 80, 146, 189, 190, 223, 326, 404; inflated, xxi; other, 325; *see also* death, Defense Intelligence, fear management/education, pathologies, regulating (systems), risk(s), viruses
Thriver, 56
Thunberg, G., xiii, xxi, 37
Tinnin, L., 361
Toffler, A., 105, 361, 382
trance, liv, 81, 194, 268, 346, 384, 400; *see also* altered state, hypnosis, learning (TBL), shamanism

transformation, xxiv, xxvii, l, lii, liii, li, lvi, lx, 20, 50, 88, 145, 204, 224, 237, 336, 356, 391; authentic, 21; change, 133, 399; learning, 18; paradigm, 9; leadership, 28; theory, 260; *see also* change(s), reformation, Reversal

transpersonal, 56, 83, 208, 222, 353, 376; theory, 405; *see also* integral

trauma, xvii, xlvi, 14, 24, 31, 49, 56, 107, 196, 269, 329, 381; post-, 331; re-(unlearning), xviii; *see also* critical literacy, Fear Problem, hurt(ing), woundedness

traumatic century, 328

Trinity, 253; *see also Matrix (The)*

Trinity (Christian theology), 385-6

True (The), cxvi, 75, 108; *see also* truth(s)

Trump, D., xxxii, xxxv, 29, 348

Trungpa (Rinpoche) C., 17, 26, 58, 204, 361, 373, 374, 376, 378, 391

trust, xxx, lxxi, lxxvii, 51, 66, 131, 166, 173, 217, 218, 355, 379; -based, xxix; radical, 27, 35; social, lxxii; *see also* hope, mistrust, social

truth(s), xxi; assumed, xv; denial of 187, 277; post-, xxx, 125, 312; *see also* false, rationality, trust, untruth

Turner, L., 361, 368

Twins, xxxii, xli, lviii : creativity and destructivity, 283; disguised, xxxvi; fear and terror, 198; Shadow, xxxv; *see also* archetype(s), depth psychology, mythology

U

ugly, xxiii, 73, 74, 81, 101, 103, 105, 126, 131, 133, 136, 302, 381; *see also* A-D/ness, evil

uncanny, xvii, xxiv, 287, 6, 89, 217, 270, 287-334, 347, 348, 358, 403, 404, 406; defined, 295; *see also* absurd(ity), anxiety, awe, psychoanalysis

uncertainty: *see* insecurity/ uncertainty

unconditional: attention, 23; loving, 10; therapy, 6

unconscious, xxvii, xxxviii, liv, ci, cxiv, 3, 5, 27, 85, 111, 174, 186, 269, 295, 296, 298, 307, 326, 381; collective, 407; fearlessness, lxviii; *see also* hypnosis, instinct(ual), negative, Shadow, slip-of-the-tongue

Uni-Bicentric Theorem, 400

United Nations, xxii, 54, 152; fearlessness and, 22

unity, xxii, 77, 78, 93, 221, 346; *see also* caring, fraternity, holistic, matrixial theory, (M)Othering

Upanishads, 255, 290, 378 ; *see also* Hinduism, *Vedas*

untruth, 279; *see also* deception, false, hypnosis, ideology, illusion, propaganda, truth (post-)

V

vaccine(s), 42, 131, 151; 'fear'-, 31, 223, 224, 225, 226; *see also* defense(s), immunity

Valentine (character), 293-4

van Kessel, C., 200-01, 202, 205, 206, 349, 361, 385, 391
van Kessel-Burke Hypothesis, 385
Vanzant, I., iii
Varela, F. J., 212, 218, 361, 391, 392-3
Vaughan, F., 362, 375
Vedas, 26; see also *Upanishads*
Ventura, M., 355, 400
Verdecchia, R., 361, 389-90
victim, xxi, lxxi, lxxvi, 24, 56, 96, 151, 306 ; not, 403; see also helplessness, woundedness
Vijayalakshmi, iii
Village (The), 277, 400
violence, xxxi, xcvi, cxviii, 32, 69, 94, 95, 116, 127, 198, 225, 228, 317, 359, 407; see also epistemic, hurt(ing), oppression
virtues: see caring, ethics, Fearlessness, Good (The), moralism
virus: culture of fear, xiv; fear, 27; of fear, xxi; see also COVID-19, ecological, 'fear'
vision(ary), xxiii; xxvi, lxxiv, 20, 172, 299, 377; logic, 236; peripheral, 5; quest, 226; Sunset vs. Sunrise, 229; see also dreams, leadership, mystic(al), prophet(ess)
Vivekananda (Swami), 27
Vokey, D., 213

W

Wachowski's (The), 253, 326, 361, 383, 390, 401
Wahinkpe Topa, liii, 267-8, 354, 362; see also Four Arrows, Jacobs, D. T.
Walker, F. N., 362, 382

walls, xvii, li, 45, 72, 93, 135, 203, 272, 275; see artificial, barriers, defense(s), enemies
Walsh, R., 362, 375
war(s), xxii, 32, 41, 109, 330, 371, 378; WW-II, lxviii; see also barriers, defense(s), paradigm(s), Fear Wars
Waterman, R. H. (Jr.), 359, 373
Watkins, A., 362, 375, 394
Watts, A., 362, 377
weaponry: egoic fear, 205; military, 56, 204
weaponization of fear, xxvi; xxxiii, 146; see also ideology
Weber, M., xxxiii
wellness: see health
Wells, H. G., 374
West, C., 342, 350
Wheatley, M., 21, 58, 60-1, 63, 362, 373
Whitehead, A. N., 367, 394
Whitfield, C. L., 9-11, 14, 15-16, 362, 372, 377
Wilber, K., xlv, 39, 59, 105, 107, 175, 184, 208, 233-4, 236, 353, 360, 362, 364, 365, 367, 370, 375, 378, 379, 382-4, 389, 394, 395, 396, 399, 404, 405, 406
Wilberian, 185, 387
Wilberland, 353
Williamson, M., xv, xxxii, xxxv, xlvi, 28-9, 31-3, 69, 133-5, 348, 362, 365, 374
wisdom, xiii, xxix, xxxix, xlv, xcii, cxv, 30, 80, 238, 364
Wittgenstein, L., 257
women, xcviii, 58, 154
worldview(s), xviii, xix, xxxi, xl, 88, 125, 381; alternative, 213; authentic, 354; big problem, xix; Biomedical, 181; culture

441

of fear and, 141; dominant, 99, Indigenous, xix, 226; Indigenous vs. Dominant, 13, 107, 227, 266, 367; kosmology and, 119; magical (natural), 301; pre-anthropocentric, 160; *see also* Biomedical worldview, paradigm(s)

worry, xiv

woundedness, 29, 51, 95, 96, 390, 395; *see also* trauma

Wright Bros., 148

Wright, R., 173, 388

X

xenophobia, 317; *see also* Other(ing)

Y

Yahweh: *see* God

Yan, S., 130, 385, 398

yoga, 225; *see also* meditation, regulating (systems)

youth, xxi, xxv-xxx, xlviii, lix, 55, 123, 130, 202, 294, 364, 384; jobless, xxii; *see also* criminalisation, fear(s), Puer (archetype), rebellious, resilience

Z

Zen, 359; *see also* Buddhism, nondualism

Zinzun, M. 244-5

Printed in Dunstable, United Kingdom